BURMA'S FOREIGN POLICY

BURMA'S
FOREIGN POLICY

A Study in Neutralism

by

WILLIAM C. JOHNSTONE
Consultant, The RAND Corporation

HARVARD UNIVERSITY PRESS

Cambridge, Massachusetts

1 9 6 3

FOR
ANNE,
DELIGHT,
AND
KATHERN

PREFACE

T his study is an analysis of Burma's foreign policy since independence. It examines, first of all, the basic concepts accepted by the Burman leadership in their initial formulation of a foreign policy for their new country. It attempts to identify those factors or circumstances which influenced the adoption of certain ideas as underlying principles of Burma's foreign policy and caused the rejection of others. In the second place, an attempt is made to trace the evolution of these underlying ideas and their translation into action in a changing domestic and international environment over the fourteen years since independence. This study is not a comprehensive review of the totality of Burma's foreign relations since 1948. Rather it is focused upon that complex of concepts, attitudes and actions described generally as a policy of "neutralism." By trying to find out the ideological content of this policy as defined by the Burman leaders themselves, and then by analyzing how these concepts of neutralism have been applied to important international issues and situations of concern to Burma, a basis is laid for some evaluation of Burma's neutralism from both the point of view of the Burmans and of the outside observer.

This volume is based on studies comprising an extensive group research project on the subject of Burma's foreign relations since independence. The project was initiated at the Johns Hopkins University School of Advanced International Studies in Washington, D. C., in the spring of 1956. It was carried on through field research in Burma between June, 1956, and April, 1959. The original research project called for a multipronged investigation of Burma's foreign relations designed to be as comprehensive as possible within the time allowed. The end product was a series of papers, each a separate study in itself and of varying lengths. These were completed in April, 1959. (See Appendix I for list of papers and authors.) After April, 1959, the author continued the collection of material from Rangoon and in January, 1962, was able to return to Rangoon, Burma, for a final evaluation of material and collection of additional data.

The group research project and this present study were made possible by the existence of the Rangoon-Hopkins Center for Southeast Asian Studies, a joint undertaking of the Johns Hopkins University School of Advanced International Studies and Rangoon University. The Center was opened in June, 1954, to serve the teaching and research needs of Rangoon University and of universities in southeast Asia. As part of its area training program, the School of Advanced International Studies provided a number of fellowships each year for selected graduates for advanced study and research at the Center in Rangoon. All the recipients of these fellowships between June, 1956, and April, 1959, worked on various papers connected with this research project on Burma's foreign policy. From February, 1957, until April, 1959, the author directed this field research while serving as Co-Director of the Rangoon-Hopkins Center and Visiting Professor of International Relations at the Rangoon University.

The initial group research project, as well as the continuing research necessary in the preparation of this present volume was substantially aided by a grant to the School of Advanced International Studies from The RAND Corporation, Santa Monica, California. The RAND Corporation regularly sponsors, with its own funds, research projects of importance to national security and public welfare. Such research is fundamentally the responsibility of the individuals involved in the project and any interpretations or conclusions offered are not necessarily endorsed by The RAND Corporation.

The author is grateful to The RAND Corporation and the staff of its Social Science Department for helpful suggestions and a variety of assistance in this project. The author is deeply indebted to those graduates of the SAIS associated with him in this research project in Burma, particularly for their conscientious and painstaking work under difficult and often frustrating conditions in Rangoon. The author is highly appreciative of the opportunity for engaging in a special kind of intellectual experience as a part of "area training" and is only hopeful that it proved of equal value to all those who participated in it.

Although the author has drawn heavily on the material provided by the individual studies comprising the original research project and on the mass of source material collected in Burma and in the United States, this present study is an attempt at coherent presentation in a single volume of the development of Burma's foreign policy of neutralism, and for any interpretations, conclusions, errors of fact, or sins of omission, the author willingly accepts responsibility.

W.C.J.
Washington, D. C.
August, 1962.

CONTENTS

— I —

INTRODUCTION

O~N~ January 4, 1962, Burma celebrated the fourteenth anniversary of its independence. For all of these fourteen years the
government of Burma has pursued an unwavering policy of nonalignment or neutralism in world affairs. It could be said that the
Burma government pioneered the policy of neutralism. Whereas in
1948, Burma stood alone with India in adopting a foreign policy of
nonalignment, today Burma is one of a large majority of neutralist
members of the United Nations. As the number of such nations increased there have been continuing references to the Afro-Asia bloc,
to the possibility that the neutralists might some day constitute a
"third force" in world politics, interposed between the major contestants in the cold war. To date no such developments have taken
place. There is no effective "Afro-Asian bloc" in the United Nations,
and at the large Belgrade conference of "unaligned" nations in September, 1961, it was apparent that neutralist unity extended no farther than agreement on vaguely worded resolutions and a unanimous
condemnation of colonialism.

The real concern of the United States and its allies, however, is
what appears to be the development of a "cult" of neutralism — a
set of beliefs which found concrete expression in the reaction of the
neutralist nations at Belgrade to resumption of nuclear tests by the
Soviet Union. The neutral nations refused to condemn vigorously
this Soviet breaking of the moratorium on nuclear testing, but instead generally condemned all nuclear tests, equating the United
States with the Soviet Union in this regard. It appeared that a policy
of neutralism involved belief in a double standard of international
morality, that neutral nations were unwilling to judge the actions of

the Communist bloc and those of the United States and its allies by the same standards. Quite apart from the understandable concern of the United States over the actions of the neutralist nations on specific issues, it is clear that neutralism is now a phenomenon in world affairs to be reckoned with.

American attitudes toward the neutralist nations have vacillated. During the early years of the Eisenhower administration, neutralism was regarded as immoral. We held that in the contest with world Communism, those who were not for us must necessarily be against us. Yet the American government continued to give economic aid to neutralist nations, from India to Yugoslavia, and American policy gradually softened to the point where the new President, John Kennedy, could call for a "neutral and independent" Laos as the American objective at the Geneva conference in 1961. Failure to obtain agreement at Geneva, the growing crisis over Berlin, and increasing Communist infiltration of the Republic of Vietnam, however, caused President Kennedy to indicate to Congress that the United States would carefully consider its future aid program with respect to "nations which share our view of world affairs." This shift caused concern among the neutrals, particularly India, and since it was obvious that the American government would not change its economic commitments to India in the immediate future, President Kennedy modified his position. At his news conference on October 11, 1961, he stated that the United States would help nations maintain their "national independence."

While there has been increasing attention given to the general problems of neutralism and to action of neutralist countries on specific international issues, there have been few attempts to subject the foreign policy of a neutralist nation to an analysis in depth, to examine the evolution of neutralism in one country and its application over a period of years to changing international issues and events.

In a great many respects Burma can be considered the prototype of a small, neutralist country. Burma's government early determined to follow a course of nonalignment in world affairs and has consistently maintained this policy over a fourteen-year period. During this period the Burma government has confronted many of the same kinds of problems which now concern the newer neutralist nations.

Armed insurrection, infiltration of foreign forces in its territory, economic growing pains, internal political upheaval, these and other difficulties have been dealt with by the Burma government since independence. As a member of the United Nations, too, the Burma government has been bound to take a foreign policy decision on a wide variety of international issues, from those involved in the Korean war, to the problems of Suez and Hungary, the recent Soviet resumption of nuclear tests, to the upheavals in the United Nations structure itself. The Burma government has had to determine the kind of foreign economic assistance it needed and decide how much to take from nations in both the power blocs in accordance with its nonalignment policy.

While it is true that each of the neutral nations occupies a particular geographic location, possesses a distinct cultural and historical heritage and that in each nation its leaders view their country's role in the world from their own particular ideological and personal preconceptions, there is much that is comparable. Burma's posture of neutralism in the cold war, therefore, provides an opportunity to examine both the evolution and the application of a neutralist policy by a small nation. Such an examination can provide some useful clues for a more careful assessment of this phenomenon of neutralism and perhaps some insights into the problems faced by the United States in its relations with the large number of neutral nations in this world of the cold war.

This study is focused on the particular concepts or principles of Burma's foreign policy since independence which, taken together, have been described as neutralism. An attempt has been made to find the answers to a series of questions which can be posed concerning the foreign policy of any nation. Was the decision of Burma's leaders in 1948 to follow a course of nonalignment the result of circumstances at the time of independence or does this policy have roots in the past? Did the Burma government have other, logical options it might have selected? What has been the ideological content of Burma's neutralist policy? How has it been changed or modified over the period since independence and what factors caused any such changes or modifications? How has Burma fared with its neutralist policy in specific situations or issues confronting it? Has the application of a neutralist policy in practice been easy or difficult? Answers to these and other relevant questions can provide a basis for rational evaluation of this policy in action.

In all of the research which forms the basis for this study an attempt was made to review the evolution and application of a neutralist policy as the leaders of the Burma government saw it, to keep in mind how these men viewed the role of their nation in world affairs. The approach to this study, therefore, has been that of empiricism, attempting to avoid prejudgment until the facts were assembled. This study is not a comprehensive review of Burma's foreign relations since 1948, nor does it attempt to include all the details of Burma's relations with its neighbors and the major nations in the two power blocs. Issues and situations which the leaders of Burma considered to be of major importance were selected for examination in terms of the application of basic concepts of their foreign policy.

In order to provide a basis for final evaluation and some judgment as to the consequences for Burma of its neutralist policy, the remaining sections of this chapter trace briefly the historical factors which influenced the leaders' choice in 1948. The chapters that follow attempt to present both the evolution and the application of neutralist policy chronologically over the fourteen years of independence. Because Burma shares a long frontier with Communist China, a major partner of the Soviet Union, such physical proximity has had a significant effect on Burma's foreign relations and this problem is dealt with in a separate chapter. The final chapters provide both a summary and an evaluation of neutralism for one country which it is believed has relevance for consideration of this relatively new phenomenon in cold war politics.

The Roots of Burma's Neutralism

The men who took control of the new government of the Union of Burma, in 1948, were not wholly free to chart the course of their independent nation in the turbulent sea of postwar international politics. The nation for whose destiny they were now responsible was not of their making. They had not determined the composition of its people. They had little to do with the extent of its territory. In their brief political careers prior to independence, they had neither shaped its history nor influenced its culture. They had been responsible only for the constitution of their new state and for the manner in which freedom had been obtained from Britain.

The leaders of the new nation, Burma, were a diverse group with varying ideas and capabilities. They had joined together to work for a single goal, independence. Although many of them shared a common orientation toward Marxism, their individual interpretations of Marxist doctrine differed widely and many of them had little attachment to Marxism either as a doctrine or as a guide to action. But no matter what their views, individually or collectively, they were soon to find that they could not divorce themselves from the historical factors that had shaped their country and its people. The leaders of the new Burma government still had to develop their domestic and foreign policies within the framework of the historical circumstances, old culture patterns, and habits of thought and conduct that were their legacies from preceding generations.

A consciousness of this legacy of the past was not immediately apparent in the actions and expressed ideas of Burma's leaders. As in most colonial territories, there was the feeling that attainment of independence would mean a sharp break, a radical change, from all that was past history. To most of the political leaders and to most politically literate Burmans, freedom from British rule meant that a wholly new, and fresh start, could be made.[1] There was little disposition to consider the operation of the new government or the formulation of domestic and foreign policies in the context of their history. They considered that by eliminating alien rule over their country they had broken with the past and in particular had finally dissociated themselves and their people from the unpalatable rule of the British.

These attitudes, of course, were delusions. No nation can wholly break with its history, its culture, or the habits of thought and patterns of conduct that have survived through generations. In the case of a colonial territory, not even the most rigorous alien rule can wholly eliminate or destroy its precolonial culture. Nor can an ex-colonial country, merely by the attainment of independence, eliminate at a stroke the effects of an imposition of alien culture or the forms and methods of colonial administration. In fact, attainment of independence is a change in only one aspect of a nation's political and social fabric — the transfer of political power from alien to indigenous rulers.

To the observer studying a new, excolonial nation's political development in the first years after independence, there is always the temptation to try to determine accurately what historical circumstances, what habits of thought and conduct, are most influential in affecting the attitudes and actions of those who control the government. There is always the temptation to try to find the answers to such natural questions as: what are the significant roots of political behavior of such a country's leaders? In what ways are they influenced by their religion? — by their own social patterns or by those acquired under colonial rule? What elements of alien culture and thought have they absorbed? In the case of a new country like Burma, such a task is full of frustration and can easily end in futility. At present too little is known about the social or economic or political history of Burma. Detailed studies by competent scholars remain to be written. Specialized studies on the nature of Burmese society, the social and political influence of Buddhism, or the sources and sanctions of conduct among Burma's diverse population are only just being undertaken.

There is also the danger that an observer, in attempting to evaluate the reasons for a particular statement of policy or a specific action of an individual official or political group, will read into this too much of his own knowledge of the country's history or his own estimates of the influence of past history and culture patterns. What must be done, so far as possible, is to estimate the degree to which persons holding political power think and act in terms of their own society or are conscious of their nation's historical development as a factor that limits their freedom of action.

In the case of Burma, the persons wielding political power since 1948 have been, for the most part, the same persons who led the prewar independence movement, who shared a variety of experiences under the Japanese from 1942 to 1945, and who were directly concerned in the successful struggle for independence after 1945. To these political leaders, the memories of their youthful prewar political activity, their experiences during the war and their more recent struggles after the war and during the period of insurrection, are all very clear. It is their own personal experiences of the immediate past that affect their attitudes and upon which they most often draw for guidance in solving their present dilemmas.

With very few exceptions, these political leaders of independent Burma have not been students of their country's history. They have had neither the time nor the inclination to analyze carefully the period of British rule or of Japanese occupation in order to determine their effects on the economic and political development of the country. In attempting to manage the affairs of a sovereign state, they are often hindered or limited by the legacies of their history and culture without being fully conscious of precisely what aspects of Burma's past affect the present.

Acutely conscious of the events within their own lives in the past twenty years, Burma's leaders have naturally drawn upon this personal experience as a guide to their actions or reactions to contemporary events. For these reasons, some understanding of the period of the independence movement in Burma, and the events between 1942 and 1948 is necessary to an evaluation of Burma's foreign policy since independence. This was the period during which the present leaders of Burma cut their political teeth. Experience in the art of politics and the operation of government was gained during this period, mainly under the Japanese.

Right at the start it is necessary to characterize Burma's independence movement. Was it a truly "nationalist" movement or not? Did the efforts of Burmans to gain independence from Britain include a conscious effort to create a feeling of national unity among the diverse population of the country? Or, did the struggle to gain freedom from British rule itself serve to unite the diverse people of Burma, bringing them together in a common effort to achieve a common aim which transcended their local differences? The answers to these questions are important for if a new government, of a new "nation," must struggle with divided loyalties among its people, and with the failure of people generally to accept their new role as citizens of a nation as one transcending their local or particular group loyalties, then that government faces grave handicaps in the execution of its domestic and foreign policies.

The area known as "Burma" today has been said to lie "within the most distinctive physical environment in the Orient, because it has but one core area placed within a framework of mountains." [2]

Throughout the early history of Burma, the bulk of the migration has come from the north, while the major cultural penetration has come from and through India from the west. The extent of these migrations from the north, the racial and linguistic characteristics of the migrants are imperfectly known, particularly for the earlier periods. It is fair to conclude with Spencer, however, that [3] "in a general way the lowlands have been the final goal of all the varied culture groups that have entered Burma, and the modern Burmese people and Burmese culture have been the final product. The Burmese of today are a lowland people, and their culture is a lowland culture, though the upland frame is home to a wide variety of culture groups with different patterns of culture." The flow of migrants from the north took place over a period of centuries. The easiest access to Burma is by the Bay of Bengal. Consequently, there have been few attempts by foreign conquerors to control Burma. Control or even political influence by outside nations was brief and transitory in the pre-British period. Unlike other territories in Asia, Burma never became a real bone of contention between rival imperialisms.

The population of Burma has been a mixture of ethnic-linguistic and geographically separate groups throughout its history. The continuing underpopulation of the country has permitted the Burmese majority and the substantial numbers of the minorities to maintain their separate identities and culture. There has been space and land enough for all. This underpopulation, when coupled with the fact that internal communication between the Burmese-populated lowlands and the surrounding non-Burmese highlands and even the coastal areas has never been adequate, produced an environment in which diversity and separatism could flourish unchecked. Today, the Burmese majority of approximately 15,000,000 lives predominantly in the lowlands, surrounded by some 4,000,000 hill people — the Shans, Kachins, Nagas, Chins, Karreni and many smaller ethnic-linguistic groups. One large minority, the Karens, are filtered throughout the Burmese population of the lower Irrawaddy delta and the Tenasserim coast.

As colonial rulers, it was only natural that the British gave no serious thought to the development of anything like a "national" culture, or a "national" society or economy that would transcend in any way the group loyalties of the Burmese and of the minority groups in the country. Such a policy would have been contrary to British economic and political interests. The Government of India, responsible for the new province of Burma, had recognized communal, ethnic and linguistic differences in India. They could not have been expected to pursue a different policy in Burma. The new British rulers took Burma as they found it — a country of diverse population.

During the first thirty years of British rule in the twentieth century, the non-Burmese groups were encouraged to retain their group characteristics and their group identity. The highland areas were separately administered from Burma proper, where the Burmese majority lived, and the Burmese were not permitted to extend their cultural domination over the non-Burmese inhabitants in any way that might have resulted in developing common ties and interests among all the people of the country. Such a development would have raised the horrid specter of "nationalism" in its modern meaning and permitted "national" aspirations to be expressed. Instead, the people of Burma became simply British subjects with the same status as the people in provinces of British India. They were governed in ways that served to perpetuate their differences rather than diminish them.[4]

Under the British, another element was added to the diverse population groups of Burma — the Indian immigrants and seasonal laborers. This influx began after the opening of the Suez Canal in 1869 when the prospect of developing Burma's raw materials for export via the shorter route to Europe caused a new interest on the part of British investors in exploitation of Burma's resources. Not only did Indians come to Burma as workers, laborers, and merchants, but they were also brought in to take positions in the British administration. For the British this was a natural step, since Burma was administered by the Government of India. For the Burmese and many non-Burmese, it meant closing the doors to employment opportunities and loss of control over much of the rich delta rice lands.

The result of British policy and of the Indian influx was to create barriers, social, political, and economic, between the British rulers and their subjects, the Burmese majority and the indigenous minorities. As Furnivall points out,[5] "Thus, merely by the working of economic forces, there came into existence a plural society, comprising many different racial elements, differing in culture and performing different economic functions and with nothing in common but the desire for gain. What had formerly been a national society was converted into a business concern." By "national" society, Furnivall, like most writers, is referring to the Burmese majority, not the people of the country as a whole. Both in administrative structure and in political policy and practice, the British administration accentuated, rather than softened, the differences among racial, linguistic, and geographic groups within Burma. Representatives of the minority races were often given preferred positions in certain fields and in the local armed forces, on grounds that the Burmese were incapable of learning discipline or were lazy. Even members of the minority groups, however, were hardly able to compete in business, in commerce, in government clerkships, or in many other occupations against the Indians and a small, but active Chinese immigrant population.

Although some attempts were made to redress this imbalance before World War II, the Burmese majority and many of the members of minority groups had developed no feeling of loyalty toward their British overlords nor any significant belief that they had a chance to eventually possess and govern a country of their own. British concessions toward self-government were grudging and gradual, lagging behind the aspirations and even demands of the small, politically conscious group of Burmans who sought independence for their country.

Compared to some other colonial territories in Asia, the independence movement in Burma came rather late in the period between the two world wars. At this point, it is necessary to emphasize that as in most Asian countries the Burma independence movement is *not* to be equated with the development of nationalism in the true sense. The movement for freedom from British rule did *not* serve to unite the people of Burma as a whole nor infuse into them any ideas of national unity — loyalty to their country, Burma, transcending any local loyalties as Shans, Karens, Arkanese and so on. Freedom from British rule was not a means toward a united Burma, a new nation in the strict sense. As in other colonial areas, independence became an end in itself and the problems of national unity were not considered important. Thus, in a realistic sense, the leaders of the Burman independence movement were seeking the creation of a new, sovereign state. They assumed that a sense of nationalism would automatically follow independence. They did indeed succeed in creating a new state, but Burma, the *nation*, has yet to be born.

The details of the "independence struggle" in Burma before 1942 have been carefully studied.[6] It is sufficient here to summarize those particular aspects of the prewar independence movement which throw light upon the postwar adoption of a policy of neutralism by the new Burma government.[7] It is now well recognized that many of the leaders of independence movements in the colonial territories in Asia found a doctrinal basis for their aspirations in Marxism. The Burman leaders were no exceptions. All, including Thakin Nu, and the key Burman politicos found in Marxism a justification, a doctrine, which supported, intellectually, their basic desires to manage their own affairs without alien control.

In considering this Marxist orientation of the independence movement several points are significant. *First,* the Thakin group got their inspiration mainly from India and from the English Communists who supplied them with literature and whose interpretations of Marxism they studied.[8] There is no available evidence yet that any concerted efforts were made to make contacts with the Soviet Union or the Chinese Communists directly in this period. Nor is there evidence that Communist literature came into Burma directly from Soviet or Chinese sources.

Second, the Thakin leaders, including those who were calling themselves Communists at this time, developed their Marxian bias pretty much on their own. They had plenty of time for heated discussion, for reading and absorption because political action and political organization were erratic and when war broke out, increasingly more difficult. There were many, many doctrinal disputes and differences among the Thakins, even among the extreme Marxists. For example, the Burma Revolutionary Party, although calling itself "Socialist," included members who preferred the "Marxist" or "Communist" label and others who refused any designation except "Nationalist." Thein Pe observed that, "Ideological anarchy permeates party ranks, as men of different shades and creeds swell them." [9]

Third, it is apparent that even at this early period, the so-called Marxists and their associates in the *Dobama Asiayone* could be roughly divided into three groups.[10] First of all there were Thakins who called themselves "Marxists" but who apparently never accepted Marxism as the only *end* of policy. Rather they patently regarded their espousal of Marxism and some of its methods as a means to the one end they were interested in — independence from Britain. General Aung San and U Nu are good examples, as are U Ba Swe and U Kyaw Nyein. These leaders seemed perfectly willing to modify their Marxist views when Marxist doctrines seemed to interfere with or inhibit them from steps they regarded necessary to the attainment of independence. This attitude has also been apparent in the actions of many political leaders since independence.

Next, there has been a smaller group of doctrinaire Marxists, some of whom call themselves Communists as well. Leaders like Than Tun, Thakin Soe, Lay Maung, Ba Hein, Thein Pe Myint and Ba Tin have adhered to Marxism-Leninism as a political goal, above anything else. These leaders, however, were not able to agree among themselves on tactics, strategy, or even on interpretation of Marxian doctrine at all times and consequently were unable to join forces in developing a single, hard-core Communist party in Burma.

The third group included a number of individuals, some among the younger Thakins and some of the older politicians, who might give lip service to Marxism, but who sought independence as a goal apart from espousal of any doctrine or political theory. Most of this group could be labelled simply "politicians," in the sense that they sought political power, and became fairly adept at using whatever appeals to their followers or to the masses they thought might work. Many emerged in top positions in the Anti-Fascist People's Freedom League (AFPFL) government after independence.

Finally, it should be noted that the division of leadership in the independence movement set forth above was not a hard and fast one. In Burma since the 1930's it has been difficult to place politicians and officeholders in precise categories. What can be said is that Burma politics has been, and still is, characterized by personal ambition for power and an individual's political power depends much more on personal relations, family connections, and personal influence than on any set of ideas or doctrines he may publicly espouse. To date, ideologies have had relatively little significance in Burma politics, a fact that must be kept in mind in evaluating the policies and the actions of the Burma government since independence. An early example of this important factor is found in the career and actions of Burma's hero, General Aung San. Although nurtured on Marxism as a leading member of the Thakin group just before the war, given a liberal dose of Japanese propaganda during the war, Aung San showed himself much more the practical politician than the doctrinaire idealist and in the immediate postwar years before his death, held fast to his single aim of independence for Burma, thus becoming the principal stumbling block to the Burman Communists in their postwar bid for power.

"Independence" — Under Japan

The effects of the Japanese occupation on the development of the independence movement and more particularly on the attitudes of its leaders have not been thoroughly studied but it was during this time that most of the present Burman political leaders gained their first significant experience in government operations. Their memory of these experiences is quite clear while they have tended to forget many of the military aspects of the war in which they were less directly concerned.

When war broke out in Europe in September, 1939, leaders of the independence movement in Burma were attempting to bring together political groups of various persuasions to form a kind of united front against the British. As in other colonial territories, such efforts could not be tolerated in wartime. By the first of the year 1940, the newly enacted Defense of Burma regulations, giving the Governor autocratic emergency powers, enabled the British administration to label the independence leaders subversive and traitorous to the state. Under these circumstances and with their connections with Indian organizations effectively broken, many Burman leaders of the independence movement began to look to Japan for succor, lured by the new spectacle of an Asian nation effectively championing the cause of colonial peoples.

A Burmese writer has observed that, "The word 'independence' hitherto unheard of in their (Burmese) lives, which Tokyo radio repeatedly held out to them, had worked like magic on their wishful imaginations." [11] U Nu adds that, "The Japanese seemed to be the only eastern people that could hold its own against the West, and we came to look confidently to Japan for leadership." [12] There is some evidence that a few of the Burman leaders were aware of Japanese efforts to woo Indian dissidents, some of whom were working with the Japanese outside of India. It is probable, however, that this did not enter into Burman thinking, since there was little actual collaboration with the Indian Independence Army brought into Burma by the Japanese after 1942.

With a warrant out for his arrest, Aung San smuggled himself aboard a ship bound for Amoy in August, 1940.[13] Subsequently, arrangements were made to smuggle several groups of Burmans to Japan for military training. The nucleus of these groups later became known as the "Thirty Comrades." Some were prominent independence leaders, but others were followers from various walks of life. These men were given military training on Hainan Island off the south China coast, and they concluded an understanding with the Japanese that the Burma Revolutionary Party would be supplied with arms.[14]

Other Burmans, outside of the "Thakin" group, were also in touch with the Japanese secretly prior to the Japanese invasion. Both Dr. Ba Maw, who had been the first Prime Minister under the 1935 Constitution, and Dr. Thein Maung, a former Minister of Commerce, had preinvasion contacts. U Saw, who followed Ba Maw as Prime Minister, was arrested and imprisoned by the British for having collaborated with the Japanese. Apparently a considerable number of students had attempted to get to Japan, even prior to the departure of the "Thirty Comrades" group. About half of this group and some others were sent to Japan through the efforts of Thakin Ba Sein and his splinter group, which had broken with the *Dobama Asiayone*.[15]

Not all the independence leaders departed so far from their Marxist teachings as to join hands with the Japanese. U Ba Choe was strongly pro-Communist consistently. The doctrinaire Communists — Thakin Soe and Thein Pe Myint — and the strongly Marxist and later Communist Thakin Than Tun seem to have opposed the Japanese from the outset. These men were the principal leaders of the Burma Revolutionary Party (BRP). Even Thein Pe Myint acted as a leader of this party for a time in upper Burma. It was largely dominated by the Marxian Socialists among the Thakin group and some of them were to claim later that it was the true forerunner of the Burma Socialist Party, organized after the war.[16]

When the Japanese armies invaded Burma in January, 1942, they were accompanied by the nucleus of what was soon to become the Burma Independence Army (BIA), which swelled in numbers as the Japanese proceeded northward.[17] Strangely enough, while this was happening, the Thakin leaders who were being held in jail by the British were offering to rally the Burmese against the Japanese in return for a British promise of independence after the war. There was no British response to this offer.[18]

The generally favorable attitude toward the Japanese in Burma was reflected by most of the population at the start, a large proportion showing no desire to resist Japan's occupation and, unless they feared being charged as British agents, they did as they were told. One major reason why many Burmans welcomed the Japanese and why many of the Burma independence leaders of diverse views initially believed the Japanese had come as liberators was the obvious unpreparedness of Britain to defend Burma adequately. The swiftness of the Japanese invasion in January, 1942 was as much of a shock to the Burmans as to the British, but to the Burmans the shock had a double effect. They had given little thought to a possible Japanese invasion or to any need for defense of their territory. They looked upon the war only as an event that caused the British colonial government to hamper their moves for independence. They assumed, as did the British themselves, that adequate provision would be made for defending Burma. The unexpected rapidity with which the Japanese routed the small British forces and cleared them from Burma led many Burmans first, to applaud the success of their Asian "brothers" and, second, to feel that they had, in fact, been liberated from British rule.

The rapid disintegration of Allied forces in Burma left the Japanese free to carry out their plans for the country as a part of the Greater East Asia Co-Prosperity Sphere. These plans had been under discussion and revision since the middle of 1940. In a plan for the "southern regions" prepared by the War Ministry in October, 1940, Burma Territory was to be used as bait in a new peace approach to Chiang Kai-Shek. In this plan, the French were to be forced out of Indo-China and the province of Tonking offered to Chiang Kai-Shek. If this was not good enough to secure his "cooperation" in a peace settlement, he was to be offered large areas of upper Burma.[19] The remainder of the country, or all of it if Chiang refused to come to terms, was to be given independence. This was to be independence with strings although the Japanese were careful not to enumerate the "strings" in their propaganda to Burma and to other Southeast Asian territories. These "strings" included a tight military and economic alliance with Japan and the use of Japanese military advisers in key positions.[20] On January 22, 1942, Premier Tojo, in a speech to the Diet, promised independence to the Philippines and Burma, provided their peoples "understood our true intentions" and were prepared to cooperate in the building of Greater East Asia.[21] Japanese intentions were clear to themselves, but were concealed from the independence leaders whom they planned to use as "a front."

There is some evidence that the Japanese hoped to place U Saw in the key position at the head of an "independent" regime in Burma, but his arrest and detention by the British scotched this plan. They therefore turned to Dr. Ba Maw. At the time of the Japanese invasion, Ba Maw was in jail at Mogok, but he escaped in the chaos of the British retreat and went to Mandalay. The apparent reason for the selection of Dr. Ba Maw in place of Aung San or one of the Thakin group with whom the Japanese were working was that the military commanders felt that the Thakins and the Burma Independence Army were getting out of hand, paying off old scores against their political opponents and against the Karens in particular. The Japanese commanders, therefore, proceeded to set up a Preparatory Executive Committee in June at Maymyo with Dr. Ba Maw as Chairman. Under his persuasion many of the Burman civil servants returned to their posts when the Committee moved to Rangoon in July. At the same time the Japanese disbanded the Burma Independence Army preparatory to its reorganization the following month under closer supervision. On August 1, 1942, Dr. Ba Maw was made head of the Burma Executive Administration, whose members included some, but not all, of the Thakin group. The Burma Defense Army (BDA) was established to include the forces of the original BIA.

On January 28, 1943, Premier Tojo declared that an independent Burma state would be created within a year. In March, Ba Maw was sent to Tokyo for consultations, and on his return to Rangoon an

Independence Preparatory Commission was established, composed of twenty-two members, of which he became Chairman. On August 1, 1943, a Burmese "Declaration of Independence" was issued, and a new "Burmese" government was formed with Ba Maw taking the title of *Nainggandaw Adipati* (roughly, Head of State or General-issimo). The end of Japanese military administration was formally announced, a treaty of alliance with Japan was signed, and the new government declared war on the United States and Great Britain.

In 1946, Ba Maw asserted that it was the Japanese who organized the work of the Preparatory Commission and drew up the "Declaration of Independence" and the "Basic Treaty" with Japan. He also stated that in addition to the treaty with Japan a secret military agreement was signed, under which the new Burma government agreed that the Japanese Commander-in-Chief in Burma could take any measures he considered necessary in respect to military operations, could order the Burma government to assist in carrying out such measures, and could veto any action of the Burma government if he so desired.[22]

The new government that assumed office in August, 1943, included many of the Thakin leaders. Aung San was made a Major General by the Japanese in command of the reorganized BDA and also became Minister of Defense. Thakin Mya was appointed Deputy Prime Minister; Thakin Than Tun, Minister for Agriculture; Thakin Nu (U Nu), Minister for Foreign Affairs; and Lay Maung, Minister for Communications and Irrigation.[23]

As the war began to turn against the Japanese and prospects of Allied reinvasion of Burma heightened, they attempted to counter a growing unrest by promoting the Maha Bama — greater Burma — movement, whose purpose was to unite all the peoples of Burma under Burmese rule with "one language" and "one country," but this movement apparently had little success. In a treaty between the Ba Maw government and the Japanese, signed in Rangoon on September 25, 1943, it was agreed that the Shan states, except the two Shan territories the Japanese had given to Thailand, the Karenni states, and the Wa territory could be incorporated into Burma. Japanese military control of these territories was to be terminated within ninety days after the treaty was signed, and they would come under the Ba Maw administration.[24]

By 1944, many Burmans had become considerably disillusioned with the disparity between Japanese promises and Japanese actions in their country. Resistance was developing, and the private talks that were to lead to open anti-Japanese activity later on had begun. The end was not far off. When it became clear that the Allied armies were capable of driving the Japanese out of Burma, General Aung San established contact with the British forces and led his army, now renamed the Burma National Army (BNA), in joining forces with the British and attacking the remnants of the fleeing Japanese troops. As the Allied forces approached Rangoon, Dr. Ba Maw and some of his close followers fled with the retreating Japanese to Moulmein and later to Tokyo, where he was imprisoned after the Japanese surrender. Later, after lengthy interrogations, he was released and returned to Rangoon to re-enter politics with a status something like that of an "elder statesman."

The development of the Ba Maw government during the war under Japanese tutelage had certain consequences. It was the first experience that many of the Burman independence leaders had had in government positions of responsibility. General Aung San, Thakin Nu, and many of their associates, who led the AFPFL after the Japanese defeat, gained their first real governmental experience under the Japanese. Yet the form and structure of the government was unlike that which they finally chose for Burma when they had freedom of choice. It is probable, however, that this wartime experience did, in fact, shape their ideas and attitudes, induce certain habits of political behavior and views about the functions of government that have affected and probably still do affect their postindependence conduct.[25] Whatever the importance or lack of importance of this first experiment at Japanese-controlled self-government, the gradual disillusionment of these Burman leaders with the Japanese and the plans made to turn against their initial "liberators" are better known and the consequences are easier to assess. This aspect of Burma politics during the war, therefore, needs some attention.

While it may be true, as U Nu described, that many Burmans welcomed the Japanese as liberators from the alien rule of the British, it was not long before the people felt the heavy hand of the Japanese military. As one prominent Burman reported:[26]

The Japanese had a wonderful opportunity of 'selling' their Co-Prosperity Sphere to the Burmese people. They had merely to pose as liberators, co-religionist brothers from the East, who had shed their blood in order to drive away the lordly whites. But unfortunately their very upbringing contained the seeds of their undoing.

They could never forget even for a second that they were descendants of a God . . . They were the lords of creation. They condescended to treat with the Burmese . . . The Japanese Army soon made the Burmans realize they were not sticking any nonsense. As in China, the Japanese resorted to slapping to secure acquiescence to their whims and behests . . . At a meeting of Upper Burma District Commissioners held in Mandalay in 1943, it was formally resolved that the Japanese authorities should be approached to prohibit the slapping of District Commissioners by anybody below the rank of Lieutenant Colonel.(!)

It is doubtful, however, that the harsh, brutal, and arbitrary treatment of the Burmans by the Japanese military alone would have caused the Burman leaders in the "independent" government to revolt against the Japanese. They could not be sure when the war would end. They heard little of the progress of the war through other than Japanese sources. It was obviously tight Japanese controls over all aspects of the economic life of the country that opened the eyes of some of the Burmese leaders like Aung San to the fact that this "made-in-Japan independence" was a sham.

For the Japanese Army kept a stranglehold on the economic life of Burma. Railway and river communications were monopolized. Large supplies of rice were requisitioned and thousands of cattle slaughtered to meet the Army's food requirements. As long as shipping was available, all resources the Japanese could obtain, such as cotton, minerals, timber, and the like, were sent out of the country. Japanese companies were given a monopoly over this business, under Japanese civilians, but the Army dominated the scene. By voluntary recruitment, and conscription where necessary, the Japanese Army organized a considerable labor force, and it is believed that as many as 30,000 Burman laborers died in the construction of the infamous "railway of death" being constructed in the south between Burma and Thailand.

All of these developments contributed to a feeling among many of the Burman leaders that their hopes for independence were not to be realized under Japan, but could only come to fruition when the Japanese armies were driven from their country. They also knew that in the country the people were finding military occupation worse than anything they had experienced under British rule. Thus a resistance movement would have some active support and virtually no opposition in the countryside. As early as August, 1944, Aung San had spoken publicly and with a certain contempt of the Japanese brand of independence.[27]

This disillusionment with the Japanese was furthered by the activities and developing organization of the Communists in Burma. After the Nazi attack on the Soviet Union, Communist parties in Asia and elsewhere were directed to do everything to help defeat the German-Japanese Fascists. In Southeast Asia, the Communists often formed the core of a well-organized underground resistance movement. In Burma, the Communists were helped by the establishment of regular channels of communication with the Indian Communist Party (CPI). Because of his open anti-Japanese views, Thein Pe Myint had fled to India shortly after the Japanese invasion of Burma began. In India he became a liaison agent between the British authorities and the anti-Japanese underground in Burma. More importantly, he took advantage of his position to develop his connections with the CPI. Many messages were apparently sent from P. C. Joshi, General Secretary of the CPI, to Thakin Nu and other Burman leaders, and Thein Pe Myint also appears to have been acting at times under Joshi's instructions.[28]

In August, 1944, which marked the first anniversary of Burma's "independence" under the Japanese, a few leaders of the Burma Defense Army, including Aung San, met with both Communist and Socialist leaders secretly to form the Anti-Fascist Organization (AFO). Thakin Than Tun became its Secretary-General and remained in that position when it later became the AFPFL. A number of Burman Communists were appointed as political commissars in several "resistance" zones established in the country in order to indoctrinate Burma National Army personnel and local leaders preparatory to an anti-Japanese uprising, which actually took place in March, 1945.[29] Thakin leaders Ba Hein and Soe, along with Than Tun, also appear to have had leading organizational roles in the AFO and in building the resistance forces.[30]

It is significant that the Burma Communist Party (BCP) was also formally organized in 1944, shortly after the formation of the AFO.[31] While actively organizing resistance against the Japanese, the Burman Communists took advantage of their position to expand their influence within the AFO and in the districts upcountry. Anti-Japanese indoctrination was combined with Communist propaganda. Since Aung San and some of his immediate non-Communist associates were much more concerned with the military aspects of the anti-Japanese resistance, with problems of eventual collaboration with the advancing British forces, and with future strategy for winning postwar independence for Burma, the Communists had a rather free hand to dominate the resistance movement politically.

By 1945 the efforts of the Communists had largely helped gain effective popular support for the open resistance movement. In the closing days of the conflict and in the rather chaotic twelve months that followed, the BCP was able to further entrench itself in many of the districts upcountry, within the trades unions, and even to an extent within the Burma Army itself.[32]

A series of circumstances, therefore, combined to place the Thakins, the younger political leaders of Burma, at the head of an anti-Japanese movement which cooperated with the Allied armies as they drove the Japanese out of central Burma in the race to Rangoon. In shifting from an anti-British movement to that of an anti-Japanese movement, Aung San and his associates not only kept pace with the feelings of most of the people but emerged at the end of the war as national heros with an enthusiastic popular support. The qualities in General Aung San that helped him attain the top position of a national leader are described by General Slim after their first meetings as follows:[33]

I was impressed by Aung San. He was not the ambitious, unscrupulous guerilla leader I had expected. He was certainly ambitious and meant to secure for himself a dominant position in post-war Burma, but I judged him to be a genuine patriot and a well-balanced realist—characters which are not always combined. His experience with the Japanese had put his views on the British into a truer perspective. He was ready himself to cooperate with us in the liberation and restoration of Burma and, I thought, probably to go on co-operating after that had been accomplished. The greatest impression he made on me was one of honesty. He was not free with glib assurances and he hesitated to commit himself, but I had the idea that if he agreed to do something he would keep his word. I could do business with Aung San.

Peaceful Transfer of Power

In Burma, the circumstances under which political decisions were made between April, 1945, and the end of 1947, as well as the nature of the decisions themselves, were to play a large part in shaping the course of independent Burma after 1948 and the adoption of a neutralist foreign policy. Two parallel political contests dominated the Burmese scene during this period. The first was carried on between the chief protagonists of Burma's independence led by General Aung San, and representatives of the British Government. The second centered on the struggle between the Socialists and the Communists for control of the AFPFL.[34] These two contests were separate and parallel, yet their outcome was interrelated and strongly conditioned the postindependence attitudes and policies of the leaders of the new Burma Government. They will be dealt with separately here for purposes of clarity.

As the British armies raced for Rangoon to gain the capital before the heavy monsoon rains should come to bog down military operations, the AFO could face the close of the war with some confidence. They had a considerable store of arms, a nationwide organization, and enthusiastic support from large segments of the population of the country, particularly in lowland Burma. The goal of Aung San and his associates was nothing less than full independence for Burma and that as soon as humanly possible.

British plans for postwar control of Burma envisaged nothing of the kind. During most of the war, a Burma government in exile, far off in the hill station of Simla, India, had been planning for postwar administration of the country. It was headed by Sir Reginald Dorman-Smith, the last prewar Governor, and included various Burman officials who had escaped Burma with the British in 1942. This government in exile was cut off from much knowledge about events in Burma under the Japanese. It was often not consulted at all by the military commanders. The plans prepared by Simla became the basis for a British "White Paper" announced on May 17, 1945.[35] This scheme called for a political retrogression rather than progress toward independence. Burma was to be under direct administration

of the Governor for three years before a Burman Cabinet and Legislature under the 1935 Constitution would be re-established. During
this period an election was to be held and the representatives invited
to draw up a Constitution. Subsequent to this, the British promised
"full self-government within the Commonwealth," but the scheduled
areas such as the Shan states and hill tracts were to continue under
separate administration of the Governor until their inhabitants had
decided what form of association with Burma proper they would
take.

Thus British plans and Burman aspirations were still far apart, and
at the time he agreed to place his forces under British command,
General Aung San warned his subordinates that they should be prepared to fight the British again to gain Burma's independence if this
should prove necessary. His remarks were in full accord with the
views of the Communists within his ranks and in keeping with the
Marxist belief that the "imperialists" could be dislodged from any
colonial territory only by force of arms.

The Thakin group under Aung San's leadership, however, did not
let their Marxism become a rigid guide to their policies and actions
in dealing with the British. Much credit for their attitudes is undoubtedly due to the treatment accorded the Burman independence
leaders by Lord Louis Mountbatten, the Supreme Commander of
Allied Forces in Southeast Asia. It was Mountbatten's view that if
the AFO was forcibly suppressed, as urged by Governor Dorman-
Smith and his aides in Simla, there would be civil war.[36] Mountbatten
was determined "that no section of the Burmese people should be
able to claim that we were returning to the country in a spirit of
revenge or reprisal." Recalling that Great Britain's traditional policy
of leniency and conciliation had convinced such ex-enemy leaders
as Generals Smuts and Botha in South Africa that it was possible to
work with the British without rancor, Mountbatten concluded that
a similar policy was needed to win the confidence of Aung San and
the Thakins and thus permit Britain to fulfill the objective of eventual
self-government within the Commonwealth. Mountbatten had received War Cabinet approval for his proposal to give support to the
AFO in resistance against the Japanese, and he now advocated treating the AFO leaders as the legitimate, although yet unofficial, representatives of the bulk of the people.[37]

According to the records of his assistants, General Aung San was so favorably impressed by the sincerity and forthright behavior of Lord Mountbatten and his leading subordinates that his confidence in the British was increased, and he was persuaded that his goal of independence could be achieved by peaceful agreement rather than by use of armed force. It was thus that Aung San agreed to place his army, renamed the Burma Patriotic Force (BPF) under British command and later to the disbandment of the BPF after the Japanese surrender. The British Commanders found Aung San "most cooperative." [38] Lord Mountbatten and his Army Commanders, Generals Slim and Rance, had so impressed General Aung San by their honesty and sincerity that he expressed his desire that "Burma should enter the British Commonwealth of Nations, if the full right of our nation to independence is recognized." [39]

Aung San and his colleagues, however, recognized that no matter how sincere Lord Mountbatten might be, he could influence, but not dictate, British policy and that he had, in fact, given them "recognition" without formal approval from London. The immediate postwar military administrations, which had attempted to restore some semblance of order, put the port of Rangoon in working order, and had partially patched up the communications and transport network of the country, gave way to the Civil Administration in October, 1945. The same colonial administrators who had been in charge before the Japanese invasion returned to Rangoon, led by the prewar Governor, Sir Reginald Dorman-Smith. Dorman-Smith had been urged to declare the AFPFL illegal and to try Aung San as a war criminal. Many of the prewar colonial administrators in Burma had supported this view and proposed that the "extremist group" (the AFPFL) be firmly handled on return to civil administration. The legal means for such action existed under the Defense of Burma Act, which had been used to break up the *Dobama Asiayone* in 1940. These emergency wartime regulations had been broadened by Dorman-Smith while in exile in Simla in 1943 and were continued in force even after the restoration of civil government in October, 1945.[40]

The attitudes of the Dorman-Smith group were known to the AFPFL leaders, and the beginnings of a mutual trust that developed between them and the military administration gave way to a growing mutual suspicion and hostility soon after civil administration was restored. The AFPFL's initial demand for their recognition as the provisional government of Burma had been set aside when the leaders believed an agreement could be reached with the British for independence. In the October, 1945, negotiations over composition of the Governor's Executive Council, the AFPFL leaders failed to reach agreement with Governor Dorman-Smith. He then formed a Council headed by Sir Paw Tun and composed of other prewar leaders, most of whom had been in exile during the war. Sir Paw Tun had been responsible for jailing AFPFL leaders during his prewar Premiership and had been an advocate of firm suppression of the AFPFL.

The brief period that followed has been characterized as a war of nerves between the Dorman-Smith administration and the AFPFL. British officials denounced the AFPFL and its activities as subversive of law and order. They continued to urge on Dorman-Smith that Aung San be arrested. In fact, an order was issued in April, 1946, for his arrest but was rescinded at the last moment on representations of the British Commander-in-Chief, General Briggs, who warned that an armed rebellion would result from such a drastic move. Although Governor Dorman-Smith left for England in June, 1946, his successor, Acting Governor Knight, continued the unconciliatory policy toward the AFPFL and threatened strong action against those persons "making subversive and inflammatory speeches," since such speeches "foster a spirit of lawlessness." [41]

The suspicions of British intentions which the AFPFL leaders developed during Dorman-Smith's brief regime were intensified by the British Government's policies, which placed heavy emphasis on rehabilitation of the large British enterprises in the country. Aung San suspected that "The British government is using their best endeavors to bring about the re-establishment of British commercial and economic domination of the country.[42] This development was hardly calculated to appeal to the Marxist-oriented leaders and the rank and file of the AFPFL. In fact, it seemed to confirm the orthodox Marxist view that "imperialists" would give up their colonial holdings only when forced to do so by use of violence.

Aung San's tactics, however, were to announce that "We want no violence and bloodshed at all," and "we are . . . determined to exhaust legitimate opportunities before resorting to violent methods." [43] To give his AFPFL bargaining power with the British administration, however, mass demonstrations were organized, and a People's Volunteer Organization (PVO) was established as a paramilitary force. The AFPFL declared that the PVO would be a large force "of ex-soldiers and guerrillas" to "rise against the British if necessary." Although there were quantities of hidden arms, collected during the war, the PVO began drilling with dummy rifles in the streets of Rangoon as a means of impressing the British with what might happen.[44]

The next move of the AFPFL was to prepare for a general strike in order to force a reassessment of British policy. This reassessment, however, was already under way. At the suggestion of Lord Mountbatten, the new Labor Prime Minister, Clement Attlee, was prepared to appoint General Sir Hubert Rance as Governor of Burma. Rance had been head of the military administration in Burma right after the Japanese surrender, and he was apparently convinced that the future of the country depended upon reaching agreement with Aung San and his AFPFL. When Rance arrived in Rangoon, the railways, postal and telegraph systems, government ministries, and the police were all on strike, and the administration and trade of the country were almost at a standstill.[45]

Governor Rance regarded Aung San as a friend, not as an ex-enemy, and was soon able to persuade him to form a new Governor's Executive Council on September 26, 1946. This AFPFL-dominated Council continued to act as the *de facto* administration of Burma until actual independence. The general strike was quickly called off as a consequence. On November 8, 1946, Aung San's Executive Council formally requested the British Government to make the necessary arrangements for transfer of power to a fully independent Burma. On December 20, Prime Minister Attlee announced in the House of Commons that a Burma delegation would be invited to London to discuss the arrangements and added that the Burmese people would have the right to choose whether they would remain within the British Commonwealth or not.

The Burma delegation arrived in London on January 8, 1947, and on January 20 a document that became known as the Aung San-Attlee Agreement was signed.[46] This agreement stated that it was designed to provide means whereby "the people of Burma may

achieve their independence . . . as soon as possible." Elections were
to be held for a Constituent Assembly, and the Governor's Executive
Council was to act as the provisional government until a constitution
was adopted and the date of independence fixed. The agreement also
provided that Britain would sponsor Burma's admission to the United
Nations, would negotiate with the new government for a loan, and
left membership in the British Commonwealth open for Burman
decision. On Aung San's triumphant return to Rangoon, he announced that Burma would have her freedom within a year.

Although the agreement was denounced as a sellout to the British
by the Communists and other left-wing groups and conditions in the
country were hardly favorable for a tranquil election, the AFPFL
won an overwhelming vote in the April elections for the Constituent
Assembly, gaining 248 of the 255 seats. The Assembly met in June,
1947, and finished its labors in September. Thakin Nu was elected
President of the Assembly and steered the deliberations in accordance with the desires of the AFPFL leaders, of which he was one.

A most important question was whether Burma would become a
member of the British Commonwealth or not. The full story of this
decision has not been revealed, but there are known factors that
heavily influenced the complete separation of Burma from the Commonwealth. Among these was the fact that Britain's immediate postwar policies had caused considerable ill-will among many political
segments of the AFPFL, and there was an emotional desire to sever
all ties with their former colonial rulers. It has been asserted that
Aung San himself would have preferred the Commonwealth connection but that Thakin u Nu and others persuaded him that such a
proposal might result in a serious split within the AFPFL. The need
for political unity overrode other considerations. Perhaps most important was the fact that the Communists and their supporters had
attacked the Aung San-Attlee Agreement as a "sham independence"
and were violently opposed to retention of any ties with Britain.
These factors were decisive, and early in its deliberations the Constituent Assembly resolved that Burma should be independent outside the Commonwealth.[47]

The Constituent Assembly's work was interrupted on July 19 when
General Aung San, Thakin Mya, and five other political leaders were
assassinated in the Secretariat Building by the hired gunmen of

U Saw. This shocking act could have thrown the country into turmoil, but U Say's "rebellion" did not occur, and the same day Governor Rance called upon Thakin Nu to form a new Cabinet.[48]

Thakin Nu carried General Aung San's work to completion, and with the adoption of the new Constitution, the British Government agreed to transfer power to a fully sovereign Burma in January, 1948. So it was that the first, important political contest of the immediate postwar period in Burma — that between the AFPFL and the British Government — was resolved by peaceful agreement and without bloodshed. This contest, however, did leave a legacy of suspicion, a very natural feeling of anticolonialism which influenced Burma's leaders against any "alignment" with the West, even membership in the British Commonwealth.

Internal Political Struggle

While this political contest was running its course toward peaceful agreement, the other internal political contest — the struggle between the Socialists and the Communists for control of the AFPFL — was continuing to mount in intensity and it eventually led, not to peaceful agreement, but to civil war. This contest, as much as the first, had a profound effect upon the postindependence policies and actions of the new Burma government, both internally and externally.

When in August, 1945, the AFO was reorganized as the AFPFL, it was announced that the primary purpose of this organization was to "marshall all available forces in the country and to . . . (utilize) the united strength in the struggle for freedom." Aung San then invited "all patriots and patriotic political parties" to join the AFPFL. The organization became, in effect, a kind of "popular front," a coalition of various political groups that included politicians of many shades of opinion and associations representing various minority groups as well.[49] Thakin Mya and his Socialist followers gave strong support to the AFPFL and its policy of avoiding the use of force and violence if peaceful means would suffice.[50]

In attempting to attain freedom from Britain by negotiation, Aung San and his Socialist supporters found themselves subjected to pressures from all sides. The newly organized PVO had been denounced by Dorman-Smith as a "danger to established authority," and various elements within the AFPFL were urging an end to negotiations with the British and an open resort to arms.[51] A correspondent for the Calcutta *Statesman* reported that "Nobody denies that he (Aung San) is a moderating influence on the forces that mill around his personality and find voice in him. But he, himself, seems doubtful sometimes as to how long he can keep them in check." [52]

The most concerted pressure on Aung San and his Socialist allies came from the various Communist groups and their extreme leftist supporters. Even before the end of the war, evidence of Communist maneuvers within the AFO had been brought to the attention of Aung San. In July, 1945, one of his officers reported that "Some of the partisans who had joined the resistance movement were Communists and had begun to convert others to their beliefs. The converted Communists then refused to take orders from non-Communist officers and discipline was fast being undermined." [53]

The Burma Communist Party had established itself in Rangoon as soon as the war ended and had intensified its organizing activities. The Communists appear to have gained many adherents among the discharged soldiers for whom they set up special indoctrination courses.[54] A measure of their success in trade-union activities was seen in the general strike of August, 1946, engineered chiefly through the Communist-dominated Ministerial Services Union.[55]

At this time the Burma Communist Party was divided into two wings. Thakin Soe was leader of one wing and an early advocate of launching a "people's war against the imperialists." [56] Thakin Than Tun, at this time more moderate in his views, was the leader of the other wing. Difference over doctrinal interpretation and tactics resulted in a party split in which Thakin Soe's group, a minority of the membership, was expelled from the Party in March, 1946. Thakin Soe and his followers immediately organized themselves as the Communist Party of Burma (CPB) becoming popularly known as the "Red Flag Communists," while Thakin Than Tun's group became known as the "White Flag Communists." Four months after this split Thakin Soe and his Red Flags began an underground campaign of violence against the Burma government which has continued to the present time.

The Burma Socialist Party was organized in September, 1945, as a "belated counter to the Communist Party." [57] The main strength of the Socialists lay in the All-Burma Peasants Organization (ABPO), which had been headed by Thakin Mya before the war and which was now reorganized and revived. The Socialists also attempted to expand their own influence in the trade unions by organizing the Trades Union Congress (Burma), [TUC(B)] as a rival group to the now Communist-dominated All-Burma Trades Union Congress.

Although there was evidence that Thakin Than Tun and his White Flag Communists aimed to eventually gain control of the Burma government, Aung San and his successor, U Nu, were able to maintain a tenuous cooperation with this group within the AFPFL until independence had been won. Than Tun at this time occupied the key post of Secretary-General of the AFPFL, and Aung San had appealed to their comradeship of the war days as resistance leaders against the Japanese to hold him and his followers in line.[58]

When the new Governor's Council was formed under Governor Rance in late September, 1946, Aung San became Deputy President of the Council, virtually Prime Minister in all but title. He also retained the Defense portfolio for himself, but in making his Ministerial appointments, Thakin Than Tun was passed over. Socialist Leader Thakin Mya got the important post of Home Minister, and Thein Pe Myint was the only representative of the White Flag Communists to be appointed. The reasons that Aung San failed to include Than Tun in his Cabinet are obscure, but the results are clear. When Aung San refused Than Tun's pleas for greater White Flag representation in the Council, he declared a general strike against the AFPFL government. Aung San responded by expelling Than Tun and his White Flag Communists from the AFPFL and members of this group from positions they occupied in the trade union organizations. Socialist U Kyaw Nyein was given Than Tun's position as Secretary-General of the AFPFL.

When the Aung San-Attlee agreement for Burma's independence was announced, opponents from both the "right" and the "left" in Burma's politics roundly denounced it as a "sell-out" to the British. Thakin Ba Sein and U Saw opposed it for different reasons, as did Dr. Ba Maw and Sir Paw Tun. Most violent in their denunciations were Than Tun and his followers, along with other pro-Communist politicians. Than Tun led his organization in fomenting "protest" strikes, and the underground Red Flag Communists increased their sabotage activities. This was the uncertain political situation in Burma as the Constituent Assembly met to begin drafting the new Constitution, and none of the political breaches had been healed at the time Aung San was assassinated in July, 1947.

When Thakin Nu succeeded Aung San, one of his first actions was to attempt to bring about political unity by a reconciliation with the White Flag Communists. This possibility had been raised by some Communist leaders themselves at a meeting with U Nu immediately after Aung San's assassination.[59]

When the Constituent Assembly had completed its work, Thakin Nu left for London to negotiate the actual transfer of power and on October 17, 1947, the Nu-Attlee agreement was signed.[60] The efforts of Thakin Nu to bring the White Flag Communists within the AFPFL fold at first seemed to have produced results. When the Nu-Attlee agreements were announced, Thein Pe Myint observed that the BCP at first welcomed the Nu-Attlee agreement.[61] But the tenuous cooperation between the BCP and the AFPFL was soon broken, and in November, 1947, the BCP began a series of attacks on the Nu-Attlee agreement. On November 17 the AFPFL announced publicly that "efforts to bring about unity between the AFPFL and the Communists had been discontinued." [62]

Two provisions of the Nu-Attlee agreement came under heavy fire from the Communists and their supporters. The first had provided for British assistance in training Burma's armed forces, and Burma had undertaken not to arrange for such assistance from any nation outside the Commonwealth. By the second provision the Burma Government had undertaken to pay equitable compensation for such British enterprises in Burma as the government might nationalize.

Recalling his negotiations with the British, Thakin Nu had remarked, "No one can deny the fact that this Labour Government are in a position to drive a hard bargain with us." Yet, "From the beginning to end the British Labour Government were at pains to win our goodwill rather than our treasure." Thakin Nu replied to his Communist detractors that the two provisions in the Nu-Attlee agreement under attack by them were reasonable and normal in international usage, that even the Soviet Government had paid compensation to private foreign enterprises and that such Communist countries as Yugoslavia had accepted this principle.[63]

After the November failure to achieve "leftist unity," relations between the AFPFL and Than Tun's White Flag Communists steadily deteriorated. The final break came within two months after independence when the BCP leaders Than Tun and Thakin Ba Tin (Goshal) established more direct connections with the world Communist movement seeking guidance as to how they should act with respect to Burma's "sham" independence. In February, 1948, these two leaders attended the Southeast Asian Youth Conference in Calcutta. This was a Communist-sponsored conference and appears to have been one of the first postwar attempts of Moscow to establish contacts with Communist leaders in South and Southeast Asia and thus exert influence and control over Communist movements in this area. At this Conference, the Moscow directive was stated to be, "that the Communist parties should initiate and lead violent insurrections and civil wars in South and Southeast Asiatic Countries." [64]

Immediately after this "youth" conference, Than Tun and Goshal attended the Second Congress of the Communist Party of India. There they came into contact with European Communist agents and party members and presumably sought for, and received, further instructions as to their course of action in Burma.[65] Thakin Than Tun is said to have told the Central Committee of the BCP in 1949, ". . . that the Yugoslav comrade who attended the CPI Congress in India in 1948 had advised him to go ahead with armed revolution in Burma." [66]

In any event, it has been revealed that when the two Communist leaders returned to Burma, Goshal brought with him a document titled "The Revolutionary Possibilities for 1948," which proposed armed insurrection against the Burma government on the grounds that independence was a "sham," that British imperialism had not been eradicated, and that Burma could be "liberated" only by violent means.[67] The BCP subsequently adopted this program and at the end of March, 1948, the White Flag Communists under Than Tun broke finally with the AFPFL government and followed the earlier example of the "Red Flags" by going underground and commencing their armed insurrection.

This development marks an important change in the position, views, and orientation of the Burma Communist Parties. It was in 1947 and 1948 that the Burma Communists began to look elsewhere than to the Communist Party in India for guidance, direction, and possible help. One reason appears to be that the Burma Communists, who were prepared to stage an armed revolt against the Government, found they had far less in common with their unarmed, aboveground Indian comrades than during the earlier stages of independence. Another reason appears to have been that the Burman Communists had become aware of developments in China and had realized that the armed revolts of the Chinese Communists against the Kuomintang Government were much more nearly parallel to their own desires and actions.

Thein Pe Myint writes that,[68]

The profound effects of the Chinese revolution on our people and on the people's emancipation movement are manyfold. . . . Firstly, so far as the Burmese people are concerned, the victory of the Chinese people is the clearest proof of the soundness and fruitfulness of the leadership of Marxism-Leninism in the struggle against foreign imperialism and native reaction, clearest because it happens in such a neighboring country as China, whose colonial and semi-colonial economic foundations are so much like ours and with whom we have so many traditional ties . . . Besides that, the victory of the Chinese Revolution teaches us, in common with other colonial and semi-colonial peoples, how to apply in true dialectical manner, the Marxist-Leninist theories to the revolutionary realities of our country.

Thein Pe Myint observes further that when U Nu raised the slogan of "Peace Within One Year," Thakin Than Tun countered with the slogan "For a Protracted Civil War." This was a copy of the Mao Tse-tung revolutionary strategy in China.[69]

The parallel struggles between the AFPFL leaders and the British government to attain independence and between the moderate AFPFL leaders and the extremists — the Communists and their supporters — have been presented in detail because they provide an important clue to the development of Burma's neutralist foreign policy after independence. As was stated, these twin contests interacted on each other but, more importantly, conditioned the attitudes of the AFPFL leadership. The contest with the British was won peacefully and led the Burman leaders to believe that postwar cooperation with Britain and the Western democracies was desirable, but their basic anticolonialisms and old suspicions of Western, capitalist nations were by no means dispelled.

The internal AFPFL contest was not won peacefully. The two Communist groups stuck to their program of seizing of power by violence and began their underground resistance, providing the spark for insurrections that nearly toppled the AFPFL government from power. There is little doubt that this later development gave to the more moderate AFPFL leaders, particularly the Socialists, a distinct bias against Communist methods. It was not sufficient to make them reject future relations with the Soviet bloc nations, but it was sufficient to make them wary of any relations which might result in outside Communist support for the Burma Communists. Thus, Thakin Nu and his colleagues, in the first year of independence, had a strong predisposition toward steering clear of alignments with either the Anglo-American group or the Communist bloc, a forerunner of their policy of "neutralism."

It had taken the AFPFL leaders only two and one-half months, from June 9 to September 24, 1947, to frame the constitution for their country. This process has been succinctly characterized by one of the few Burmese specialists in government as follows:

The main task for the framers of the constitution was to seek ways and means of getting the best of all worlds: state socialism, without any drastic surrender of the liberties and rights of the individual in a democratic society; detailed enumeration of fundamental rights and their safeguards, and directive principles to further express the socialist spirit of the constitution; parliamentary government and the rule of law; a federal structure in which the minorities and racial groups can feel happy enjoying some autonomy, with a strong central government which will ensure unity and a strong Union; separation of powers with safeguards against the Executive and the Judiciary becoming too free and independent of the Legislature. Once compromise arrangements were found to collect these elements and principles and put them together in one document, the details and the drafting were quickly done, for all the model constitutions were at hand to consult and borrow from. The Yugoslav constitution was perhaps the most frequently consulted, and the constitution of the Republic of Ireland. On federal government the American constitution was a helpful guide, while on parliamentary democracy the unwritten constitutional conventions and practices in Britain were already familiar to most Burmese lawyers. The resulting document therefore showed traces of those constitutions and a few others, but the main thing was that the document was finished in record time and it serves the purpose.[70]

True to their Marxist background, the AFPFL leaders set as the goal for their nation, the establishment of state socialism, the first and only new excolonial Asian nation to do so unequivocally. In moving the adoption of the draft constitution before the third session of the Constituent Assembly on September 24, 1947, U Nu had asserted,

And I might say at once, that it (the new Burma) will be Leftist. And a Leftist country is one in which the people working together to the best of their power and ability strive to convert the natural resources and produce of the land, both above ground and below ground, into consumer commodities to which everybody will be entitled, each according to his need. In a Leftist country there will be no such thing as a handful of people holding monopoly over the inexhaustible wealth of the land while the poor and the starving grow more and more numerous. Then again, in such a country the aim of production is not profit for the few but comfort and happiness of a full life for the many. Lastly, in a Leftist country there will be no distinction between employer class and the employed class, or to put it simply, there will be no such thing as the master-class and the slave-class, the governing-class and the governed.

After stating that the new government would welcome all groups who agreed with the aim of making Burma a "Leftist country" — British, Chinese, Indian, and Burmese — and thus "enable the Burmese masses to live a full life," U Nu then elaborated on his definition of a "Leftist country" in terms of contending ideologies:

However, to proceed. After the Russian revolution of 1917 two ideologies became current—one was to start revolutions in all countries of the world and another was to secure firm and sure foundations for Socialism in Russia itself. The adherents of the former school of thought were led by Trotsky and the latter by Lenin. A study of both these ideologies reveals that both exponents are agreed that Socialism will stand safe and secure in Russia only when there are revolutions all over the world and Socialism is established in all countries. There is but one point of difference, and that is immediate action *versus* deferred action; action only after one has made oneself strong.

In the post-Revolution feeling of excitement, the general feeling was that Trotsky's 'immediate action' rang true and sound. But looking back now it will be seen that history has proved the soundness of Lenin's view.

Now, Sir, the ideology that Burma needs today is not Trotsky's 'immediate action regardless of consequences,' but Lenin's 'Get strong first, everything else afterwards,' The Credo of our late and lamented Bogyoke is the latter. The House and the whole country know this so well I hardly need dilate on it.

At the end of this speech, U Nu added the following:

And now, may I be permitted, Mr. President, to take this opportunity to say a few words to those who can speak and act only in terms of Moscow. I have every reverence and respect for and rely on the Soviet Union which stands as the bulwark of all depressed countries of which Burma is one.

But, I do wish the House to agree with me when I say that in formulating our schemes which are to be put into practical application it will not do to place sole reliance on the Soviet Union like Czechoslovakia, Bulgaria, and Yugoslavia, there is reason to think the situation in Burma may be quite different.

But, Burma which is at least 3,000 miles away from the U.S.S.R. cannot think in terms of such countries as Czechoslovakia, etc.[71]

These statements reveal clearly the importance of certain factors influencing the formulation of Burma's policy at the time of independence, and noted in the preceding sections. First, Thakin Nu and many of his colleagues, while regarding state socialism as having its basis in Marxist doctrine, did not equate this with Communism. Nor did the AFPFL leaders fully accept Communist methods. Their adoption of parliamentary democracy as their system of government was heavily influenced by their experience under Britain, particularly their brief period of self-government after 1935. They were more familiar with this British system of government and administration than any other. Furthermore the methods and goals of Britain's Labor Government under Attlee were much more akin to their own goals and habits of action than those of Stalin.

The AFPFL leaders, whatever their other qualities, have shown themselves to be political realists within the limits of their knowledge and capabilities at any time, and far less concerned about ideologies and doctrines than many of their counterparts in other new nations. As they viewed the tasks of creating a socialist state in their new country, Burma, they were well aware of formidable obstacles. First and foremost was the tremendous job of rehabilitation and reconstruction to be undertaken because of war devastation.

Although prewar Burman economy had been largely controlled by British and Indian interests, it recovered from the effects of the world economic depression of the thirties and could be generally described as "sound." There was always an export surplus and the level of living was above the average for southeast Asian countries no matter how much the Burmans objected to British rule. The principal commercial commodity since 1870 had been rice and in 1940, out of 18,800,000 acres under cultivation, 12,500,000 were in paddy.[72] During the British period the other most successfuly commercially exploitable resources had been petroleum, lead, zinc, tin concentrates, tungsten, nickel speiss, and cobalt. Teak wood, the oldest commercially used product in Burma, along with some of the other many varieties of woods, had contributed nearly ten percent of the gross national product before the war. Likewise, under British rule, a river and rail transportation network, keyed to support of the extractive industries, was well developed.

The Japanese invasion wrecked Burma's economy. British demolitions destroyed the oil wells at Chauk and Yenangyaung, the pipeline to the refineries and the largest refinery at Syriam near Rangoon. The Bawdin mine, a source of lead and silver ores, was put out of production, and the Mawchi mines, site of some of the richest wolfram and tin ores in Southeast Asia, were demolished. The four-year process of girdling, cutting, and then floating the teak logs to port was stopped on the Japanese invasion and most of the sawmills were burned. Likewise, almost the whole transportation complex — railways, river transport, bridges, dock and port installations, and coastal shipping — either was destroyed or seized by the advancing Japanese armies.

Japanese occupation was directed to the support of their military effort. All commodities and resources that would be useful in their home islands were exported. A large proportion of the cattle population was slaughtered to provide food for their soldiers and civilians in the occupation administration.[73] The transport complex was restored only to the extent needed to support their military campaigns. Almost every aspect of the prewar economic system was disrupted and drastically altered by the Japanese occupation.

It is probable, however, that Burman economy suffered more in the last stages of the war than initially. The reinvasion of Burma by the Allied forces in 1944–45 in the face of stubborn Japanese resistance again destroyed roads, railways, bridges, canal embankments, and all of the water transport. Intensive Allied bombing caused extensive damage in the towns and cities, for the fighting was carried throughout almost the whole country. By 1945 it is probable that Burma had suffered more devastation and disruption than any of the Southeast Asian countries.

In the two and one-half years of British administration after the Japanese surrender, some progress was made toward economic rehabilitation. Rice production was brought back to 75 percent of its prewar yield by 1948. Offsetting this, however, was the fact that the Japanese invasion plus the political demands of the AFPFL prior to 1948 resulted in a complete breakdown of the prewar land tenure system. The owner's status was completely confused by 1948 and remained so until the new government could put into execution its new land-tenure policies.[74]

Other primary industries were much slower to recover. Production of minerals and of teak in 1948 was far below prewar figures. While a serious effort was made by the British military administration to reconstruct the transportation system by bringing in new ships for the river fleet and new rolling stock for the railways, several key bridges and most of Burma's port facilities were still unusable at independence. In view of the new government's declared policy of nationalization, there was only a small reinvestment of capital in oil-refining and some processing industries by Indian and other foreign owners. All of these circumstances caused a shift in Burma's export position, making the government dependent on rice exports for nearly three fourths of its foreign exchange earnings as against one half before the war.

The new Burma government, therefore, had a double economic liability to overcome as a result of the war. First, it had to proceed with a formidable job of economic rehabilitation and reconstruction that would require very large amounts of capital, and if undertaken rapidly, amounts far in excess of its expected foreign exchange earnings. Second, it was committed to undertake, hand-in-hand with economic reconstruction, the development and execution of wholly new and untried economic policies and plans consistent with its socialist goals. Quick recognition of the new Burma government by Britain, the United States, India, Pakistan, France, and the Republic of China, coupled with the peaceful arrangements for independence made by the British, convinced the AFPFL leaders that they could obtain economic help from Britain and the United States when they were ready for it.

The policy of the Kremlin, too, in 1948, served to support the above view. Moscow's instructions to Communists in Southeast Asia were to resort to violence against a sham independence. This was hard for the AFPFL leaders to understand. It is likely that many of the convinced Marxists among them believed that establishment of state socialism as a goal and refusal to join the British Commonwealth would result in quick offers of assistance from the Soviet Union which they regarded as their model. Instead, they were rebuffed. No overtures were made and even an early attempt at diplomatic relations was received cooly. Moscow radio poured out diatribes against Thakin Nu, Nehru, and Sukarno as the "running dogs of the capitalist-imperialist" warmongers and Burma was accused of remaining under the "yoke" of British imperialism.

The aloofness of the Soviet Union, however, did not lead the AFPFL leaders to close the door to future collaboration. The intransigence of their domestic Communists, their resort to insurgency under Moscow's orders only served to instill a fear that the Soviet Union's coolness toward Burma might be translated into active support for the Burma Communists in their struggle against the new government. These various circumstances induced the Burman leaders to believe that they could ill-afford to take any action which might antagonize any powerful nations. Their experience with their own Communists, Moscow's cool reception and their own pride made them refrain from any direct approach to the Soviet Union for economic aid. Wisely or not, the AFPFL leadership decided at the start that since their first tasks were to establish the authority of their government in the face of rebellion and to get on with the task of economic reconstruction of their country, they should make every attempt to remain uninvolved in cold war politics — that they should do their best to remain on terms of "friendship with all nations." Thus they established the cornerstone of a foreign policy later labelled as neutralism.

— II —

THE FORMATIVE PERIOD

1948–1953

Eᴀʀʟʏ on the morning of January 4, 1948, at a time chosen as most propitious by astrologers, the new flag of the Republic of the Union of Burma was raised in front of the old, rambling Secretariat Building in Rangoon, for over half a century the seat of British rule. The Burma ship of state had been launched. There were those among the British onlookers and older Burmans who were certain that Burma had been cut adrift in uncharted waters and that the new ship of state was hardly seaworthy. For the Prime Minister, U Nu, and his colleagues this hour marked the attainment of their dreams. They were free at last to chart their own course. If they saw shoals ahead they were convinced that these were but the shadows British rule had cast on their country. Since they now commanded power, they believed that what they willed, would be. It was much later, in 1953, that U Nu confessed, "I had not expected that the work of building up a nation would be so difficult. I had thought that everything could be accomplished at the stroke of a pen when one becomes the wielder of political power." [1]

The AFPFL leaders plunged immediately into the multifold tasks of organizing their administration and deciding how and in what ways they should proceed to turn Burma into a socialist state. In doing this they also were forced to give much of their time to internal politics, to the grave problem of holding the AFPFL coalition together. In this task they failed to prevent the White Flag Communists from going underground to join their Red Flag comrades. During these first months, there must have been many dark hours for U Nu and his close colleagues. There must have been times when they felt very much alone and wondered whether their "small, weak nation" would be able to survive.

If they had doubts, these must have arisen most often when the AFPFL leaders thought about Burma's foreign relations, for this was the one major function of an independent government they were least prepared to carry on. These Burma leaders were not at home in the highly competitive world of cold war politics. They were neither students nor practitioners of international diplomacy. As practical politicians, however, when facing an uncharted course, they were predisposed to play it safe until they could learn by experience in foreign relations. Inexperience, then, was also a factor in shaping Burma's policy of nonalignment and neutralism.

Whatever U Nu and his associates felt about their problems, they knew very well that their first task was to keep control of the government. In mid-March, the Burman Communist leaders, fresh from their meetings with other communists in India, staged a rally of the All-Burma Peasant's Union at Pyinmana, some 300 miles north of Rangoon on the road to Mandalay. Encouraged by the enthusiasm of an estimated 75,000 people at this rally, Than Tun staged a public "resistance" rally in Rangoon on March 27, on the same day that U Nu was making a "Resistance Day" speech to his AFPFL followers in the capital.

Fear of a possible coup had led U Nu to order the arrest of Than Tun and other Communist leaders two days earlier, but certain PVO leaders had intervened and urged U Nu to continue negotiations. The speeches of Than Tun and others at his rally calling for an armed uprising against the government were decisive and U Nu proceeded with an attempt to arrest these opponents. Action was too slow, and Than Tun and his associates fled to the stronghold of their support in Pyinmana. Here they established the headquarters of armed revolt against the government and the Communist insurrection was in full swing.

With both Burma Communist groups in armed revolt, U Nu was urged to make more strenuous efforts to patch up his weakening AFPFL coalition. Among the remaining groups within the AFPFL the two most important were the PVO organizations with their supporters and the Socialists. Much of the PVO organization was Communist infiltrated. The PVO leaders demanded a disproportionate share in a coalition government and the inclusion of the Burma Communists in the government as the price of their cooperation. Such demands were unacceptable to the Socialists and to U Nu, but unlike General Aung San, the Prime Minister seemed incapable of "knocking heads together." [2] He continued his attempt to formulate an ideological accommodation to the Communists and the PVO left wing which would enable him to strengthen his AFPFL coalition (which he said had become "corrupt" and "privilege-seeking") and which might prevent or lessen armed resistance to his government. He announced that he would retire from politics in June and turn over leadership of the AFPFL to his old associate, Bo Let Ya. At this time, U Kyaw Nyein, leader of the Socialists and one of his key advisers, was out of politics for health reasons and Thein Pe Myint an aboveground Communist, therefore, was reputedly the chief draftsman of U Nu's "Leftist Unity Program."

The fifteen-point "Leftist Unity Program" was announced in a statement by U Nu on May 25, 1948.[3] The Prime Minister said that, "when the above programme has been generally accepted by the representatives in the Cabinet, the Parliament of Leftism should discuss how the programme could be implemented by the Union Government of Burma." On June 13, U Nu spoke before a mass rally in Rangoon and presented an elaboration of his fifteen-point program which he called, "The Nature of Leftist Unity." The speech was full of communist terminology. While some of the points affirmed socialist goals of abolition of private property, "nationalization of monopoly industries," and strict government management of foreign trade, there was the considerable emphasis on transformation of "popular government" for the frontier areas, and the setting up of "people's courts" in the villages. Point Fifteen called for organization of a "Marxist League," presumably under government sponsorship, to propagate Marxist doctrines and the writings of Marx, Lenin, and Stalin among the people.

Taken at its face value, as a statement of policy, the speech by the Prime Minister seemed to be setting Burma firmly on the path toward becoming a communist state. Both the tone and the terminology alarmed the representatives of the western nations in Rangoon and some reported that this was the first move which would put Burma into the communist camp. If the speech is viewed in the context of Burma politics at the time, however, it is patent that it was less an affirmation of long-range policy than a tactical maneuver by U Nu by which he hoped to resolve the differences among the left-wing factions in his weakening AFPFL coalition. To gain the political support he needed, he was persuaded to demonstrate publicly that he could be a better Marxist than his left-wing opponents who had been bitter in their criticism of the British Defense Assistance Agreement and the proposed plans for paying compensation for nationalization of foreign-owned businesses. In actual fact, U Nu and his less extreme supporters were able to refrain from putting the Leftist Unity program in practice. The "Marxist League" idea was quietly and finally dropped and many others of the fifteen proposals were later sharply modified or remained inactive.

The reaction of the western diplomats in Rangoon to this speech and their expressed alarm reflected in some of the western press is a good illustration of the dangers inherent in evaluating public policy statements in the Burman political setting. *What* is said by public officials publicly is important, but *why* it is said at a particular time is much more important. In this instance, the domestic program set forth in the "Leftist Unity" speech should have been taken with severe reservations if the reasons for the terminology and the particular points were understood. Although there is no reason to doubt that Thein Pe Myint was advancing a radical communist-sounding program in all good faith since that was and is his conviction, U Nu, the politician, was voicing these points to gain a purely internal political end without commitment to the execution of the program. Had his maneuver succeeded, however, in keeping the PVO leaders in the AFPFL fold and perhaps even in bringing back Than Tun, U Nu would undoubtedly have found it most difficult to avoid activating the "Leftist Unity" program. The danger, therefore, did not lie in accepting this program as a statement of the Burma government's policy and objectives, but rather in whether this tactical maneuver succeeded in changing the character of the AFPFL coalition to one more committed to communism.

This same observation holds for policy statements on foreign relations. At every point, as will be seen in the subsequent exposition of foreign policy evolution in Burma, it is necessary to determine *why* particular statements were made in terms of both Burma's internal politics and external relations and situations. Because of an almost visceral reaction to the communist terminology used by U Nu in describing the domestic parts of his "Leftist Unity" program, his exposition of foreign policy in this speech was little mentioned in the western press and almost disregarded by at least some of the western representatives in Rangoon.

Need for a more detailed explanation of the fifteen-point program was soon apparent and an opportunity was made on June 13 at a mass rally organized for the purpose. In this speech, U Nu spent some time explaining the policy of nationalization of his government and payment of compensation to foreign property owners. He took pains to justify this policy, to explain further the reasons for repayment of the debt to Britain and again to justify the necessity for the British Military Mission in Burma by asserting that the government was free to request arms and assistance from any country. These were all items under heavy attack by the Communists. After attempting to prove that the action of the government with respect to the three above items still left Burma a completely free and sovereign independent state, U Nu proceeded as follows:[4]

I have now set out the three principal points of disagreement with regard to the Treaty (with Britain). I would now explain the disagreement in regard to foreign policy.

Of the three great Western Powers, the United Kingdom, the United States and the USSR, the Communists (i.e., the Burmese Communists) wish to be in friendly relations only with the USSR, whereas the AFPFL wish that Burma should be in friendly relations with all three. The Communists doubtless have their own reasons but the Government of Burma's policy of seeking friendly relations with all the big three among the powers is based on three considerations:

1. Geographically, Burma is situated close to the sphere of Anglo-American influence.
2. Weight must also be given to the wishes of the Shans, the Chins, the Kachins, the Karens and the Karennis.
3. The majority of those who are in effective political life in Burma have great regard for Soviet Russia and believe that Soviet economics will solve the problem arising from the poverty of the Burmese peasants.

In deciding on the foreign policy of the Government of Burma, no person, whether inclined to the Right or the Left, can disregard the three considerations I have set out above. Any mistaken policy will be detrimental to the interests of the whole of the Burma Union.

To support his point, U Nu quotes several of his favorite proverbs and then attempts to show that the "great and powerful" Soviet Union "has expressed the wish to live on terms of peace with Britain and the United States." He cites as evidence the Soviet-British-Twenty-year Friendship Treaty, remarking that "we ourselves have as yet no such treaty with the United Kingdom." He quotes Stalin's statement on the twenty-seventh anniversary of the Russian Revolution (1944) about the firm alliance with Britain and the U.S.A. He adds quotations from Stalin's answers to questions by Hugh Bailie of the American United Press on October 23, 1946, and by Alexander Werth of the Sunday *Times* (London) on September 20, 1946. His final proof is a quotation from an interview given by Stalin to Mr. Harold Stassen on May 4, 1948. The theme of all these quotations from Stalin is that "peaceful" relations between the U.S.S.R. and the U. S. and Britain are possible and desired by the Soviet Union. He follows this with an attack on the Burmese Communists for inconsistencies in their "line," and evidence that in spite of peaceful overtures, the Burmese Communists were under directives to seize power by force.

Later in the speech, after again justifying the agreement with Britain, U Nu stated,

Let me now explain these 15 points in detail. Firstly, we propose to seek political and economic relationships with Soviet Russia and the New Democracies of Eastern Europe in the same way as we have achieved such relationships with Britain and the United States. According to the law of nations, independence involves the freedom to enter into relationship with all countries.

Our country suffered the most by the war and seeks peace for the whole world. We do not wish to see dissension between the Big Powers, and we shall support any measure for securing unity between Britain, the United States, Russia and other powers. Only if these great Powers are in harmony will the peace of the world be secured. That is why we say that Burma should seek friendly relations with Russia and the New Democracies of Eastern Europe. We must understand these countries. We must derive use and benefit not only from the way of life, methods and culture of Britain and America and other Western countries, but also from the way of life, methods and culture of countries like Russia.

Further, as an independent country we need to sell our produce at the best prices available in the markets of the world and to obtain imports that we need at the most favourable world prices. It is necessary therefore that we should have a larger sphere of world contacts in the economic sphere and that is why it is necessary that we should seek political and economic relations with Russia, Poland, Yugoslavia and other countries like these.

Fifthly, the Programme provides for the refusal by Burma of any foreign aid which would be detrimental to the political, economic and strategic freedom of Burma. This is a point which must be enforced with due regard to our old saying that by debts we do become enslaved. Independence includes economic as well as strategic independence. Thus when foreign aid is offered to us, we must consider very carefully whether it is in the nature of a charitable gift like a contribution to the Red Cross, or whether it is just an extension of friendly mutual aid between two countries, or whether it is aid of the kind through which we shall be enslaved.

Burma has, however, fertile land and is full of rice, teak and minerals, so that we can obtain the goods we want in exchange for the goods produced here and needed by other countries. And there will be need for us to seek foreign loans or to seek foreign aid with humble demeanor. But if we fight among ourselves so that the people are unable to work, we shall produce no rice and no timber and that may be our difficulty. Otherwise, we shall not have difficulty obtaining foreign aid.

Friendly relations with all nations and refusal of any kind of foreign aid that might compromise Burma's political, economic or strategic independence thus became the first two basic principles officially and publicly announced by the Prime Minister as a guide to his government's relations with other nations. Burma's need for assistance in reconstruction and economic development and the internal political pressures on U Nu at the time dictated the formulation of these principles and particularly his justification and explanation of them. As with his domestic "Leftist Unity" program, U Nu hoped his first official statement of what Burma's foreign policy was to be would not antagonize his extreme left-wing opponents. His emphasis on opening relations with the Soviet Union went only part way in appeasing the Communists and their aboveground adherents who would have preferred exclusive relations with the Communist bloc states.[5] On the other hand, he had no wish to antagonize the U. S., Britain, and members of the Commonwealth from whom he hoped to get further assistance.

U Nu had emphasized "friendly relations with all countries" and "no economic aid with strings attached" as the two principles his government would follow in its foreign policy. To these two concepts was added an obvious corollary — that of avoiding alignments or entanglements with any power blocs. On June 16, U Tin Tut, then Foreign Minister, clarified Burma's position at a press conference,[6] by stating,

What the government seeks is to extend its political and economic relationships with the outside world. Burma has no desire to be entangled in any alignment of World Powers, and wishes to be in friendly relationship with all countries. She desires to adhere to the friendly relationship already entered into with the U.S.A., Britain, and other countries in western Europe, and China. These countries are themselves in friendly political and economic relationship with Russia and other countries under the 'new democracy,' and in seeking to do the same Burma hopes her relationship with the Western democracies and China will in no way be impaired.

In response to questions, he asserted that Burma was not turning communist and its attitude toward the West would not be changed by the relationship it was seeking with the Soviet Bloc.

These three themes, therefore — friendly relations with all countries, no alignments with power blocs and no economic aid that would infringe Burma's sovereignty — became the cornerstones of Burma's foreign policy. Each was repeated over and over during the next ten years. The AFPFL leaders established the basic concepts for their government's foreign policy as practical politicians taking account of the weakness of Burma and its needs for the future as they saw them, but equally considering the exigencies of Burma politics and the problem of political survival for themselves as the officials in power. The AFPFL leaders were soon to recognize the value of these very general and rather vague principles. For in any specific action in foreign affairs, they found that they could interpret their basic policy to fit the circumstances of the moment. No political leader at the time, nor indeed for several years thereafter, attempted to set out publicly a criteria by which they, the Burman public, or foreign governments could test whether a specific action by the Burma government was in conformity with their basic foreign policy or not. U Nu and his colleagues thus began with a set of foreign policy principles general enough and vague enough to provide considerable flexibility for government action in foreign relations. The AFPFL leaders discovered that they could usually find ways to justify what they wanted to do or what they were forced to do by circumstances as being compatible with their foreign policy principles.

Communist and Karen Insurrections

U Nu's program of "Leftist Unity" failed completely to appease the Burma Communists and their PVO supporters. These extremists did not want to share in a coalition government, they wanted to control the government. They did not want a foreign policy of nonalignment, they wanted the closest relations possible with the Communist bloc. By July, it was obvious that agreement between the Socialists and the extremists was impossible. On July 16, U Nu offered his resignation as Prime Minister in accordance with his earlier promise. It was soon evident, however, that the Socialists alone could not muster enough parliamentary support to form a government and U Nu was persuaded to remain in office heading a "caretaker" government. On August 1, it was announced that U Nu and his "caretaker" cabinet would stay in command until the regular parliamentary elections, scheduled for April, 1949.

Immediate results of all this futile political maneuvering were soon seen in the increasing disaffection of large numbers of the PVO's who began to collect arms and to go underground in resistance to the U Nu government. During July and August, approximately sixty percent took up arms against the government and several units of the Burma Army mutineed, joining the Communist and PVO contingents in seizing government treasuries and arms stocks in the country districts.[7] U Nu and his associates were now faced with a dangerous armed rebellion against their government.

Between August, and December, 1948, Burma politics and government operations were in a state bordering utter confusion. Aboveground politicians were constantly maneuvering for political position and carrying on varied negotiations among themselves and often with insurgent groups of all colors. The various groups of Communist and PVO insurgents all thought they saw in this confusion an opportunity to seize control of the government. At one point an Army march on Rangoon by two rebellious battalions from Mingaladon and Thayetmo was only narrowly averted by quick action on the part of loyal Army commanders under General Smith Dun, a Karen. The survival of U Nu's government in the fall of 1948 was due more to the inability of the various insurgent groups to unite under a single leadership and agree on a program of action and to their general lack of experience than to any actions of the U Nu government. Toward the end of the year, more vigorous action by the loyal elements of the Burma Army succeeded in preventing unity among the insurgents and removing any immediate armed threats to the capital.

When it seemed that the danger from the Communists and PVO insurgents was not enough to topple the government, and just at the time U Nu and his associates believed they could contain and break up these insurrectionists, the government faced an equally serious rebellion from another quarter — the dissatisfied Karens. As the second largest minority within the Burma Union, the Karens had been promised autonomy in a separate state. In September, 1948, a Regional Autonomy Commission met with representatives of the frontier peoples at Panglong to settle frontier problems and details of the relationships between these frontier minorities within the Union government. Karen observers had arrived late at this meeting and took no part in the proceedings. U Nu stated publicly that he was opposed to creation of Mon, Arakan, or Karen states within the Union and this sharpened the growing fears among the Karens that in a Burmese-dominated government they would suffer severe discrimination. Again, there were many differences among the Karen leaders as to the proper course of action.[8] The disclosure that two British subjects, Tulloch and Campbell, were involved in a plot to get arms aid to the Karens, hardened the Burmese AFPFL leaders against the Karens in spite of continuing negotiations in Rangoon on the composition and geographic confines of a Karen state within the Union.

The more extremist elements among the Karen groups, mindful of their many past grievances against the Burmese and fearful of their future security in a Burmese-controlled government, urged forceful action and an end to negotiations. In September some of these leaders began the organization of the Karen National Defense Organization (KNDO) a para-military force formed supposedly to protect Karen communities in the delta area of the Irrawaddy, but quickly becoming an organized insurgent force for action against the government. In the last months of 1948, all efforts at compromise failed primarily because neither the U Nu coalition nor the Karens could achieve a strong and unified command of the situation. By

January, 1949, the KNDO rebellion was in full swing and soon part of the capital itself, the Insein district, was under control of the Karen forces. General Smith Dun resigned as Commander-in-Chief of the Burma Army on February 1 and was replaced by General Ne Win. It was not until the late fall of 1949 that the KNDO insurgents were so broken up and sufficiently dispersed as to remove the threat to the capital.

The Karen insurrection resulted in more intense guerrilla activity by the Communists and the PVO's. Had these groups been able to unite under an able leadership, the Burma government could not have survived. As it was, the Communist and PVO's held virtual control of the Irrawaddy corridor for several years and sizeable groups of KNDO's continued to operate and control parts of the hill districts for an equally long time.[9] Hardly a district was free from marauding bands of Red Flags, White Flags, Yellow Flags, KNDO's and dacoits.[10] Export of commodities other than rice could not be brought back to anything like prewar levels because of the disorders. Refugees from the country districts flocked to Rangoon and the larger towns in Burma, placing almost insurmountable burdens on local government.

The outbreak of the Karen insurrection in early 1949 posed an even greater threat to existence of the AFPFL government, but it did serve to bring the plight of the government more forcefully to the attention of Britain, India, and the United States. Although Burma had refused to join the Commonwealth, there were many members of Parliament in London who felt a sense of responsibility toward the new nation. Many British who had served in Burma became alarmed at the possibility of warfare between the Burmese and the Karen minority. Although charges that the Karens were aided by British agents were denied by the British government, U Nu and his colleagues began to worry lest the Karen insurrectionists might get aid from the West and thus provide an excuse for Soviet intervention. This concern reinforced the belief of U Nu and his associates that the safest course for Burma was to steer clear of alignments with major nations in either the Communist or Anglo-American bloc.

The policy of nonalignment, however, was never designed to prevent Burma from receiving help from other nations when proffered "without strings attached." In late February, India invited representatives of Britain, Pakistan, Australia, and Ceylon to a conference in New Delhi to consider the problem of the insurrection in Burma. At the same time the Burma government sent a request to London and the Commonwealth countries for urgent financial aid. The conference in Delhi terminated with a joint statement that it had been agreed that peace should be restored in Burma through conciliation and that certain suggestions had been sent to Prime Minister U Nu as to how this might be achieved.[11] The conference proposed conciliation of Karen differences through Commonwealth mediation apparently through a good-offices committee of Commonwealth representatives in Rangoon. This proposal was sharply rebuffed by the U Nu Government as undue interference in internal affairs. The AFPFL leaders could not tolerate this kind of assistance in the face of the strong antiwestern and pro-Communist opposition they faced. With U E Maung's assumption of the post of Foreign Minister in March, 1949, a series of conferences was projected which took E Maung and General Ne Win to London and to the United States. Additional arms were provided under the British Defense Assistance Agreement and by June the main threat of the combined Communist-PVO-Karen insurrection to the government had been considerably lessened. Nevertheless it was estimated that the AFPFL government in June, 1949, could exert its authority over only slightly more than thirty percent of the Union Territory. The main thing was that this government still controlled the capital, Rangoon, and was still the government of Burma dealing with foreign powers.

In June, 1949, the Burma government seemed much less full of Marxist zeal than a year earlier when the program of "Leftist Unity" had been announced. Financial stringency, daily becoming more acute, the grim dangers of defeat at the hands of the insurrectionists, and the apparent willingness of the Commonwealth countries to come to Burma's assistance, all combined to cause a change of attitude on the part of the AFPFL leaders. This change was noted in an editorial in the *Nation*:[12]

The most important factor influencing Commonwealth to aid Burma is probably the change of attitude in Burma . . . The foreign embassies cannot help noticing that there has been an almost unanimous stoppage of abuse where the Western democracies are concerned. The campaign of villification against the Anglo-Americans (the British in particular) did not spend itself, it was cut short by momentous events outside this country: first Nehru declined the role of leader in a S.E.A. bloc; and then the reverses of the Nationalists in China brought the menace of Communism to our doorstep. Burma found the physical proximity of Communist jarring, and there has been a tendency to swing toward the devil we know, which could not be such a bad devil after all if Pandit Nehru, who was also acquainted with him, decided to remain in his society.

In June, 1949, the Burma government faced its first real test of its foreign policy principles. The AFPFL leaders became aware that the civil war in China seemed to be going in favor of the Communists. Events moved swiftly and by fall it was apparent that the Chinese Communists had gained control of virtually all of mainland China. Whether or not to recognize the new Chinese regime and sever relations with the Nationalists was no easy decision. The Burma government was still uncertain of its tenure. It had swung of necessity toward closer economic relations with the Commonwealth countries but final arrangements were not yet complete. The AFPFL leaders were aware of the alarm which Communist victories had caused in the United States in particular. U E Maung and General Ne Win were abroad having discussions in various western capitals. It was in the midst of this interplay of circumstances and pressures from all sides that U Nu and his colleagues had to take action with respect to their big northern neighbor.

The Recognition of Communist China

As early as June, 1949, the possible effects of the situation in China were being discussed within the AFPFL top echelon and had been aired in the Burma press. Continued rumors of Chinese refugees crossing into Burma and of Chinese Nationalist army units fleeing across the border had begun to cause apprehension.[13] The dilemma posed for the AFPFL leaders is illustrated by the following extracts from editorials. On May 22, 1949, an editorial in the *Nation*, Rangoon, asserted,

As usual, we are beholden to *The Statesmen*, published in Calcutta for information on our foreign policy in regard to China. Yesterday it said that the Government in Burma and authorities in Yunnan agreed on joint measures to maintain order in the frontier area. . . . but it didn't say which authorities in Yunnan had done this. Our border with Yunnan is extremely long and we betray no military secrets when we say that it is at the same time an exposed and vulnerable one. The Nationalists also cast acquisitive eyes on Mytkyina. The Communists, if they come, will come to join forces with the Burmese Communists and warnings from Britain or the U. S. are not likely to have much effect.

On May 28, another editorial, "Border Confusion" in the same paper stated in part,

In regard to the editorial of May 22, other papers have since reported the danger of Communist Chinese infiltration . . . yesterday one or two reported an interview with an official from the Shan Ministry denying infiltration. The head of the Kachin State, Sima Duwa Sinwa Nawng, a 'realist,' in a statement carried in yesterday's *Statesman,* said that 10,000 Chinese Communists are within thirty miles of the Burma border waiting for a chance to cross it. He is reported arming 20,000 Kachin troops . . . but if the Communists have designs in Burma, Burma must seek diplomatic support . . . against Red China. Burma cannot stand alone.

On June 7, the Burma Socialist Party issued a public statement that was published in full in many of the English language and vernacular papers in Burma.[14] The tenor of this statement was a rejoicing in ". . . successive victories won by the people of China . . . the people's revolution can never fall . . . the victory of the people of China means also the victory of the people of Burma." Since the Socialists were the major political group on whom U Nu had to rely for support, informed observers in Rangoon concluded that internal political pressure from the "left" in Rangoon would force U Nu to prepare the way for close relations with the Chinese Communists. Such action would be even more necessary to offset the Burma Government's request for financial aid from the Commonwealth countries, approved in May, and the introduction in Parliament of legislation to permit participation of foreign capital in the exploitation of Burma's natural resources.

In the debate following U Nu's June speech before parliament, U Kyaw Nyein, as leader of the Socialists, asserted that friendship with one's own neighbors was necessary and that it was also necessary for Burma to enter into agreements with some countries but this should be done in such a way as not to offend others. He urged that Burma should follow a course similar to Nehru's in foreign policy. Other Socialist and moderate leaders agreed with Kyaw Nyein. In concluding the debate on foreign policy, U Nu expressed himself as having some fears of alliances and pacts. He asserted that neither the United States nor Russia was always right, but "It is necessary to give something in order to get something." "The question is," he said, "what sacrifice is entailed in getting something." [15] He concluded by stating that he would consult party leaders and members of Parliament before any major decisions were taken.

If the AFPFL leaders were uncertain as to what position their government should take regarding events in China, they were not alone. From July until the end of the year, as the Chinese Communists expanded their control over the mainland area, other governments in the West and in Asia appeared equally uncertain. The rapid disintegration of the Chinese Nationalist government and its armies and the imminent possibility that the huge mass of the Chinese people would come under Communist control was an event unpredicted and for which no nation had planned. The implications of Communist expansion, not only into China itself but also into Korea and Vietnam, were apparent, widely publicized, and widely discussed, but the nations opposed to such expansion or potentially threatened by it did not seem capable of concerting their policies and actions effectively.

While U E Maung, Burma's foreign minister, and General Ne Win were conferring in London and Washington, the Chinese Communist press and radio were attacking the AFPFL government as "aligned with the imperialist-capitalist" camp. Although giving no hint that they intended to extend material aid to the Burma Communists and underground groups fighting with them, the Chinese Communists adhered to their line that Burma, India, Pakistan, and Ceylon were still really under the "imperialist yoke" and that only a "people's democracy" would be truly independent. At a meeting of the World Federation of Trades Unions in Peking in November, their attacks became more virulent and were directed personally against U Nu, Nehru, and Sukarno. Chinese Communist speakers emphasized that they were only supporting the "fighters of national liberation wars in Burma and other countries." [16]

From the public record it would seem that the Burma government had become directly involved in discussion with western nations looking toward some sort of agreement, even a defensive alliance as a check to Chinese Communist expansion. The AFPFL leaders, however, were constantly aware of their country's vulnerability to any action or interference by the Chinese Communists. They also had become dimly aware at this time that if any large numbers of Kuomintang troops took refuge in Burma territory, the Chinese Communists might well intervene to eliminate any possibility of a reinvasion by the Chinese Nationalists. In these circumstances, U Nu and his colleagues followed Indian reactions closely, and were inclined to follow Nehru's lead. When the Indian Premier indicated that his government would not join a Pacific Union, but might be interested "in a general way" in close cooperation among the southeast Asian nations, the Burma government took the same position.

In his speech before parliament on September 28, 1949, U Nu explained the position of his government as follows:

> . . . Let me now make a few observations regarding foreign affairs.
> I want to speak on the so-called anti-Left or anti-Right pacts which are now in fashion. We are not in the least interested in anti-Left or anti-Right pacts. An anti-Left pact smacks of aggression on Leftists and in the same way an anti-Right pact smacks of aggression on Rightists.
> We hate aggression on our territories and we equally hate to aggress on others. Therefore, on behalf of the Government let me announce from the floor of this House that we are not interested in any anti-this or anti-that pact except an anti-aggression pact.

On October 2, 1949, the Chinese Communists proclaimed the inauguration of the "People's Republic of China" in Peking and invited recognition from all nations.[17] The new government was immediately recognized by the U.S.S.R., followed by similar action by the Soviet satellite states of eastern Europe. The issue of recognition was now out in the open and very shortly most of the diplomatic representatives of major non-Communist nations to the Chinese Nationalist government were called home for consultation, including U Myint Thein, Burma's Ambassador in Nanking. With the formation of the Chinese Communist government, all of the leftists in Burma began a campaign of pressure on the AFPFL government to recognize the Peking regime. This pressure was buttressed by some forty Chinese associations in Burma led by the Chinese Chamber of Commerce and the Chinese Trade Association, all favoring recognition. According to the Burmese press, the majority of the Chinese in Rangoon were "disinterested" in political ideology, but a small nucleus of a Chinese

Communist party which had been formed within the Chinese community was alleged to have pushed through the decision in the Chinese organizations.[18]

During November and early December, the AFPFL government was under continuing pressure from almost all the left-wing groups in the country to hasten recognition. There appears to have been pressure also from many in the Chinese business community who argued that Burma had to be able to do business with the new government. With internal pressure for recognition mounting steadily, Foreign Minister E Maung, again in London, was reported to have said on December 3,[19]

We shall have to recognize the new government of China very soon. Nothing has been decided yet, but it is a question of recognizing facts. It is not that we want to hug each other as friends . . . Communism is not gaining ground in Burma . . . We have, of course, reason to be nervous of the spread of Communism in China across our borders. At the best of times there have always been border raids on both sides between Burma and China. These have been regular for many years. But with the Communists gaining ground in China, these raids are likely to change in meaning and become tainted with political ideology.

Back in Rangoon on December 6, U E Maung told press reporters that Burma would recognize Communist China before Christmas and that this would mean automatic breaking of relations with the Nationalist Chinese government.

Although the Indian government was hesitant to rush into recognition and other governments of the British Commonwealth were holding off, the Burma government apparently decided that something was to be gained by speed. In deciding to take action before the new year, the AFPFL leaders were virtually sure that Britain and India would follow suit. The position of the United States at this time was not clear, although a strong Senate resolution against such an act had forced Secretary of State Acheson to announce that no steps would be taken without Congressional approval.

On December 16, the Burma government sent a telegraphic message to Peking extending recognition to the Chinese People's Republic. By this action, taken somewhat hastily and under pressure from a considerable segment of political groups, Burma achieved the dubious honor of being the first non-Communist nation to recognize the new Peking regime.[20] If the Burman government hoped to achieve any immediate advantage from this action, they were soon to be disappointed. On December 18, the Chinese Communist government replied to Burma's telegraphic recognition by coldly stating it was "willing to enter into negotiations for diplomatic relations."[21] The Burma government then sent U Myint Thein (former Ambassador to Nationalist China) to Peking to conduct negotiations as Burma's first Ambassador to the Chinese People's Republic. Apparently the Chinese Communists were in no hurry and U Myint Thein did not get to present his credentials as Ambassador until August 7, 1950.[22] (The first Chinese Communist Ambassador to Burma, Yao Chungming, presented his credentials in Rangoon on September 27, 1950.)

After the decision to recognize the Peking regime had been made, but before it had been announced publicly, Prime Minister U Nu once more explained the rationale of his government's basic foreign policy concepts. In a speech before a mass rally in Rangoon on December 11, 1949, he said,[23]

In regard to our foreign policy also, we are convinced that the course we have adopted is the best in the circumstances of our country and we are therefore pursuing it steadfastly no matter how strongly it is criticized. Our circumstances demand that we follow an independent course and not ally ourselves with any power bloc. We are therefore determined to follow this course no matter what critics say, and we will march breast to breast with any country that respects our sovereignty and association which will be of mutual benefit both to ourselves and to that country.

In drawing up a political programme, it will just not do to lay down, for example, a pro-Anglo-American programme simply in the belief that the Anglo-American powers will crush Soviet Russia in the event of war. Similarly also we must not lay down a Communist programme merely because Chinese Communists are overrunning China and therefore we must adopt a pattern acceptable for them. Such political programmes adopted without conviction are the work of opportunists. The only political programme which we should pursue is the one which we genuinely believe to be the most suitable for our Union whatever course the British, the Americans, the Russians, and the Chinese Communists might follow. Our salvation lies in our own hands, and no matter what help foreign capitalists or foreign Communists may give us it will be of no avail if we are divided and lack the ability to steer our own ship of state. They will not merely form a low opinion of us but they will take full advantage of our weakness and meddle in our affairs until our sovereignty vanishes.

Just look at the world today, and be they Capitalist or Communist they behave in exactly the same way.

Therefore in our attitude towards foreign powers we should do away with any inclination to 'long for the aunt at the expense of the mother' and all opportunistic tendencies.

Be friendly with all foreign countries. Our tiny nation cannot have the effrontery to quarrel with any power. If any country comes with an offer of a mutually beneficial enterprise, welcome it by all means and work closely and honestly. But do not forget to strengthen yourself and to be fully equipped for your dealings with foreign countries. In laying down political programmes do not forget to ensure that it is fully suited to the requirements of the Union.

In emphasizing his government's need to follow an "independent" course and one that was "most suitable for our Union," U Nu foreshadowed his later and broadened interpretation of the principles of nonalignment, an interpretation which permitted the AFPFL government to take whatever action it decided was "right" on a given issue or in a given situation, so long as it did not tie Burma's hands or resulted in political or military alignment with the members of either power bloc. The Burman leaders believed then, and still do, that their nonalignment policy with its corollaries allows them a wide freedom of action in foreign affairs as they interpret them at any particular time. Since they make the assessment of an issue or situation it is hard to deny to them the privilege of this belief.

Economic Growing Pains and Foreign Aid

While the change of government in China was the first political testing of Burma's foreign policy, its need for foreign economic assistance represented not a single issue which could be resolved quickly, but a series of decisions which had to be taken continuously over the formative period between 1948 and 1953. U Nu had made it plain that his government would take aid from any country, in fact sought aid from the Soviet Union and its satellites, but only if such assistance did not infringe upon Burma's sovereignty and security. In asserting this principle as basic to his government's foreign policy, U Nu and his associates were consciously attempting to avoid partiality, to act in the spirit of a neutral in the cold war.

During the first year of independence the AFPFL leaders had little time for economic planning. Although they fully recognized the seriousness of wartime economic dislocation and the need for rapid reconstruction, they seemed to assume that Burma's "natural resources" would be in great demand and could easily be exchanged for those commodities necessary to the country's development. By the fall of 1948, Burma was in greater financial and economic difficulties than at the time of independence. The AFPFL leadership had begun to recognize the economic plight of their country but shied away from consideration of drastic remedies which might have to be adopted. The AFPFL leadership apparently concluded that the seriousness of the country's economic plight was due almost entirely to the insurrection. In his summary of the current situation on February 27, 1949, the Prime Minister stated,[24]

It is vital to know how much we have suffered politically and economically all on account of these mischiefs. (referring to the Communist and Karen insurrections at that time in full swing.)

. . . Our Union at one time stood high in the estimation of the World just after it had regained independence. But now, owing to disruptions, the whole world has opined that our days are numbered.

Because of that low estimation, we look small in the eyes of the world in our international relations — be it with regard to national economy, finance or politics. If we were reduced to abject poverty and forced to beg for our *dole*, this low estimation was quite understandable. We should have had nothing to complain of.

But our Union has a profundity of natural wealth after which every other country is hankering with avidity. If only the people of the Union did not err in their ways but followed the democratic path, if only peace reigned supreme in the country, there would have been absolutely no cause for us to drink the cup of humiliation. We could live on the fat of the land, sitting back at comfortable ease. Then, countries that needed the produce of our land would have to pay us off in advance.

But now instead of sitting back at comfortable ease, we have come to such a state that we can hardly raise a loan. I am not surprised in the least that no one wants to lend any money to a country seething with disruptive elements.

The first attempt by Commonwealth nations to assist Burma was made at a meeting in New Delhi the week following this speech but produced no concrete results. In mid-April, U Nu conferred with Prime Minister Nehru in Calcutta and was able to announce that India and Pakistan would support Burma's request for financial and arms aid at the formal meeting of Commonwealth Prime Ministers in London later in the month. On May 11, the British Labor Government announced that Commonwealth members were preparing to assist Burma financially. The next month the British government announced it was sending 10,000 rifles to the Burma Army to take the place of those seized by the insurgents. In June, negotiations on financial aid stalled over a proposed "committee" of Commonwealth representatives to be set up in Rangoon to coordinate economic assistance and to help in efforts to halt the insurrections.

By the fall of 1949, the Burma government was in dire straits. The costs of fighting the insurrection were eating away its financial reserves. The 1949 rice crop was fifteen percent below that of the previous year. The AFPFL leaders were willing to concede that their Socialist state was likely to be a more distant goal than they had anticipated. In June the Prime Minister told parliament that it was "now time" to enter into economic and other agreements with foreign governments which he amplified as follows:[25]

> We have a lot of things to do in the economic sphere. Our country's economy now depends to a large extent on agriculture but this dependence cannot be perpetual. Independence has brought in its train increased responsibilities. Defense, rehabilitation and uplift of the people's economic status are heavy responsibilities to shoulder. To face these problems squarely and solve them successfully, increased National Income is necessary. To achieve this we must rely not only on agriculture but also on industries.

> To be candid, we cannot set up the industries by our own efforts alone. For this purpose we need, (1) capital, (2) equipment, (3) skilled technicians and (4) experienced executives. We cannot get these essentials of industrialization by merely looking on. We must seek the aid of friendly countries whose interests are the same as ours. I have laid on the table of the House a comprehensive statement of policy in regard to this aid.

The Government proposed to enact new legislation regulating foreign investment and to obtain approval for foreign capital in domestic industries jointly with the Government on a roughly 50-50 basis.

During the first half of 1950, Burma's financial situation eased as sales of surplus rice provided a larger amount of needed foreign exchange. Negotiations for the Commowealth loan continued amid disputes between the Burma and British governments over the compensation to be paid to British-owned teak extraction firms and for nationalization of the Irrawaddy Flotilla Company. Private talks were initiated with American representatives looking to direct aid under the U. S. Economic Cooperation Administration. In March the first of a succession of agreements with Japan was signed by which Japan was to purchase £17,500,000 of rice for the first of a two-year contract.[26] Short-term loans from Pakistan, from the U. K. and from India helped to finance rice purchases and further ease Burma's financial problem.

In March, the House of Commons voted approval of the Commonwealth loan of £6,000,000 to be supplied by Britain, Ceylon, India, Pakistan, and Australia. The final agreement was signed in Rangoon on June 28. With the imminent prospect of American aid in the form of an outright grant, the Burma government did not draw on the Commonwealth loan. The U.S.-Burma agreement providing for a sum of $8,010,000 was signed in Rangoon in September.[27]

By the fall of 1950, therefore, the AFPFL leaders had become confident that they could move ahead in the economic development of their country. The gross production in the country had recovered from the near collapse of 1948–49 and Burma's foreign exchange position had improved, markedly aided by the U. S. dollar grant.

For the next three years, Burma profited from the Korean War. However much the Burma representatives might deplore the devastation in Korea or the international tensions produced by the conflict, the fact remained that the very considerable increase in the world market price of rice provided the government with far greater foreign exchange earnings than had been anticipated. Nationalization of rice exports controlled by a government agency, the State Agricultural Marketing Board (SAMB), enabled the government to fix the purchase price of paddy (unhusked rice) and to make huge profits by exporting rice at approximately twice the domestic price. It was under these favorable economic circumstances that the AFPFL leaders went rapidly ahead in development of economic relations with other countries and with development of their economic planning.

Between 1950 and 1953, high Burman officials were sent on missions abroad covering countries of western Europe, the U. K., and the United States. Partly as a result of these missions, the government concluded a large number of treaties and trade agreements with a variety of countries. General treaties and trade agreements were concluded with India, Pakistan, Indonesia, Yugoslavia, Egypt, and Israel in addition to previous agreements with the U. K. and the United States. A trade agreement with Occupied Japan was signed in August, 1951. This led to a formal termination of the state of war with Japan the following April and in December, 1953, a four-year trade agreement between Burma and Japan was signed. These agreements with Japan paved the way the following year for a reparations agreement under which the Burma government would receive a total of $250,000,000, the largest amount of aid from any single outside source.

While Burman missions of various kinds and numbers were coming and going, the Burma government also moved to formalize its participation in international organizations. By virtue of its UN membership, Burma automatically became a member of ECAFE (UN Economic Commission for Asia and the Far East). In January, 1952, Burma joined the International Bank for Reconstruction and Development and the International Monetary Fund by subscribing the necessary capital. By March, Burma had become a full participant in the Colombo Plan and a member of the ILO, the FAO, the WHO, and UNESCO. To all of these international organizations, the Burma government made appeals for assistance and by mid-1953, these agencies plus the UN Technical Assistance Board were supporting a variety of projects costing about $500,000.

In 1951–52 a series of economic surveys, undertaken by the American engineering firm of Knappen, Tippets, and McCarthy and a staff supplied by Robert Nathan Associates of Washington, D. C., were pulled together in an ambitious scheme called the Pyidawtha welfare state program.[28] This scheme as explained by Prime Minister U Nu at a special conference called in Rangoon in August, envisaged an eight-year capital investment program, large-scale development of local welfare activities and democratization of local government. The economic development envisioned in the scheme was based on estimates of a realization of large sums of investment capital from local savings, both private and public. Economic expansion in a variety of activities, however, was handicapped by many factors. The scheme was overambitious in terms of the capacity of the government and the capabilities of the Burmans. The whole budgeting of the scheme was based on the assumption of continued high prices for rice in the world market, and when the end of the Korean War in 1953 caused the market price to drop severely, it fell below even the minimum anticipated, with disastrous results for Burma's foreign exchange position.

The course of the Burma government's economic planning, the assistance received in the process from the two American groups and other western sources, plus the expansion of economic agreements with western nations led many persons to conclude that these events signalled a fundamental shift toward the west in Burma's basic foreign policy — a shift away from strict "non-alignment." When the Burma representatives defended vigorously these agreements at ECAFE meetings against charges of western alignment, many were further convinced that Burma was leaning toward the West and modifying its original socialist goals toward a more democratic orientation.

Those who accepted this line of reasoning received a rude shock in the spring of 1953, when the Burma government announced abruptly that it had requested the termination of the United States aid program by June 30 of that year.[29] Some took this as a sign of another reversal of direction, while others took it as an evidence of ingratitude and fickleness on the part of the AFPFL leaders. For these reasons it is worth while recapitulating the causes for this sudden move and its relationship to Burma's basic foreign policy principles.

In its inception, the U. S. economic aid program had been received with good will by the Burmans. It is probably true that they were somewhat less suspicious of the United States at that time and generally believed that the program served the interests of Burma. The sudden action of the Burma government was the result of a combination of events and circumstances and of the application by the AFPFL leaders of their particular concepts of "right" and "justice" in foreign relations. The events and circumstances can be summarized briefly. First was the fact that in the very nature of conditions in Burma in 1950–51, any substantial aid program must have included considerable planning and involved for the most part, long-term development projects. Thus, no immediate results could be foreseen, particularly results visible to the public and to the press. Unfortunately, the U. S. TCA Mission approved assistance to two immediate projects already begun by Burma Government Boards, both of which were unpopular with the Burmese press. One example was the Housing Board, which with services of four TCA experts began a construction program for housing government workers at a time when Rangoon was more than full of refugees from the upcountry insurrectionist areas living in makeshift, crowded, and unsanitary conditions in almost every vacant space in the city. The press viewed refugee housing as the most urgent problem and decried American assistance going into lengthy construction projects for the benefit of higher-paid civil servants and political henchmen.

A second factor was found in what appears to be poor public relations on the part of the TCA officials. Shortly after the first TCA officials arrived, it was reported in the press that they were approached informally by representatives of the Burma Journalists Association, a powerful group of the Burmese press, who inquired whether the TCA might be prepared to assist in expansion of the press facilities for the Burmese newspapers. According to press reports, the request was "curtly denied" and all the journalists got was a lecture on the virtues of self-help. Whether the press exaggerated this incident or not, it was widely believed and at the next annual meeting of the Burma Journalists Association, a group presented a resolution asking all members to ban all news of the American aid program. Although the resolution did not pass, the press became increasingly hostile. The TCA office in Burma was accused of mismanagement, unfair allocation of funds, and even of corruption because of association with an AFPFL group headed by U Hla Maung.[30]

A third event bearing on the cancellation of the U. S. program was the change in the U. S. government from the TCA to the new aid agency, the Mutual Security Administration, in October, 1952. Under the new law, the aid agreement with Burma had to be renegotiated and the question was debated in the Burma Parliament for over a month. The very use of the words "mutual security" was alleged to be evidence of "alignment" with the United States. Government spokesmen had to reassure the opposition that signing the new agreement did not mean a violation of the principle of "no-aid with strings attached." The leading English language daily, the *Nation*, commented at length, as follows:[31] ". . . the doubtful advantage of stringing together a few high-sounding phrases to make American Congressmen feel good has been more than offset by the embarrassment caused to friendly governments that have accepted the Mutual Security Program and by popular suspicions aroused concerning America's motives."

In its review of the TCA effort, the *Nation* editorialized,

. . . To a certain extent we agree that much of the criticism against ECA is undeserved . . . ECA in Burma is not anti-Communist, nor anti-anything. It is simply pro-U Hla Maung. Its accomplishments can be measured in terms of how they pulled U Hla Maung's chestnuts out of the fire, beginning with the Cotton Spinning and Weaving Factory and resting with the Mingadalon airport. How many more follies Mr. Abbot Moffat will perpetrate before ECA earns universal opprobrium in this country depends upon how many more "white elephants" projects will be initiated in the fertile brain of U Hla Maung, and then sustained by American raw products and American dollars . . . It would seem hard on some of the technical experts who came out with the sole objective of doing an honest job of work that they should find themselves hamstrung by prejudice, suspicion and hostility on the part of the people whom they have come to help, but that is nothing more nor less than the penalty they have to pay for the mission as a whole playing politics in Burma, by trying to please one or two people and ignoring the rest.

The foregoing circumstances and factors were not enough in themselves to have led the Burma government to cancel the U. S. aid program. They were sufficient, however, to tip the scales when the AFPFL leaders became fully aware of the seriousness of the presence of refugee Kuomintang troops in northeastern Burma. Just at the time when it believed the main force of the Communist and Karen insurrections had been broken, here was a new armed force with the capability of linking up with the insurrectionists and threatening both the stability and the internal security of the country. More than this, there existed the possibility that the presence of this sizeable body of alien troops in Burma might be used either as an excuse for Chinese Communist incursion into Burma or a basis for more concerted Chinese Nationalist attack on Communist-held Yunnan. The KMT problem, then, was both a threat to Burma's internal *and* external security.

Since the Burma government did not recognize the Chinese Nationalist regime on Formosa, the AFPFL leaders turned to the United States for help in solving the problem. They were convinced that the KMT troops were being supplied from Nationalist-held Taiwan and with tacit American agrement. Rumors of direct American military assistance appeared continuously in the Rangoon press. The Burma government believed that the Nationalist government was so obligated to the U. S. it would yield to strong American pressure. When that pressure was not forthcoming soon enough and when the United States seemed unwilling to exert real pressure, the Burma government used counterpressure. The AFPFL leaders justified their action in terminating American aid on moral grounds. They explained they could not continue to receive aid from the U. S. on the one hand when U. S. aid to the Chinese Nationalists was encouraging them to assist the KMT refugee troops on the other hand. The Burma leaders also felt that their case before the United Nations would be strengthened if they were not the recipients of U. S. help.

One final factor was influential, although it is hard to evaluate to what extent this element governed Burma's action. In March, 1953, the Burma government was beginning to see a much rosier economic picture for the country than at any time since independence.[32] Foreign exchange earnings had topped the billion-kyat mark and the end of the Korean War with its consequent sudden drop in world rice prices was not anticipated. Therefore, in the minds of the Burma government leaders, there was far less need for U. S. aid than two years previously and they believed that a termination, which would still permit completion of going projects, would not substantially harm or affect economic development of their country.

The period from 1950 to the fall of 1953 was a period of economic growing pains for Burma. The government, with expert foreign assistance, drew up its first basic economic plans. It rapidly expanded its relations with other countries, with the members of the British Commonwealth and established beneficial ties with the United Nations specialized agencies. These developments proceeded rapidly and under the impetus of getting things done without much of a look farther ahead. What is most important about this development of Burma's foreign economic relations at this time is the fact that there is no evidence that the AFPFL leaders regarded their expanding economic ties with western nations or the UN agencies as in any way modifying their policy of "non-alignment" with the two power blocs. Severance of U. S. aid was decided with little reference to power bloc relationships. In the minds of the Burman leaders, aid from western nations did not mean that Burma was "leaning" politically to the West, nor did termination of the U. S. aid program mean that Burma was "leaning" away from the U. S. and toward the Communists. Generally speaking, Burma's foreign economic relations were being conducted from necessity and were judged in practical, pragmatic terms of what Burma needed, where it could be got soonest so long as the AFPFL leaders convinced themselves that such aid from any one foreign country did not affect their security and independence of action.

Termination of the American aid program, obviously with little animus toward the United States or Americans, also illustrates a very important factor in the application of Burma's foreign policy, soon to be called "neutralism." This abrupt action by the AFPFL government caused but a momentary stir in Rangoon and in the American press and the American government. If the American government believed this act was prejudicial to American interests or that Burma's attempts to obtain American and United Nations help in evacuating the refugee Chinese Kuomintang troops from upper Burma was an indication of undue sensitivity toward the Communist bloc, it gave no sign and Burma suffered no penalities from the United States. The above event was, for Burma, the forerunner of a later attitude or belief implicit in neutralism and expressed openly after 1957–58, that Burma, as well as other neutral nations could deal with the United States and its allies as they saw fit without fear of serious reprisal, but that any action which might antagonize the Soviet Union or particularly Communist China must be weighed carefully in terms of its possible harmful consequences. For Burma, the United States was far away and Uncle Sam was benign and friendly, but Mao Tsetung and his Chinese hordes were near at hand and no Burmese could guess at what moment the olive branch of peaceful coexistence would be lost in a deluge of China's millions moving south.

Reluctant Acceptance of "Neutralism"

Between the beginning of 1950 and the end of 1953, the AFPFL leaders continued to emphasize the basic elements of their foreign policy described in the preceding sections. Western officials, journalists and publicists, however, increasingly expressed the idea that the new nations in the world had but two choices — to align themselves with the anti-Communist western coalition or align themselves with the Communist bloc. In the minds of many Americans and other westerners, pursuit of an "independent" foreign policy was a sign of weakness and the words, "neutral," "neutralist," and "neutralism," were increasingly applied to the uncommitted nations, always with the implication that those who were "neutralist" were, in effect, pro-Communist.

The AFPFL leaders, even more than their Indian and Indonesian counterparts, resisted efforts to put their country's position in foreign affairs in such a category. While being virtually forced to accept the labels of "neutralist" and "neutral" they nevertheless attempted to so define their "neutralism" as to give themselves as much freedom of action in conduct of their foreign relations as possible. The attitude of the Burma government was explained by Prime Minister U Nu in a speech before Parliament, March 8, 1951, as follows:[33]

This House is perfectly aware of the existence of the two power blocs led respectively by Anglo-Americans and Soviet Russia. Although our country is a tiny mite compared with these countries, we have consistently pursued an independent line in tackling international problems with the sole purpose of achieving the Union's peace and world peace without any regard for the wishes of these powers. Because of this independent policy, both the Anglo-American bloc and the Soviet bloc suspect our motives. Not only the Russophiles accuse us of being stooges of the Anglo-Americans, but the Anglo-Americanphiles also accuse us of being renegade Communists and stooges of Soviet Russia.

Mr. Speaker, Sir, on page 14 of an American Journal, 'News Week' dated the 12th of February, we come across a commentary under the caption, 'United Nations.' With your permission, Sir, let me read an extract from this item. It relates to the United States resolution in the General Assembly of the UN on 1st February, to brand Communist China as aggressor in Korea. 'Newsweek' observes 'The vote on this American sponsored resolution was 44 in favor, 7 against and 9 abstaining. The 7 nations which openly favoured Peking were the Soviet Union and its satellites, Burma and India.'

Sir, I am not citing it as a strange phenomenon. We know that such comments are but natural. Any country which we happen to oppose will not view us in a favourable light. Although the Russophiles are branding us as traitors, stooges of imperialists and henchmen of Anglo-Americans, they will, in the twinkling of an eye, reverse their opinion if we offer ourselves as Russian stooges or Russian henchmen. They will then laud us as decent people with right views and progressive ideas. In the same way, although the Anglo-Americanphiles accuse us as renegade Communists and Soviet satellites when we do not side with them, they will suddenly reverse their opinion if we declare ourselves to be their camp followers.

To be candid, we can never be the camp followers or stooges of any power. As our present actions will be recorded for posterity, we must be extremely careful in what we do. We do not want our decisions to be swayed for example, by consideration of financial assistance received nor out of fear or love or hatred. The sole criteria for all our decisions is *our sense of what is right and proper*.[34]

In June, 1951, U Nu was quoted as stating that, "Burma's foreign policy is not framed on the basis of political ideologies, therefore, Burma has no intention of taking sides in the struggle between Communist and anti-Communist forces."[35] The first of the next month, Burma's Foreign Minister, Sao Hkun Hkaio, expressed the view that Burma was not likely to be the next target of the Cominform in the Far East. Referring to anxieties expressed in America, he said there were interested parties "deliberately trying to influence the Burmese government to abandon its independent foreign policy of neutrality" and that such tactics "would not work."[36] In his annual Martyr's Day speech the same month, the Prime Minister, under fire from leftist opposition to his foreign policy, stated that Burma "will ask the Soviet Union and Communist China for economic aid." "We want to see if Russia and New China will give aid to any country like ours which will refuse to become their satellite," he said. American aid to Burma had come without any strings and "we want to know if similar aid will be forthcoming from Russia on the same terms, though Burma follows an independent and neutral foreign policy."[37]

By August, Burma's ambitious economic plan was adopted and a large conference was convened in Rangoon so that it could be explained fully prior to its implementation. At this conference, in a very long address, Prime Minister U Nu again defined his government's foreign policy in the following words:[38]

Before the advent of independence we did not have any foreign relations. Our external affairs were all handled by the British Government. Thus we had no opportunity to play our part in shaping the affairs of the world, either for good or bad. We were nothing better than onlookers at the British handling of foreign relations. But independence changed all this. We now have full rights to participate in world affairs.

Now we could play our role in world affairs to the fullest extent of our ability. We are now like the proverbial prawn, which, despite its tiny proportions, could yet swim in the ocean. But we abhor the very idea of acting as a disciple to any big power or as a satellite of any political bloc. We do not like to lift our fingers or nod our heads at a signal from anyone.

For these reasons we have steered clear of membership in any bloc and have openly declared our policy of strict neutrality. The cardinal prerequisites for pursuance of a policy of neutrality are as follows:

(1) We must use our own consideration to either support or object to any matter on its own merits.

(2) We must establish the friendliest relations with all nations whenever possible.

(3) We must accept from any country any assistance for the creation of a Welfare State provided such assistance is given freely and does not violate our sovereignty.

(4) We must render our utmost assistance to any country which needs it.

By upholding the above four prerequisites for neutrality, our Union has gained a high prestige in the international sphere. Some nations may feel piqued because we have not supported their cause, but even such nations cannot despise us for having followed this step through sinister and ulterior motives. The most they can say of us is: 'These people will never be our followers nor of anyone else.'

U Nu goes on to say that certain people "label us tools of the Anglo-Americans because we accept aid from England and America." He points out that the Soviet Union accepted aid from America during the war and on the basis of this reasoning, Russia could be considered a "tool" of America. He implies such reasoning is manifestly absurd and that any nation must have outside help when it is in trouble. And he makes his point that, "If any assistance is given on two conditions, which are (1) non-infringement of our sovereignty and (2) creation for the new era, we shall accept this assistance from any source, be it Britain, the United States, Soviet Russia, the People's Republic of China, Abyssinia or the Andamans."

After criticizing those people who take sides and say that everything done by the Anglo-Americans is good and by the other side is bad and vice versa, he concludes,

Why, then, must we join any group when these are all devoid of the right outlook and are consciously or unconsciously trying to destroy the world?

Distinguished guests and gentlemen, it is immaterial whether or not we get assistance in the course of our foreign relations. If any nation wishes to render assistance because it may be of mutual benefit, it could do so. Otherwise it can also withold assistance. In any case, we object to the idea of joining any bloc, relying on such bloc and attacking the opposite bloc. This is the road to ruin. Both on behalf of the AFPFL and the Government, I give you this assurance that we shall never accept from any nation such assistance which will bring the Union into a humiliating and disgraceful position before the world.

For these reasons, distinguished guests and gentlemen, in consideration of our internal and surrounding external situation —
   (1) We must use our own discretion to either support or object to any matter on its own merits;
   (2) We must establish the most cordial relations with other nations whenever possible;
   (3) We must accept from any country any assistance for the creation of a Welfare State, provided such assistance is given freely and does not violate our sovereignty;
   (4) We must render our utmost assistance to any country which needs it. I can assure you that no Foreign Policy can be better than ours which has embodied these four principles.

By the end of 1953, the AFPFL leaders had accepted the label of "neutralism" for their country but only with reluctance and qualifications. Burma's "neutralism" did not connote aloofness or withdrawal from world affairs. Nor did it connote a refusal to take a positive stand on international issues. To the Burman leaders their foreign policy first of all was "independent" of ties with either of the power blocs and they arrogated to themselves the right to judge each international issue on its merits and take their stand on what they believed to be "right" at any given time. U Nu and his associates were always at pains to explain that any action which seemed to align Burma with one bloc or the other, was in fact only the exercise of their independent judgment of what was "right." On many occasions, U Nu pointed out that in pursuit of these principles his government had supported the admission of Communist China to the UN consistently, but had voted against the Soviet Union on many Korean issues. Burma's vote with the Soviet Union against the U. S.-sponsored resolution declaring the Chinese Communists aggressors in Korea was justified on moral grounds and on the premise that such action would not contribute to peaceful settlement of the Korean War.

The AFPFL leaders, between 1950 and 1954, stuck to their contention that Burma was to be a Welfare State, not on the Soviet model, but one to be achieved by the slower processes of democratic procedures. They believed, and continued to assert, that arrangements for economic assistance with any country, whether associated with one of the power blocs or uncommitted like their own, had no relevance to the fundamental foreign policy of "independent neutrality" or "non-partisanship." Thus, it would be incorrect to state from the record that the conclusion of many economic agreements with the western nations in this period represented any shift in Burma's foreign policy toward possible alignment with the Anglo-American bloc, just as it would be incorrect to assert that termination of the American economic aid program in March, 1953, represented a more favorable attitude toward the Communist bloc.

The basic foreign policy which the AFPFL government gradually evolved between 1948 and 1953 was one that in their own minds allowed them considerable freedom of action. Intent on their economic goals, they sought economic assistance wherever they could get it. Thus Burma's foreign economic policy was based on a simple, single premise — aid from any nation so long as it did not infringe Burma's independence — and this policy bore no relationship to their basic political-military foreign policy in the minds of the Burman leaders, as they were constantly trying to explain to the left- and right-wing oppositionists.

The policy of "independent neutrality" was reinforced in the minds of the Burman leaders by a series of circumstances. The swift UN action at the start of the Korean War removed the necessity of seeking any kind of military arrangements for defense of their independence which would have involved them with one of the power blocs. Reliance on the UN for protection did not violate their "independent" course. As the necessity for economic aid led to a series of arrangements between 1950–53 with the U. S., the U. K., and other western nations and to Burma's participation in the help from the UN agencies, there were many in Rangoon who urged closer ties with the British Commonwealth and the U. S. In resisting these pressures (which were never overwhelming or concerted) U Nu and his colleagues tended to follow the lead of Prime Minister Nehru, generally. More important, the Korean War led to devastation of that country and the Burman leaders were bound and determined this would not happen again to Burma if it could be avoided, a determination which reinforced their belief that Burma must be friendly with *all* nations. The issue of the KMT refugee troops in upper Burma plunged the Burma government into the midst of cold war politics in the UN. They suffered the disillusionment of idealists, who, though familiar with clean and dirty politics in their own country, try to convince themselves that international politics, particularly under the aegis of an international organization, are somehow conducted on a higher plane.

By the end of 1953, the AFPFL leaders were more experienced in the conduct of foreign relations. Many of them had gone on missions to Europe, the U. S., and a few to the Soviet Union. Their experience had induced a firmer belief in the validity of their "independent neutralism" and had also led them to develop a certain cynicism. This attitude was reflected in a speech by U Nu to the Rangoon University students in December, 1953, in which he gave a somewhat lengthy exposition of the thesis that the "leaders of the two great power blocs, namely England, America and Soviet Russia are not working for the interests and benefit of anybody else, they are purely working for their own interests." In this speech he said,[39]

As they are building up strength for global control, they are making rival claims, and shouting each other down, for the defense of Democracy, respect for human dignity, liberation from imperialism and the building of heaven on earth.

But, whatever ideologies they have, whatever policies they outline, whatever resolutions they pass, whatever slogans they shout, in actual practice, whenever there is a conflict with their interest, they are not ashamed to discard their policies, to shelve their resolutions, and to change their slogans as easily and quickly as a woman of no character changing her loves.

Since these great powers are not acting for the interests of anybody else, but their own, do not let yourselves be their stooges . . . But, although these great powers cannot bring us beneficial advantages, they can injure and damage us. Therefore, we must not insult them. We have to get on as best we can with them. Where there is a question of mutual interest, or where there can be mutual advantage, we should act in concert with them sincerely and cleanly. Nevertheless, never trust them completely to the extent of leaving our all in their hand.

These assertions of U Nu's reflect some of the cynicism and wariness of the politician who regards anyone outside his own circle with a certain amount of suspicion and takes his opponent's platform speeches with several grains of salt. The evolution of Burma's neutralist policy during these first five years is also a reflection of the fact that the Burma government was managed by men whose primary ability lies in the rough and tumble politics of a power struggle, whether internal or international. By 1953, the Burma politicians had gained enough confidence to feel that they understood the rules of the game of international politics. They tended to scorn polemics about the free world versus Communism or to see in this struggle any great moral crusade by either side. They had convinced themselves that for Burma's foreign policy the concepts of "non-alignment with power blocs antagonistic to each other," "no economic aid with strings attached," and "maintenance of friendly relations with all countries" were sound cornerstones and had been successful because they worked for Burma. They had interpreted these principles in action under a variety of circumstances without loss of freedom and with the belief that their "small, weak nation," had emerged, by the end of 1953, unscathed by the cold war and commanding a growing respect in world affairs.

The AFPFL leaders, as politicians, were not accustomed to look very far ahead or take a very long-range view of where their neutralism might eventually lead them. By and large they were practical men of action, not idealists or planners. As such, most of the AFPFL leaders tended to shun doctrine or rigid formulas in the conduct of foreign relations, for they had emerged to lead their nation after a chaotic world war into a rapidly changing world, often bewildering, in which old values, customs and beliefs were being challenged or cast aside.

The Burma politicians' approach to foreign affairs in a world of cold war politics was well illustrated in their reluctant acceptance of neutralism as a label for their foreign policy of nonalignment. U Nu and his colleagues sensed that neutralism, as a label to be commonly applied to all unaligned new nations, might well be a semantic trap. For by strict definition, the neutral is the careful nonpartisan, must never show partiality to one side or the other, and to protect his neutrality must assume a passive role in the world. Consequently, the Prime Minister and his colleagues constantly sought to interpret neutralism as something different than it should be by strict definition. U Nu used the phrases, "independent and neutral," "non-alignment" and began to insist his government would judge an issue or situation on its own terms, taking the action it believed to be "right" in each case. When accused of partiality toward one or the other of the power blocs, the AFPFL leaders found they could also show that if they had acted favorably toward one side in one instance they had balanced such acts by favorable action toward the other side in other cases, thus maintaining their "independent neutrality."

Since U Nu and his associates had little time for any long-range planning or for careful analysis of world events or even for some attempt at a prognosis of future problems, they found it easier to convince themselves that their foreign policy had succeeded because by 1953, Burma was still free, wooed by nations in both power blocs as well as others, and had survived crises which might well have destroyed another small nation under a different foreign policy. This attitude points up a major weakness in the formulation and execution of Burma's neutralist policy during the first five years. Throughout this period there is little evidence that the AFPFL leaders gave more than passing consideration to two aspects of their neutralist policy.

First, in none of the foreign policy speeches by U Nu and his associates is it possible to find more than very vague and general limits fixed for the pursuit of their policy of neutralism. In different terms, there seems to have been little thought given to establishment of criteria by which the leaders of the Burma government could determine what kind of action, what kind of arrangements or agreements might transgress the bounds of neutralism and, in fact, result in an alignment with either the Communist bloc or the West from which there might be no turning back. To be sure, specific political or military "alignment" with either contending power bloc was to be eschewed, but this leaves a wide range of actions which over a period and in combination could create such economic or other ties with one group as to make it necessary for Burma to reduce greatly or virtually to sever its economic or other ties with the opposing group of nations. Such a development for a small nation is far from unknown in the history of international politics, and the leaders of a government are never directly confronted with a decision on the end result for it is a slow and gradual process in which a series of separate decisions finally are compounded to force a nation into a position of something less than independence.

Second, in their desire to spread Burma's economic commitments among a large group of nations, to maintain impartiality among the donors of economic aid by accepting it from both power blocs and from uncommitted nations, the AFPFL leaders, after the first few years showed evidence in their speeches and in the actions of their government that they were very close to taking Burma's position in the world for granted. There was a tendency to assume that the major nations of both camps in the cold war and others as well considered Burma a nation worthy of help or were convinced that assistance to Burma would somehow serve their selfish interests.

To put it bluntly, it was probably very natural and very human that the AFPFL leaders did not stop to consider how much Burma was a beneficiary of cold war rivalry. Nor did they apparently stop to consider that their five-year policy of "independent neutrality" might only be possible because of the struggle between the two behemoths, the U.S.S.R. and the U.S.A. Such considerations are not palatable thoughts for prideful politicians directing the policy of a small nation.

The foregoing considerations point to a tentative appraisal of Burma's neutralism, not as a policy which provides for maximum freedom of action by its government, nor as the most likely policy designed to preserve Burma's sovereignty and territorial integrity, but as one which induces a growing *dependence* upon the vagaries, sudden changes, and swift developments in the struggle of the giants. On the sixth anniversary of Burma's independence, there is evidence that some AFPFL leaders felt or sensed these things without benefit of cold, rational analysis. Their country's close proximity to the Chinese end of the Communist bloc axis would tend to induce thoughts along this line. But by this time, the AFPFL leaders were not only committed to a neutralist posture in world affairs, they had also become bound by the psychology of neutralism which might be paraphrased as, "speak softly to everyone and don't even carry a stick."

"POSITIVE NEUTRALISM"

1954 – 1958

Burma's first five years of independence was a period of severe trials. One crisis followed another in almost dizzying succession. One by one these crises were surmounted and by the end of 1953, the AFPFL leaders could look to the future with some confidence. They had been able to obtain economic aid without compromising their policy of nonalignment. From a position of virtual isolation in 1948, Burma had reached the point where more active participation in world affairs seemed both possible and desirable.

The next four years, from 1953 to the beginning of the political crisis in 1958 was a period in which the AFPFL government had ample opportunity to put the basic concepts of its neutralist policy to test. U Nu and his colleagues had said many times they could take economic aid from any country so long as "no strings were attached." The problem of Burma's rice exports, following the drop in world prices after the Korean armistice, gave them an opportunity to test this principle through trade agreements with the Communist bloc states. On more than one occasion, U Nu had implied that neutralism should not dictate a passive role for his government in foreign relations. After five difficult years as Burma's chief executive, he was now ready to assume a more active role in world affairs. Also, U Nu and his associates had implied that neutralism as a foreign policy still left the Burma government free to follow any course with respect to a particular international issue or situation that its leaders determined was morally "right." A series of issues and events in this period afforded the Burma government the opportunity to make such choices.

During this four-year period, in the actions of the Burma government, as well as in views expressed by its leaders, are to be seen some of the difficulties and possible contradictions inherent in a posture of neutralism by a small nation. They provide further insight into those beliefs or views about world affairs underlying neutralist thinking. For U Nu and his colleagues, like Prime Minister Nehru and leaders of other neutralist nations, appear to have developed a set of beliefs or attitudes about the politics of the cold war which differ in many important respects from those held by its chief protagonists on both sides. For the Burmans and other neutralist leaders, dedicated to rapid modernization of their respective countries and forced to give detailed attention to problems of internal economic, political, and social development, the cold war contest often seems a nightmare. Therefore, any formula which seems to them likely to "relieve tensions" is attractive. They see "peaceful co-existence" as a worthy end, not in Khrushchev's terms as a means to a Communist world. Almost any kind of negotiated settlement of disputes between the cold war contestants appears to the neutralist leaders preferable to the risks of nuclear *or* limited warfare. These and other ideas, seemingly inherent in the "cult" of neutralism as it developed in this period are illustrated in the actions of the Burma government and the views expressed by U Nu and his AFPFL colleagues before the beginning of 1958 when they all became enmeshed in their internal struggle for political power.

Expanding Foreign Economic Relations

By January, 1953, Burma's foreign exchange reserves equalled more than one fourth of the gross national product for the preceding year.[1] Having gained such a favorable position, the government set about investing its earnings. Up to this time the burden of reconstruction and introduction of new industries had been carried by the American grant through the Technical Cooperation Administration. With the termination of the American aid program and with growing foreign exchange reserves, the Burma government now assumed financial responsibility for economic development projects and, in addition to large capital goods orders already made, dispatched missions to a number of countries to place new orders for planned projects. In terminating American aid, neither the press nor the government mentioned the fact that the Burman economy was approaching a greater stability than it had experienced since independence, but the Cabinet was in possession of favorable indicators of this stability in a rising national income, large foreign exchange reserves, conclusions of favorable trade agreements with Japan and India, and substantial rice contracts with Japan, India, Ceylon, Indonesia, and British Empire countries.

By mid-1953, payment for these foreign orders, however, had become a heavy drain on the foreign exchange reserves. The Korean armistice, concluded at the same time, caused a rapid fall in worldwide government purchases for stockpiling. These purchases had pushed prices of most primary commodities, including cereals, to a postwar high. Although world rice prices began to decline immediately after the Korean armistice, the Burma government initially refused to lower their offer price. Consequently, two important customers, India and Japan, cut purchases to an extent that Burma's rice exports fell by over thirty percent during the latter half of 1953.[2] In addition, a Japanese government press release stated that imports from Burma were stopped because Burma rice was inferior to that which could be purchased elsewhere for the same price. Indian reasons appear to be similar.[3] Although world economic conditions appeared less favorable after the Korean armistice, the Burma government was somewhat slow to react. As late as February, 1954, at the tenth meeting of ECAFE, the Burma representative stated that, ". . . Burma would, in all probability, be able to meet a substantial portion of foreign exchange requirements for those programs (economic development programs) without resorting to loans from abroad. Burma planned to increase its exchange position by developing its exports of rice, timber and minerals and by producing within Burma many of the products which were now available only from abroad."[4]

Both India and Japan, after reducing rice purchases from Burma, turned to the United States and over the next twelve months India bought US$50 million and Japan US$150 million worth of wheat and other surplus cereals. Although the U. S. Department of Agriculture declared that the grain was supplemental to regular rice purchases, the Burman officials and the press drew different conclusions. The *New Times of Burma,* a progovernment newspaper, editorially declared that,[5]

A broad hint was also implied in press reports that the United States Government may be behind an insidious plan to cut off rice markets from Burma so as to force the Burmese to come to terms, economic as well as political, which will once again envelop Burma in the American sphere of influence. To support this trend of thought, observers have mentioned the recent decision of the Japanese to cut Burmese rice imports by half . . . The fact that this decision came on the eve of the departure of a Burmese economic mission to India where the mission hopes to barter Burma rice for Indian products was also taken as a mischievous intent to discredit Burma rice in Indian markets . . . Anyone who can prevent, prohibit or otherwise make Burma rice unsalable at normal market prices will be holding the whip hand against Burma . . .

In the following months all the Burman press joined in general criticism of United States surplus cereal sales, hunting for any facts to substantiate their arguments that these sales were a deliberate infringement on Burma's traditional rice markets. Immediate rice exports were not bright in the last half of 1953, but three long-term trade agreements provided some compensation. The first was a barter agreement with Yugoslavia, of unlimited duration, signed on June 29. Although this particular agreement had little effect on Burma's trade position for the immediate future, it was important because it became the model used for later agreements with the U.S.S.R. and countries of the Communist bloc. Ceylon agreed to a four-year rice trade agreement in September, effective in January, 1954, calling for purchase of from 200,000 to 400,000 tons of rice annually at annual prices ranging from £50 to £44 per ton, in each succeeding year. This was a major drop in Burma's selling price which had reached as high as £60 per ton the previous year. The agreement with Japan on December 8th called for export of from 200,000 to 300,000 tons per year for four years. These agreements were greeted by a wave of optimism in the press and predictions that the Burma government had ably survived the midyear crisis for which the United States was blamed.

In the first months of 1954, additional rice contracts were signed with Ceylon, Japan, India, and the Ryukyus which relieved Burma of the carry-over 1953 rice crop, but Indonesia and Malaya, two heavy purchasers previously, contracted for only half of their usual amounts. Prospects for excellent rice yields for 1954 throughout southeast Asian countries and for India and Japan as well brought new pressures to bear on the world rice market causing prices to decline still further. By March, 1954, the Burma government was faced with a more serious rice export problem than in the previous year. A quick survey revealed that prospects for complete disposal of the 1954 rice crop in normal markets appeared to be very bleak.

The decline in rice prices and in normal market outlets for Burma, plus the pressure of dwindling foreign exchange reserves, influenced the Burma government to modify its earlier policy of self-support for economic development and to seek assistance from two sources — the United States and the World Bank. In early April, Finance Minister U Tin announced in Parliament that the Burma government would have to seek foreign loans if economic expansion was to continue at the planned rate. Negotiations with the American government and with the World Bank were continued through the summer of 1954 as the Burma Government became more and more apprehensive over its rice surplus. In October, Prime Minister U Nu acknowledged that negotiations for a resumption of U. S. aid had been going on, but stated that,[6] "Burma is willing to accept United States economic aid but we do not want it free. We prefer to pay for it as this forms a more solid basis of friendship than acceptance of gifts." Burma's offer to pay for American assistance in rice, however, was not acceptable to an American government involved in disposal of its own cereal surpluses and no agreement was reached. At the same time, the World Bank refused a loan to the Burma government, allegedly because of continuing disorder in the country which was claimed to be a substantial barrier to any kind of orderly economic development.

Again, the United States was roundly criticized in the press for refusal to accept Burma's terms, while pouring in military aid to certain countries in Asia. A press editorial concluded,[7] "While the United States is still haggling over its ultimate policies, the Russians have efficiently switched emphasis from exporting consumer goods, thus entering the struggle in Asia through the back door . . . the economic field. The Soviet Union and Communist China frankly state that they can absorb much of the surplus production of raw materials in the Asian states."

Declining rice prices and foreign exchange reserves, smaller sales to previous customers and the failure of negotiations for assistance from the World Bank and from the United States at this juncture were mainly responsible for the decision of the Burma government leaders to barter 150,000 tons of rice with Communist China by an agreement signed on November 3. This agreement was immediately hailed in some of the western press as a sign that Burma was being drawn into the Communist bloc since it was followed by similar agreements with the U.S.S.R. and its eastern satellites. This was not quite the case, however.

The rice agreement of November was not a sudden decision and the groundwork for it had been well laid. On the previous April 22 Burma and the People's Republic of China had signed a three-year trade agreement to be later implemented by the two governments. The agreement of November 3 was for one year and called for Burma to exchange 150,000 tons of rice, food beans and lentils, oil cakes, mineral ores, timber, rubber, and raw cotton for materials and products from Communist China.[8] Trade was to be conducted through national trading organizations or their agencies. An unusual clause in the protocol called for a separate account to be maintained by both parties for twenty percent of the purchases which would be paid in goods from the U.S.S.R. and East European countries.

In June, Chou En-lai had paid his first visit to Burma and after long conversations U Nu and Chou announced adherence to the "Five Principles of Peaceful Co-Existence" which Chou and Prime Minister Nehru had publicly agreed to earlier. In September, a Burma trade mission spent three weeks in Communist China. In October, Prime Minister Nehru had visited Burma for talks with U Nu and his colleagues. In August the Prime Ministers of the Colombo Powers had met and discussed common problems. In September, a new Russian Ambassador arrived in Rangoon. By November, the AFPFL leaders had ceased to feel that they and their small country were alone in the world. The meeting of the Asian Prime Ministers in Colombo, calling themselves the "Colombo Powers" at which the Burma Prime Minister met as an equal with his opposite numbers from India, Pakistan, Indonesia, and Ceylon, had shown the world Burma's new status. The visit of Chou in midsummer was the beginning of closer and more extensive relations between Communist China and Burma, and U Nu had accepted Chou's invitation to visit up north. The new Soviet Ambassador was reported to have brought information that the U.S.S.R. was in a position to assist Burma and was willing to do so "without strings."

The intimations of the Soviet and Communist Chinese representatives to U Nu and his AFPFL colleagues were that no long or protracted negotiations would have to take place for Burma to get assistance. Further, the Communist bloc representatives apparently did not haggle initially over terms but gave the impression that they applauded the Burmese desire to "pay" for aid and not to accept "gifts."

The Burma government had made no official comment before the barter agreement with the Chinese Communist regime was signed, other than occasional references to the need for a wider market,[9] and referred to economic arrangements with the Soviet bloc only in the context of assistance.[10] When the barter agreement was signed, U Nu assured the Press that it had exceeded the expectations of the government:[11]

Because we did not know what to do with the rice surplus, we were prepared to let China have it on a straight barter basis — Chinese goods of an equivalent value in exchange for the rice — but the Chinese as a gesture of friendship went out of their way to offer 20 per cent cash and another 20 per cent in goods from Russia and East European countries. That's why I said earlier that we got better terms than we should have been content with.

Questions: 'Then the suggestion is that although China has rice surpluses of her own, she is extending a helping hand out of friendship?'

Answer: 'That is correct.'

However, the press had debated the issue of trade with the Soviet bloc for at least a year prior to the agreement. Since 1953 some trade, on a small scale and consisting mostly of raw rubber shipments, did take place between Burma and China; this was viewed favorably by all but the most pro-American papers. In June, 1953, the *New Times* asserted that trade should be expanded:[12]

It is particularly interesting for Burma, and advantageous also, to develop trade relations with China, her great neighbor and friend. Burma and Communist China stand to gain together by developing their mutual trade and commerce. The fact that these two countries are adjacent geographically and that the neutral port of Rangoon is as much an open backdoor to China as any other, make possible greater trade exchange than exists today . . . Burma's raw materials, strategic as well as non-strategic, have a wide range of appeal to the Chinese Communists. Communist China can be a bargain counter, literally, if anyone has enough foresight and boldness to grasp the chance.

In the following months, other, more independent newspapers gave increasing support to Communist bloc trade:

> . . . India, Ceylon, Japan and Malaya have been our rice buying countries ever since the pre-war years. We have not had trade relations with New China yet. China with her big and increasing population never has food sufficiency . . . Therefore we should seriously consider to open (sic) new trade relations with Red China. The foreign exchange in China is unfavourable, but we can get their goods in exchange for the sale of rice to them.[13]

> If local reports regarding news that Burma is considering entry into trade relations with China, Russia and Czechoslovakia are true, she is, in the best interests of herself and her people exercising a right which she enjoys as a sovereign state and as a subject of international law. We are aware that Burma possesses raw materials which she would like to export on the most advantageous terms and she stands in need of finished articles and other commodities which she would do well to import on reasonable terms.

> She has been trading with the Western bloc countries with a plan for rapid industrialization of the country. If Burma considers that it would be best for her to extend her trade relations so as to include countries from the Communist bloc, we would think that she is indeed following a wise course.[14]

After the Peking regime signed the agreement in April, 1954, the *New Times* voiced government expectations in the following editorial:

> The Sino-Burmese agreement to barter Burmese rice with Chinese manufactured and agricultural goods is a welcome aspect of the growing friendliness between the two peaceful neighbors. The Chinese Government's decision to buy Burmese rice is doubly welcome in this country when it is well known that China herself is exporting her rice to such countries as Ceylon. Burma can therefore look forward to China as a vast and untapped market for selling her surplus food stocks and thereby assist the Chinese workers to concentrate more time and energy on rebuilding their industry . . .[15]

The *People's Daily* supported the government's decision with this reason:

We heard that the U.S.S.R. and the People's Democracy countries are willing to trade with Burma. But trade agreements have been executed with China only. Nothing has been sold or bought under this agreement yet. Clever countries trade with Communist countries . . .[16]

Finally, an editorial from the *Taing-Lone-Kyaw,* a liberal Burmese language daily, appears to be the essence of most press opinion about barter trade at this time.

"Burma has found a new customer in China for her sale of rice. We want to urge authorities to find new markets in the U.S.S.R. and Eastern European countries, through China, for the sale of Burma's rice." [17]

In spite of the government's fears, Burma exported fifty percent more rice in 1954 than in the previous year, but what the nonexpert public did not understand was the fact that even with this increase in export tonnage, receipts rose only by twelve percent. In the same period there was a continued heavy drain on foreign exchange reserves, which by the end of 1954 were down to the 1950 level. During 1955, the Burma government signed rice barter agreements with Czechoslovakia, Hungary, East Germany, and Poland. The most important barter deal, however, was concluded with the U.S.S.R. which contracted to purchase 150,000 to 200,000 tons of rice within one year. Contracts with Burma's older customers were also concluded so that by the beginning of 1956, the Burma government had advance sales of nearly one million tons of rice contracted for.

During 1956, the government renewed rice barter agreements with Communist China, the U.S.S.R., and the other Communist bloc states so that the amount of rice sold to the Communist bloc under barter arrangements accounted for over half of the total rice exports. Earnings from increased rice exports, however, rose only a little, being only six percent over the 1955 level. Even this increase was not actual since the statistics included sales of barter rice which were valued at a sterling price comparable to the Burman asking price on the open market. In terms of goods to be imported in exchange from Communist bloc countries, whose prices were in some cases higher than similar goods on the sterling market, it can be seen that real earnings from barter trade were questionable.

The impact of barter trade on imports was substantial. To protect dwindling foreign exchange reserves the Burma government instituted more and more import controls on consumer goods beginning in 1955 and cancelled considerable numbers of orders for capital goods from the non-Communist countries. The Burma leaders hoped their economic development projects would be supplied by commodities and capital goods from the Communist bloc countries, and consequently placed some of their orders in these countries in 1955 and 1956. Although on some specific projects, where Soviet technicians were employed, the Burma government received adequate materials as planned, the general effect of barter trade on economic development was to substantially slow down the implementation of planned projects. The well-publicized shipments of cement from the Soviet Union at the monsoon season and in a quantity which tied up the port of Rangoon for weeks only served to dramatize some of the drawbacks to barter trade.

Part of the problem was frankly stated as follows:[18]

It is difficult for Burma to find qualified representatives to go on trade missions. Persons of unusual qualifications are required to understand the complex of goods required by Burma's economic development program. Furthermore, there is the difficult language barrier. For the Burmese, the pricing is very important. The goods offered by the Soviet Union in barter do not have to be priced competitively. There is no competition. If the Burmese do not want to pay the Soviet price, they have no choice but to move along to the next item.

Shortly after the cement crisis in May, 1956, Prime Minister U Nu stated in a press conference,[19] "Do you think we have accepted barter through choice? A man who takes barter when he can have cash must be out of his mind. Our experts have laid before us all the implications of the barter trade, that prices are so manipulated as to place us at a disadvantage of 10–30 percent on the goods exchanged. But it was either barter or throwing the rice in water . . . Where we have made commitments we will honor them. Otherwise we envision a reduction and cessation of barter deals."

In March, 1956, Burma was able to conclude a five-year agreement with India covering two million tons of rice and late contracts with Japan, Ceylon and Pakistan gave Burma a guarantee of sale in 1957 of over 700,000 tons of export rice. With sales thus increased to non-

Communist countries, as he had promised, U Nu reduced the amount of rice to the Soviet Union from 400,000 tons to 100,000 tons and the contract for the year made with Communist China involved only 50,000 tons as against a contemplated 150,000. Similar reductions were made in rice barter exports to other countries of the Communist bloc.

By 1956, too, the Burma government was more successful in obtaining aid from sources other than the Communist bloc states. The International Monetary Fund provided a loan of $15,000,000 against Burma's basic kyat deposit and the World Bank granted a loan of $19,350,000 for improvement of Rangoon port facilities and improvement of the railway system. At the same time, the United States agreed with Burma to provide $21,000,000 under the surplus agricultural commodities act (P. L. 480) in addition to an earlier offer to buy 10,000 tons of Burma rice in return for which American technicians would be sent to assist in specific economic projects. In November, the Indian government agreed to provide a 200 million rupee loan to Burma which, in March, 1957, was further implemented when it was agreed that this fund would be freely exchangeable in sterling to be drawn on by Burma as needed to bolster its foreign exchange reserves. The net result of these developments was to stabilize Burma's foreign economic commitments and reduce its dependence on Communist bloc states for surplus rice disposal.

Perhaps these very developments, and similar ones in India and elsewhere in southeast Asia led to increased Communist attention in the shape of the well-publicized visit of Bulganin and Khrushchev to the area in the fall of 1956. In Burma, where "B and K" stayed longest, Khrushchev denounced the "Anglo-American imperialists" in strident terms. Before leaving, he also announced that the Soviet Union was prepared to "give" Burma a technical institute, a hospital, hotel, theater, and a cultural and sports center. Actually, the Burman leaders insisted that they would accept no outright "gifts" and a resulting loan agreement was signed between Burma and the Soviet Union on January 17, 1957, valued at K. 210,000,000, which provided that the Soviet Union would supply technicians and materials not available in Burma, while the Burma government would pay for local labor and all materials procurable locally, making up the difference in rice shipments to the Soviet Union's account. Thus, the

Russian "gift" projects were comparable to the earlier rice barter agreements.

Not long after the conclusion of the initial agreement for the Soviet "gift" projects, the Burma government signed another agreement with the United States providing for $42,200,000 to finance development projects under the International Cooperation Administration, successor to the Mutual Security Administration. A small ICA mission was assigned to the American Embassy to work out implementation of the projects to be supported from these American funds.[20] All of these foregoing agreements, plus the earlier Japanese reparations agreement which provided Burma with $250,000,000 over a ten-year period furnished Burma with approximately K. 920,000,000 worth of foreign economic aid over the four-year period, 1957–61.

By 1958 the Burma government had established firmly a pattern of "seeking aid from any country which does not infringe Burma's sovereignty or independence." And this policy was successful. It enabled the government to surmount some of the difficulties of economic development and to avoid severe economic dislocation because of their essentially monoculture economy and large dependence on rice exports. At each step taken in relations to nations with the Communist bloc or the Anglo-American group, the government was under criticism for violating its policies of nonalignment. In each case the AFPFL leaders defended these arrangements as having nothing to do with alignment one way or the other and as being wholly "without strings attached." Perhaps more significant, was the growing complex of trade agreements and rice contracts with India, Indonesia, and other nations described as "uncommitted." The Indian loan and the five-year rice agreements mentioned earlier undoubtedly strengthened Burma's ties with India and placed India in a kind of "Big Brother" relationship with its former province.

U Nu as Mediator

Burma's expanding economic relations with a variety of countries in Asia, the Middle East, and Europe naturally gained the country some attention in world capitals. It was the eruption of warfare in Indo-China in 1953–54, however, which focused the attention of the major countries on all of Southeast Asia. In the United States, both officials and journalists were evoking the "house of cards" theory —

e.g., that if Indo-China fell to the Communists, the other countries of Southeast Asia, Laos, Cambodia, Thailand, Burma, and Malaya, would go down before the Communists like a house of cards. And it was the United States that moved hastily and belatedly to bolster free Asia's defenses by a series of defense and mutual security arrangements culminating in the Manila Pact of September 8, 1954, and the establishment of the Southeast Asia Treaty Organization (SEATO).

The oligarchs in Peking and Moscow, however, were beforehand and prior to the preliminary moves by the United States Chou En-lai laid the groundwork for closer cooperation between India and Burma and the Chinese Communist regime. Moscow followed suit, or perhaps their moves were coordinated. At any rate, it must have seemed to the Burmans in 1954 that both Peking and Moscow had suddenly discovered Burma. Burma's need to dispose of its surplus rice and the negotiation of the barter arrangements with the Chinese Communist government, the U.S.S.R., and the East European Communist states conditioned the AFPFL leaders to look with favor on further overtures from their economic rescuers.

All of these circumstances, combined with a very real fear by the Burman leaders that the Indo-China war might expand to seriously threaten their security, led U Nu to attempt the role of mediator between the two principal Far Eastern antagonists, the United States and Communist China. There is no doubt, also, that U Nu as a politician conceived of his new role on the stage of world affairs as a means of adding to the prestige of Burma and to his personal prestige. U Nu's initial participation among equals as the Prime Minister of one of the "Colombo Powers" in several previous conferences had served to break down the earlier Burman feeling that they had isolated themselves by refusing to join the Commonwealth or to make definite "alignments" with the larger nations.

U Nu's role, and therefore Burma's role, in international affairs for the next few years can be understood against a chronological backdrop of the Government of Burma's visitors and of U Nu's journeys abroad. On June 28, 1954, Chou En-lai, then Chinese Communist Foreign Minister, paid his first visit to Burma. Significantly he came to Rangoon from New Delhi, where he and Prime Minister Nehru had just announced their joint adherence to the "Five Principles of

Peaceful Co-Existence" which were to play a large part in the Chinese propaganda effort for the next four or five years.[21] In the brief visit of Chou and U Nu, the two leaders discussed Burma-Chinese trade and, reportedly, exchanged views on the problem of Indo-China. It is possible that there was some talk about a large conference of Afro-Asian nations, such as had been proposed by the Indonesian Prime Minister, Ali Sastroamidjojo, at a meeting of the Colombo powers held in Ceylon the preceding April and May. It is certain there was discussion of a visit to Communist China by Prime Minister U Nu, at a future date.

In September, U Nu's trusted colleague U Tin headed a Burman trade mission to Communist China and the U.S.S.R. The Indonesian Prime Minister visited Rangoon and Delhi to arrange details of what was to be the Bandung Conference. On October 16, Prime Minister Nehru paid an official visit to Rangoon accompanied by his daughter, Indira Ghandi and the Secretary-General of the Indian External Affairs Ministry. At the end of November, U Nu paid his first visit to Communist China, stopping en route in Hanoi for a brief meeting with Ho Chih-minh, head of the "People's Democratic Republic of Vietnam." After two weeks and a series of talks with Chinese Communist leaders, U Nu returned to Rangoon briefly and then went to Bogor, Indonesia, for a meeting of the Colombo Prime Ministers to agree on final plans for the Asian-African Conference to be held the next spring at Bandung, Indonesia.

On January 6, 1955, President Tito of Yugoslavia paid an important eleven-day state visit to Burma, one result of which was to make the Burman leaders develop a special affinity for Tito and his country, for they felt that Yugoslavia had comparable problems and was pursuing a policy of "independent neutrality" much like their own. (Later a similar affinity was developed for Israel.) In February, U. S. Secretary of State Dulles paid a quick one-day visit to Rangoon. U Nu went to Delhi in March. April was the most important month for the Burma government and to the people of Rangoon it must have seemed that many world figures were beating a path to Burma's door.

On April 12, the Deputy Premier and Foreign Minister of the Ho Chih-minh regime in North Vietnam arrived for a brief state visit. On April 14, Prime Minister Nehru of India, President Gamel Nasser of Egypt, and Naim Khan of Afghanistan stopped in Rangoon and these dignitaries were joined by Chou En-lai. After brief talks and state dinners, the whole group left with U Nu for the Bandung Conference on the 16th. On the 27th all were back again in Rangoon before going their separate ways to their own countries.

A month later, in part to demonstrate Burma's "independent" policy in redressing what seemed to some as a "leaning" toward the Communist bloc, U Nu set off on an extended trip, first to Israel, and next to Yugoslavia, the two countries with which Burma had developed a special affinity. From his visit with President Tito, U Nu went to London for a week and then for his first experience in America from June 23 to July 19 when he left for Tokyo and his return home.

Again in October, U Nu redressed his middle-of-the-road course by a state visit to the U.S.S.R., Poland, and then Finland, Sweden, Norway, and Denmark. Perhaps to return his visit and most certainly to show their nation's interest in Asian affairs, Bulganin and Khrushchev took their well-publicized swing out to Asia at the end of 1955, arriving in Burma on December 1 for a week's stay. In January, Madame Sun-Yat-sen was a state guest in Burma as if to keep attention focused on the other half of the Moscow-Peking partnership. More important to the Burmans, however, was the visit of a Yugoslav economic mission in February. During the remainder of 1956, the Israeli Prime Minister paid an official visit to Burma, Soviet First Vice Premier Mikoyan appeared in March, Soviet Deputy Foreign Minister Federenko came in December, and in February, Soviet Marshall Zhukov paid a five-day visit to Burma. Although Chou En-lai came to Rangoon for the third time in December, 1956, Soviet visitors outnumbered those from Communist China or any other country in the fourteen months between November 1955 and February 1957.

To this brief account of the comings and goings of foreign dignitaries and of U Nu's travels, must be added the increased flow of foreign missions of one kind or another to Burma and an increasing number of Burman missions to a variety of countries. Under these circumstances, it would have been difficult for any political leaders not to feel that their country had attained an enhanced position in the world. This view was reflected in the Burma press and particularly in the press reports of the deference paid to Burma leaders by representatives of the Soviet Union, Communist China, and other Communist bloc states.

It was during this period and in this atmosphere, that U Nu attempted to assume a more active role in the world stage as a participant, rather than as an observer from the wings. His first opportunity for such a role had occurred earlier when he had been invited to participate in the two conferences on Indonesia, called by Nehru to meet in New Delhi in January, 1949 and again in March. By this time, the chief participants, Burma, Ceylon, Indonesia, and Pakistan, were being nominated by the press as a new "Asian Bloc" or combination of some sort. In April, 1954, the Prime Ministers of these nations met in Colombo, Ceylon, for a general conference on Asian and world problems. The participants were immediately labelled the "Colombo" powers and hope was expressed by the press that this grouping would take a more active role in representing Asian interests in world affairs.

It was at this first Colombo Conference, that Prime Minister U Nu presented a resolution calling on the five Prime Ministers to form a committee to explore ways and means of economic cooperation among the new Asian states. This resolution was tabled and nothing more came of it. The Burma press, however, had hailed its presentation as an act of leadership by U Nu and many papers expressed disappointment that it had not been even considered. Although the deliberations at Colombo were secret, the evidence suggests first, that U Nu's resolution had been hastily prepared before he left for Colombo so that Burma would have something to contribute to the deliberations. Either U Nu was poorly briefed on his proposal or was unprepared to defend its basic concept in concrete terms of implementation. On the other hand, it is more likely that his resolution was shoved aside by Prime Minister Nehru's insistence on limiting conference discussions to those subjects he was personally interested in and on which he wished to take the lead.

At the Bandung Preparatory Conference in Bogor, Indonesia, in December 1954, and at the Bandung Conference itself in April 1955, U Nu was only one of many leaders who sought the limelight. Or, perhaps it is fairer to say he was overshadowed by more vigorous individuals, particularly at Bandung by Nehru and Chou En-lai. At the second Colombo Powers Conference in New Delhi in November

1956, U Nu seems to have played only a passive role. If it is true that U Nu and his close associates had begun to feel that their country was becoming more important in international affairs and consequently, that they would be listened to by leaders in other nations, their experience at the Colombo Conferences and at Bandung seemed to have cast Burma in a minor role. They expressed pride in the fact that U Nu had been successful as a behind-the-scenes conciliator.

It was in part simultaneous with the foregoing developments that U Nu made his one attempt to act individually as a mediator in the cold war by privately and publicly working toward a rapprochement between the United States and Communist China. There is no question but that he viewed the sharp conflict of interests between the United States and Communist China as one which could easily lead to conflict and thus affect Burma's vital interests. There is also no question that he sincerely believed it was possible for these two nations to compose their differences through bilateral negotiations around a conference table. He expressed this concern in public for the first time on July 19, 1954. This was his annual Martyr's Day address and on this occasion he began by asserting,[22] "Today, instead of dealing with internal problems, as on previous occasions, I will deal with international problems since they are assuming great importance." Then he continued,

Once, it was speculated that World War III, if it broke out, would start in Europe. Now the general belief is otherwise. Southeast Asia is considered the likely fuse for conflagration. . . . As it is generally anticipated that war will mean almost global destruction, the peoples of the world are in a perpetual state of nightmare, so to say.

. . . I think the present hostility between America and the People's Republic of China is far more intense than that which existed between the three Axis powers: Hitler's Germany, Mussolini's Italy and Fascist Japan on the one hand and the democracies headed by the Anglo-Americans on the other.

U Nu asserted that, "Since we are a neutral nation, our view of these two countries (the United States and Communist China) however, is unclouded by prejudice." U Nu then describes America and concludes that it is a "nation of great men and women capable of making the world a better world . . . heroes who saved the world from the scourge of Nazism and Fascism . . . playing the unprecedented role of benefactors showering the needy with billions worth of free gifts, when most countries are indulging instead of giving."

The Prime Minister then gave a much longer eulogy of Communist China praising the "courage" of the regime and extolling its merits for what it was giving to the Chinese people. U Nu then concluded, "Therefore, we feel that as neutrals in power politics we ought to do something to enable both America and China to achieve their ends without resorting to bloody warfare."

After giving some very general and vague advice as to how these two great nations should conduct their affairs, he concludes,

Hydrogen and atomic bombs will have one result. If these weapons are resorted to, of course countries will be laid waste. Out of the ashes will grow the inevitable hatred against the Anglo-Americans who wield the terrible weapon, and out of these ashes will grow Communism which thrives on destruction and poverty.

Therefore a Southeast Asian today requests that his voice be heard by those who are principally concerned so that a worldwide conflagration does not break out.

I pray that the United States of America and the People's Republic of China may be able to work jointly and with understanding for world peace and progress.

U Nu attempted to bring the two nations together through public speeches and private talks first in Peking at the end of 1954 and then in Washington during his visit in the summer of 1955. In the course of his long five-hour speech on September 27, 1957, over a fourth of which was given to a report on Burma's foreign relations, in this section of his speech, U Nu described his efforts at mediation between the United States and Communist China and concluded:[23]

The reception which was accorded me in both these countries was most heartening, and spoke volumes for the deep seated desires of their people for peace. I cannot and do not claim to have performed wonders. In any event the attitudes of both sides have hardened to such an extent that it would be unrealistic to expect spectacular results. But this does not absolve us from the responsibility of doing all that is humanly possible to reduce these dangerous world tensions, and even if I have achieved nothing I have the satisfaction of knowing that the Union of Burma has done all that lies in her power to save mankind from the threat of extinction, and to this cause I shall devote all my energies.

U Nu's private talks with high Chinese Communist officials were reportedly more specific and to the point about his attitudes toward both the Communist Chinese government and the United States than what he said in public. Although Prime Minister Nehru took the lead in the negotiations at the Bandung Conference, U Nu shares a great deal of credit with Nehru and others for whatever success the Conference may have had. It was U Nu who used his acquaintance of Chou En-lai and his position as head of a small nation to persuade the Chinese Communist Premier that he had little to gain by bluster or threats and much more to gain by a posture of "sweet reasonableness" at Bandung. The resulting agreements between the United States and Peking regime to open talks on certain questions in Geneva between official representatives was credited in Burman eyes to U Nu's efforts.

Apart from this slight progress, however, U Nu's one venture in the role of active mediator between two great powers cannot be counted a success. It is important only because the Burman leaders and many of their supporters believed it was important. For them it marked in many ways the point at which Burma, even though weak and small, came of age in international affairs and achieved recognition as an equal of even the greatest nations — a position which had been the goal of every independence leader in Burma since colonial days. Regardless of whether U Nu's efforts on the world stage bore lasting fruit, he and his AFPFL colleagues from 1955 on exhibited a greater degree of self-confidence in directing the foreign relations of their country. Their experiences in world capitals, their talks with world leaders who came to Rangoon, and their participation in the Bandung Conference and other international meetings convinced them that the foreign policy concepts they had formulated were workable. They generally believed that these principles gave to their nation a position of dignity and stature that could not have been achieved by any other course. What was most important in their own thinking was the fact that the basic principles of their foreign policy had preserved the Union in times of great internal difficulties and external threats. These principles, therefore, were fixed enough to steer a course by, but were flexible enough to enable their government to shift and change the course of its foreign relations in accord with changing circumstances and changing needs, thus avoiding the rocks and shoals so numerous in international politics. This seemed to be their analysis by the end of 1955 which U Nu confirmed again in his speech of September 1957, quoted above. What U Nu and his colleagues did not say publicly, however, was that the basic principles of their government's foreign policy were suitable to Burma's needs because they and they alone could interpret them for a given action or in a given situation.

Positive Neutralism

U Nu's venture in international diplomacy was in accordance with an evolving interpretation of the basic principles of "non-alignment with power blocs which are antagonistic to each other" and of "developing friendly relations with all countries." In earlier statements, he and his colleagues had asserted that pursuit of an "independent" foreign policy or a policy of "non-alignment" did not mean aloofness from international issues and problems. It was not isolation or withdrawal and on several occasions U Nu and his Ministers had asserted that the Burma government must contribute positively to the easing of international tensions — must make some contribution to international peace.

It was not until the Burma government, together with those of India and Indonesia and other "un-committed" states, came under fire from the West for their "neutrality" in the cold war that U Nu and his colleagues sought for a more concise definition of the "neutralist" label they had been forced to accept as a characterization of their basic foreign policy. The groundwork for the idea of "positive neutralism" had already been laid by Prime Minister Nehru of India, whom the AFPFL leaders relied upon for their chief inspiration in formulating foreign policy, even though they did not always follow India on specific actions and issues. In several speeches between 1950 and 1953, in attempting to explain India's foreign policy, Nehru had linked principles similar to those of the Burma Government to the idea of positive neutrality. In a speech before the Indian Parliament in March, 1950, Nehru asserted,[24]

We wanted to follow not merely a neutral or negative policy, but a positive one, naturally helping those forces that we consider right and naturally disapproving of the things that we do not like, but fundamentally keeping away from other countries and other alignments of powers which normally lead to major conflicts. This does not mean that, in our economic life, or in other spheres of life, we do not incline this way or that; it does, however, mean, in the jargon of the day, that we do not line up with this or that set of forces but try to maintain a certain friendliness and spirit of cooperation with both the great and small countries of the world.

Again, during a debate on foreign affairs in the Indian Parliament on March 28, 1951, Nehru said, ". . . we would do our utmost to avoid a world war or any war for that matter, we shall judge all issues on their merits and act in conformity with our objective." Again the following June, the Indian Prime Minister stated that,[25]

I submit that this is my approach to foreign policy. You may call it neutral or whatever else you like, but I, for my part, fail to see how this approach is neutral. Neutrality as a policy has little meaning except in times of war . . . If you think there is a war on today, we are neutral. If you think there is a cold war today, we are certainly neutral. We are not going to participate in a cold war which, I think is worse than a shooting war in many ways. . . . Nations must act with dignity and strength, adopt what they consider is the right course and adhere to it.

Again in February, 1953, Prime Minister Nehru said,[26]

Our foreign policy has been criticized from various points of view. The most common criticism is that it is not a policy at all because it is too vague. Some honorable members believe that we are tied up with the Anglo-American bloc because we expect help from it. Others talk frequently of building up a 'third force' or 'third bloc.' An honorable member wants us — he says so — to align ourselves with the rival bloc. According to the general consensus of opinion in this country, we should follow a policy independent of this or that bloc . . . I am not saying that we should not cooperate with others or consult with them but at the same time we must follow an independent policy . . .
A country's foreign policy is really a collection of different policies, though they have a common basic outlook . . . The only rule we can lay down is that we shall try to be friendly with all the countries.

The first use by Burmese officials of a somewhat different terminology to characterize their policy of "independent neutrality" is found in two speeches, first by U Nu and then by U Ba Swe made on successive days at a Conference of Commanding Officers of the Burma Army in Maymyo on September 13 and 14, 1954, respectively.[27]

The phraseology used in these two speeches was not only repeated subsequently, but official statements emphasized that this modified concept of "neutralism" was the "core" of Burma's foreign policy. These ideas were given special prominence since they were repeated in almost identical words by both U Nu and U Ba Swe. In his speech to the Army officers on September 13, U Nu said he wanted "to explain our neutral policy. It has a negative aspect," he said, which is "non-involvement" but "we do not stop at non-involvement, we do our utmost to shun any activity which is likely to create misunderstanding in any quarter." He asserted that Burma's neutral policy also had a "positive" aspect in that "we have endeavored our utmost to be on the best of relations with all countries of the world in spite of non-participation in any power bloc . . . Besides we have played our little part in the establishment of friendly relations between countries and the promotion of mutually advantageous activities." He continued,

It may be asked on what factors this policy and these relations are based: (a) Is it due to the fact that the Union of Burma is geographically within the two spheres of influence of the contending power blocs? (b) Is it due to the fact that our nation is weak militarily and economically? (c) Is it based on our selfish motives generated by our desire for self-preservation even though the two power blocs may be flowing with blood? To tell the truth, we have our own human weaknesses, our own fears, our desire to swim with the tide and our anxiety for self-preservation, and therefore, in the formulation of our foreign policy, the above considerations might have played their part consciously or otherwise. But the greatest consideration that has influenced me in the formulation of this policy and the adoption of these foreign relations is our unshakable belief that war, instead of solving the problems of the peoples of any region: East, West or neutral; will only complicate matters. . . . however small a country may be its alignment with a power bloc will more or less help to increase world tensions. In the circumstances we must try in concert to act with other neutral countries which have an implicit faith in the futility of war, to exert our utmost to prevent World War.

After pointing out that in both previous World Wars, no nation achieved its goals, he commented on the recent formation of the Southeast Asian Treaty Organization (SEATO) apparently to scotch rumors that Burma might consider joining it. He said, "The formation of such organizations increases the chances of World War III. I am firmly convinced that war will not solve any of the problems we want to solve. Therefore we will not be a party to the proposed SEATO. We must not be caught under the clash of swords."

The next day, U Ba Swe, Deputy Prime Minister and also Minister for Defense, returned to the same theme of "positive" neutrality. He asserted that the foreign policy of Burma was being understood as a neutral one by the countries of the world, and it was necessary to explain how this policy was being carried out in practice. "It was possible," he said, "that this policy could be understood as one of indifference towards international developments. There were two aspects of a neutral policy — inactive and active." "An inactive neutral policy," he continued, "consisted of an attitude which was concerned only with one's betterment regardless of others. The active aspect of a neutral policy, on the other hand, was the non-participation in any power bloc whose objective was to bring about a third world war, but participation in measures for bringing about world peace." The struggle between the power blocs was the cause of international tension, U Ba Swe stated, "Accordingly, the Union Government had kept clear of power bloc politics. On the other hand, in order to give prominence to her policy of neutrality, Burma had supported international issues based on right policies and withdrawn her support on those based on wrong policies."

On September 29, U Kyaw Nyein, another top AFPFL leader and Cabinet Minister, gave out a statement to the press in Tokyo, evidently in response to questions, where he was negotiating with the Japanese on the reparations issue. In this statement, he compared Burmese relations with Communist China to that of Finland to Soviet Russia and forcefully reaffirmed the neutrality of his government as a basic policy. "We could not afford the luxury of antagonizing any bloc. Our foreign policy is dictated by domestic conditions, that is the need for peace, just like India and Indonesia. We are subject to pressure from both sides, Communist fifth-column and some western diplomatic pressure outside. But we are determined to do our utmost to prevent a new war from breaking out at least in our part of the world." [28]

In October, when he made public his plans to pay his first visit to Communist China before the end of the year, and stating that he would also like to visit the U. S. after that, U Nu asserted "Burma could not join any bloc just now." "We must be friendly with all states," he said, and then described Burma's foreign policy as one of "dynamic neutrality." Again, in November in his National Day speech, the Prime Minister referred to Burma's foreign policy as follows:[29]

. . . Due to our neutral policy, we do not align ourselves with any power bloc. For this non-alignment, both blocs would not of course view us as favourably as they would their own close colleagues. But, one fact is certain. Both these power blocs now know fully well we are not playing second fiddle to any bloc.

Because of our neutral stand, we are in a position to be on friendly terms with all countries of both blocs. It may perhaps be difficult to understand that our friendly dealings with all countries are important for the stability of our independence. But, a perusal of the world map and the geographical position occupied by our country and a close study of various countries will convince us, beyond a shadow of a doubt, how far our friendly relations with all countries based on our neutral foreign policy have contributed towards the stability of our independence.

. . . We have been able to be on the friendliest of terms with both power blocs because of our correct foreign policy. I have not the slightest doubt about it.

The visit of President Tito of Yugoslavia in January, 1955, opened the way for development of an "affinity" between the Burman leaders and Yugoslavia which may or may not have been reciprocal. It was no secret that Tito was attempting to gain support wherever he could for his own "middle course," and there was talk that he was attempting to promote a "neutralist" third force. The AFPFL leaders, however, were pleased to find that Tito apparently understood their basic aim of building a socialist state and that he seemed to be a firm supporter of their policy of "positive" or "active" neutralism. In the final communiqué issued after his eleven-day visit, Tito and U Nu affirmed that nothing was to be achieved by either a "passive" neutralism which would mean "withdrawal from the battle for peace," or by an alignment with either of the power blocs which would perpetuate the biggest barrier to peace. Only through "active" or "positive" neutralism in support of all efforts to achieve peace could progress be made. U Nu was undoubtedly encouraged by Tito to continue his efforts at mediation between the U. S. and Communist China which he planned to further by his American visit in the late spring.[30]

During the period of the talks in Rangoon preceding the Bandung Conference and at the Conference itself U Nu, as well as his colleagues from India and Indonesia, heavily emphasized the importance of the "Five Principles of Peaceful Co-Existence" initiated by Chou En-lai the previous year. Nothing was said during any of these meetings about "active" or "positive" neutrality. The public position of the Burma government was that it stood by the "Five Principles" and at Bandung was demonstrating Burma's willingness to be on friendly terms with all nations. There were continuing denials that Burma would ever join SEATO, but privately, many high Burmese officials expressed their belief that SEATO was a good thing and might well serve as a protection of Burma's independence, even though the Burma government could not afford to join it for fear of antagonizing Communist China.

Probably the most detailed explanation of Burma's foreign policy was made by Prime Minister U Nu during his visit to the United States in late June and July 1955. U Nu had been made aware that Burma's policy was being criticized widely in America. He knew he would be under a certain amount of fire from the American press and would have to explain what appeared to many Americans a decided bias toward the Communist bloc. His speeches before the United States Senate and before a large audience at the National Press Club in Washington, therefore, had been carefully prepared and the texts carefully checked by his aides. Two sections of this speech emphasize the evolution of basic foreign policy concepts:[31]

For a little over seven years now Burma has been a sovereign, independent nation. We are independent of foreign rule. And we are independent of any power blocs based on military treaties. Nations that choose not to participate in military blocs usually are referred to as neutrals. If my impression is correct, this word "neutral" has acquired a distinct and unfavourable semantic coloration. Apparently the word suggests the image of the ostrich with his head in the sand, a negative attitude towards world politics, a blind withdrawal from reality. The implication seems to be that a nation which does not choose sides and join irrevocably with one or the other camps in the armed truce that exists in the world today lacks courage and conviction. And very often the inference which seems to be drawn is 'if you are not with us, then you are against us.' And if you are not with us, you must be either openly or secretly in tow with communism.

At least these are the impressions which I have received from my conversations about neutralism with American friends and visitors, including representatives of the press. And if this is the case, there is real need for clarification so that we can better understand each other. That is why I want to discuss with you some of the meanings and the implications of independence to the people and Government of Burma.

. . . In the present circumstances of Burma her membership in any alliance with a great power military block is incompatible with her continued existence as an independent state. This may seem to be putting it strongly, but is a fact.

What is the practical effect of this? It is that Burma at the present time has no choice but to pursue her policy of neutrality if she wishes to preserve her independence, and that to us is more important than anything else. It is part of her defense, an important part, against subversion . . . But in another way, she cannot abandon her neutrality without increasing the risk of losing her independence through subversion . . .

. . . In this talk I have been trying to explain how our love of independence — call it preoccupation if you will — leads us logically and inevitably to the foreign policy of independence from any alignment of major powers on the basis of a military treaty. This policy has been called neutralism in the cold war. Perhaps that is the right name for it.

On July 19, 1955, at a Martyrs' Day mass rally in Aung San Memorial Stadium in Rangoon, U Kyaw Nyein (Minister for Industries) pointed out that the world had been on the brink of global war on four occasions since the end of World War II: during the Berlin airlift; during the Korean hostilities; during the siege of Dien Bien Phu; and during the evacuation of some off-shore islands near Formosa. Affirming the "positive" aspect of Burma's neutral policy, he affirmed that, with tensions at the breaking point, Burma, together with Ceylon, India, Pakistan, and Indonesia, had "successfully welded a neutral bloc." At first, he stated, the efforts of these Asian powers had been treated lightly, but the current world situation showed how successful they had been. Tension had lessened, and the change in atmosphere had culminated in the present "Summit" conference in Geneva, for which, U Kyaw Nyein asserted, "Burma and her fellow-Asian colleagues could rightly claim credit for having brought about a brighter international picture." "For herself," he stated, "Burma had succeeded in forging closer relationships with not only her neighbors, but also with both power blocs . . . and she had been successful in rousing world feeling against colonialism."

On January 4, 1956, Ba U, the President of Burma, in his Independence Day speech, asserted that, "Burma gained world-wide recognition due mainly to her steadfast pursuance of the policy of maintaining strict neutrality between the two Power Blocs." In the same month, U Nu resigned as Prime Minister, and U Ba Swe, who had been Defense Minister, succeeded him, stating that Burma's foreign policy would remain unchanged. On January 13, 1956, in his new capacity as Prime Minister, U Ba Swe stated that Burma's policy was, "active neutrality aimed at bringing about understanding and better relations between the two opposing blocs." Again on July 3, 1956, U Ba Swe affirmed the policy of "active neutrality," and later in the same speech said, "We will accept aid from any country provided it does not conflict with our policy of independent neutrality."

On July 19, 1956, U Nu, as President of the AFPFL made his annual Martyrs' Day speech. In this speech he explained that Burma's "neutral foreign policy" had three features: "1. Non-alignment with any power bloc; 2. Friendship with all countries; and 3. Positive endeavours to bridge the gulf between opposing blocs and to promote peace." Striking at the oppostion political groups in Burma as "stooges" (a favorite label), he asserted that, "Stooge-breeding will end up with the loss of independence." To combat this danger, U Nu asserted that the AFPFL Government must "use the following weapons: 1. Support for the UN Organization; 2. A clean and straight-forward policy of neutrality; and 3. Activities directed toward conversion of the foreign stooges without our country."

On September 18, 1956, President Ba U asserted that, "The policy of active neutrality will continue."

On October 4, 1956, U Win, recently appointed Burman Ambassador to the United States, said in a press interview in New York that Burma "does not adopt an attitude of strict neutrality," but "judges each issue on its merits." [32]

U Nu's lengthy speech before Parliament on September 27, 1958, was concerned with a long discussion of domestic problems and explanations of the new four-year plan for the country's economic development. The foreign affairs section of this speech knowingly or not was modeled somewhat after the general format of an American President's "State of the Union" address before the opening session of a new Congress. The speech was carefully prepared to cover all major developments in Burma's foreign relations and specific passages were devoted to Burma's relations with all major countries and those in all main geographic regions. At the beginning of the foreign affairs section, the Prime Minister quoted from the international relations section of the Constitution and stated he would try to show how, in the development of Burma's foreign policy, his government had endeavored to attain the objectives stated in the Constitution. After reviewing briefly the major problems which his government had encountered since 1948 — all of which have been referred to in previous discussions in this and preceding chapters, U Nu then went on to say, "Our foreign policy is directed towards

(1) securing a world peace based in international justice and morality,

(2) establishing and maintaining friendly relations with all other nations and cooperating with them for our mutual benefit, but at the same time avoiding any entanglements which might entail the loss of our freedom of action in foreign affairs."

The Prime Minister then proceeded to give a lengthy review of Burma's relations with individual countries and groups of countries. In the section on relations with Communist China, he asserted, "However, as years passed and the Chinese saw from our actions that we were stooges of nobody and that we were embarked on an independent foreign policy, they changed their attitude." U Nu repeats this reference to an "independent foreign policy" in the sections of his speech dealing with the Soviet Union and with Yugoslavia. It is significant that U Nu completes his rather long explanation of foreign relations with the following statement:

Finally, I would like to submit that we have succeeded in making all these friends without sacrificing our freedom of action in foreign affairs. Our right to decide each issue on its strict merits, without dictation or pressure from any external source, remains unscathed. It was this which has made it possible for us in the course of one session of the General Assembly of the United Nations to condemn the French for their policy in Algeria, the British, French and Israelis for their attack on Egypt, and the Soviet Union for its armed intervention in Hungary. For a small country in our position, I am convinced there is no better foreign policy, and I can assure the House that it is the policy which will be followed as long as the Government which I have the honour to lead remains in power.

From this time on the AFPFL leaders apparently felt that their foreign policy had been explained in public at sufficient length and in enough detail as to make it understood both within the country and abroad. Subsequent references by officials were confined to statements on specific issues, and what the Prime Minister said in this speech was often given as a reason for not making any further explanations at length on Burma's "neutralism."

Burma's Policy Tested — 1956

By the summer of 1956, the Bandung Conference was history and mild suggestions for a second conference had evoked little response. The large flow of Communist bloc official visitors had slackened, and with new agreements concluded and under negotiation for American aid, rice barter deals were no longer necessary. Furthermore, the Burmans were able to appraise the results of the hasty barter deals of 1954–55 and found that they were by no means satisfactory. Burman leaders admitted they had been undertaken to meet the emergency of their rice surplus but that the returns in goods and capital equipment had not met their needs. Renewal of American aid redressed the balance of Burma's economic relations with the two power blocs and the truce in Indo-China plus the Geneva summit conference induced the Burman leaders to feel that international tensions in Asia had slackened. Although U Nu and his colleagues took credit for this in part, as a result of effort to bring the United States and Communist China together, there was little disposition on their part to continue such an active role in Asian and world affairs. Their attention was urgently needed at home.

It was in this changed atmosphere, that the Burma government found its basic policies tested in three specific situations in the fall of 1956. A serious border dispute broke out with Communist China. The Israeli invasion of Egypt and the Anglo-French occupation of the Suez Canal again posed the threat of a general war. At the same time the Soviet armed intervention of Hungary raised the issue of Communist imperialism. The first problem was bilateral, but the other two issues, while not directly affecting Burma's security, were brought before the United Nations where Burma, like all other members, had to formulate a position and take a stand.

In July, 1956, the Rangoon English language paper *The Nation* began to print stories indicating serious infiltration of Chinese Communist troops across the northern border, much of which was undemarcated. The details of this dispute are presented in Chapter V, as part of a case study of Sino-Burmese relations. It is sufficient here to see how the AFPFL leaders both applied and interpreted their basic foreign policy principles to this situation. It was obvious from the start that the Burma government feared involvement with Communist China and the possible active support of the Peking regime for the Burman Communists.

The problem of the Burman government, in applying their foreign policy to this particular dispute, was to avoid real trouble with Communist China if at all possible but not at the price of significant loss of territory or any real compromise of their independence. By the beginning of September, it was apparent that to achieve a peaceful settlement without compromising their territorial integrity or freedom, the Burma government must regard the dispute as wholly of concern to the two nations involved. Any action must be kept on a bilateral basis. A suggestion from the Premier of Thailand that the border incursion constituted "aggression" and that Thailand was willing to participate in any measures, including military, that the UN might decide evoked nothing but horror in the minds of the AFPFL leaders.[33] The last thing they wanted at this time was to see this border dispute become involved in the politics of the cold war. It was perhaps fortunate for their objectives that the Suez crisis and the Soviet intervention in Hungary occurred during the same period as their border dispute with Communist China and thus drew the attention of the world away from the reaches of upper Burma and Yunnan.

From the evidence gathered, the incursions of Chinese troops was not a planned invasion or even a carefully planned capture of border territory. It was not accompanied by more active support for Burma's internal insurgents, nor is there evidence that the Peking regime was putting significant pressure on Burma to change its policies or reshuffle its government in a way more favorable to the Communist cause.[34] In these circumstances, U Nu and his colleagues reached agreement among themselves that negotiation was necessary. At this time, U Ba Swe was Prime Minister and U Nu was presumed to be devoting his time to rebuilding the political fences of the AFPFL. It was decided that because of U Nu's personal acquaintance with Chou En-lai, he should initiate the negotiations. Whether planned or not, this move had the advantage to the Burma government of leaving it free to accept or repudiate any settlement U Nu might arrange, since he was not an official. Whether his colleagues could have repudiated his negotiations or not, is another question.

U Nu went to Peking in October and Chou En-lai was in Rangoon in December. A border conference and, of course, continual communications between Rangoon and Peking, finally produced an agreement in principle. This was the so-called "package deal" which U Nu made public in November and which he justified largely on two grounds. First, Burma had achieved a peaceful settlement and nothing had really marred the friendly relations between Communist China and Burma. Second, U Nu revived a principle stated in an earlier speech on foreign policy, namely, that in the interests of maintaining peace and friendly relations between two countries, it is sometimes necessary for one nation to forego its legitimate rights if this does not impair its independence.[35] It was agreed that Burma should give up certain pieces of territory and that a final border demarcation would be arranged. Settlement of the border question in principle led the AFPFL leaders to again publicly assert that their foreign policy was proved right for Burma in practice as well as in theory, thus reinforcing their earlier beliefs that peaceful relations with all nations were vital to a small country.

The Israeli attack on Egypt and subsequent Anglo-French intervention posed no problems for Burma's relations with Communist China or the Soviet Union. While the Burman leaders realized the explosiveness of the situation, it really did not touch Burma's vital interests and hence the Burma government could easily take the position they regarded as "right" in this case, thus evoking another of their basic principles. It is interesting to note, however, that on this issue as on others before the United Nations, both the Burma votes and the justification of the Burman position differ from that chosen by India, Indonesia, and other "neutrals." On September 23, 1956, Prime Minister U Ba Swe stated that he believed President Nasser had done right in nationalizing the Suez Canal Company, but that he believed that as an international waterway it should be kept open to all nations.[36] The Prime Minister also asserted he thought that the Colombo Powers should be consulted about the matter and felt that they could bring about a peaceful settlement. "Burma," he said, "did not want to see any party suffer as a result of the settlement on Suez, and she did not want to see the dispute flare up into war."

This view of the Prime Minister, somewhat elaborated in more formal language became the official government position made public on October 2, 1956.[37] When the Anglo-French military intervention occurred, U Ba Swe was in Bombay attending a meeting of the Asian Socialist Conference. It was in his capacity as Prime Minister, however, that he issued an official statement on this new aspect of the situation which was somewhat different in tone and wording than of the Indian and the Indonesian governments, and for this reason is worth quoting in full:[38]

Sensational and almost incredible developments are taking place in West Asia. War, as an instrument of national policy, is being employed once again with renewed vigour by certain nations, and the United Nations Charter is faced with the distressing prospect of becoming a mere scrap of paper.

I feel rather strongly that in the present crisis, mere condemnation of certain countries will not help to solve the problems confronting the world today. Rather than condemn, I would place all possible emphasis on constructive and effective action for the immediate restoration of peace.

Steps must be taken for the immediate cessation of hostilities, the withdrawal of all foreign troops from Egyptian territory, and the countries concerned must, without reservation, refer the cases of dispute to the United Nations, which it must be remembered, is the only hope of mankind. In any collective action under the auspices of the United Nations, Burma is prepared to put in her share of contribution towards the successful consummation of any constructive and effective action for the solution of the problem.

I have instructed our Foreign Office to take immediate steps for implementation of this policy and Burma's representatives at the United Nations have also been instructed to render all possible help in the peaceful solution of the problem and to work in close concert with the Colombo countries for the realization of these objectives.

Ceylon alone of the Colombo Powers joined with Canada and other UN members in sponsoring a General Assembly resolution creating a United Nations Emergency Force. Burma joined in a much weaker resolution introduced by nineteen Afro-Asian bloc members. Nevertheless, Burma voted in favor of creating the UN Emergency Force. The Burma representative, U Pe Khin, making his maiden speech to the Assembly, called for "scrupulous" observance of the 1949 armistice agreement and urged that the UN Emergency Force be put into the field immediately. He announced that Burma "will contribute its share of forces, however small, to the UN Emergency International Force." [39] The position taken by Burma on the whole Suez crisis represented a firmer support for the United Nations than that taken by India. It is more difficult to determine whether U Ba Swe and his associates in the cabinet at that time gave full consideration to the implications of their support for UN action particularly with respect to use of a UN Emergency Force in future situations. [40]

The Hungarian revolt and its subsequent brutal suppression by the intervention of the Soviet Union's armed forces raised a different kind of a question for neutralist nations like Burma. In the Suez crisis, Burma could hardly lose any friends by condemning the Israeli attack on Egypt, and Burma logically could not have taken any other position than to condemn the Anglo-French intervention. It was to the credit of U Ba Swe and his government that Burma was not content to merely condemn but from the beginning adopted a stand in positive support of United Nations action in the crisis. In the case of Hungary, the Soviet Union's position naturally was to assert that Soviet forces had been "invited" into Hungary to "suppress a revolt against a legitimate government," and that this was an "internal affair." Although all facts seemed contrary to this position, nevertheless, nations could and some nations did, virtually accept this "explanation" as a means of avoiding any actions which might antagonize the Soviet Union. In the politics of the United Nations Assembly, every uncommitted nation was under extreme pressure from both power blocs when the time came to vote on resolutions on the Hungarian question.

The position taken by India, Indonesia, and other "neutral" nations was in general accord with the Soviet position, that the Hungarian matter was one of internal affairs — a "domestic" question and that, therefore, the United Nations should not condemn Soviet action. On the amendments to this effect offered by the members of the Afro-Asian bloc at the UN to the resolution sponsored by the United States and other nations condemning Soviet armed action in Hungary, Burma abstained and in the final vote in the Assembly, Burma abstained. This drew immediate criticism since Prime Minister U Ba

Swe, then at the Asian Socialist Conference in Bombay, had strongly condemned the Soviet action. The action of Burma was explained in a series of statements. First, U Pe Khin, Burma's representative at the UN General Assembly, announced that Burma's abstention on the General Assembly resolution condemning Soviet action in Hungary was due to the fact the Burma delegation lacked instructions. He said, "My delegation wishes to go on record that the Government of Burma views with great concern the act of Soviet intervention, especially armed intervention, in the internal affairs of Hungary." He urged the Soviet Union to withdraw its troops and continued, "My delegation will support any effort of the United Nations which is consistent with the Charter and which in the opinion of my Government does not amount to interference by some other power." In a press conference in Rangoon, U Tun Shein, permanent secretary of the foreign office explained, "We worked desperately, but we received notice of two resolutions on Saturday and the vote was taken on Sunday night. Instructions just failed to reach our delegate in time." U Nu added bluntly, "We should have voted. You can quote me as saying the abstention was wrong." [41]

On the return of Prime Minister U Ba Swe to Rangoon, he was questioned sharply at his press conference about his statements made in India on the Hungarian situation. *The Nation*, Rangoon, reported that during the conference U Ba Swe stated, "When one country interferes in the internal affairs of another to the extent of setting up in it a Government of its own choice, that is aggression. That was the view I expressed in India, and I did it as Prime Minister of Burma, and not as a mere Socialist leader . . . I consider what is taking place in Hungary as aggression." [42] In the UN General Assembly, U Pe Khin continued to take a strong stand in asserting that the position of the Burma government was that of condemnation equally of the Anglo-French intervention in Suez and of the Soviet armed intervention in Hungary.

Intervening in the debate on a Cuban resolution asking for immediate cessation of deportations by the Soviet-backed Hungarian government and repatriation of the deportees, U Pe Khin noted that the delegation of Burma had abstained on the previous General Assembly resolutions on Hungary, particularly on the November 4 resolution because, he said, "time and tide had not afforded it the opportunity of acting in conformity with its own principles." "Now," he said, "the Burma delegation was faced with what seems to be strong evidence that the intervention which we so moderately condemned, is unwarrantedly continuing." He asked why the representatives of Hungary and the U.S.S.R., who on the day before had denied that deportations were taking place, did not now comply with the General Assembly resolution which asked that UN observers be permitted to visit Hungary. In the absence of such compliance and continued refusal to even consider it, he did not know how the conscience of the world could fail to vote "to disapprove Soviet interference in the internal life of Hungary, an interference which had already cost many thousands of lives and is now depriving other thousands of their own country." U Pe Khin concluded his rather long speech by the statement, "There, but for the grace of God, go we." [43]

In a press interview on November 26, reported by the New York *Herald Tribune* on November 30, U Pe Khin was quoted as saying that Burma's policy of "positive neutrality" does not "preclude us from speaking our minds." He stated that although Burma was a small country and wants to remain peaceful, "if something is wrong or unjust, we will not hesitate to speak out." Thus, he was reported to have said, the invasion of Egypt by Anglo-French forces was "wrong" and the intervention of Russian forces in Hungary "cannot be justified." This stand taken by the Burma government at the UN was endorsed by U Nu as head of the AFPFL. In the Burma Parliament, a heated debate was touched off by a motion introduced by one member seeking approval of the Burma stand at the UN condemning Soviet intervention in Hungary. The left-wing opposition of the National United Front attempted to substitute a motion condemning Israeli action in Egypt. As the debate became heated, it was obvious no satisfactory conclusions could be reached and the House of Deputies was adjourned without a vote being taken. The debate occurred in March, 1957, and showed the continued significance of the whole problem of the cold war for a small country when two wholly different issues were presented to it in the UN for action.

In his speech before Parliament on September 27, 1957, Prime Minister U Nu stated that evidence that Burma's foreign policy was determined by "independent" action or "positive" action on issues according to what the Burma government believed was "right" in a given situation was to be found in the Burma government's position on the Hungary and Suez issues in the United Nations. On these issues, U Nu stated, the Burma government acted regardless of relations with either of the power blocs, but acted by judging each issue on its merits.

Between 1953 and 1958, the Burma government expanded its economic relations with the Communist bloc states, with those associated with the United States in opposition to the Communist bloc and with other neutral nations. The rice export emergency of 1953–54 forced the government into barter deals with the Communist bloc which could hardly be regarded as more than stop-gap measures. By expanding its trade arrangements with nations outside the Communist bloc, the AFPFL leaders were able to reduce commitments to the nations of this bloc and thus redress the balance of their neutralist position in the economic field.

An enhanced economic position by mid-1954 was coupled with a worsening international situation in southeastern Asia, leading U Nu to essay more active attempts at conciliation between the United States and Communist China as well as to take an active role in Asian and Afro-Asian meetings. Rightly or not, U Nu and his associates took credit and were given credit generally in the Burma press for helping to ease tensions over Indo-China and between the United States and the Peking regime.

In 1956–57, three situations provided tests of Burma's neutralist policy. The border dispute with Communist China was settled amicably. In the Suez affair and the Hungarian revolt Burma's membership in the United Nations forced the government to take sides. In doing so, the AFPFL leaders sought to interpret their neutralism in the widest possible manner in order to give their government as much freedom of action as possible. The record, as U Nu pointed out with understandable pride in his lengthy summation of foreign policy on September 27, 1957, before the parliament, pointed to the success of Burma's basic principles of "non-alignment" "friendly relations with all countries" and "no aid with strings attached." He and his associates had used the terms "positive" and "dynamic" to characterize their neutralist policy as it unfolded in these years.

A more detailed look at the record of the AFPFL's conduct of foreign affairs in this period, however, points to certain weaknesses in their neutralist policy and illustrates certain of the attitudes and beliefs which have come to mark the actions of most neutralist countries in the arena of cold war politics.

First, as has been stated earlier in this study, the AFPFL ministers gave no evidence that they had carefully analyzed the kinds of economic relations which their government might undertake with other nations which might well lead to economic dependence on one or the other of the contending power blocs, and thus prejudice their economic independence. U Nu and his associates dealt with each annual surplus rice disposal crisis as it occurred. They reacted to the economic conditions of the moment. Thus, to a large extent economic circumstances dictated policy. They should not be blamed for such action. For it is difficult to see where they might have obtained guidance. There has been little attention paid to analysis of the postwar economic relations of the neutralist nations, particularly with the states of the Communist bloc, to determine the kind and scope of economic arrangements which, in fact, make a nation more dependent upon closer relations with one group of advanced nations or another. U Nu and his advisers would have found it hard to obtain a concrete and expert assessment of just how and where a small nation can or should draw the line between economic independence and economic dependence.

Second, in the actions of U Nu on the world stage during this period there is revealed a certain quality which characterizes the views of many neutralist leaders, and which can best be described as parochialism in international affairs. It is a fact that U Nu and his associates, like many politicians who led the fight for independence in other small nations, are not great students of history and international diplomacy. Such studies were not fostered by colonial powers for even the few who had an opportunity for advanced education. With the advent of independence, these leaders were almost overwhelmed by the many internal problems they faced, by the necessity of planning for their nation's defense and for the conduct of foreign relations, functions of a sovereign nation for which they had very little preparation.

National pride and their previous isolation from the main currents of world politics tended to make them view the world with a certain suspicion. They seemed to overestimate, at times, what they believed to be the predatory intent of the big nations, particularly those which their Marxist beliefs dubbed the "capitalist-imperialist" states. Thus, it is fairly certain that U Nu and his colleagues believed they could treat with Communist China over the border dispute as equals — as sovereign states, one with another. Their estimate of Burma's progress by 1956 may well have led them to believe they had a certain bargaining strength. Their adherence to the concept of maintaining friendly relations with all countries may have led them to assume that such a policy would naturally be reciprocated by all other nations.

In the attitude of the Burma government toward obtaining aid from a variety of sources and in expressions of its leaders at international meetings and in bilateral conversations in world capitals this parochialism can be detected, for it seemed that by 1958 they had begun to take for granted foreign aid would be forthcoming when needed and that because of their constantly repeated principles of foreign policy, such aid would be offered "without strings." Their neutralism seemed to be getting for them the best of all possible worlds.

Third, in their natural concern to preserve their political independence in the face of distressing situations in Indo-China and the Formosa straits, U Nu exhibited the belief that the cold war did not really represent a clash of moral principles but that tensions between the two power blocs, particularly the United States and Communist China during this period, constituted little more than the type of historic clashes of interest which had always occurred between powerful nations. This reasoning easily led to the conclusion that such tensions were negotiable, could, in fact, be negotiated away, if only the contending powers could be persuaded that there was some good on each side and would sit down at the conference table together. Such reasoning also was quite in keeping with Burman leaders who espoused Buddhism as a way of life. By his attempts to undertake what he always regarded as a modest effort at "peacemaking" U Nu was applying the idea of "positive" neutralism as a position which did not mean "sideline" impartiality, but active efforts, where possible, to induce a state of "peaceful co-existence" between the powers arrayed against each other. This was not wholly idealistic, but in the minds of the Burman leaders a necessary condition of world affairs if their nation was to have the opportunity to attain their goal of a socialist welfare state while retaining their independence.

Finally, in advancing the thesis that the Burma government would endeavor to take the "right" action on each international issue as it arose, U Nu and his advisers seemed to attribute to their own government the capability of taking action on the basis of moral principles, without, it may be noted, carefully defining those particular principles. In this stand there appears one of the contradictions of a neutralist policy. For the AFPFL leaders appeared to arrogate to themselves the privilege of justifying a foreign policy action on the basis of a moral principle of "right" while seemingly denying the same privilege to the United States and its allies, and attributing to them only selfish, materialistic motives.

In U Nu's foreign policy summation of September 1957, he spent some time presenting evidence that his government had conducted itself in the spirit of its concepts of neutralism. As evidence he stated Burma had supported Communist China's admission to the United Nations, had opposed the Israeli invasion of Egypt, had opposed the Anglo-French intervention in Suez, and had firmly stated its opposition to Soviet armed intervention in Hungary. Observers could hardly fail to note that only in the latter case did the Burma government's "right" action place Burma on the opposite side of the Communist bloc position. There was at least the inference, expressed obliquely by a few officials that there was developing a double standard by which Burma and other neutralist nations judged the actions of the Communist bloc states on the one hand and those of the United States and its allies on the other. Evidence of this attitude and of other neutralist concepts were to be more clearly revealed in the next four years.

— IV —

POLITICAL MALAISE—*AND ITS AFTERMATH*
1 9 5 8 – 1 9 6 2

For ten years, the men who had largely engineered Burma's independence had ruled the country through a political coalition, the AFPFL. Their government had surmounted all manner of internal and external crises, and in their eyes, had weathered them all successfully. Economic development had proceeded, not always as planned and not always with a marked success of specific projects, but with the promise that by a gradual approach to their goal of a socialist state, the nation would gradually grow in economic strength with a concomitant increase in the people's welfare. Although the AFPFL had suffered a setback in the general elections of 1956, this had caused only momentary alarm among the leaders. If there was discontent within the electorate it was only manifest sporadically. Press criticism of the government was frequent and often carping, but taken with a certain easygoing tolerance by the politicians. At the end of the first decade, there were few observers who would have predicted stormy political waters ahead and some of the AFPFL leaders, including Prime Minister U Nu, dared to assert the AFPFL rule and AFPFL policies would "last for forty years, even for four hundred years!"

Scanning the international horizon, these AFPFL leaders could take satisfaction in what seemed an enhanced position for Burma in world affairs. It was a fact that their country was effectively maintaining friendly relations with all countries. A final settlement and demarcation of the troublesome frontier with Communist China was in sight, carried out in the spirit of the "Five Principles of Peaceful Co-Existence." No serious disputes with any neighboring nations

had developed. To the consistent practice of their policy of neutralism, there had developed no serious objections by any important
groups within Burma nor had this policy antagonized any major
powers in either bloc. U Nu's many travels had projected before the
world the picture of the friendly, benign, but articulate political
leader, and a consequent image of Burma as a "peace-loving,"
"friendly" country, almost a kind of Buddhist paradise.[1]

Underneath this surface harmony, however, all was not well.
Within a few months of the tenth anniversary of Burma's independence, the AFPFL coalition split wide open amid mutual castigation
and recrimination on the part of its leaders. In retrospect, two causes,
among others, stand out as responsible for the political disintegration
of the Burma government and its politics in 1958. In the first place,
the men who had guided the destinies of the AFPFL government
through the first decade represented a wide diversity of personal and
political conduct. As the threat of successful armed insurrection diminished and the hard and complex tasks of governing a country
more and more intruded, these men reacted in varying ways. Many
became increasingly impatient with delays and inefficiency. Many
became more selfish in furthering their personal interests or those of
their own particular political clique. More and more, these political
leaders, who had been in almost daily association with each other for
over ten years, began to get on each other's nerves. They became
supersensitive to rumors and suspicions, overanxious about their personal prestige and power position, for at the end of ten years it was
no longer possible to blame British rule for mistakes and failures.

A second, and equally important cause for the near-political chaos
of 1958 could be found in the fact that the continuous process of dividing and redividing the spoils of political power and of apportion-
ing patronage among an increasing number of claimants tended to
exacerbate the irritations arising from clash of personalities. Appor-
tionment of spoils to various politicians and political groups had begun to have diminishing returns for U Nu as a means of holding the
top AFPFL leaders and their followers together in common policy
and action. On the other hand, the more widely political power and
the spoils of office were shared, the less satisfactory it was to these
top leaders whose natural political ambitions led them to work for
concentration of power and control of patronage in fewer hands.

In the end, there had been too much talk, too many unfulfilled promises and too few real accomplishments by Prime Minister U Nu's AFPFL government. The active politicians in the government began to choose sides, either throwing in their lot with U Nu or turning against him as the author of all past mistakes. What seemed apparent in the spring of 1958 was the fact that this diverse group of AFPFL leaders had worked together too long. They knew each other's personalities, strengths, and weaknesses too well. In the end, long familiarity had bred contempt and the desire for more power and fewer power-sharers led them to risk political chaos in their attempt to gain a new alignment of power in keeping with their individual ambitions.

The deterioration of politics in Burma during the first nine months of 1958 which led to eighteen months of rule by the military and was followed in turn by the re-election of U Nu as Prime Minister in February, 1960, did not directly change Burma's foreign policy nor alter the basic concepts of Burma's "neutralism" in foreign affairs. The political crisis and subsequent military rule did have consequences for the conduct of foreign relations, however, which are still being felt. First, the nine-months' crises revealed clearly the aims and strategy of the aboveground and underground Communists in Burma. It provided a clearer picture of the weaknesses of the Communist movement in the country, a picture not at all lost on the hierarchy in Peking. Second, the crisis revealed inherent weaknesses in Burma's political system and its susceptibility to Communist pressure and infiltration. The main weaknesses seemed not to be in political structure but in the paucity of politicians who were willing to put the welfare of their nation above personal and political gain. Finally, the denouncement of the crisis in September, 1958, provided a unique instance of the take-over of a government by a military group pledged to fulfill limited commitments in a limited time and of that military government turning the country back into the hands of the politicians through the normal electoral process. Burman pride in their maintenance of constitutional processes, however, should not obscure some of the less happy consequences of these developments. Because of these factors and because there was a repetition of this political crisis which led to a second military take-over in March,

1962, it is worth while examining the events of this period in some detail.[2]

On April 24 and 28, 1958, the Rangoon newspaper, *The Nation,* published two editorials which gave a succinct summary and a key to understanding the essence of the political crisis. After referring to mass arrests in the Insein District of Rangoon and elsewhere and to the fact that two top AFPFL leaders, Thakin Kyaw Dun (a supporter of U Nu) and U Kyaw Nyein (U Nu's principal opponent) were both convinced that their personal followers were being attacked and in danger of being jailed, the first editorial stated:

It is this which fills us with foreboding. For as the arrests proceed the tension between the two factions will mount, and there is no saying when an explosion might result. While the top leaders may not try to bump each other off, we see no guarantee that the lower echelons will not reach for their guns when the time comes for them to be arrested. It is all very well for U Nu to say he has sent directives to them to submit voluntarily, but the AFPFL rank and file is not made up of such docile and obedient people. If some of the thugs whom the AFPFL have reared lose their heads, it might well touch off a shooting match which will confound the already existing chaos in the country . . . Already, thinking people, who genuinely love their country are beginning to look with disgust upon the top AFPFL leaders who are so petty, so narrow, so self-seeking that they are willing to jeopardize the whole future of this land for the sake of personal vanity and power.

The second editorial was entitled "No Hope Now." It described the Insein "battle" between U Kyaw Nyein's Youth League and Thakin Kyaw Dun's All-Burma Peasant's Organization. It noted that U Nu had relieved Thakin Tha Khin as Home Minister and taken this cabinet portfolio himself. This move placed directly in U Nu's hands control of all police and internal security forces except the army. It was feared this presaged more extensive mass arrests of U Nu's opponents and increased the risk of civil war. The editorial continued,

It does not require a very skilled political eye to realize that the rifts in the AFPFL are growing wider by the minute and that a final and irrevocable split is very near. The cleavages in the AFPFL leadership have apparently gone too far now to be repaired. Furthermore, though some sections of the AFPFL are now trying to drag in labels like 'democratic socialism' or 'Marxist socialism' and other terms, the tragic fact is that the splits have nothing to do with ideological questions, and are purely personal prejudices which have turned into a struggle for personal power.

Thus as we predicted several years ago, the AFPFL is going to be destroyed by the AFPFL. It has withstood onslaughts by the underground Communists and by the above-ground Communists, and has even survived the expulsion of some of its own trusted leaders. But this time the crisis is so deep and so grave that we believe nothing can save the AFPFL. It is now only a question of time before the form and manner of the final split will be made known to the country.

By April 30 the split was an accomplished fact. After fruitless attempts to "divide" the AFPFL assets between the two factions, neither of whom wanted to give up the AFPFL label, U Nu, supported by U Tin, U Raschid, and others named their faction the AFPFL (Clean) and their opponents chiefly led by U Ba Swe and U Kyaw Nyein adopted the label, AFPFL (Stable). The opposing factions did agree that an emergency session of parliament would be held on June 5 and that they would test their parliamentary strength on a "no-confidence" motion — whichever faction gained a majority of the parliamentary vote would then form a new government. It was strongly urged by members of both factions that a general election should be held as soon as possible, November being the earliest predicted date. For no one believed that the Nu-Tin faction or the Ba Swe-Kyaw Nyein faction could muster a sufficient majority in parliament to be able to carry on the government without facing a general election.

In public statements, leaders of both the Clean and Stable factions pledged themselves to continue Burma's foreign policy of "neutrality" and nonalignment. Neither faction, however, committed themselves to details. In the charges and countercharges which flew thick and fast and were thoroughly aired in public, the Ba Swe-Kyaw Nyein faction was accused of favoring the "Anglo-American bloc," more because of their opposition to the Communists than anything else. Likewise, the Nu-Tin faction was accused of favoring the Communists and in this there was more substance.

The Role of the Communists

When the split in the AFPFL occurred, the first question confronting the aboveground Communists was whether they should throw their support to the U Nu-U Tin Clean AFPFL or remain as a third political group in the coming contest for a parliamentary majority. This was not an easy decision, mainly because the aboveground Communists and their followers had been unable to constitute a cohesive Communist-front coalition. They were themselves divided into some fifteen political organizations, with some overlapping of leadership. They had formed a loose coalition, the National United Front (NUF) to contest the 1956 elections. This amalgamation of convenience included Communist and left-wing groups and the then largely right-wing Justice Party led by U E Maung. They had won forty-five of two hundred-fifty seats in the Chamber of Deputies in the election, but the NUF candidates and others in opposition to the AFPFL had polled nearly forty-six percent of the popular vote. Between 1956 and 1958 the NUF was the only organized parliamentary opposition to the then monolithic AFPFL.

When the split occurred, some leaders in the NUF realized that if they joined the Nu-Tin faction and helped it survive a vote of no confidence in parliament, they would become part and parcel of a government in power and no longer the opposition. The Burma Worker's Party led by U Ba Nyein and Thakin Chit Maung and the People's Unity Party, led by the Communist "elder statesman" U Thein Pe Myint, hurriedly assured U Nu of their support and on May 10 the NUF leaders announced that their coalition would support the Nu-Tin faction, claiming that they controlled forty-seven votes in parliament.[3]

Since it seemed certain even at this date that the Ba Swe-Kyaw Nyein group would hold the majority of AFPFL MP's on their side, this NUF decision gave to U Nu his only assurance that he might muster a bare majority when the parliamentary vote was taken. The NUF leaders, too, were perfectly aware that they might thus get into a position where they would hold the balance of power in parliament and in a Nu-Tin government.

NUF strategy, however, was not limited to the parliamentary session, but looked beyond to a general election in which, with the help of the underground Communists in various ways, they hoped to gain a much larger parliamentary representation, even a working majority. To carry out this strategy the NUF leaders supported the idea of a dissolution of parliament immediately after the regularly scheduled budget session (normally held in late August or early September) and the calling of a general election for November. In order to strengthen their support and attain a larger vote in the general election, the NUF leaders pressed for direct negotiations with the underground Communists so as to "end the insurrection" and "bring peace to the country." There was nothing wrong with this strategy and it came close to being successful. The difficulty lay in the fact that the NUF leaders had to compose differences among leaders of between nineteen and twenty-three political parties belonging to their coalition and here specific issues entered into the politics of the Communist and pro-Communist groups, complicated by the fact that the Justice Party, an important element of the NUF, was generally non-Communist in its composition and had a few strong anti-Communist elements in it. The specific issues, which in the end caused a split in the NUF no less significant than that in the old AFPFL, were: (1) the nature and degree of NUF participation in the Nu-Tin government after the close vote in parliament on June 9; (2) release of political prisoners; (3) terms to be offered the underground insurgents; and (4) the problems of reorganization or disbandment of the local defense forces called *pyusawhtis*.[4]

Again it must be emphasized that even within the groups composing the NUF, although issues were fought over, debated and discussed, the focus of politics was still the personal and factional struggle for power. The leaders of individual parties which formed the NUF coalition were constantly maneuvering, trying to hold their followers together and attempting to strengthen their position by mergers with other parties. Thus between May and September, the parties within the NUF split, merged, suffered defections, and often opposed each other more vigorously than the opposing political faction, the AFPFL (Stable). NUF leadership consisted of leaders of these variegated political groups organized collectively into a praesidium. Each leader had his own party, there were none who, like U Nu in the old days of the AFPFL, stood above this factional strife and hence were in a position to weld these parties into a workable and effective coalition. In this defect were the seeds of defeat for the Communists.

So intent were the politicians and parties on their contest for power that on May 27 a new Burma-U. S. economic aid agreement was signed involving some $17,000,000 of U. S. assistance with hardly a

notice being taken of it. Two days later it was announced that the
U. S. had agreed to provide $10,000,000 worth of equipment for the
government's internal security forces, an arrangement worked out
with the U. S. Export-Import Bank through the International Cooperation Administration. With these two agreements, a program of
American economic aid to Burma was fully reinstated. Although
there were one or two protests from NUF leaders and the local Communist press accused the government of "leaning" toward the Anglo-
American bloc, the Burma Communists were, after all, supporting
that government in a bid to gain more power and this was the focus
of their attention.

In spite of all kinds of rumors, charges and countercharges, the
June 5th session of parliament passed off without incident. A vote
was agreed to for the 9th and on a no-confidence motion, the Nu-Tin
Clean faction was upheld by a vote of 127 to 119. Thus U Nu retained
control of the premiership and the government by the close margin
of eight votes.

Once the life of the Nu-Tin government was assured at least until
the budget session of parliament due at the end of August, there
was increasing public evidence that the Communists and their supporters were going to take advantage of their position in support of
U Nu to do everything possible to strengthen their own position and
weaken that of their opponents in the Swe-Nyein group. Reports of
arrests of followers of the Stable faction began to appear almost
daily. The leaders of the Communist-controlled All-Burma Federation of Student Unions (ABFSU) sent a directive to all schools on
June 15 stating that the previous order by the government banning
the student unions was illegal and that the "imperialists who imposed
the ban had been got rid of," hence the Unions could be revived.
During the next two and one half months, all parties and politicians
were active throughout the country and tension among the contestants mounted steadily. Charges and countercharges filled the air and
dismissals of civil servants and office holders coupled with a general
public knowledge that numerous factions possessed arms or were
known to be arming their followers all contributed to a growing fear
of turmoil which could easily lead to civil war.

A major factor contributing to increased tension at this time was
the existence of numerous "pocket armies." The development and

use of small armed forces by politicians and political organizations is not a new phenomenon in Burmese history. In pre-British times, whenever the authority of the king was weak, armed bands were organized both for protective purposes and for possible offensive use to further the ambitions of a local leader, provincial governor or a particular minority group which hoped to become independent of Burmese royal authority. Thus, in 1946–47, General Aung San organized the PVO as his private army partly to intimidate the British and partly for political purposes. In the ensuing insurrections of 1948–49, a large proportion of the PVO's went underground and became fragmented under the control of various insurgent leaders in the countryside. In October, 1955, the AFPFL had inaugurated the *pyusawhti* town and village defense scheme. Under this scheme, the *pyusawhtis* consisted of locally recruited volunteers as an auxiliary force to aid the army in repelling rebel attacks, defend town and villages against robber bands and insurgents. The plan provided for a security council in each district headed by the senior military officer but including administrative officers and local political leaders. In practice, these local forces often became a bone of contention between vying political leaders and there was an increasing tendency for units to act on their own initiative as a kind of vigilante group or turn into a criminal gang with looting and robbery their primary object. In villages and districts where no *pyusawhti* force was formally organized, a local defense force was frequently raised or one was recruited by a political organization such as the ABPO which had its "Peace Guerrillas" in many areas.

After the June vote in parliament the status of the *pyusawhtis* became a political issue, hotly debated by the contending political factions. It was obvious to everyone, particularly the politicians with experience in past elections, that the country was far from peaceful and that an orderly and free election could not be held unless the activities of these private armies were brought under strict control. It was feared that unless this could be accomplished, the contending factions would most certainly use these local forces to intimidate the voters and in a struggle for control over them or in their use by opposing sides disorder and even civil conflict could well result. This issue, like others, became prominent because of rumors circulated by almost every faction that the private armies and local forces of other factions were being armed heavily and were already being used to intimidate officials, party organizers and the *ludu* (the Burmese word for the "common man").

On July 4 it was announced that the underground PVO's had organized themselves into the "People's Comrade Party" (PCP), and that their leaders had sent a letter to the Army saying that they were ready to accept the government's offer to "enter into the democratic fold." On August 15 the People's Comrade Party was legalized and established headquarters in Rangoon. Large numbers of the PVO insurgents came out of the jungle giving up their arms under their stated aim of "altering the form of the struggle from armed action to parliamentary action." It was later revealed that not all PVO's surrendered nor were all their arms turned over; thus this organization, Communist in all but name, was in a position to act both above and below ground in furthering the Communist cause. Once the exinsurgent PVO's obtained legal recognition for their PCP, their leaders attempted to strengthen their position by talks with leaders of other parties of similar persuasion looking to a possible open and legal Communist front which might or might not continue a part of the NUF coalition.[5]

Originally, the annual budget session of parliament was scheduled for August 28, but on the 19th, U Nu announced in a press conference that, "a situation had arisen in which smooth passage of the budget could not be ensured." He stated that the June 9th majority of the Nu-Tin AFPFL in parliament could not be maintained "without interference" if parliament met on August 28, therefore, he proposed to ask the President to dissolve parliament at some date in the near future and hold a general election. It was assumed that the dissolution would be requested some time in September, which would mean that elections would begin in November. The Swe-Nyein faction were jubilant over this seeming admission that U Nu had lost his parliamentary majority and they demanded that the budget session should be held because it was constitutionally necessary.

During the latter part of July and early August considerable numbers of political prisoners had been released which satisfied one demand of the NUF and the Communist parties. No action had been taken, however, on the problem of the *pyusawhtis*. The original NUF proposition had been that these local defense forces should be disbanded. On August 21, however, the PCP Central Committee issued a statement which almost amounted to a list of "demands." The Committee insisted that all "repressive laws" should be abolished, that the amnesty for the insurgents should be made complete, that "administrative power" should be taken out of the hands of the military in certain districts, and that the *pyusawhtis* should be "controlled." This position on the *pyusawhtis* caused a new round of debates and talks among the NUF leaders and those heading its constituent parties.

On August 22 a conference was held between the Nu-Tin AFPFL and the Ba Swe-Kyaw Nyein AFPFL factions, the first since the June parliament session. After this session it was announced that U Nu had proposed that the budget be passed by Presidential decree and that a National Convention be held to gain views of all people and, presumably of the insurgents who would be pardoned and would "come into the light." Nu asked the Swe-Nyein faction to propose a candidate for Organizing Secretary-General of the proposed convention. Apparently the idea of a convention was another effort on U Nu's part to find a way of strengthening his rapidly weakening AFPFL faction. It was never called. The proposal that the budget be passed by a Presidential decree provided a diversionary opportunity for the constitutional lawyers and all politicians in interpreting the Constitution. Few doubted, however, that some means would be found to justify such an action legally for it was by now apparent that the Nu-Tin government dared not face parliament and the real question was *when* elections could be held.

The holding of anything like orderly elections depended upon what action could be taken to control the private armies, *pyusawhtis*, and remaining insurgents and robber bands. The Burma army was still carrying on its task of flushing out the insurgents and robber bands, but was also undertaking the general task of maintaining law and order in many of the upcountry districts. Whenever an army unit attacked a particular armed band, or seized a cache of arms or prevented armed action for purposes of intimidation by the *pyusawhtis*, they stepped on the toes of some political group whose leaders were quick to charge "repression" and "interference" by the army. Criticism of alleged army "excesses" and "interference" mounted steadily in the latter part of August and occasioned conferences between

General Ne Win and U Nu. The Army reacted to this criticism by instituting a campaign in a number of districts denying the charges in speeches, and posters and stating that the three main enemies of Burma were the Communists, the KNDO's (Karen National Defense Organization — an insurgent group) and "selfish politicians."

On September 8 U Nu announced the formation of a Central Security Committee whose job would be to transform *pyusawhti* units into "special police reserves" beginning in eighteen village areas. The original Security Councils were to be abolished and the "transformed" *pyusawhtis* were to be under direct control of the local army commander and the district superintendent of police. At the same time U Nu felt obliged to vigorously defend the integrity of the army from continuing attacks by followers of his own Clean AFPFL. On September 11, the NUF leaders showed clearly how far the factional struggle had split the Clean AFPFL and its supporting groups by holding a press conference in which they attacked the Nu-Tin government for its policies, asserting "it was time for the government's guns to be turned away from the Burmese people and used to guard against external emergencies."

On the same day of the NUF attack against the government, Colonel Tun Sein, later to play a key role in the military caretaker government, spoke to the Commanding Officers of the Second Burma Army Brigade and stated the "army has politics and our politics is to bring peace and insure democracy. We are fighting the insurgents because Communism means the end of democracy." He charged that the KNDO's were the "walking sticks of the Anglo-Americans" and that the Communist insurgents were the "walking sticks" of the Russo-Chinese. The Colonel added, "There is a rumor that the army is going to seize power. That is entirely untrue because that is not the method of democracy. As believers in democracy we will defend the government that rules according to democracy."

This speech confirmed the fact that various politicians were spreading the rumor that an army *coup d'état* was a possibility to forestall a general election in which the Communists and their supporters would show substantial gains. In fact, however, the Communist's parties were even more divided in September than they had been earlier. The NUF leaders had begun to realize that far from winning any substantial majority in a forthcoming election, it was more likely that the Nu-Tin and Swe-Nyein factions would register the largest block of votes or that at best, the NUF and its coalition of parties would not be able to cooperate closely enough to wage a very successful election campaign for their candidates, even if they could agree on candidates whom they would all support. There also seems to have been the realization on the part of some of the NUF leaders, that the failure of left-wing Communist parties to unite or at least form a better organized and disciplined coalition within the NUF or otherwise had only strengthened U Nu and his chief supporters and that at this date U Nu was more unlikely to take the NUF parties and leaders really into his government even if it should be formed largely with their support after the election.

During the first three weeks of September, the Rangoon newspapers reported dissension in the Communist parties and among the NUF leaders almost daily. A large part of the dissidence was still due to the personal ambitions of the politicians, but it also appeared that almost every left-wing group was split internally between moderates or "go-slow" communists and extremists who thirsted for action — any action by which they could seize power. By mid-September and certainly by September 20, careful observers were agreed that the political crisis was coming to a head, that almost all of the factional parties were mobilizing their followers in the country districts and that many political groups were arming their supporters or had gained control of local *pyusawhti* forces or similar armed bands. Between September 15 and 20, there was increasing evidence that various factions were pulling a larger number of followers into Rangoon and that other local leaders were converging on the capital. It was reported that by September 22, there were ten thousand armed men in the Rangoon area. By this time, the integrity of almost every group, including the army, seemed in doubt. The police and the Union Military Police were said to be ready to take sides and rumors continued that the army itself would seize the capital rather than permit civil conflict to break out.

While these developments had been taking place in the open political arena, the underground Communist insurgents had been making strenuous attempts to enhance their bargaining position with the government. Their opportunity arose after the vote of June 9 when the Nu-Tin government became more amenable to some sort of negotiations with these insurgents and more lenient on the terms by which they could "come into the light" and resume open and legal activities. After June 9 *The Nation* commented editorially that with experienced ministers now out of the government, the previous singleness of purpose in dealing with the insurgents would be lost in the days to come. Almost immediately, there were reports that the underground Communists had sent out word demanding the legalization of their armed forces before any negotiations on surrenders would be agreed to. By mid-May, Thakin Kodaw Hmaing, called by some "the grand old man of Burma politics" and by others "a foolish idealist," had called together a group to discuss arrangements for an "All-Burma Peace Conference." This group later was formed into a sixteen-man "Peace Committee" and undertook to make contact with the rebel leaders. It also was proposed by the NUF as a vehicle through which the government could conduct talks without the need for formal and official negotiations.

During the June session of parliament, *The Nation* printed a roundup report on the insurgent situation. This paper reported that the Communist Party of Burma (Thakin Than Tun's group) now felt strong enough to demand not only face-to-face negotiations as equals but also to insist that its armed forces be legalized.[6] The report stated that during May the CPB's Major Chit Myaing (later proved to be Major Hla Myaing) had conferred with high-ranking Burma Army officials and had "demanded" that the CPB Army be legalized. *The Nation* continued,

Not only are they (the Communist Party of Burma) not prepared to surrender, but the political situation is deemed sufficiently favorable for them to press their demands for equality and negotiations in an imperious manner. The implication to be gathered from their documents is that their rebel army, rather than the existing Burma Army, should take over the defense of the country. If there is any concession on their part, it is that they are prepared to over-look the crimes of murder, arson, and rape committed by the Burma Army or, in short, that they are offering a general amnesty for the Burma Army!

The Burma Government War Office confirmed the details of the *Nation*'s story.

On June 21, the War Office released the text of a letter from Thakin Than Tun, dated May 7 and addressed to U Nu as Prime

Minister. In this letter, Than Tun asserted that the CPB had decided to support the Nu-Tin AFPFL and not the Swe-Nyein faction. He then set forth five conditions for "ending the insurrection": (1) free all political prisoners; (2) repeal repressive laws; (3) disband all pocket armies; (4) legalize all parties, including underground groups; and (5) give firm guarantees to wipe out all crimes committed during the course of the civil war. These terms were practically identical with those proposed earlier by the NUF on April 30.[7]

By mid-July it was known that the PVO's had been carrying on talks with army representatives looking toward their surrender and the legalization of their newly formed People's Comrade Party. On July 23 over 1,000 insurgents surrendered and the Army announced that the PCP's (ex-PVO's) would surrender on August 15th. On July 30 the Burma government announced the proclamation of a Presidential Amnesty Order absolving all insurgents of all crimes committed up to midnight of July 30. When the surrender of the ex-PVO's took place on schedule on August 15, the NUF announced that it would not renew its appeals and efforts to get the CPB under Thakin Than Tun to come into the democratic fold since there had been nothing but silence from the CPB since the first appeal nearly a month earlier and this the NUF leaders felt was a deliberate insult.

In the next several weeks up to September 22, the aboveground Communists became more widely split and all factions intensified their efforts to win new supporters and hold those they had. The press reported that the Army had seized considerable quantities of arms left behind by the surrendered ex-PVO insurgents and that villagers were being told that the *pyusawhtis* were to be disbanded and the now aboveground PCP supporters would be armed in their place. Posters and loud speakers urged the villagers to vote only for PCP candidates. Clashes between the rival workers' and peasants' organizations of the Clean and Stable AFPFL factions became more frequent in Rangoon, Mandalay, and the upcountry districts. The PCP was making strenuous attempts to form their own workers' and peasants' organizations. Thakin Kodaw Hmaing's Peace Committee was still very active and on September 7 the Committee held a meeting with representatives of all the Communist and left-wing parties, including the NUF leaders, at which it was generally agreed to attempt talks between the "peace Committee" and the rebel leaders.

One proposal had been received on September 1 from the Chairman of the Central Committee of the KNDO insurgents of their willingness to talk with the Peace Committee. On September 20, at Akyab over 250 CPB rebels surrendered to the Burma Army, one of the largest single groups of underground Communists to do so. The army announcement stated that 176 arms, and 1600 rounds of ammunition were turned in, but it is interesting to note that in a press interview in Rangoon with Bo Hla Sein and Bo Chan Sein, two of the leaders of this CPB group, they calmly and positively asserted that they were still Communists and surrendered only because they believed that peace could be won without insurrection.

It should be noted here that each of the major factions had its own rough estimation of the crucial point at which the political contest could be resolved decisively in its favor. For the Swe-Nyein group, the budget session of parliament due in September was the point at which they felt power could pass to their hands. They believed that they could muster a substantial majority of parliamentary members in favor of a no-confidence vote on the budget and thus form the government. For the NUF and its Communist affiliates, the key point was the general election. The more astute NUF leaders realized that the shaky Nu-Tin majority of June had diminished significantly. They believed that the substantial gains registered in 1956 could be increased in a new election with the help of surrendered rebels and those still underground. They believed that Communist and pro-Communist parties might win close to a parliamentary majority, but at least would hold the balance of power in any government. They counted on other methods to gain virtual control when the time came. The Nu-Tin group were convinced by September that they would lose power if the budget session was held, consequently U Nu had planned to dissolve parliament on September 29, pass the budget by presidential ordinance, and hold fresh elections in November.

A Military Caretaker Government

Prior to mid-September, General Ne Win and his staff officers had made great efforts to keep the armed forces apart from the political struggle for power. Yet he and his officers fully realized that if civil conflict did occur and if the Nu-Tin Government was unable to maintain order, the Burma Army was the sole force which could save the country from political disintegration.

For some time continuing efforts had been made by politicians and political factions to woo and win individual officers and individual units. The armed forces were well aware of these efforts, nor could the officers and men of many of the army units avoid observing the general political deterioration in the country, the petty local struggles for power, the prevalence of graft and corruption and the lack of visible economic and social progress in the country. It is fair to say that, if the Burma Armed Forces were partisan at all, they were "against the politicians of all colors." If there was any partiality among the top officers, it is probable they were more sympathetic to the Swe-Nyein faction than to the Nu-Tin group, for they had become deeply suspicious of Communist influence within the Nu-Tin government.

In order to forestall army help to its opposition, the Nu-Tin faction moved in two directions. First, the Nu-Tin government took steps to purge the government of known Swe-Nyein followers and to bring under their control through the Home Ministry, the Union Military Police, and all local defense forces such as the *pyusawhtis*. This was attempted gradually, and with some success, by removal of Swe-Nyein sympathizers in many units. Second, some of U Nu's followers began a campaign of rumors to discredit the armed forces which reached a point at which U Nu publicly inveighed against such maneuvers, as previously noted.

Failing to win adherents within the armed forces, the Nu-Tin faction, supported by the NUF leaders, apparently planned to bring in to Rangoon two and one-half battalions of Union Military Police to protect their position in the government. These and *pyusawhtis*, as well as some Forest Guards were to be brought to the capital in small groups quietly and then given arms in order to meet any emergency resulting from the passage of the budget by ordinance and the official dissolution of parliament. According to later reports, these forces were to be used to check any forceful action by the Swe-Nyein faction or even an attempt by the Army to take command of the government.[8] If all went well, there seems no doubt that the Nu-Tin faction, presumably retaining control of the government until the elections, would have undertaken or possibly been forced to undertake a reorganization of the armed forces in order to ensure subservience to their designs.

This was the situation on September 22, when U Nu returned to Rangoon from an electioneering trip through the lower delta districts. Between this date and the evening of September 26 when U Nu announced he had asked General Ne Win to assume control of the government, all signs pointed to the fact that the nine-month political crisis was coming to a head. On September 23, the Army, working with local police, began an extensive system of security checks within Rangoon, establishing road blocks along all main highways leading to the city and on main streets within the city itself. The *Nation*, and other newspapers expressed grave concern at the unusual security precautions, the secrecy surrounding movements of cabinet ministers and other government officials and reports of unusual concentrations of armed men in certain districts in the capital. The feeling of unease and uncertainty in Rangoon during this week was a tangible thing. People stayed close to their houses, shops closed early and the usual night sounds of people singing on their way home, and the traffic of jeeps, horse carts, and trucks were absent. Even the *pi* dogs were quiet. Rumors of an army *coup d'état* were widespread. Rumors of arrests of the leaders of the Swe-Nyein faction and even of a planned flight from the country by U Nu were being circulated. There is little question that had this unusually tense situation continued much longer, no one could tell what might have happened.

In this tense and uneasy atmosphere and unknown to the public or even the press, U Nu was negotiating with the Army. While there is dispute over the exact details and timing of events, it is clear that after September 22, the top staff officers had to act to avert trouble. Underlying this conclusion was a growing belief that the danger of Communist control of the government was real and present. The demand of Thakin Than Tun that the Communist underground forces be legalized as well as that for legalization of the Communist Party of Burma only underlined the fact that whatever happened there would be strenuous efforts made by the Communists to somehow gain control of the Burma Armed Forces in order to ensure their political success.

Under these circumstances, the Commanding Officers of the Army decided to move. While Colonels Aung Gyi and Maung Maung were acting as intermediaries between U Nu and General Ne Win, the Army had not only instituted much tighter security precautions in the capital and its environs, but also quietly moved a sizeable contingent of fully armed and reliable troops into the capital and dispersed them at key points but more or less out of sight.[9] At the same time, one armed battalion of Union Military Police, upon which some politicians of the Nu-Tin faction had relied for support was ordered upcountry toward the Mandalay district.

On the evening of September 25 the Rangoon press reported that Army intelligence had received many reports of trouble brewing as a result of Communist infiltration in large numbers into Rangoon. The *Nation* noted that the underground Communists, supported by most factions in the NUF had been stepping up their demands that "face-to-face negotiations" be permitted in Rangoon between emissaries of the CPB and Thakin Kodaw Hmaing's "Peace Committee," but that the general impression was the Nu-Tin government had not yet guaranteed safe conduct to the rebel emissaries. It was inferred, however, that the pressures of the Nu-Tin government might very likely force it to accede to the Communist demands.[10]

On the morning of September 26, the leaders of the NUF issued a long statement accusing the United States of attempting to "use the Nyein-Sein-Maw gang" (U Kyaw Nyein, Thakin Ba Sein, People's Democratic Party and Dr. Ba Maw) to destroy Burma's neutralism and to take Burma into SEATO. The statement charged that the Americans planned first "to smash the people's anti-imperialist forces, then to get the Shan States to secede from the Union." With this accomplished, they would try to dislodge the "indecisive" U Nu Government and power would be handed over to the "Nyein-Sein-Maw group" who were "ready to sell themselves for dollars to wipe out Communism and drag Burma into the SEATO pact."[11] Later evidence has shown that this statement was issued at the instance of Soviet officials in Rangoon and was probably drafted by them. Since no responsible politicians had even hinted that Burma join SEATO, nor was any effort being made by any western government to bring this about, the statement had little effect. It proved to be a last minute effort on the part of the Communist bloc to intervene in Burma politics and is one bit of evidence which shows that Soviet understanding of politics in Burma or of effective means of influencing political developments hardly lived up to their reputation for such maneuvers elsewhere.

On the evening of September 26, Prime Minister U Nu spoke to the public over the Burma radio and announced that he was asking General Ne Win to assume charge of the Burma Government, stating that parliament would be called into session on October 28 to elect him formally as Prime Minister. U Nu made it clear, however, that General Ne Win and the armed forces were already in control of the capital. The Prime Minister's voice sounded weary as he made his report to the people in the following brief announcement:

People of the Union of Burma,
I would like to make a few important remarks. We had intended to hold a general election in November of this year. But, in the light of existing circumstances and events in the whole country, we came to realize more and more, day by day, that the General Election to be held in November could not at all be a free and fair election.

It cannot be denied that so long as the people of a country cannot freely elect the government they want, without let or hindrance, without intimidation and undue influence, there will be no democracy at all in that country. Therefore, for every lover of democracy, a free and fair election is as precious as life itself. I invited General Ne Win to make arrangements essential for holding such a free and fair election before the end of April, 1959, for the sake of maintaining a firm and durable democracy, I earnestly appeal to the entire people of the country to give their support to General Ne Win in the same way as they have given their support to me.

At the conclusion of this brief message from the Prime Minister, the announcer read the texts of an exchange of letters between U Nu and General Ne Win — the formal method used to obtain the General's assent to his succession to the premiership. The procedure proposed by U Nu and accepted by General Ne Win was for U Nu to advise the President to call a session of parliament for October 28, at which session U Nu would resign his post and immediately nominate General Ne Win as his successor. U Nu enjoined Ne Win to: (1) make arrangements for holding "free and fair" elections not later than April, 1959; (2) to take particular care that government servants and the armed forces do not encroach or interfere in political affairs; (3) to give "prior and particular attention" to suppression of such misdeeds, as acts of oppression, murder, and violence committed by some of the armed forces; (4) to give "prior and particular attention" to the suppression of such crimes as rape, robbery, dacoity, kidnapping and murder"; (5) "to secure to the fullest extent this glorious prize of internal peace"; and (6) "in foreign relations also, I would like the government formed by you to continue and maintain the policy of strict and straightforward neutrality." At the beginning of the letter, U Nu had stated it would not be necessary for General Ne Win to include members of the Clean AFPFL in his government. General Ne Win replied by accepting the injunctions laid down by U Nu. That this sudden change in the political situation caught most of the politicians by surprise, there is no doubt. The Communists apparently had not counted on this kind of maneuver and were unprepared to act quickly enough before it was too late.

On September 27, General Ne Win made a speech to the armed forces urging the exercise of greater self-discipline than ever before and saying that the armed forces must so conduct themselves as to enhance the prestige of the military.[12] On the same day the NUF, on behalf of nineteen constituent parties denounced the transfer of power to General Ne Win, and asserted that it was "a seizure through military strength." This stand was endorsed by a joint statement issued by the leaders of the Rangoon University Student's Union (RUSU), the All-Burma Federation of Student's Union (AGFSU) and the All-Rangoon Student's Union (ARSU) in which it was charged that, "the Army's action could only mean that the principle of governing by the people's consent would disappear and there was every likelihood that violent means would be adopted in the future to seize power." [13]

The Swe-Nyein Stable AFPFL leaders took a few days to agree on what their position should be regarding the transfer of power to the military. On October 1, the Stable AFPFL leaders issued a statement in which they attacked U Nu, "whose Fascist government" had allowed the country to deteriorate so much that he had no alternative but to invite General Ne Win to form a caretaker government.

On October 1, the budget was passed by Presidential ordinance and it seemed a foregone conclusion that General Ne Win would receive the votes of both AFPFL factions and some of the non-Communist elements of the NUF of October 28 in parliament. There was now no opportunity for any political faction to gain power or seize control of the government until the general elections, which were tentatively planned for February, 1959. Under the Constitution, a nonmember of parliament may be elected Prime Minister for a period of only six months and this clause defined the length of Ne Win's term of office.

On October 28 in the Chamber of Deputies, U Nu announced his resignation as Prime Minister and immediately nominated General Ne Win to succeed him. On the vote, one NUF MP walked out of the session, the other NUF members abstained from voting and General Ne Win received the affirmative votes of all other members present. There thus began eighteen months of a military caretaker government which also marked a low point of Communist political influence in Burma.

On October 9, the *Nation,* in an editorial entitled "Communists Fall Back to Third Place," summed up the position of the Communists in Burma as follows:

The Swe-Nyein group, it can readily be seen, are treating the Communist propaganda onslaught with indifference, if not with contempt. As old campaigners they realize that the publicity which the Communists are giving them is not bad at all for election purposes. The Communists are a thoroughly discredited lot, and any group which they denounce as a strong arm party, far from frightening the people, is likely to win the support of men and women who want to be rid of the Communist nuisance and are looking for a Government which will do something effective toward this end.

For too long the Communists have hung like a millstone around U Nu's neck. In the process of soul-searching that he must indubitably have gone through before deciding to transfer power to General Ne Win, his sense of humor could not fail to have been provoked by the thought that after his broadcast speech the above-ground Communists, who were fattening on him politically, would be out in the cold. Observers are not slow to notice that by giving up power, U Nu may have jolted his own party, but that is as nothing compared to the beating the Communists have taken.

Time was when we put the Communists' chances as lying somewhere between the two AFPFL's. With the coming of General Ne Win, the Communists have fallen to third place and they are likely to remain there until the ballots are counted. Regardless of whether it is Nu-Tin or Swe-Nyein who win at the polls, the prospects of a Communist victory or a coalition government with the Communists in it, have receded. Many years from now it is possible that people will look back on this era and conclude that

U Nu's unorthodoxy in ensuring free and fair elections was the greatest set-back to the Communist movement in Asia.

Two days after General Ne Win took power, there were reports of large quantities of hidden arms seized in Rangoon and environs belonging to the PCP followers. Other reports indicated the Army had seized quantities of weapons "left behind" by surrendered Communist insurgents. The NUF continued to charge that the Ne Win government was "against the Communists" because it "condoned" attacks on NUF members, alleging that twenty-seven politicians had been murdered and over 155 arrested in the first six weeks of military rule. What seems to have happened is that prior to October 28, the Nu-Tin government, under pressure from the Communists, released large numbers of political prisoners from jail, evidently in the hope that this would help their cause. On February 9, 1959, the Ne Win government issued a statement that between July and October 1958, the Nu-Tin government released 855 political prisoners from nineteen jails, half of whom were released in the month immediately preceding Ne Win's election as Premier. It was claimed that most of these were Communists or Communist sympathisers and several were recognized top Communist leaders. In effect, therefore, the Ne Win government was arresting or detaining for trial a large number of Communists and troublemakers who had previously been released from jail by the Nu-Tin government. These new arrests were made under an emergency detention law passed by parliament at the instance of the Ne Win government.

The arrests and detention of political leaders as well as rank-and-file members of Communist parties and organizations continued for over twelve months as the Ne Win government appeared, on the whole, to prosecute troublemakers, and known law violators without fear or favor. The general effect of this on the Communist groups was to keep their organizations in turmoil and prevent crystallization of leadership within contending groups.

Although the over-all influence of the Burman Communists steadily declined during the Ne Win regime, the Communists continued their vocal opposition to the caretaker government. Through their controlled press and at public meetings they charged the Ne Win government with violation of democratic rights, predicted that democracy in Burma was not likely to be restored, and insisted that

Burma's neutrality was being compromised by the military which still plotted with the Swe-Nyein faction to take the country into the American camp and SEATO. This propaganda line was at least an echo and more likely the result of a directive from Moscow.

On July 30, 1959, for example, *Pravda* published an article by a P. Mayorov charging that "reactionary elements are persecuting democratic organizations and political leaders who advocate Burma's neutrality thus working to disrupt good relations between Burma and the Soviet Union and the People's Republic of China." In another instance, the Soviet Journal, *International Affairs*, published a long article in its issue of October, 1959, on "Events in Burma." [14] In this article the author describes the history of the AFPFL and events leading up to the split in the AFPFL. He states that the ending of civil war by opening negotiations with the insurgents on a "fair and equal basis" did not at all suit certain circles in the country or "foreign imperialist politicians." He cites an Indian *Nav Bharat Times* article which stated that certain foreign powers were hatching a plot to overthrow Prime Minister U Nu and draw Burma into SEATO.[15] The theme running through this article is that opponents of the NUF are destroying democracy, suppressing citizens' rights, and taking Burma into the SEATO camp.

The one place where the Communists retained some strength was in the RUSU which had been dominated by them since 1952. Although the government arrested a number of the old-line leaders of this organization who had been "students" for a long time, this apparently did not break their organization. In the regular university elections for the RUSU in 1959 and 1960 the Communists continued to win with a complete ticket. This exception had no immediate significance, however, since the RUSU had lost much of its off-campus support from the NUF and were fully aware that the Army could, and would crack down on their activities at any time they became dangerous.

It was generally assumed that elections would be held in April, at the expiry of the Constitutional six months during which General Ne Win as a nonmember of parliament could serve. By December it was apparent to many observers that while the military caretaker government had moved with vigor in performing its tasks, a great deal remained to be done and that, in fact, law and order had not yet been restored sufficiently in the country to permit "free and fair" elections. The NUF proposed that on the expiry of Ne Win's term as Prime Minister, a coalition government be formed with all parties represented. The Clean AFPFL leaders were unable to agree on their course of action but finally came up with a proposal that if they formed a government they would include the army in cabinet posts. There was considerable confusion about the exact nature of the proposal. It was assumed by many politicians that when parliament met in February, 1959, there would be a proposal for a six-months' extension of the caretaker government. It was also clear, to the chagrin of U Nu and his Clean faction, that the Swe-Nyein Stable AFPFL would have a majority of the votes in this forthcoming parliamentary session.

When parliament met, General Ne Win announced that he was not prepared to guarantee that free and fair elections could be held in April. Therefore, he intended to resign together with his Cabinet because he could not remain in office and assume responsibility for April elections. He stated that if the parliament desired his government to remain in office, it would be necessary for the parliament to repeal section 116 of the Constitution temporarily so that he could be re-elected Prime Minister and continue his task of preparing for free and fair elections, which he hoped might be accomplished by February, 1960, the date for general elections under the Constitution. While there was much grumbling from many politicians, particularly those in the Communist factions, no one could suggest a workable alternative to this proposition and both houses of parliament acted to repeal section 116. The wording of the bill was such that it became void immediately on election of a new parliament.

The Cabinet appointed by General Ne Win were all civilians (with one exception) who had no direct connections with any existing political parties. The number of cabinet posts was reduced from thirty to around twenty, most Ministers assuming charge of several activities.[16] Although there was much speculation as to just how the military caretaker government would function, General Ne Win moved decisively and within three months, almost every ministry, major department and the principal government boards and corporations had assigned to each of them an officer of the armed forces to oversee their work. These officers became, in fact, the bosses in the administration. The phrase "I'll have to see what my Colonel says" soon became the stock reply to people seeking decisions from government departments. On the whole, these officers were vigorous, intolerant of red tape, and anxious to get things done. All they lacked was detailed knowledge and experience. This lack was made up in part when they relied on the civil servants whose morale improved noticeably in the first few months. As many explained, it was a relief to "have the politicians off our necks for a change."

In general structure and operations, the military caretaker government was remarkably like that of the Japanese occupation. Civilian officials carried out orders of the military, and they brooked no nonsense. At the end of the first nine months, half way through his tenure as Prime Minister, there was little doubt that General Ne Win and his colonels had accomplished much. Hundreds of "disturbers of the peace" had been arrested. Several hundred political appointees had been dismissed and the payrolls of many government boards and corporations cleansed of patronage appointees. All firms dealing in import licenses had been investigated and some 2,000 were deregistered as having violated the law. Utilizing the Defense Services Institute as a kind of holding corporation, the Army went directly into business — shipping, fishing, banking, food distribution, and the like, "in order to purge the economy and halt a rising inflation." Rangoon and some other cities and towns were cleared of garbage piled on the streets and vacant land. Streets were repaired in the capital and a start was made in resettling thousands of refugees in Rangoon in newly constructed satellite villages.[17]

Nevertheless, there was a certain unease among the people. After nine months, many accomplishments of the Ne Win government were visible, disorder and banditry had been curbed, but all this was done with the power of the armed forces behind every move. Many people began to wonder whether the standards of vigorous action could be maintained by the politicians of a new government after the general elections. Although General Ne Win adhered strictly to his directive — "to establish law and order" and make possible "free and fair elections" in early 1960, there was no doubt that many of his officers, tasting political power for the first time, enjoyed the experience. They were responsible to no one but their superiors and while many simply did their duty and looked forward to the day when they could return to their strictly military duties, others felt that they could run the country better than the politicians.

The politicians and politically conscious Burmans began to chafe at military rule and at arbitrary acts of military officers. After nine months, it was realized by many that while the government continued to function, well-planned economic development had virtually come to a standstill. Existing projects somehow went forward, but over-all development designed to enhance the welfare of the people of the country had slowed down. Political factionalism, which had destroyed the old AFPFL coalition, had not abated.

In foreign affairs, the Ne Win government was pledged to continue the policy of neutralism. In pursuit of this policy, General Ne Win was in a more favored position than U Nu for his government had no political debts to pay nor was it concerned with keeping disparate political cliques together in some sort of unity. On the other hand, his government was handicapped by its status as an interim government and no foreign government could be sure what actions would be taken by its then unknown successor. Within these limitations, the Ne Win government moved to obtain additional economic aid from the west, to develop further its ties with nations outside the two power blocs and to stabilize finally the problem of the Sino-Burman border.

One announced principle of the Ne Win government was to economize as much as possible in the administration, and within a few months it was reported that all economic aid projects and the Burma government's employment of foreign advisers and technicians would be carefully reviewed. On December 2, 1958, speaking in his capacity as Chancellor to the Rangoon University convocation, General Ne Win said, "Speaking for myself, I want to hide my head in shame that during eleven years since our independence we had had to rely entirely on foreign technicians and experts." The next day, it was announced that a ninety-day termination notice had been served on the two American advisory groups under contract to the government, requesting that their personnel be out of the country by March 1, 1959.[18]

This action was followed later by announcement that the government would not renew the contracts of twelve Soviet agricultural experts who had been attached to the Agricultural and Redevelopment Corporation and during 1959 a number of contracts with Soviet bloc countries for technical assistance were similarly not renewed. As a further economy move, the government announced on October 24, 1959, that it would give up implementation of the Soviet "gift" projects as too costly and unnecessary. Only three had been scheduled for completion — the technical institute and hotel in Rangoon, and a 200-bed hospital in Taunggyi in the Shan states.

Meantime the Ne Win government proceeded to avail itself of American aid, as its predecessor governments had done during the past two years. Agreements were concluded with a number of western countries such as Japan, the U. K., and the Netherlands for import of cotton textiles and yarn against payment in cotton to those countries on Burma's account with the United States under Public Law 480 providing for sales of surplus agricultural produce. On December 10, Colonel Tun Sein, in charge of the Rangoon Corporation, signed an agreement with the International Cooperation Administration for over $700,000 worth of equipment to improve Rangoon's water supply and sewer system. On April 2, 1959, another agreement was signed for financing the completion of nine projects for which the United States had agreed in 1957 to provide some $7,000,000 to cover the foreign exchange costs. In July, the Ne Win government signed a new aid agreement with the United States by which $37,-000,000 was to be provided, part in Burmese currency and part in dollars, as grant aid to finance a four-lane highway from Rangoon to Mandalay and to construct a number of buildings for Rangoon University. From the time of the AFPFL split in April, 1958, until the end of the military regime's term of office in February, 1960, the ups and downs of internal politics showed no appreciable effect on relations with the United States nor any desire on the part of the Burma government to turn to the Communist bloc for help and stop American assistance as had been done once before.

When it came to more complex aid negotiations, in the one major case where this became necessary, the army officers again showed their impatience and lack of experience. This case involved the reparations agreement with Japan. In negotiating the original agreement on reparations with Japan in 1954, the then Burma Government had included what amounted to a "most-favored-nation" clause which provided that should Japan conclude a reparations agreement with another country for a larger amount than given Burma, the Burma agreement would be subject to renegotiation. In the summer of 1959, the Japanese did conclude such an agreement with the Republic of Vietnam and a Burma mission was sent to Tokyo headed by army officers to attempt to obtain an additional $150,000,000 in reparations. The mission was also charged with attempting to persuade the Japanese government to purchase a substantially larger quantity of rice than in previous years. The Japanese refused to increase their reparations payment and also refused to purchase more rice, but instead, offered to extend US $50,000,000 to Burma in grant-aid. The military officers on the Burma mission were unused to the requirements of diplomatic negotiations. Instead of attempting to bargain with the Japanese and more particularly exhibiting some understanding of the complexities of Japanese domestic politics and bureaucracy, the Burmans terminated the negotiations in a huff and on their return to Burma helped organize a boycott of private Japanese business and trade. This impatient action accomplished exactly nothing, and was soon given up.

During the first decade of Burma's independence, diplomatic relations had been established with all major nations and a good many smaller ones as well, but "close and friendly" relations had developed with India, as was natural, and with Yugoslavia, the U.A.R., and with Israel. Of the new Asian neutrals, the Burma government almost alone had been able to maintain relations with both Israel and the leading Arab state, the U.A.R. In June, 1959, General Ne Win made his first trip abroad as Prime Minister to further consolidate Burma's relations with these nations. In Israel, the Prime Minister conferred at length with his Israeli opposite number, David Ben Gurion. He also visited the Burman families living in the south and in training as settlement-defense communities in preparation for location along the Sino-Burman frontier.[19] As a result, arrangements were made for further visits and additional Israeli military "good-will" and technical assistance missions to Burma.

Although U Nu was reported at one time to have fancied himself as a mediator in the Arab-Israeli conflict, President Nasser had been cool toward Burma and reportedly had expressed his displeasure at Burma's Israeli ties. Nevertheless, General Ne Win arrived in Cairo on September 25, 1959, at the invitation of Nasser and apparently received a warm welcome. He also visited Damascus and returned to Cairo for a final talk with Nasser on October 5. On his way home, Ne Win stopped briefly in Pakistan and also in New Delhi, where he had a private hour and a half's talk with Prime Minister Nehru.

Friendly relations with Yugoslavia had been further solidified early in 1959 by a state visit to Burma by President Tito who arrived on his yacht in January. This was followed in November by a five-man Yugoslav military "good-will" mission when it was reported an agreement was reached for purchase of Yugoslav military equipment. In these visits it is generally agreed that there was considerable discussion among Ne Win, Nasser, Tito, and Nehru concerning the role of the neutralists in the cold war. Although there was much speculation that these neutral nations might take steps to concert their policies, no significant results were apparent.

The Ne Win government's relations with Communist bloc states remained friendly but more on the polite and formal side than during U Nu's incumbency. Good-will missions and cultural troupes came and went, but it seemed obvious that the oligarchs in Moscow and Peking were uncertain about the military caretaker government and wanted more firsthand information on political conditions in Burma.[20] There is little doubt that the sudden change-over to military rule had caught both Moscow and Peking by surprise. In the subsequent campaign by the Burma military to establish law and order, the whole Communist movement, both aboveground and underground had been seriously weakened. Then in April and June, 1959, two officers of the Soviet Embassy defected, the first unsuccessfully and the second successfully to asylum in the United States. These events took place with wide publicity and created considerable reaction against the Soviet government.[21] The true image of the Soviet state was more sharply revealed to the Burmans.

In this same period, the Tibetan revolt occurred, bringing on a brutal suppression by the Chinese Communist Army destroying the fictitious autonomy agreement of 1950 and causing the flight of the Dalai Lama and thousands of refugees to India. The events in Tibet caused a profound shock to people in India, followed as it was by public knowledge of the seriousness of the Sino-Indian border dispute. It shocked many Burmans, too, but not sufficiently to cause any significant change in attitude toward Communist China. The Burma government's reaction to the Tibetan revolt affords another example of seeming contradictions in its policy of neutralism.

In essence, the events in Tibet were almost a replica of those in Hungary, three years earlier. A revolt was brutally suppressed by alien military forces and as many people as could fled to neighboring countries. The one vital difference in the two cases was the fact that China's suzerainty over Tibet as an integral part of China had been acknowledged and Tibet was never a sovereign state as was Hungary. Hence there was some justice in the Chinese claim that the Tibetan revolt was a purely internal affair. Nevertheless, in both instances there was a brutal suppression of revolt by alien armed forces, yet it did not appear so to the neutrals. While India offered asylum to the Dalai Lama and the Tibetan refugees, and resistance to Chinese Communist claims on Indian territory stiffened, the Burma government reacted with only mild disapproval.

In the case of Burma, the border problem with Communist China was in process of settlement and the Burmans had become acutely conscious of the bulk of Communist China looming on the other side of its long northern boundary. Hungary was far away, and so was the Soviet Union for that matter, while Tibet was close at hand and Communist China even closer. It was obvious that the principle of taking the "right" action on an international issue to which U Nu had pointed with pride in the Hungarian case as an example of Burma's neutralism, had to be modified in any situation affecting Burma's vital interests close at home. Even the strong anti-Communist feelings of high officers in the Burma armed forces did not extend to any act which might antagonize their big northern neighbor.

Thus the Ne Win government did not breach the policy of neutralism firmly established by the AFPFL government under U Nu. One final act by General Ne Win, before he relinquished the premiership, served to offer further proof that the policy of neutralism had paid off. This was the formal signing of a border settlement with the Chinese Communists. As early as November, 1958, there were rumors in Rangoon that U Nu might head a government deputation to Peking to reach formal agreement on border demarcation. Knowledgeable politicians dismissed these rumors as an attempt on U Nu's part to keep in the public eye. In late December of that year, General Ne Win held a series of conferences with leaders of the Kachin state, which stood to lose some territory under the "package deal" earlier agreed to by U Nu and Chou En-lai "in principle." At this time, it was made quite clear that if any official mission went to Peking it would be headed by General Ne Win himself.

Toward the end of 1959, it became apparent that the Chinese Communist leaders were ready to reach agreement on a definitive settlement of the border. On the Burma side, Ne Win moved to strengthen his hand by reaching agreements with both the Kachin State Council on December 26, and the Shan State Council on December 28, providing that each state should transfer to the Union Government "the task of developing remote frontier areas for a specified length of time." [22] The Union Government was to bear all costs of development and plans were to be carried out under a Department of Frontier Administration. This move served to establish more clearly the sovereignty of the Union Government along the borders of the Kachin and Shan States adjacent to China.

It is quite possible that some such move was discussed by General Ne Win and Prime Minister Nehru at their meeting the previous October when it was rumored that both premiers had agreed their governments would stand firm for a demarcated border with Communist China along the so-called "MacMahon Line." [23] It is likely that Indian officials may have pointed out to General Ne Win the advantages of direct administration of frontier areas such as India maintained through the Northeast Frontier Agency over the upper reaches of Assam.

Consequently, just before the scheduled elections in February, 1960, General Ne Win headed a sizeable delegation to Peking and was able to announce on his return that he had signed definitive border treaties with Communist China, in which the "MacMahon Line" was recognized and only a small transfer of territory was to take place. With this final act in foreign relations, the Ne Win government prepared to turn back control of Burma to the politicians — to whatever party won in the general elections. On the whole, most Burmans who were interested in or knowledgeable of politics felt that the stewardship of the military caretaker government had been good. No miracles had taken place for none were expected, but there were positive accomplishments in economy in government and progress in restoring law and order to the country.

The Third U Nu Government and Its End

U Nu's first premiership lasted from 1948 until June 9, 1958, if one excepts the short period in 1956–57 when he retired voluntarily to "re-organize the AFPFL." His second premiership was a short one when he headed the Clean AFPFL government until he turned the government over to General Ne Win and the armed forces. His third "government" began with the general elections of 1960, when his Clean AFPFL won a resounding victory at the polls capturing two thirds of the popular vote and 200 of 250 seats in the Chamber of Deputies. Even the two principal opposition leaders of the Stable AFPFL, U Ba Swe and U Kyaw Nyein were defeated in their own constituencies and lost their parliamentary seats.

The immediate effect of his victory was to cause U Nu to finally drop the old AFPFL label and rename his party the "Union Party." Since great promises were made and few people expected a second take-over by the Army it is worth while summarizing briefly the main reasons for U Nu's sweeping victory in 1960. In the first place, the Clean AFPFL campaign for electoral votes seems to have been better organized and managed than most people believed at the time. How this was achieved is difficult to determine since there have been no objective analyses made of this election. Second, in addition to good organization, U Nu's campaign was politically clever. He got off to a good start in October by holding an All-Burma Conference of the Clean AFPFL at the Peace Pagoda in Rangoon. At this meeting U Nu promised that he would make Buddhism the state religion, if elected. He promised the government servants that they would no longer be under the thumbs of politicians but that they could write their own charter of independence on his return to power. To the people, he promised a government faithful to the "five precepts" of Buddhism, a government of democracy and a new "Union Plan" which would cure all the economic ills of the country. Actually the improvements in law and order and general government efficiency under the caretaker government were such that U Nu would have received votes had he but promised to carry on with the kind of government handed over by General Ne Win.

In the third place, U Nu's promise to make Buddhism the state religion undoubtedly won him many, many votes. This was due not only to the appeal of U Nu to the Buddhists of Burma, but to the active campaigning and vote solicitation of the Buddhist *phongyis* (monks). While some worked for the opposition faction, the large percentage of monks and their organizations actively supported U Nu. Observers believe that this support greatly strengthened the Clean AFPFL in the countryside since monasteries and monks are everywhere in Burma and constitute a potent political force if mobilized. The Stable AFPFL was slow to react to U Nu's platform plank of making Buddhism the state religion. Their eventual counter to this was to promise an eleven-point program which included state primary schools in the monasteries, compulsory teaching of Buddhist lessons, and a separate teachers' college and university for the Buddhist monks. This platform fell considerably short of the blanket promise to make Buddhism the state religion, although U Nu was careful not to specify timing or details on when this would happen after the elections.

Fourth, the Ne Win government had ordered that no political party could use the picture of Burma's hero, General Aung San, in any way in the election campaign. The Clean AFPFL, therefore, used U Nu's picture on all its posters, campaign literature, and ballot boxes. Although the Ba Swe-Kyaw Nyein faction protested this tactic, there was nothing they could do about it. Many observers believe that the use of U Nu's picture was the decisive factor in obtaining his landslide vote. There is little doubt that many Burmans, perhaps many thousands, believed they were voting for U Nu personally, although he only ran for election in his own constituency. One story, which seems typical, was of an elderly lady who had pledged herself to vote for the Swe-Nyein candidates, but was seen at the polling place kneeling in front of U Nu's picture, praying.

Political analysts, if such had been present in Burma, would probably conclude that over the years U Nu had become to the Burmans a "father image" or in Burmese style, the national "uncle." Somehow or other, and in spite of the bitter charges flung at him by his opponents, in the minds of the people he escaped the tarnish of corruption, and even the blame for having to rely on the Communists and insurgents to stay in power. He is also the symbol of Buddhism to a large majority of people, a position acquired by his constant citation of Buddhist "precepts" and the widespread publicity given to his leadership at the 2,500th Buddhist anniversary celebration in Rangoon in 1954 for which he built the "Peace" pagoda.

Fifth, U Nu's lieutenants had been assiduously cultivating the peoples of the various states and playing on their general disgruntlement with discrimination by the central "Burmese" government in Rangoon. In addition, even before General Ne Win took over the government, he had promised the people of the Arakan coastal region a separate state and he repeated this in the election campaign.

In summary, it seems that all U Nu's past mistakes or the sins or failures of his AFPFL government were forgotten and that the people, tired of the push and "drive" of military rule, as well as for other reasons noted, gave U Nu their overwhelming vote of confidence. It is possible that Dr. Ba Maw put his finger on a main cause for U Nu's victory when he was reported to have said that, "The Burmese have believed for a thousand years or more that a government exists only to promote their religion, especially by building pagodas and other rich and costly edifices; to collect taxes which it may use as it likes; to punish the lawbreaker, and for nothing else. Whatever else government does is quickly suspected as tyranny." He went on to assert that the Burmans "just want to be left alone by the government." He said that, to the Burmans, progress means change and all sorts of rules and regulations and other things they cannot understand and which they regard as an interference with their lives. It is possible that in this election, tradition and religion won out after twelve years of socialist planning, national schemes of one kind or another, and the uncertainties of insurrections and rebellion.

In his first policy speech to the parliament on April 4, 1960, after his sweeping election victory, Prime Minister U Nu reaffirmed full support for Burma's neutral foreign policy which he noted had been successfully maintained during the eighteen months' rule of the military caretaker government under General Ne Win. On the following day, Thakin Tha Khin, who had been declared opposition leader in the Chamber of Deputies representing the now weakened Stable AFPFL, declared that his party fully supported the neutral foreign policy of the U Nu government. In the following weeks the controlling body of the NUF, also weakened politically by U Nu's victory, was mainly concerned that the U Nu's Union Party (successor to the Clean AFPFL) government continue Burma's neutral policy.

In commenting on accomplishments of the Ne Win government, the *Guardian Monthly* asserted:[24]

One of the most positive stands of neutrality General Ne Win's Government succeeded in taking was the visit to Peking followed by the signing of the Border Agreement and the Non-Aggression Treaty. If Communist China lives up to terms of the agreements the common frontier will be delimited to mutual satisfaction and Burma will deny the use of its territory and resources for hostile purposes against China. We doubt that such a positive and peaceful attitude of neutrality can be exceeded by any subsequent government that may be formed here. In West Asia, the Caretaker Government has strengthened relations with Pakistan and the United Arab Republic without hurting relations with either India or Israel. . . . The goal of most neutral Asian countries is to promote neutral policy abroad without it having the effect of strengthening the Communist influence at home. The Caretaker Government of General Ne Win has achieved this goal. And there is no reason to doubt that U Nu's next government will maintain it.

The two years of the third U Nu government appeared to have proved out the editorial comments given above. The Prime Minister vigorously followed to a conclusion the Sino-Burman border settlement. The Border Treaty and the Non-Aggression Treaty were duly approved by the parliament and Sino-Burman *rapprochement* reached its high point in January, 1961, at the annual independence day celebrations. Documents for the formal exchange of ratifications of the treaties were signed in Rangoon by U Nu and Chou En-lai who was awarded a specially created decoration by the Burma Government. The Chinese Communists reciprocated by announcing a £30 million credit to Burma for stimulation of trade and promotion of various projects in the country requiring technical assistance. The celebrations were enhanced by the presence of a total Chinese Communist delegation of over four hundred persons.[25]

In both 1960 and 1961 there was a continued flow of missions from Burma to many countries and an even greater number of trade, military "good-will" missions to Burma from Indonesia, India, Pakistan, Israel, Yugoslavia, West Germany, and others. This exchange of missions led the *Guardian Monthly* to comment wryly on U Nu's prosecution of his neutralist policy during one month, September, 1960, as follows:[26]

So many missions with so many important persons have left for abroad, some East and some West, towards the end of the last month that it has truly been a month of exodus. . . . While the Prime Minister goes East to make Burma safe in friendship with the giant country of China, others have gone West in search of money and help to keep us solvent. The foremost among the West-bound government journey men is the Finance Minister Thakin Tin with his financial experts who left the country to attend the conference of the International Monetary Fund. It is Thakin Tin's task to wheedle money out of the World Bank, and possibly out of the United States Government, so that the four-year plan being prepared at home by the politicians and the bureaucrats may get to a good start. Meanwhile, another government group, on a lower level, got busy negotiating in Pakistan and Ceylon to unload Burma's new rice crop and bring back precious foreign exchange. The Trade Development Minister will soon go south to Indonesia, the Philippines and then to Japan to get rid of the rest of the rice crop. . . . We now have members of the Government scattered abroad who are governing us by not being with us but by talking, dining and wining with foreigners in acquisition of friendship and cash.

Burman efforts to obtain economic aid and to dispose of its rice surplus were generally successful and a profile of the sources of foreign economic assistance would show a larger number of countries and agencies providing assistance, although in financial terms, the Chinese Communist credit was by far the largest segment of aid received from abroad. In only one major attempt to obtain aid from outside, was the U Nu government unsuccessful. Under General Ne Win, the government had sought a large increase in Japanese reparations without success, as previously related. U Nu's delegations to Tokyo were no more successful. Although the Japanese government increased its original offer, the Burmans apparently insisted that another $200,-000,000 was the only "fair" amount and negotiations were broken off.

One important modification was made by the U Nu government in the application of its principles of neutralism. Beginning in 1949, U Nu had taken the position that Burma would not recognize the governments of "divided countries." This was applied to Korea in 1949 when the Burma government refused to follow a United Nations resolution calling on members to recognize the Republic of Korea. This "principle" was not applied rigidly since Burma entered into relations with the Peking regime and broke with the Nationalist Government on Taiwan. More pertinent, the Burma government entered into full diplomatic relations with the Federal Republic of Germany, but not with the East German Communist regime. In August 1960, the Burma government received a five-man delegation from the East German regime, headed by the Deputy Prime Minister, Max Sefrin. At the end of their stay, it was announced that the two governments would establish consular relations and enter into trade arrangements, but that this did not involve "diplomatic recognition" by either party.

In May, 1961, an eight-man delegation from the "People's Republic" of North Korea was received in Rangoon and a joint committee was set up to map out a "detailed program for bi-lateral trade expansion" between Burma and North Korea. The final communiqué announced that the two countries would develop commercial relations and exchange consular representatives, "without involving diplomatic recognition." The Burma government has also received delegations from the North Vietnam regime and from the Republic of Vietnam, but no formal agreements have been made for commercial and trade relations. In view of the development of much closer ties between Burma and Communist China during 1960 and 1961, these actions with respect to the East German and North Korean Communist regimes pose some interesting questions regarding the application of Burma's neutralist principles. If neutralism for Burma means "friendly relations" with all countries but not with some because they represent divided countries, then just what criteria are being used by U Nu and his colleagues? On the surface it would seem that Burma's actions have been contradictory to its announced principles of neutralism. Or, the suspicion could be voiced that closer relations with Communist China influenced the Burma government toward closer relations with the Communist regimes of East Germany and North Korea.

During 1961, the Sino-Burman boundary was finally delimited and joint survey teams had placed markers along the whole frontier with the exception of the northwest corner where the boundaries of Burma, India, and Communist China meet. In the maps attached to the Sino-Burman boundary treaty and final protocols, the Indian government formally protested the line shown as including Indian territory and being south of the watershed. U Nu made a special trip to New Delhi to explain Burma's position but the matter remains a part of the Sino-India border dispute, as yet unsettled.

U Nu accompanied Prime Minister Nehru to the Belgrade Conference of Unaligned States in September, but unlike the Bandung Conference of 1955, the Chinese Communists were not present and so far as can be learned U Nu did not play a decisive part in the proceedings. While it is reported that he generally supported the more moderate views of Nehru against the more extreme antiwestern views of President Tito, it would be understandable if he were chary of offending either of these two leaders with whose countries Burma has had "close and friendly" relations.

As the time for the fourteenth anniversary of Burma's independence was approaching, there seemed little doubt that the Burma leaders had developed considerable pride in the success of their neutralist policy in world affairs. U Nu's "positive neutralism" had received full endorsement from all political parties in Burma and even from the underground Communists under Thakin Than Tun. If U Nu and his colleagues foresaw any hazards ahead in their closer political and economic ties with Communist China, there was little evidence of it in their actions or public statements. And there is no reason to believe that these did not reflect generally their private views. The real hazard to continued success of their neutralist policy was to be found in domestic problems.

It took over twelve months for the third U Nu government to produce a new four-year plan for economic development and several major elements in this plan had to be adjusted in the light of reduction of their 1961 rice crops by severe floods and in view of the problem of how Burma was to "spend" the large Chinese Communist credit. The Peking regime agreed to take some 300,000 tons of rice annually from Burma and the Burma government agreed to try to stimulate more Sino-Burman trade as well as deciding on those projects in Burma which could be undertaken with Chinese Communist assistance. One effect of the Sino-Burman agreements was to limit severely the market for foreign textiles within Burma in favor of Chinese Communist goods.

The economic picture in Burma at the end of 1961 was by no means better than it had been under the military caretaker government, but it was far from being worse. It was largely in the realm of politics and government administration that Burmans themselves were having more and more doubts. By midsummer of 1961, it was generally known that U Nu's Union Party had become plagued with factionalism as had the old AFPFL before it. There was dissension among the political leaders and dissatisfaction with U Nu's attempt to subordinate the various mass organizations such as the ABPO to Union Party control. Civil servants were again complaining of political control and politically conscious Burmans were highly critical of continual appointment of committees and commissions to "investigate" and "make recommendations" on a growing number of internal problems. Certain rumblings of discontent were heard in the armed forces, particularly since progress in the establishment of internal security achieved under General Ne Win, seemed to have slipped badly as reports of armed robberies, insurgent raids, and unrest in the Shan states and upcountry districts increased in number almost daily.

By the end of January, 1962, the political climate in Burma bore a striking resemblance to that of 1958 which brought on the first military caretaker government. U Nu and his Union party colleagues seemed to have lost their sense of direction and their ability to provide any kind of effective administration or management of Burma's affairs. In spite of his many speeches calling for national unity, U Nu, in February, was negotiating for establishment of separate Mon and Arakanese states within the Union, thus feeding the tendencies toward separatism already being manifest vigorously by many Shan state leaders and young extremists.

The Union Party had become irrevocably split between the "Thakin" and the "Bo" factions, each struggling to gain control as did the Clean and Stable factions of the old AFPFL four years previously. U Nu's chief confidant, U Ohn had been named "Organizing Secretary-General" of the Union Party and the showdown came during the last week in January with elections for party offices. The Thakin faction, reportedly backed by U Nu and his henchmen, won all offices and thereby control of the party machinery, such as it was. This "victory" was interpreted by many observers as a decided swing toward the extreme left and it was predicted that both above and underground Communist groups would intensify their attempts to gain more political power as they had during the summer of 1958.

At this same time, a twenty-five man American business group was in Rangoon prepared to spend a number of weeks in negotiations with government officials on expansion of private capital investment in Burma. They had hardly begun their talks when U Nu suddenly announced that all private import licenses were revoked, effective in March. This act was taken to mean the end of private business, both domestic and foreign, in Burma and resulted in an unusual three-day "strike" by the whole Rangoon business community.

Most serious of all, however, was the growing disorder and the disaffection of all minority groups in Burma. Again, as in 1958, there were rumors of "pocket" armies prepared to take local government into their own hands in many sections of the country. In such circumstances, with U Nu's government almost daily losing its ability to exercise its authority over the country or to maintain even a minimum of law and order, there was the danger that Communist or pro-Communist groups might be able to join forces this time and gain the upper hand in the Burma government. If this happened, their first move would almost certainly be to dismiss the Commanding General of the Armed Forces and his immediate staff, and attempt to control the one cohesive organization in Burma, the Burma Armed Forces.

In the early morning hours of March 2, the military quietly and efficiently took control of the capital and the country, this time on their own initiative. This time the Constitution was ignored. This time U Nu, many of his Cabinet Ministers, and over half of the Shan State Sawbwas were jailed or placed under house arrest. In his broadcast announcement, General Ne Win stated that henceforth Burma would be ruled by a seventeen-man "Revolutionary Council" and that the Constitution would be "revised" at some later, unspecified date. General Ne Win said, "The army has taken control of a vastly deteriorating situation. The people must remain calm. The government servants must carry on their duties as usual. We assure you that we will make all possible efforts to serve the Burmese people's interests." [27]

Thus, after less than two years, U Nu's third government was ousted by the military and for a second time General Ne Win and his officers were running the Burma government. These officers, under the leadership of Brigadier Aung Gyi, moved swiftly, as they had before, to cleanse the government agencies of political appointees, and take the politicians off the necks of the civil servants. The Su-

preme Court and High Courts were abolished and new tribunals
with military appointees instituted in their stead. As in 1958, the
military exhibited an impatience with Burma's need for foreign advice and assistance. On April 19, it was publicly announced that
orders had been issued on April 12 terminating the activities of both
the Ford and the Asia Foundations in Burma. These two private
American foundations had been supporting a wide variety of development projects over a considerable period of years. In announcing
this action the Revolutionary Council stated that henceforth all foreign aid to Burma would be arranged on a "government-to-government" basis.

The second Ne Win government, the result of a military *coup
d'état*, was recognized by all the major nations of both power blocs
within days after its assumption of power. It reaffirmed Burma's policy of "positive neutrality" and maintenance of "cordial relations
with all nations." It was clear that this time the military would remain in power for an indeterminant period. For this time they were
under no obligations to hold "free and fair elections." It was equally
clear that the politicians had failed to make parliamentary democracy work in Burma. To many Burmans, Army rule was unpalatable
but still to be preferred to civil disorder and political disintegration.
By the *coup d'état* of March 2 the military in Burma have given
themselves a free hand. It will remain to be seen how they discharge
this responsibility.

— V —

BURMA'S RELATIONS WITH COMMUNIST CHINA

In a discussion of Burma's policy of "neutralism" a seasoned Burmese politician remarked, "Back of all of our public statements about 'non-alignment,' 'friendship with all countries,' 'positive neutralism,' and the like, is a constant awareness of our big and powerful neighbor to the north. We do not fear Communism as an ideology so much as we fear the day when China's masses must find living space in our under-populated country." This relationship of a weak, unstable nation to a large, well-organized and powerful neighbor, was succinctly expressed in the famous Lansing-Ishii notes of 1917. In this exchange of notes, the United States and Japan agreed that, "territorial propinquity creates special relations between countries, and consequently . . . that Japan has special interests in China, particularly in that part to which her possessions are contiguous." Substitute Communist China for Japan, and Burma for China in this statement and it would provide an accurate description of the key to Sino-Burman relations today. For these reasons, the development of Burma's relations with Communist China deserves special attention.

The Burma government's establishment of diplomatic relations with the Chinese Communist regime has already been described. In analyzing the development of Sino-Burman relations from 1949 to the present, it is necessary to note certain changes in Chinese Communist policies toward Burma and other Asian nations. Between 1948 and late 1953, the Chinese Communists and the Soviets generally promoted the line that the new governments in Southeast Asia were not truly independent, but were still under the domination of the "capitalist-imperialist" western nations. The Chinese Communists have consistently contended that their goal has been and still is the "liberation" of all Asian nations from this western "domination." In pursuit of this policy, however, both the Chinese Communists and the Soviets have altered their tactics and changed some of their specific policies. Until about 1952–53, they supported vocally the efforts of the Burma Communists to seize control of the government by force. When it appeared that the underground Communists in Burma had neither the strength nor the skill at organization to accomplish this and when efforts of Communist groups in the same direction in Indonesia and Malaya were equally unavailing, the Chinese Communists changed their approach to that of developing "friendly relations" with the nations in South and Southeast Asia. There then began the period of the "Five Principles of Peaceful Co-Existence" which lasted until sometime in 1957–58 and to which the rulers in Peking still pay lip service. Since this time, Chinese Communist actions along the Indian frontier in Tibet, and toward Laos and Vietnam have been a negation of their "peaceful" pretensions.[1]

During these two periods there was a significant shift in Chinese Communist policy regarding their southern frontier areas which was relatively unnoticed until the Sino-Indian frontier disputes broke out into the open in 1959. At first, both the Soviets and the Chinese Communists were inclined to accept the colonial boundaries of Burma and India as valid. It was only after recognition that the new governments were not going to be captured by internal Communist insurgents or subversion that the Peking regime changed its attitude. In 1953–54, it became evident that the Chinese Communists were giving close attention to the ethnic-linguistic groups along their frontiers with both India and Burma. The creation of autonomous areas in Yunnan including Kachins, Thais, and other tribal groups whose members lived astride the frontier, and the position taken that the people of Ladakh were essentially an irredentist group because of their Tibetan origins, religion and culture, are illustrative of this new policy. The operation of this policy, taken together with the action of the Chinese Communists in Tibet in 1959, had the effect of unstabilizing the whole long frontier area of India and China. Furthermore, it provided the Chinese Communists with a means of establishing claims to thousands of square miles of territory which both Burma and India had considered theirs. Even more important, it gave the Chinese Communists a large area of maneuverability. By infiltration of the border areas and by subversion, the Chinese Communists might hope at least to stir up trouble among the trans-border peoples for whom the concepts of a frontier and of national-ity have little meaning. At the most, it could mean that the Chinese Communists might be able to detach some or all of these ethnic-linguistic groups from control of India or Burma and thus establish their power on the southern slopes of the Himalayan mountain bar-rier. The danger to Burma and India from such eventualities is ob-vious.

Between 1953 and 1959, Chinese Communist propaganda hinted at claims to large slices of territory which both Burma and India re-garded as theirs. Suppression of the Tibetan revolt in 1959 produced public acknowledgement in India that the Peking regime was in occupation of a considerable portion of Ladakh in the state of Kash-mir adjoining Tibet and had built a road and established new fron-tier posts to reinforce their claims. With these developments, and in the face of Indian resentment, Communist Chinese border diplomacy took a more complex turn as the Chinese Communists proceeded to accept virtually the prewar Burma frontier with only minor adjust-ments and to agree with the government of Nepal on a definitive border settlement. No agreement was reached with India. All of these permutations in Chinese Communist policy and tactics, as well as the "special relations" of geographical propinquity between Burma and China made it necessary that the Burma government develop a care-fully thought-out China policy.

Fortunately for Burma, its relations with Communist China since 1948 have not been subjected to any really severe strains. Conse-quently, it is possible to consider four main aspects of Sino-Burman relations: first, the formulation of a China policy by Burma; second, the merging of Burma's China policy with Chou En-lai's "Five Prin-ciples of Peaceful Co-Existence"; third, the problem of Chinese Com-munist subversion and infiltration in Burma; and fourth, the Sino-Burman border settlement and its consequences.

The Formulation of a China Policy

Once diplomatic relations with the People's Republic of China had been established, the AFPFL leaders were quick to recognize that they faced a problem peculiar to their geographic position as a southern neighbor of a huge Communist state. Their immediate concern, however, was whether the new Chinese Communist regime would take any active steps to assist the Burman underground Communists in their fight against the AFPFL government. It would have been consonant with Communist policy at the time for Peking to do so. Consequently, what U Nu and his colleagues hoped for was a "correct" relationship with the new Communist regime so that "friendly relations" would have time to grow and ripen. Privately, the AFPFL leaders fervently hoped that internal problems and international situations elsewhere would induce the Chinese Communists to let Burma alone. In this respect the AFPFL leaders correctly estimated the future. The Korean War, the problem of Taiwan and the Formosa straits, the war and subsequent troubles in Indo-China, in Laos and Vietnam, plus severe internal strains seem to have induced the Chinese Communists to go along with the Burma government's goal of developing "close and friendly relations."

On September 8, 1950, Ya Chung-ming, the first Chinese Communist Ambassador to Burma, gave a luncheon in which he had his initial contacts with the Burman press. He read a long speech, the chief burden of which was that both Burma and the "new China" had won their independence after a "prolonged struggle" and that successful development of Sino-Burman relationships would help promote peace in Asia and in the world. He repeated the theme of the "prolonged struggle to free their peoples" as the point of common interest between China and Burma several times in this speech. With the Peking regime's involvement in the Korean War, Mao Tse-tung and his colleagues evidently felt it was time to soft-pedal the idea of "liberation" from the remnants of "capitalism-imperialism" and talk about "beautiful friendship." [2] Burma reciprocated this gesture when its United Nations' representative made a strong plea for admission of Communist China to the UN at the fall session of the General Assembly.

There is little evidence that the establishment of Chinese Communist control over Tibet in the fall and and winter of 1950 was a cause of serious concern to the Burman Government. The Burman position was stated by U Thant, then secretary to the Information Ministry, in a radio broadcast on November 5, when he asserted,[3]

"Our country has not the least desire to take sides on the Sino-Tibetan affairs but Burma with its policy of abhorrence of aggression of any type is certainly not happy at the news of the People's Republic of China ordering the units of the Chinese army into Tibet. Burma believes in the settlement of differences by peaceful means, and therefore, the Union Government cannot but regret that the Central People's Government of China should have seen fit to take this drastic action on Tibet."

In January 1951, Burma was confronted with the issue of Chinese Communist aggression in Korea, which was brought before the United Nations. On this issue, the Burmese Government hedged, finding a justification for their refusal to brand Communist China as an aggressor in the fact that they did not believe such action would contribute to international peace, particularly since there seemed no likelihood that sanctions would be voted against Peking.

It has been the lot of the AFPFL leaders that any move they made toward closer relations with the United States and Western nations produced immediate charges that they were departing from their announced nonalignment policy. These charges came from elements within the AFPFL, as well as from the opposition — elements that were politically important to the Government. On the other hand, whenever some move has been made toward closer relations with Communist bloc countries, the AFPFL leadership finds itself accused of being pro-Communist in the Western press and by some fairly important political elements at home. Many of the foreign policy statements made by Burman leaders, therefore, include attempts to demonstrate that Burma does not favor one side more than the other. These justifications hardly show that Burma's policy is one of strict neutrality, but rather are designed to show that a particular move toward one power bloc is really balanced by previous Burman moves with respect to the other power bloc.

Typical of these official "explanations" is the statement made by U Ba Swe in a May Day speech to the Trades Union Congress (Burma).[4] In his speech he said he wanted to refute the charges made that Burma leaned toward the Anglo-Americans. Proof of the falsity of this was the fact, he asserted, that Burma had sought Communist China's admission to the United Nations, had refused to join in naming Communist China as an aggressor in Korea, and had refused an American military mission.

In the early part of the year 1951, stories appeared in the Burman press and elsewhere that plans to expand Rangoon port facilities and rebuild the Rangoon airport were part of an American plot to secure military and air bases. These reports became numerous enough that U Nu chose to refute them to the Rangoon press. In doing so, he said that talk of Communist China being a menace to Burma was a "myth" fostered by persons who were trying to "disrupt Sino-Burmese relations." U Nu stated that relations with China were most cordial, and that reports that Chinese Communist soldiers were bolstering the Burmese Communist groups fighting the Government were "completely baseless." U Nu asserted to the press that the Peking government had assured the Burma Government it had no territorial ambitions regarding Burma and that this assurance had been given regarding the contested border area. U Nu concluded his statements on Sino-Burmese relations by saying,[5] "There are no problems which Asian countries like China, India, and Burma cannot solve through normal diplomatic channels. The Chinese government has not had time to draw new maps and only reproduced old maps showing the China-Burma border undemarcated. We see no difficulty in sitting down together and demarcating a boundary. The Chinese have no territorial ambitions."

U Nu's reference to maps arose because of press reports of maps published in Peking showing a Chinese claim to considerable Burmese territory and Indian territory as well.

The Burman position on membership for Communist China in the United Nations is illustrated by the speech made at the UN General Assembly session in November 1951, in Paris by the delegate U Myint Thein, Burma's first Ambassador to Communist China. In the course of this speech, he said:[6]

In other words we are to forget the existence, for so long as we are in Paris, of what is unquestionably one of the most important and one of the most urgent of the issues facing the U.N.

. . . the stern fact that stares all of us in the face is that the real China, one of the Big Five, is not represented in our midst.

As our Foreign Minister stated in his U.N. day speech last year, we have faced the facts of the Chinese situation, and I would urge the assembly to face these same facts without prejudice or bias and to accept the position that the People's Republic of China on the mainland of China is the effective and legitimate government of the Chinese People.

My personal conviction is that the People's Government is effective, honest and sincere.

The sensitivity of the Burman leadership to charges of leaning toward one power bloc or the other in the conduct of their foreign relations was again shown in U Nu's speech at the Union Welfare Conference in Rangoon on August 4, 1952.[7] With considerable vigor, U Nu attacked people who "say that the Anglo-Americans are always right," or accuse Burma of "leaning toward the Anglo-Americans." With equal vigor, he attacked those people who say that "whatever is done by Soviet Russia or Red China is always right." No nation can always be right or wrong, U Nu went on to say, and then he paid tribute to the good things he found in the United States, the U.S.S.R., Communist China, and the U.K.

This same "explanation" or "justification" line was followed at the United Nations. In September, 1952, Burma rejected Chinese Communist charges that the United States forces had been using "germ warfare" in Korea as "completely untrue." Nevertheless, in his speech at the UN assembly in which he stated his Government's position on this question, Ambassador Barrington also took time to deny that this meant that Burma was "inclined to the U. S. side." He firmly asserted that Burma had "maintained her neutral character in international relations."

By the middle of 1952, the main lines of Burma's China policy were established. The AFPFL leaders believed that maintenance of friendly relations with the Peking regime was the only course compatible with the preservation of their nation's interests and security. They accepted at face value the Peking regime's assurances that Chinese intentions toward Burma were honorable and that it had no desire to interfere in Burma's internal affairs. They rejected Western notions that Chinese Communist expansion or "imperialism" toward Southeast Asia was a clear and present danger. They sincerely believed that internal problems would so occupy Chinese Communist efforts that Peking would have neither the heart nor the capability for concerted action in or against Burma.

The original apprehension that the Chinese Communists might assist the insurrectionists against the AFPFL Government had been largely dissipated by the end of 1952, and there was a growing confidence among the AFPFL leaders that the threat of the insurrection to the existence of their Government was no longer serious. The border demarcation issue was unsettled, but U Nu and his colleagues seemed convinced that a posture of friendship and willingness to compromise in the interests of peaceful relations with Peking would prevent this problem from becoming a source of friction.

The only remaining issue at this time which concerned the AFPFL leaders was that of the refugee Kuomintang troops in upper Burma. For the Burma Government, this was the most delicate international problem they had so far faced. In 1952, rumors and press charges of American assistance to the KMT troops were a continuing sore point to the Burma Government. Fears were expressed that the KMT fighting in Kengtung province might turn Burma into another Korea.[8] U Nu publicly stated that he had received assurances from Peking that the Chinese Communists would not intervene. At the same time, the Burma Government was considering the best means of getting this problem before the United Nations for action.

During 1952, new economic agreements were concluded with the United States, and these brought the usual left-wing criticism that Burma was leaning toward the "Anglo-American bloc." As in past years, the Burman leaders felt it necessary publicly to refute these charges, and U Nu stated that Burma would request aid from the Soviet Union and from China "to see if it would be offered without strings." Burma's decision to participate in the Colombo plan, and the fact that economic aid might be obtainable from a variety of sources, seemed to give additional confidence to the Burmans that their "independent" and "neutral" course in foreign relations was paying off.

With the beginning of 1953, a more concerted drive to liquidate the KMT forces was possible, and it became apparent that the problem was more complex than had been anticipated. On March 2, the Government decided to take the whole KMT question to the United Nations, and on March 17, the Government notified the United States that American economic aid must be terminated by June. During 1953, efforts in and out of the United Nations to settle the KMT problem consumed the major attention of the Burman leaders, along with their problems of economic development. In this period nothing arose to mar the "friendly" relations between Burma and the Chinese Communists. The evacuation scheme, assisted by the governments of Thailand, the United States, and the Chinese Nationalist Government on Taiwan, was declared completed in May 1954, although it was reliably reported that only about half of the KMT troops had been taken out of the Kengtung province. In the meantime, the Burma government had signed their first trade agreement with Communist China amid an aura of official statements about "Sino-Burmese friendship" and "cooperation for peace."

Adhering to their principle of nonalignment, the AFPFL leaders based their China policy on the corollary principle of "maintaining friendly relations with all countries." By supporting Chinese Communist membership in the United Nations and by consulting Peking at each step in the crisis over the KMT troops in Burma, the government hoped it had shown the Chinese Communists that it had nothing but peaceful intentions and friendly feelings toward them. A shift in Chinese Communist tactics in 1953–54 evidenced by a willingness to aid Burma by rice barter agreements, was coupled with a sudden increase of exchange of good-will missions and visits between U Nu and Chou En-lai, all of which enabled the Burma government to consolidate its China policy around its original principles of neutralism. And, what is more, many Burman leaders believed the change in Chinese Communist attitudes toward Burma was primarily due to Burma's desire for "peaceful and friendly relations."

"The Five Principles of Peaceful Co-Existence"

June, 1954, marks the beginning of a period of close and "friendly" relations between Burma and her big northern neighbor, signalized first by agreement on a set of guiding "principles" which Burma henceforth accepted as a basis for its own China policy. The peripatetic Chinese Premier, Chou En-lai, visited Prime Minister Nehru in that month, and they jointly announced their adherence to the "Five Principles of Peaceful Co-Existence." From Delhi, Chou came to Rangoon for his first meeting with Prime Minister U Nu, and at the end of his visit, U Nu, too, joined with Chou in declaring adher-

ence to the "Five Principles."[9] Obviously this joint declaration did
not constitute an alliance between Burma and Communist China,
but the fanfare attending its announcement caused much speculation.

A sampling of editorial opinion given below indicates the nature
of some of this speculation:

> Chou said that his meeting with Nehru was a great help to world peace.
> If all the nations observe the preamble to the Indo-China (India-China)
> agreement on Tibet, world peace could be secured. The preamble lays
> down respect for sovereignty, non-aggression, non-intervention, equal
> status and co-existence. If these were observed we can expect to live in
> Utopia. Russia also pronounced these some time ago. But what do we see?
> She has annexed some small European countries, while in the east she is
> planning to make China her tool. One method she used is to instigate trou-
> ble from within. In this there is little to choose between China and Russia:
> Relation with other countries is aggression while their interference is
> called "Liberation." Poland and Tibet have been liberated. They have the
> plan to liberate Southeast Asian countries. China is giving training to Naw
> Seng with a view to overthrow the Burmese government. Like Chou En-lai
> other people also believe in the 5 points. But the Communists themselves
> do not observe these. Communists should demonstrate by giving up ag-
> gression and withdraw their big boots and guns from the countries they
> have occupied.[10]
>
> Mr. Chou's visit to Burma will give the local people a chance to see at
> close quarters this remarkable man from a remarkable country and per-
> haps even gain a better understanding of the New China that dangles so
> tantalizing between the extremes of independent Asian nationalism and
> subservience to the dictates of the Kremlin. Those whose hackles rise at
> the very mention of the word Communism have spent millions trying to
> convince Asia that the Mao-Chou regime has been foisted on the people
> of China by Moscow. This is a distortion of the truth that has never been
> equalled by even the most vociferous propaganda machines that the world
> has known.
>
> The visit of Mr. Chou to India and Burma has also given rise to the
> speculation that China is planning a new "peace offensive." This seems
> to be giving an unfortunate and unwarranted interpretation to a gesture
> of goodwill from the People's Republic. Mr. Chou's visit certainly will tip
> the balance in favour of friendship and closer ties with the People's Re-
> public, but to see in this a defeat for what is popularly called the "free
> world" would be foolish.[11]
>
> The relations between Communists and non-Communists are specially
> important and we must be cautious in all matters . . .

. . . Communists' plan is to isolate small countries and when time comes Communists will devour these countries (being weak and defenseless) like a tiger. East European countries and China are examples.

Communists in Southeast Asia are revolting against their governments in Southeast Asia. Burmese Communists even go to Red China to be allies with Red China for planning against Burma. Such questions should be asked to the Chinese Premier who is now in Rangoon for a visit. Action should be taken with regard to such affairs.

Democracies both in Europe and Asia should unite and face Communists' constant threats and aggressions. Only united action will meet with success. All Burma should be careful not to fall a victim to Communists' intrigues.[12]

Just before the departure of Chou En-lai, Chou and U Nu issued the customary joint statement. In affirming support for the "Five Principles" they expressed hopes for a peaceful solution of international disputes such as that in Indo-China. The most significant point in this joint communiqué was that "The Prime Ministers affirmed that the people of each nation should have the right to choose their own state system and way of life without interference from other nations. Revolution cannot be exported; at the same time outside interference with the common will expressed by the people of any nation should not be permitted."

The Burman leaders did not accept this declaration wholly at face value, but were willing to believe that it would apply to Sino-Burman relations regardless of what the Chinese Communists did elsewhere. Some high officials stated privately that their attitude was a pragmatic "wait and see" whether the Chinese Communists would live up to it. "If they do, fine, but if they don't, we shall face that problem when the time comes." This Burman attitude emphasizes a basic element in Burma's China policy, namely, that the Burman leaders regard their nation's relations with Communist China as having a special, bilateral character, only in part because of their common frontier. They either do not see or tend to ignore what the Peking regime does and says in relations with other nations. For there are few, if any, high Burman officials who have studied Communist strategy, particularly Chinese Communist doctrine and strategy in depth. What the Chinese Communists do or say with respect to situations apart from Burma is not considered relevant to the conduct of Sino-Burman relations. This view was implied in U Nu's Martyr's Day speech on July 19, 1954, when he said,

. . . Then let me tell you how we also see the People's Republic of China. To start with, this viewpoint is different from that of most of those who are anti-Communists. As we do not like Communism, we do not want to see the spread of this creed into our territories. We have, therefore, been doing our best to prevent such a contingency here. But, it is far from our intention to meddle in their (Communist Chinese) affairs. They have chosen Communism in order to suit their own circumstances.

. . . The unity of the Chinese people under Chairman Mao Tse Tung gratifies us as Asians . . . His China has earned the respect of many foreigners, and as Asians we take pride in this new phenomenon . . . As Asians we are delighted at the great strides made there.[13]

In September, 1954, it was announced that Prime Minister Nehru would go to Communist China to return Chou's visit to India and that U Nu would follow him sometime in November. At a press conference following this announcement, U Nu stated that his forthcoming visit was "symbolic" of the cordial relations between Burma and China and that he had no "triangular" connection with Chou and Nehru. When asked whether his visit and that of Nehru's would culminate in a nonaggression pact, U Nu denied this as a possibility. He added that the "Five Principles" were self-explanatory and that no further detailed discussions were required.[14]

During the period between Chou's visit and the press conferences noted above, there were continuing reports that Chou had warned U Nu not to join the Manila Pact and SEATO or engage in any kind of military agreement with the United States. This was reported by *The New York Times* correspondent, Robert Trumbell, in a roundup piece on October 24, 1954, following a stay in Rangoon and interviews with a number of Burman leaders. His story is confirmed by data collected from interviews, and it underlines the privately expressed apprehensions of the Burmans about Communist China's intentions, their determination to stay clear of involvement, but their awareness, nevertheless, that good relations with a potentially powerful northern neighbor were a necessity.

On his return from Peking, Nehru held a press conference which *The New York Times* reported as follows:

He said that Communist China's pledge to India and Burma of non-interference bars 'encouragement or help' by Peiping to subversive Communist movements in other Asian countries . . . Observing that 'sub rosa activities' of international Communism were 'intimately connected,' Nehru implied that time would show whether the five principles adopted recently by China, India and Burma would mean an automatic end to Chinese involvement to Communist subversion abroad. He said the Chinese regime had accepted the principle that Chinese residing abroad should either become citizens of the host country or disassociate themselves from local political activities and that China wished to take up this question with the governments involved with a view to making bilateral agreements on their status. Nehru mentioned particularly Burma and Indonesia in this connection.[15]

On the same day, U Nu gave a radio broadcast celebrating Prime Minister Nehru's birthday and paying tribute to him and his career. In the course of his broadcast, U Nu asserted:[16]

. . . His wise policy of non-alignment with any of the two power blocs has also come in for a good deal of misunderstanding and criticism. We have heard of the fantastic allegation from one side that Sri Nehru is the spearhead of the Anglo-Americans, and there is the equally fantastic allegation from the other side that he is pro-Communist. Neither of these allegations is, of course, true.

His visit to the People's Republic of China has been a great revelation to him. I had a brief discussion with him on his return from Peking and he was genuinely impressed with all that he had seen. One thing that struck him most was the extraordinary discipline of the Chinese people under the new regime.

On his departure for his tour of Communist China, U Nu said that his own policy was "one of anti-Communism," but that he had found Chou En-lai quite agreeable during their previous talks; Chou had not wielded a "big stick," but, rather, had "seemed liberal." [17] U Nu added that after his two-week trip to China, he hoped to make a six-weeks' trip to the United States.

During his visit to mainland China, U Nu carefully followed the policy of "friendliness." He told a Peking audience that Chiang Kai-shek had been a failure because he had lacked moral integrity, and he said he was proud that his country had been the first to recognize the Communist regime. He praised Communist China's "abundance of goodwill, regard, and brotherly feeling" toward Burma, which had been proven by its rice purchases and its decision not to

pursue KMT troops into Burmese territory.[18] These friendly manifestations, Nu continued, had shown that although Burma and the
Peking regime differed in political ideologies, Communist China had
a "keen desire to help her neighbors."

On his return from China, the following exchange took place at a
press conference in Rangoon:

Q. Did you discuss a non-aggression pact with China?
A. Since we subscribe to the Five-Point Principle, non-aggression pacts
   are unnecessary . . .

Q. Did the Chinese categorically state they had no connection with the
   Burmese Communists?
A. Yes.

Q. How about the question of citizenship of overseas Chinese?
A. We discussed this, too. Our decision will have to await the negotiations
   now taking place between China and Indonesia. The same problem is
   involved . . .

Q. Mr. Prime Minister, you have gone to China as the eyes and ears of
   this country. From what you have observed, can you give the assurance that the Chinese are sincere when they say we have nothing to
   fear from them?
A. So long as we do not think and plan evil against them, and so long as
   we are sincere when we say that they have nothing to fear from our
   direction, and we do not give them any cause for apprehension by al-
   lowing ourselves to be used as bases against them, I am convinced the
   Chinese will not wish us harm. I believe the Chinese are sincere; they
   wish to live in peace with us.[19]

After his return, U Nu also reported to an AFPFL convention that
he had given three assurances to Peking: first, that Burma would
not be used as a stooge by any power; second, that Burma would
never "betray the people's trust"; and third, that Burma would "exert
her utmost towards the achievement of world peace." At the same
time, he testified to China's desire for peace and said that her claim
to Taiwan should be considered. He reported that Chou En-lai had
told him that peace and friendship with the U. S. would be possible
if America would withdraw her forces from Formosa and stop inter-
fering in China's internal affairs.[20]

One of the main purposes of the Afro-Asian Conference, which
took place at Bandung from April 18 to 24, 1955, was to bring about

a meeting between Chou En-lai and the leaders of other Asian states. On his way to Bandung Chou was invited to stop over in Rangoon with Nehru, Nasser, and Naim (of Afghanistan), and later on, at the Conference itself, U Nu appears to have devoted his greatest efforts toward an avoidance of difficult issues and of friction between Chou En-lai and the proponents of pro-Western attitudes. According to one report, Nehru and U Nu had a hand in the resumption of discussions on an ambassadorial level between the U. S. and Communist China in the summer of 1955 (less than a week after the termination of U Nu's American visit).[21]

During U Nu's visit to the United States (June 23 to July 19, 1955), in an interview which he gave to the *U. S. News and World Report,* he defended his signing of the "Five Principles" agreement with Communist China in the following way: "If I think a principle is right, I am happy to have anyone subscribe to it. If he later fails to live up to it, the onus is upon him." U Nu implied, however, that security could not be guaranteed by words alone, for he also pointed out the importance to Burma of building up the United Nations and eliminating "the conditions on which subversion thrives." [22]

U Nu emphasized to Americans his belief that Communist China wanted peace, that its leaders were sincere, and that these men were primarily interested in China's internal problems. He added that it was the Burmans who had "much more to lose in the event that I am wrong in my estimate of Chinese sentiment," and that it was "in full realization of this that I say I sincerely believe that the present government of China truly wants peace." [23]

As far as tension between the U. S. and Communist China was concerned, U Nu told the National Press Club in Washington that Burma was fully prepared to mediate between the two countries, if they should so desire. He voiced the conviction that U. S. policy makers were not opposed in principle to Chinese Communist membership in the United Nations, but that it was just a question of timing. He then went on to accuse America of an exaggerated fear of Red China. The joint statement issued by Eisenhower and U Nu at the conclusion of the latter's stay in Washington said that U Nu had discussed frankly with Eisenhower and Dulles the problem of U. S. airmen imprisoned in China, but nothing has been made known of what was actually said during these discussions.[24]

Toward the summer of 1956, there were increasing rumors of Chinese Communist infiltration along the northern border, and in July the Burmese press broke the stories of incursions of Chinese troops in considerable numbers. From this time on, until the late spring of 1957, the border issue assumed major importance in Sino-Burmese relations, and U Nu's attempts to bring about "reconciliation" between Communist China and the United States seemed all but forgotten. As with the KMT problem earlier, this border issue was a real test of Burma's policy toward the Peking regime and of the effectiveness of the "Five Principles." (Details of this dispute are discussed in a final section of this chapter.)

The agreement "in principle" on the border issue resulted from U Nu's presence in Peking in November, 1956. This time he was not there as Prime Minister, but as President of the AFPFL. Although he was treated as a state guest, not a high government official, U Nu did, in fact, discuss the Sino-Burmese border problem which resulted in his "package deal" announced in Burma at a later date after his return. It seems clear, however, that the AFPFL leaders had become gravely concerned over the implications of the border issue and of what seemed to some, an increasing amount of Chinese Communist infiltration over the border. Because of his nongovernment position at the time, U Nu apparently felt he could speak more frankly than as a Prime Minister. In a speech before the Political Consultative Conference in Peking on November 2, 1956, U Nu took this opportunity to expound his version of the meaning of the "Five Principles of Peaceful Co-Existence." That this was done deliberately, there is little question. Furthermore, it was well known in Peking as well as in Burma, that U Nu's private role was only temporary. (He was back in office as Prime Minister by February, 1957.)

The pertinent parts of this speech are given below:[25]

. . . The impression may arise that for such friendship to be sincere and lasting there might be difficulties in the way. The basis for such a conclusion may be that China is a Communist country while Burma is not, and that difference in ideology would keep the people apart.

But . . . the cultivation and the commentation of friendship should be based on common factors which mark the characteristics of the two peoples . . . The Chinese are entitled to decide for themselves what is best for them, and they are free to adopt the kind of ideology that is best suited for themselves, just as the Burmese are entitled to make their decision for themselves . . . Thus, the Chinese, considering all that is relevant, have decided it is for their good and to their advantage to adopt Communism and the Burmese should have no quarrel with what the Chinese have decided for themselves. Similarly the Chinese should not quarrel with the Burmese for adopting the form of democracy which they consider is best suited to them.

Let me explain the first principle of mutual respect for each other's territorial integrity and sovereignty . . . To say it candidly, the Burmese dislike intensely any kind of subjugation or control direct or indirect and any attempt to control or subjugate us would be resisted. I know that, like us, the Chinese would similarly repel any attempt to fetter their freedom. Such control would be accepted only by lackeys . . .

Having dealt with the first principle, I proceed to the second, the principle of non-aggression. If we look at the history of China and Burma, there is evidence that there were times when the Burmese committed aggression in the territory of China just as the Chinese did likewise in the territories of Burma . . . What has happened in the past was bad. If it should happen again it will also be bad . . .

The Chinese and Burmese travel in the same boat. It was but yesterday that we managed to shake off the shackles that fettered our freedom . . . The two of us have neither the inclination nor the time to quarrel or to fight or to commit aggression on each other's land. Thus from this rostrum I declare plainly that the second principle also has the whole hearted support of the Burmese.

. . . Now the third principle, the principle of non-interference in each other's internal affairs . . . It need hardly be emphasized that a mere declaration of acceptance of a principle is not enough. Both our countries must make special endeavour to their utmost that the principle is strictly observed. It is erroneous to suppose that only the big countries can indulge in such interference. Small countries are also capable . . . From this rostrum, I make this declaration to the Chinese leaders and Chinese people. It is not our intention to make a convenience of Sino-Burmese friendship and to use it for our own selfish ends. Such a base motive is unworthy and we have no such thoughts. Apart from ties of friendship with China we have similar ties with other great countries . . . In her relations with the big and mighty countries it is not Burma's intention merely to receive. The thought is ever present in her that she will repay the many kindnesses whenever the opportunity should occur and I assure you that we are always ready to render such help or aid.

I now come to the fourth principle, that of equality and mutual benefit . . . Both from the point of view of area and in population and also the wealth of natural resources, China is, in fact, one of the greatest countries in Asia and also in the world and it would be lamentable if pride in her greatness should cloud her perspective.

Burma is one of the smallest countries. We would like to be friends with all countries but we would not like to be merely the appendage of the mightiest countries in the world. Therefore, the fourth principle which eliminates distinction between a big country and a small country is one that appeals to us and one that we accept without reservation. I come now to the fifth principle, the principle of co-existence.

Does anybody doubt that in this age of atomic and hydrogen bombs, if peace should end, the world would be converted into a huge ash-heap? It is said that even with this realization, because of distrust and suspicion, the idea of co-existence unfortunately is not universally accepted. Apart from four or five countries no country has even seriously considered its acceptance . . . Some wonder with dread if the talk for peace is but a facade, and whether the aim of the other party is to breed fifth columnists and lackeys. All this is lamentable and should be eradicated . . . if we practice these principles honestly with full sincerity to eradicate mistrust and suspicion, China and Burma will go down in history as the two countries which turned a world of turmoil, suspicion and distrust into a world of peace and contentment.

In his long review of Burma's foreign relations during his five-hour speech to the Burmese parliament on September 27, 1957, U Nu spent some time dealing with Sino-Burmese relations. He related his efforts to "bridge the gap" between Communist China and the United States with extensive quotations from his speeches in both countries. After complimenting both Communist China and the United States for their attitude toward the KMT problem, U Nu summarized the evolution of Burma's China policy as follows:

Let me now deal with another neighbor, China. When we regained our independence, the Kuomintang Government was still in control of China though they were fast losing ground to the Communists. In accordance with our policy of establishing friendly relations with all countries, we made necessary arrangements in Nanking even before independence for setting up our Embassy there. Our relations with the then Government of China were cordial, despite the existence of a Sino-Burma border problem even at that time. In fact the Kuomintang Government was one of the Governments which sponsored Burma's admission to the United Nations. It was a friendly act which we shall not forget. But things moved fast in the Chinese Civil War, and by the end of 1949 the Chinese Communists had obtained control over the whole of China except the island of Formosa on which Chiang Kai-shek took refuge. Faced with this reality, we recognized the new Government of China as the legal Government at the end of 1949, and immediately took steps to establish our Embassy there. This proved successful and by June, 1950, we had entered into normal diplomatic relations with the new Government of China. From then on we have tried hard to get the new Government of China to be given her rightful place in the United Nations and other world organizations. But our relations with the new Chinese regime remained uncertain for a number of years. The Communist rebellion was still going strong, and the new Chinese Government seemed inclined to give our Communists their moral support, apparently regarding us as stooges of the West. Broadcasts from Peking Radio at that time did not attempt to disguise this attitude. However, as the years passed, and the Chinese saw from our actions that we were stooges of nobody and that we were embarked on an independent policy in internal affairs, they changed their attitude. Premier Chou En-lai's visit to India and Burma in 1954 proved to be the turning point in Sino-Burmese relations, and since then both of us have been guided by the five principles which were embodied in the Joint Statement issued by Premier Chou En-lai and me at the time. Consequent of a firm understanding on a political level, we have developed rapidly expanding economic and cultural relations, which is as it should be between two friendly neighbors.

Between September 1958 and April 1960, the military caretaker government continued to pursue U Nu's policy of "close and friendly relations" with Communist China. Final conclusion of the border settlement and further development of economic and cultural relations took place since U Nu's return to power in April, 1960. Underneath all this talk of Sino-Burman "friendship" however, there remained a gnawing internal problem which at any time could erupt into a major crisis in Burma's relations with her northern neighbor. This was the problem of continued subversion and infiltration within Burma by the Chinese Communists and the Soviets as well. At no time has this activity been so extensive as to affect either internal security or endanger the Burma government, but the fact that it has continued and is of the pattern of Communist activity in other countries, has been cause for concern.

Communist Subversion and Infiltration

From the beginning, Burman officials and politicians have been conscious of attempts at subversion of their people by the outside Communists. Members of the government and particularly the top officers in the armed services have been quite aware that the presence of both Soviet and Chinese Communist Embassies in Rangoon, together with the easy access to Burma afforded citizens of Communist countries offered opportunities for Communist espionage, recruitment of Communist agents, and subversion of officials and political organizations within Burma. Whatever the Russians have been up to, and there has been little evidence available to the public concerning their activities, the Burma Government, quite naturally, has been more concerned about Chinese Communist operations.

In the first place, the Chinese community in Burma, though small in comparison to those of Indonesia or Thailand, nevertheless provides a potential source for recruitment of agents and the conduct of a variety of subversive action. In the second place, connections were established at an early date between the underground Burma Communists and their Chinese counterparts across the border. So far as is known, the leaders of the underground Communists in Burma never established any significant contacts with the Soviets either in Burma or in Moscow. They would more naturally look to the Asian Chinese Communists immediately adjacent Burma for aid and assistance. Finally, the Sino-Burman border area presents a prime opportunity to the Chinese Communists for stirring up trouble. The frontier terrain makes it most difficult for the Burma government to police border crossings and to prevent infiltration by Communist agents, tribal refugees from Yunnan, and others. Transborder tribal groups all along the frontier offer an excellent opportunity for training agents and provocateurs whose presence inside Burma among their kinsmen is much harder to detect than that of the Chinese-speaking peoples.

In facing the problem of Communist subversion and infiltration, the Burma government is not alone. It remains a major unsolved problem for many states of southeast Asia of real concern to the United States and its SEATO allies. Conditions in Laos and Vietnam over the past eighteen months have demonstrated how easily efforts at subversion and infiltration can become serious threats to a government's existence when the ingredient of guerrilla warfare, supported from outside a country, is added. So far, Burma has escaped what Laos and Vietnam have suffered and evidence of the extent of Communist subversion and infiltration is understandaably not available to an outsider. It is the public recognition that such a problem has continued to exist, however, which is important particularly as the Burmans see it and themselves define its significance.

The danger of subversion and infiltration from outside the country was quickly recognized by the AFPFL leaders. Between 1948 and 1951, the AFPFL government believed that the greater danger was from outside help to the Communist and other underground insurgents. In public statements, U Nu and others almost always pointed to dangers from both the Communist bloc and the Anglo-American bloc. British sympathy for the Karens was well known and evidence of individual attempts to aid the Karen revolt enabled Prime Minister U Nu to assert that both sides in the cold war might very well act in support of insurgent groups. He was thus able to project Burma's posture of neutrality to any who were worried about interference from the outside in Burma's internal affairs.

After 1951, the chief fear of the AFPFL leaders was that the presence of refugee KMT troops in northeast Burma might be used as an excuse for interference by Communist China. When this did not happen and when the Communist Chinese regime indicated it would regard this as a wholly Burman problem, the AFPFL leaders were impressed and were consequently more than ever willing to accept the later "doctrines" of the "Five Principles of Peaceful Co-Existence" at face value.

The Burma government has been well aware that both the Soviet Union and the Chinese Communists have been making attempts at subversion and infiltration of the government, the Armed Forces and of political and student organizations. There is a duality about such attempts, however, that often tends to confuse the issue. Since the inception of independence there have been aboveground Communist and pro-Communist politicians and organizations which have naturally been active in trying to win followers and gain more support. This activity has been well known to the government and many such individuals and groups have been publicly identified in the press. It was also recognized that both the Soviets and the Chinese Communists have been giving varying kinds of support to these individuals and groups. On the other hand, both the Soviets and the Chinese Communists seem to have made separate efforts to win over certain individuals and groups to their cause and to plant their agents in various government departments and in the Armed Forces. These efforts have had as their purpose espionage, intelligence gathering, and, more importantly, the building of a hard core of Communist agents and party workers who can be relied upon to take orders from Moscow and Peking. There is no overt evidence to date that Soviet and Chinese Communist efforts have been carefully concerted or coordinated as part of a broad Communist plan for Burma. From sources available, it appears that efforts at subversion by the Chinese Communists as well as by the Soviets have been quite similar to the common pattern of their activity in any country which is not a prime target of the Communist bloc.

Although recognition of all this by the AFPFL leaders has been present from the beginning, they have been understandably cautious in expressing their views about this danger in public. Two references by U Nu are typical of public recognition of the problem of sub-version and infiltration. On June 23, 1956, shortly before the news of Chinese military incursions on the frontier were made public, U Nu gave a radio broadcast devoted to his exposition of problems facing his AFPFL government. In the course of this talk, he said,

We can no longer afford to drift like this indefinitely . . . if the prob-lem (the evil of opportunists and persons corrupted by power) is not at-tacked systematically . . . then it is certain that sooner or later we will be confronted by the following three dangerous consequences:

(1) History will record us as the destroyers of the AFPFL which had been meticulously nurtured by Bogyoke Aung San with a view to national unity and independence.
(2) When AFPFL falls on the no-confidence of the people, it will be the fall of the dog and not of the cat, as the Burmese saying goes.
(3) Political power will pass into the hands of the unscrupulous stooges and agents of foreign powers.

. . . I dread the third consequence more than the first or the second. Our hard won independence, long cherished and fought for by our fore-bears and by several generations at great suffering and sacrifice, will dis-appear from the Union once political power passes into the hands and agents of foreign countries.

Our times are not like olden times. In the past a great and powerful country could conquer a less powerful country by force of arms. It is no longer the case now. No country, however big and powerful it may be, can aggress another country by military means. Open aggression will in-evitably result in open hostilities between the big powers. Therefore, tactics are undergoing a great change. The method of planting stooges and agents in small countries is being increasingly adopted by big countries, and by subversive means small countries are roped in. Subversion and infiltration have replaced the old and obsolete military methods. With this end in view some big powers are exerting their utmost to breed their own hirelings and fifth-columnists in small countries.

Our country has a liberal sprinkling of these stooges and hirelings and it is not very difficult to ascertain who they are. Their own actions and utterances reveal their real identity.[26]

Again on August 17, 1956, in a speech to the students of the School of Journalism in Rangoon, U Nu expounded on the same theme:

. . . Let us also remember that a country can be conquered in several ways, and that the use of overt force is only one of them. The other means are even more dangerous and sinister precisely because they are not open. If we are wise we will assume that there are those who are interested in sabotaging the independence of the Union of Burma and who will not abandon their attempts merely because it has become too dangerous for them to try to secure this objective by overt means. On the contrary, we must assume that they will be continually seeking alternative means of securing the same objective; and we must be ever vigilant to discover what these means are, expose them and take measures to counter them.[27]

These two speeches were given at a time when U Nu was out of office as Prime Minister with the self-assumed task of "cleansing" the AFPFL.

In his five-hour speech to the parliament on September 27, 1957, which involved a long review of Burma's foreign relations, Premier U Nu again referred to the dangers of internal subversion, but only in general terms. In this speech he reaffirmed the wisdom of Burma's neutral foreign policy with praise for countries in both power blocs as well as Burma's neighbors. The AFPFL leaders always tempered their public statements for fear of openly antagonizing Communist China. Privately, government officials and officers of the armed forces continued to be concerned with this problem. The effectiveness of their knowledge of subversive activities in the country can be judged by the largely successful efforts of the military caretaker government in rounding up Communists and their supporters for law violations between 1958 and 1960.

Directly related to the problem of subversion within Burma has been the problem of direct contacts between the underground Burmese Communists since 1949 with Communist China. For example, early in 1952, reports on the activities of an "Asian Revolutionary Committee" which had been set up by the Chinese Communists indicated that Burma was the second target for revolution, Indo-China being the first.[28] On January 4, the Chinese Communist Ambassador protested to the Burma Foreign Office over the display of the Nationalist flag by KMT sympathizers in independence celebrations; the Burmese Government ordered the flags removed.[29] According to a January 14 editorial in *The Nation*, the Peking radio and the Chinese Communist press were continuing their attacks on Southeast Asian governments, but the "unapproachable attitude" of Chinese diplomats, together with Chinese military action in Tibet, Korea, and Indo-China, had resulted in decreased Burman support for the Communist regime.[30] Early in 1953, some Burmese Army officials reported that thirty Burmese Communists had gone to Communist China for military training. Editorial comment on this report in one Burmese newspaper pointed out with a certain amount of indignation that, while Burma was doing her best to rid the countryside of Chinese Nationalist troops, the Chinese Communists were busily giving aid to other rebels in Burma.[31]

The Rangoon press has regularly reported contacts between the underground Burmese Communists and the Chinese Communists. These press reports have been substantiated by at least two public reports on connections between the Chinese Communists and their underground comrades in Burma. The first appeared as a series of articles in *The Nation* in June, 1954, at the time of Chou En-lai's first visit to Rangoon. In this series *The Nation* recalled the history of Soviet directives to the Burman and other Southeast Asian Communist parties in 1948. It then asserted that in late 1949 or early 1950, two of the top leaders of the CPB under Thakin Than Tun, Ko Aung Gyi and Bo Than Swe, were sent to China to establish regular channels of contact with Peking. It was reported that Ko Aung Gyi was supposed to handle political affairs and Bo Than Swe was to handle military affairs and that they were received in Peking almost as plenipotentiaries from one government to another.

In 1959 a comprehensive account of relations between the Burma Communist underground and the Chinese Communists was presented in a series of three articles written by Than Maung of the *Mandalay Sun*.[32] These two series, as well as other press reports appearing regularly, provide overt evidence of connections between the Burma Communist underground and the Chinese Communists.

During the past decade there is evidence of varying directives sent from Peking to the CPB and also evidence of Chinese irritation with the split between Thakin Than Tun and the Thakin Soe White Flag Communists. Generally the Chinese Communists were working to get the Burma Communist underground to move north and establish themselves along the frontier where support from China would be easier. Such moves of any large numbers of the Communist insurgents were frustrated by Burma Army operations against them and by the inhospitality of the border people such as the Kachins and the Shans.

There are authenticated reports of upwards of one hundred Burmans having gone to Communist China for training since 1951. Than Maung states in his articles that this has so far been a one-way street and that these Burmans are still in Communist China. On the other hand, *The Nation* reported on April 19, 1958 (before Than Maung's articles appeared in *The New Burma Weekly*), that some eighty members of the Communist Party of Burma (CPB) "who went to China nine years ago for training" were believed to have slipped back into Burma disguised as Shan Tayoks and that they were led by Yebaw Than Swe who went to China in 1949 with Yebaw Aung Gyi.[33] It was not possible to verify completely this report. Burmans who have visited Communist China have reported talking with a few of these "trainees" from the underground who appeared to be unhappy that they were not permitted to return to their country and put their training to use.

More important than these contacts between the Burman underground Communists and the Chinese to the north have been the efforts of the Chinese Communists to infiltrate the transborder tribal groups. Again, these efforts have been continuous as can be seen from a selected sampling of newspaper reports. As early as May, 1949, *The Nation* stated in an editorial, entitled "Border Confusion" that,[34] "In regard to our editorial of May 22, other papers have since reported the danger of Communist China infiltration yesterday one or two reported an interview with an official of the Shan Ministry denying infiltration. The head of the Kachin State, Sima Duwa Sinway Nawng, was reported to have said that ten thousand Chinese Communists are within thirty miles of the Burma border waiting for a chance to cross it." An Associated Press report from Rangoon of

January 31, 1951, asserted that a force of nearly 3,000 Chinese Communists were operating freely in North Burma in the northwest area of the Kachin state. The report stated that they had crossed over the border ostensibly to check on rumors that the United States was helping the Burma government construct an air base at Putao (Fort Hertz) and alleged that this was the same force whose infiltration was publicly denied by the Burma government the preceding November.[35]

In March, 1951, shortly after the Burman Ambassador to the United States had denied any tension with the Chinese Communists over the border, U Nu stated that there was no truth in reports that Chinese Communist soldiers were aiding the Burmese Communists.[36] Two months later Ambassador Yao in Rangoon also denied any contacts between the Chinese Communists and Burmese rebels, although Peking propaganda was still denouncing U Nu and supporting the "liberation struggle" in Burma, according to a report published in June.[37] In June it was also reported that a "Central Committee of the People's Liberation Armies of Southeast Asia" had been established in Kunming (Yunnan), with a Chinese advisory board and two Burmese Communist leaders, Bo Ye Htoot and Bo Than Shwe, as members. This report estimated that two hundred Burmese youth were attending Communist Chinese indoctrination classes.[38]

In a background article in August, 1953, describing a political split in Kachin politics, it was stated in part that,[39]

Fears of political instability in this loosely administered home province of 200,000 primitive Kachins are reinforced by persistent Chinese Communist propaganda for a "greater Kachin State" comprising Kachin-inhabited areas of Yunnan, Burma and India. About 300,000 Kachins live in China, and 70,000 in India. Fearing a possible incursion of Chinese agitators, the government of India closed the war-time Ledo road from Margherita, in Assam to China via Myitkyina (Burma) in March, 1951. The closing of this vital trade route has affected the prosperity of the Burmese Kachins and led to demands for a re-opening of the roads . . . Kachin State is free of Communist rebellions so far, but many disaffected Kachins are known to have migrated to China to receive training in Marxist ideology and techniques of class warfare. Forty, wearing the uniforms of Chinese Communist guerillas, are reported to have penetrated 180 miles into Burma and linked up with Burma Communists at Tagaung.

Several (Kachin) hereditary chiefs have authority on both sides of the border and reportedly are carrying Communist ideas among the Kachins.

Than Maung also refers to similar activity among the Kachins.[40] During the period of Chou En-lai's first visit to Rangoon in 1954, a number of Burman newspapers openly expressed their anxiety over infiltration among the Kachins, the Shans, and the people of the Wa State.[41] Similar reports continued to appear between this time and the outbreak of the serious border incursions in mid-1956.[42] On the Chinese side, the change in Chinese Communist tactics as previously noted led to the creation of various autonomous areas in Yunnan beginning in 1954, which could well constitute a springboard for stimulation of separatist movements along the frontier area. Such a development still remains a real possibility.

Still another aspect of the general problem of subversion and infiltration has been the border crossings of whole groups of tribal people who apparently have been able to leave Yunnan as refugees and settle in with their compatriots on the Burma side. From 1951 to date, there have been public reports of what may be called "refugee infiltration." Since it is difficult for either the Burma or Chinese Communist Government fully to police all possible transborder routes along the 900-mile frontier, it is impossible to determine the numbers of persons entering Burma or to determine the extent to which the Chinese Communist authorities have been lenient in permitting this flow. Some Burman officials and some Army officers have expressed anxiety over this "refugee" problem as marking the beginning of a larger migration, not only of transborder tribal groups, but also of Chinese, which could have serious political and economic implications for Burma. It is also suspected that the Chinese Communists may be sending agents with these groups of refugees who will establish themselves on the Burma side and can be used later to stir up trouble and disaffection.

During late 1957 and into 1959, there were constant reports of border crossings by groups numbering anywhere from 50 to 500 and over 1,000. On November 22, it was reported that there were more than 10,000 illegal immigrants from Yunnan in the area of the Wa State and the northern Shan states. These numbers, mostly members of transborder tribal groups, also were reported to include many hundred of persons of Chinese stock who were alleged to have fled to Burma to escape the harsh restrictions of the Chinese Commune system.

During the first half of 1959, three events occurred which many observers believed would have the effect of opening the eyes of Burmans to the evils of Communism as seen by the West. The first was the brutal suppression of the Tibetan revolt by the Chinese Communists and the consequent flight of the Dalai Lama and thousands of Tibetans to India as refugees. Here, believed some observers, was an Asian equivalent of the Hungarian affair close at home where the facts seemed clear and abundant. Burman public reaction was one of immediate shock, soon to be followed by indifference to a problem about which the Burma government could do nothing and a cause which it would certainly not wish to make its own. Passive interest in the Tibetan affair perhaps illustrated as much as anything the effects of long isolation by Burma from the main stream of world events and the consequent lack of desire to be participants in any way in them.

The other two events occurred within Burma, amid considerable press publicity and were similar in character. In April and again in June, there were two defections of officers of the Soviet Embassy in Rangoon, the first unsuccessful and the second successful. Both served to demonstrate the nature of Communist regimes and provide evidence on the problem of subversion. On April 28, 1959, an officer of the Soviet Embassy (later identified as Colonel Mikkail Stryguine) was brought to the Rangoon General Hospital, suffering from what the press described as "hypnotic poisoning." While there he voiced "invectives" against the Soviet Union and was reported to have jumped from the hospital window to avoid arrest. He was overpowered by fellow officers of the Soviet Embassy, and according to the press, taken home and given strong sedatives. It was intimated that he would be taken out of the country by the Embassy at the first opportunity. Here was a story which the Soviet Embassy could not keep quiet. On the next day a number of reporters from *The Nation* and *The Guardian Daily* began a vigil at the airport in an attempt to see whether he would be spirited out of Rangoon and, if possible, to interview him before his departure. On May 3, Colonel Stryguine was taken to the airport by Soviet Embassy officials and hustled aboard a Chinese Communist Civil Aviation Company plane. The reporters who attempted to intercept him for an interview or state-ment were "manhandled" by Soviet officials.

The next day some forty newspaper reporters demonstrated in front of the Soviet Embassy and a near riot ensued. According to press reports in *The Guardian* and *The Nation*, officials of the Em-bassy attempted to break up the demonstration, using chairs as weapons against the "tomatoes and other fruit" hurled by the report-ers. It was stated that a press photographer was dragged into the Embassy, beaten, and that his camera was taken away from him. The Burma Reporters Association next day convened an emergency meeting in protest and passed a resolution asking all newspapers to black out all publicity materials issued by the Soviet Embassy in retaliation. The circumstances surrounding this attempted defection of the Soviet Military Attaché was given a full airing in the Burma press. On June 8, a new Soviet Ambassador presented his credentials to the Burma Government.[43]

On June 26, the American Embassy announced that one Alex Urevitch Kaznacheev, twenty-seven years of age and an Informa-tion Officer in the Soviet Embassy, had asked for, and had been granted protection in the Embassy. The next day, the Embassy ar-ranged for him to meet the press and answer questions. He stated that he was disillusioned with Communism and with the kind of work he was doing and was seeking asylum in the free world. The same day, the Burma Foreign Office issued a press communiqué stating that, since the Union Government does not recognize the right of any Embassy or Legation to offer asylum which covers protection, the Government was "considering" the position of Kaznacheev. There was also a press report that a "U.S. Air Force Globemaster" had arrived at Mingaladon airport from Manila.

On June 29, the American Ambassador, Walter McConaughy, pro-duced Kaznacheev before the Burma Foreign Minister at the Na-tional Defense College and transferred him to the protection of the Burma Government. It was reported that the Foreign Minister and "other appropriate officials" interrogated him at length. It was also reported that the Burma Government had offered the Soviet Am-bassador an opportunity to meet and question Kaznacheev but that this offer had been declined. With this development, the Burma Government took the position that since Kaznacheev had left the

Soviet Embassy of his own free will, the government would permit him to go anywhere he liked. This statement was apparently made at the conference at the National Defense College, whereupon Kaznacheev announced that he chose to go to the United States. At the end of the conference he "stepped into the American Ambassador's car and made for the airport where he boarded the special U. S. Air Force plane which took off for Manila at 4:47 P.M."

On July 1, the tape-recorded statement made by Kaznacheev at the American Embassy was released to the press. In the statement, according to the Burmese press, Kaznacheev revealed "the miserable living conditions of the people in the Soviet Union and their growing hatred of the Communist regime." More importantly, his tape-recorded statement gave a rather full account of espionage and intelligence activities in Burma and also of some of the activities of the Chinese Communist Embassy. It is known that in his interviews with Burma Government officials prior to his departure, he was quite specific, naming Burmese who were employed as agents by the Soviet and Chinese Embassies in Rangoon and giving amounts of money paid to various persons. This successful defection, coming right on top of the case of Colonel Stryguine, and being fully reported in the press, represented concrete evidence to the Burmans of the nature of Soviet and Chinese Communist activities in Burma. The circumstances of both cases constituted open, visible evidence of Communist subversion, as one reporter put it, "right in our own front yard." These facts and events could not be dismissed as propaganda.

Dramatic as these two events were, they were soon forgotten by all except those few in the Burma government whose business it is to deal with problems of subversion and espionage. Certainly, as far as the public and the politicians were concerned, this firsthand view of Soviet methods did not seem to affect their attitudes toward the Communist bloc. The government contented itself with asserting that Burma's internal security forces would increase their vigilance against subversion and espionage. The basic principles of Burma's neutralist policy remained unquestioned and unchanged.

The Sino-Burman Border Settlement and Its Consequences

Throughout fourteen years as a neutralist nation, Burma has faced no international problem as vital to its security or to its future as that posed by the border dispute with Communist China. In essence, this had been a territorial dispute between two states with conflicting claims like many such disputes in the history of international frontiers. In a broader context, however, this dispute has involved basic issues in cold war politics as well as providing one more instance of the essential struggle between the two power blocs for influence over the unaligned nations. The dispute was the only serious territorial problem the Burma government inherited from British rule, for the British had neglected or failed to provide the new Burma state with an internationally defined northern frontier. The problem was settled peacefully only after thirteen years and the Burma government's resolution of this difficult issue may yet produce results which will bear directly on its fixed policy of neutralism.

From the beginning, the Burma government considered that the problem of their inherited undemarcated frontier with China was wholly bilateral, a problem for settlement between the two parties concerned. Fortunately, perhaps, for Burma, this territorial dispute with their big northern neighbor never assumed the importance of a Kashmir or a West Irian (Dutch New Guinea), both of which were legacies left by colonial powers to newly independent nations. Even in the fall of 1956, when it appeared that real trouble between Burma and Communist China might be brewing on the frontier, the dispute remained bilateral and little attention was paid to this border problem. The Suez crisis and the Hungarian revolt seemed far more important, and probably were more important as issues in the cold war. Furthermore, since the dispute was settled by peaceful agreement, little attention has been given to the terms of settlement, for too many other problems await solution, are causing international concern and demand "headline" treatment.

It is not necessary here to present all of the details of this dispute. The technical and legal points at issue have been covered elsewhere.[44] As a concluding section of this discussion of Burma's relations with Communist China, the border dispute provides an example of how the Burma government applied its principles of neutralism in a case clearly affecting its vital interests. The dénouement of this dispute also provides some sidelights on Chinese Communist policy toward Burma and the rest of Asia.

From the beginning, many Burman officials were concerned about the Sino-Burman frontier area. The difficulty of policing the border both to prevent infiltration of persons from Communist China and to control smuggling, as well as the variety of problems presented by the existence of transborder tribal minority groups have been mentioned. All Burmans in the government or in the Burma Army who had any responsibility for the northern border areas were also aware that until a demarcated boundary had been agreed to with the Chinese Communist regime, their difficulties would not lessen and might, at any time, grow worse. Likewise, a number of high Burman officials were aware of British attempts to obtain China's agreement to the so-called MacMahon line and the later "Iselin" line in the northeast without success. Establishment of Chinese Communist control over Tibet in 1950 served to emphasize the desirability, from Burma's point of view, of reaching agreement for border demarcation along both the northwest and the northeast sectors of the border with China.

Until 1952, it appears that the Chinese Communist regime regarded the border question with Burma as a relatively unimportant matter which might be dealt with eventually, since it was not responsive to reported queries on the matter by the Burma government. A principal cause for this apparent lack of interest seems to have been due to the uncertainty in Peking over the outcome of the Communist armed rebellion in Burma. As long as there was some chance that the Burma Communists might overthrow the AFPFL government, it was unnecessary for the Chinese Communists to question the traditional prewar frontier. By 1952, the situation had changed. It was obvious that the underground Burma Communists and their aboveground supporters were too divided and had neither the organization nor the discipline to seriously threaten the existence of the AFPFL government without outside help. The Burma government, however, was facing a threat from another source: the large number of refugee Kuomintang troops who had fled into northeast Burma from the Chinese Communists. At this time the Burman leaders were unsure whether these refugee troops would find means to link up with the Karen or even the Communist insurgents and thus provide the extra support needed for a successful rebellion. They were even more afraid that the presence of these refugee troops would provide a rational excuse for a "mopping up" operation by

Chinese Communist forces from Yunnan. Past experience indicated that Chinese troops of any color in Burmese territory were difficult to dislodge.

In retrospect, it would seem that if the Peking regime had had any ideas that occupation of territory in northeast Burma, from which infiltration of Thailand and Laos would have been possible, would serve its interests, then the presence of the Kuomintang troops in Burma was an opportunity worth exploiting. The leaders of the AFPFL government believe that their pursuit of a neutralist policy and their sincere efforts to demonstrate Burma's friendliness toward Communist China in this period were responsible for saving the Burma government from getting into serious trouble with their northern neighbor before "friendship" had begun to ripen. It is also possible that the situation in Korea, that of Formosa and the offshore islands, and the war in Indo-China were all regarded by Mao Tsetung and his colleagues as of far greater importance than the KMT problem in Burma. It is fairly certain that the Peking regime, anxious to protect its southern flank, was quite content to let the Burma army fight the Kuomintang troops and the Burma government take the responsibility for getting them out of Burma.

The attention focused on this KMT problem and on the pi tion of Burma's request for help to the United Nations by Burma government officials tended to obscure for a while what now appears to be a shift in Chinese Communist policy and border diplomacy. As mentioned earlier, both Communist China and the Soviet Union seemed to have "discovered" Burma in 1953–54. As far as Peking was concerned, the basis of closer relations, begun in 1953, was firmly established by the joint acceptance by U Nu and Chou En-lai of the "Five Principles of Peaceful Co-Existence" in June, 1954. During this year and in 1955 when U Nu and Chou En-lai were cooperating at Bandung and exchanging friendly visits, some Burman leaders and some segments of the Burma press became disturbed by reports of Chinese Communist publications being distributed in Asia containing maps which showed large areas in northeast and northwest Burma as well as larger areas of Assam and Kashmir apparently claimed by Communist China.

This "battle of the maps," reported with some facetiousness in the western press on occasion, led to denials in Peking, Delhi, and Rangoon that any serious disputes over the undemarcated frontier existed which could not be amicably settled in accordance with the "spirit of the Five Principles." In Burma, there was more privately expressed concern because of a reported direct clash in 1955 between Burman army units and Chinese Communist troops in the northeast Wa State, within traditionally Burma territory. At a suggestion that both Burman and Chinese forces withdraw behind the 1941 "Iselin line" it was reported that the Peking regime informed the Burma government it did not recognize a boundary "imposed by the British." [45] Available evidence suggests that the Chinese Communists seeing little hope of successful "liberation from within" in Burma or India, decided that the undemarcated portions of both the Burman and Indian frontiers gave them a good bargaining weapon. By making large claims of territory south of the traditional frontiers, Peking could later appear magnanimous in giving up all or part of such claims in the interests of peaceful settlement of "differences" and "friendly relations." This is exactly what happened when the Sino-Burman border negotiations finally took place. [46]

The foregoing analysis, however, does not fully explain the sudden and seemingly serious border trouble that flared up in July, 1956, and continued to the early part of 1957. As seen by some of the leading Rangoon newspapers, this trouble amounted to no less than an armed "invasion" of Burman territory by Chinese Communist forces. Reports filtering into Rangoon of border incursions by Chinese Communist troops were denied by the Burma government prior to this time, but enough information accumulated in June and July, 1956, to cause the Rangoon newspaper, *The Nation,* to dispatch a team of reporters to the frontier for an on-the-spot investigation. [47] On July 31, *The Nation* broke the story with a three-column front-page report of "an invasion" by Chinese Communist troops into the northeast Wa State. Almost daily reports were published in *The Nation* and other papers for the next six months. Border crossings and the destruction of boundary pillars by Chinese Communist troops were reported from the Kachin state and along part of the wartime Ledo road.

At first the Chinese Communists denied that any border crossings had taken place asserting, as did the Burma government initially, that military units seen were really Burma army troops, a case of "mistaken identity." When these denials could no longer serve because of eyewitness accounts of Red Chinese troops seen within Burma territory, the Burma government acknowledged the incursions but insisted that press accounts were greatly exaggerated. The Peking regime, in turn, admitted its troops had crossed the border, but insisted they had only gone into "disputed territory" and hence their action could not be called "an invasion." Alarm was expressed by the Kachins and other minority groups along the frontier that Chinese Communist infiltration was only a prelude to occupation of all disputed territory shown on the maps.

During this period, U Nu was out of office and U Ba Swe was premier but the border problem was deemed sufficiently serious so that when the Peking regime intimated there was really no cause for alarm and the whole matter could be adjusted, U Nu accepted an invitation to go to Peking for a conference on September 22, 1956. Although he went in his capacity as President of the AFPFL, he was welcomed almost as a state guest and an official Burma government delegation followed him in less than a week with "full powers to negotiate a border settlement." [48] On his return to Rangoon, U Nu announced that Communist China had agreed to a border settlement "in principle," along the traditional frontier except for three Kachin village tracts of Hpimaw, Gawlun, and Kanfang which were to be transferred to China along with the "Namwan assigned tract." The latter had been held by Britain under perpetual lease with the predecessor Chinese government which the Chinese Communists had ousted.

The Rangoon press immediately dubbed this settlement "in principle" a "package deal." Although there were protests by the Kachins and some mild mass demonstrations, the final border settlement did not vary greatly from this "package deal." It involved transfer to Communist China of three small areas which might be regarded as having some strategic significance, but hardly of great importance to the security of Burma's frontier. Before the transfer of territory actually took place, the inhabitants were removed to new settlements within Burma territory.

It is difficult to see what this flare-up of border trouble in 1956 gained Peking. On-the-spot reports indicated that those Chinese Communist troops which did cross the traditional frontier were not prepared to remain and establish a new boundary nor was there any evidence that any force was being readied in Yunnan for occupation or "invasion." It was unnecessary for the Chinese Communists to use the troop movements to bring pressure on the Burma government to negotiate a border settlement which it was only too anxious to do. Two factors may have influenced the Peking regime. First, by sending troops into "disputed territory" Mao Tse-tung and his colleagues could withdraw them behind the traditional frontier as part of their magnanimous gesture of "peace and friendship." Second, there may have been more than a coincidence in the fact that by July, 1956, it was public knowledge that the Burma government was negotiating with the United States for a resumption of its economic aid.[49] It is possible that the leaders in Peking believed a border threat and show of force might deter the Burma government from close U. S. ties. Whether the above is correct or not, the border incursions did give both the Chinese Communists and Burma armed forces an opportunity to get better acquainted with the terrain of the frontier area, an advantage to both sides.

The border trouble of 1956 now seems to be a rather minor episode in Sino-Burman relations, but the delay in negotiations following U Nu's agreement to the "package deal" has more significance. During all of 1957, U Nu was frequently questioned about the progress of negotiations with the Chinese Communists and usually replied that matters were proceeding. It now seems clear that the Peking regime was in no real hurry to complete the negotiations. Minor questions were raised concerning the exact pieces of territory to be transferred to Communist China and still no real agreement was reached. Until late September, 1958, the Burma government was torn by the split in the AFPFL and little could be done. There is evidence that General Ne Win was anxious to achieve a definitive border agreement and that during 1959 attempted to arrange for negotiations. The Chinese Communists frequently changed their position, but finally permitted General Ne Win to crown his term of office as head of the military caretaker government by signing a border treaty in January, 1960.

General Ne Win returned to Rangoon, not only with a treaty providing for a demarcation of the whole Sino-Burman frontier, but also with a new treaty of "Friendship and Mutual Non-Aggression." [50]

In October, 1960, U Nu once again Prime Minister, went to Peking to sign the border agreement by which joint survey teams were to be put to work actually establishing the boundary and placing markers along the whole frontier. Late in December, Chou En-lai arrived in Rangoon with a delegation of over 400 and remained to help celebrate the thirteenth anniversary of Burma's independence. As a part of the ceremonies, the two premiers exchanged ratifications for their respective governments of two Sino-Burman treaties. U Nu and General Ne Win both went to Peking again in October, 1961, to celebrate the anniversary of the Chinese Communist "revolution" and to sign the final agreements and protocols of the border settlement.

Publicly, at least, the border settlement was hailed by the Burman leaders of all factions as an outsanding demonstration of the efficacy of Burma's neutralism which emphasizes friendly relations with all countries. In both Burma and Communist China, the border settlement was publicized as a triumphal application of the "Five Principles of Peaceful Co-Existence." Officially, the two treaties were said to signalize a "new era" of peace and friendship between Burma and Communist China. As a concrete demonstration of this closer relationship, when Chou En-lai was in Rangoon in January, 1961, he announced that the Peking regime had granted Burma a credit in the equivalent of 30 million pounds sterling, with interest repayable only after the first ten years. Trade missions were exchanged and arrangements made to expand commerce overland between the two countries.

Both publicly and privately, most politically conscious Burmans felt that Burma had gained a great deal from the final border settlement. Those who were somewhat cynical about China's adherence to the "Five Principles" usually asserted that with a demarcated frontier, there would be no future disputes over aggression by Chinese troops into "disputed territory" and that Burma would be foolish not to develop friendly and closer ties with the big nation on her own border. If anything was needed to vindicate Burma's neutralist policy in the minds of the Burmans, the Sino-Burman treaties clinched the argument.

Enough time has passed since General Ne Win signed the border treaty and the nonaggression pact in Peking to be able to assess the results and to determine some of the consequences of this new Sino-

Burman *rapprochement*. It could not be expected that any Burman politician of consequence would publicly admit that a result of the border settlement was to draw Burma much closer to Communist China and make Burma "less neutral" toward the West. Burman leaders could point out that their government had agreed to additional aid from the United States, accepted another World Bank loan, and arranged for a series of technical assistance projects from West Germany and other non-Communist countries. They could easily deny that there was any special significance in the fact that Communist China had become the largest single customer for export rice, for the Burma government will still sell to any nation willing to buy at a good price. Burma leaders also see no special significance in the expanding trade and commercial relations with Communist China, pointing to this as a natural development resulting from elimination of any difference between the two countries. Similarly, they believe sincerely that the border settlement and nonaggression pact prove the efficacy of Burma's neutralist foreign policy as well as attesting to Peking's good faith in following the "Five Principles of Peaceful Co-Existence."

These developments in Sino-Burman relations must be viewed, not just through Burman eyes, but in the broader context of Chinese Communist policy in Asia and Burma's future position vis-à-vis her big neighbor. The first question to be answered concerns the motives of the Peking regime in finally agreeing to a definitive border settlement and nonaggression pact. One obvious motive, recognized by the Burman leaders, was to enable Chou En-lai to demonstrate to Prime Minister Nehru that a border settlement could be reached by peaceful negotiations in which the traditional border lines were accepted with only slight adjustments. In the Burma settlement, only three small pieces of territory were transferred to China and in return the Chinese presumably gave up claims to much larger territory.[51] The record of the Sino-Indian border talks indicate that Chou En-lai reportedly was willing to forego claims to considerable territory in northeast India in return for Indian agreement to "give up" a considerable portion of northern Ladakh where the Chinese Communists were in occupation and had built a road and several frontier posts. To the Chinese Communists, such an offer would seem reasonable and in accord with the precedent set with Burma. To date, the

Indian government has stood firm on claiming sovereignty up to the traditional prewar boundary.

A more significant motive is found in the conclusion of the treaty of "friendship and mutual non-aggression." To the Burmans, signing such a treaty and giving up small bits of Burman territory, seemed a fair bargain in return for agreement on a fixed frontier. In Rangoon and Peking, the nonaggression treaty was hailed as a firm restatement of the "Five Principles," which it is, but there is one important clause in this treaty which seems to have escaped public comment. Article III provides that "each Contracting Party undertakes not to carry out acts of aggression against the other and *not to take part in any military alliance directed against the other Contracting Party.*" [52] This is the first such treaty Burma has signed with any nation and the first such treaty signed by Communist China with any non-Communist state.

By agreeing to this treaty, the Burma government has formally limited its freedom of action in respect to its self-defense. It would bar the Burma government from making any defense arrangements with non-Communist nations in Asia or elsewhere or providing for outside military assistance in future contingencies if the Chinese Communists wanted to object under the terms of this treaty. In effect, the treaty gives to the Peking regime a veto over Burma's future foreign relations in respect to military defense since it is clear that the Chinese Communists would interpret this clause to suit their own purposes at the time. Since the Chinese Communists already have their mutual defense agreement with the U.S.S.R., this treaty does not tie their hands. On the contrary, it would seem that the Peking regime regards this type of nonaggression treaty as an instrument of its Asian policy, having earlier concluded such treaties with the North Korean and the North Vietnam regimes and with Afghanistan in April, 1960. It has been reported that Chou En-lai proposed such a treaty in one of his discussions with Prime Minister Nehru and that it was suggested by the Chinese Communists in their border negotiations with Nepal. A first consequence of the Sino-Burman border settlement, therefore, is that the nonaggression pact with Communist China now constitutes a limitation on Burma's freedom of action in foreign affairs for the future.

A second consequence flows from the agreement between Burma

and Communist China to develop closer and more extensive economic and cultural ties, embodied in Article IV of the nonaggression
treaty. The very process of negotiations and subsequent surveys of
the border and of implementation of trade agreements and the use
of the large Chinese Communist credit have all resulted in more extensive and closer contacts between Burma government officials at
all levels and their Chinese Communist counterparts. When two
countries expand their official and trade relations across a common
border there is always a net residue of greater understanding and
accommodation toward each other. When one country is a big power
and its neighbor is small and weak, however, the net result is to increase the influence of the larger over the smaller associate. Before
1960, there were high-level official missions between Burma and
Communist China and exchange of good-will missions but these exchanges were sporadic and beyond the desire to have "friendly relations" the Burma government had developed no fixed pattern in its
relations with its big neighbor.

After General Ne Win's trip to Peking in January, 1960, to sign the
border treaty and nonaggression pact, Chou En-lai visited Rangoon
in April for talks with U Nu and his colleagues before going to New
Delhi to see Nehru about the Indian border problem. In October,
1960, U Nu and a delegation of nearly 300 went to Peking to sign
the treaty establishing procedures for the border demarcation. At
the same time a Chinese Communist delegation came to Rangoon to
begin a survey of Sino-Burman trade possibilities. In December,
1960, Chou En-lai brought a delegation of over 400 from Peking to
Rangoon, where the ratifications of the border and nonaggression
treaties were exchanged, the public offer of the large Chinese Communist credit to Burma was made, and further talks on trade were
held. In April, 1961, U Nu and Chou met for a special conference in
Yunnan and there was a further exchange of agricultural and trade
missions. Again, in October, 1961, U Nu, General Ne Win and a
large delegation attended celebrations in Peking on the final border
demarcation.

Meantime the Burma government established two official committees with Chinese Communist counterparts to work out the details of implementation of the Chinese Communist credit, which
although stated in terms of pounds sterling does not apparently in-

volve use of any other than Chinese Communist and Burman currencies for the various projects to be agreed to. While it is too early to assert that the Chinese Communist credit provides the Peking regime with a lever not only to open up trade between the two countries, but also to exert influence on the Burma government's acceptance of economic aid from other sources, the amount, approximately $85,000,000, must necessarily force considerable expansion of Sino-Burman trade and use of Chinese Communist technicians in Burma, with the natural consequence of diminution in economic aid and use of technicians from other countries.[53]

Here indeed, unless unforeseen events cause a rupture, is a new era in Sino-Burman relations. The Burmans and the Chinese appear to get along very well with each other. Burmans have always been impressed with the "discipline" they saw in Communist China, and they have an inherent respect for Chinese culture and civilization which is "Asian." Continued and increased "working together" by the Burmans and the Chinese Communists will most probably exert a subtle influence on Burman attitudes, and result in an increase of Chinese Communist influence in many aspects of Burman life, and even on the conduct of Burman foreign policy. It should be noted too, that there has been an increased number of "good-will" military missions traveling back and forth, and it is quite possible some informal "understandings" have resulted regarding the problem of the remaining KMT troops and other insurgents in northeast Burma. All of these developments would incline the Burma government to be even more reluctant than in the past to take any action or position which might be contrary to Chinese Communist policy. In reality, it would seem that maintenance of "friendly and peaceful relations" with Communist China has now become a principal cornerstone of Burma's neutralist policy.

There is still a third consequence of the border settlement which should be noted. This relates to the new position of Burma within the broad framework of Chinese Communist strategy in Asia. Assuming that western analysis is correct in asserting that both the U.S.S.R. and Communist China have concluded since 1957–58 that the real balance of strength in the cold war has shifted to the side of the Communist bloc as a whole and assuming that the leaders in Peking will continue to act on their premise that "wars of liberation" are just wars and hence must be supported, it is valid to conclude that in Burma the Chinese Communists have found a new outlet to the world and a potential position of strength for activity elsewhere in Asia. Burma is the one Asian country with which the Chinese Communists have had the longest and most consistently friendly relations. The Burma government has consistently supported the admission of the Peking regime to the United Nations and on all crucial questions such as the KMT problem, has acted in full consultation with the Chinese Communists.

In the evolution of Chinese Communist policy toward Burma, therefore, the recent Sino-Burman *rapprochement* has given to Communist China an open door to the world through a friendly country and has enabled Chinese Communist influence to reach the shores of the Bay of Bengal. Burma is the only friendly non-Communist territory through which the Chinese Communists can come and go, and through which delegations and official missions from Africa, Latin America, and the rest of Asia can come and go with ease. The Chinese Communist airline terminating in Rangoon provides this easy means of communication for people and the port of Rangoon provides an easy means of ingress for critical commodities through a country whose government is not allied in any way with Peking's enemies, the United States and its allies.

On the Burma side of this picture, it may well be that the new entente between Burma and its big neighbor to the north will compromise Burma's traditional neutralism so that in the future, it will be more difficult for any Burma government to take any position on an international issue on the basis of "right" action unless it is in accord with the interests of the Peking regime. In all of U Nu's speeches since the summer of 1956, he attempted to justify Burma's neutralism by the assertion that his government has acted on what it believed was "right." He asserted that actions in support of positions taken by the Communist bloc states was balanced by Burma's condemnation of the Soviet armed action in Hungary. This is the only crucial international issue in the past six years on which Burma aligned itself against the Communist bloc. There have been other international issues in the cold war of equal import, but these have found Burma taking a passive position or openly aligned on the side of the Communists.

Burman leaders will argue that the geographic location plus the small size and weakness of their country dictates no other course than that of "close, cordial and friendly" relations with Communist China. It is hard to refute the logic of this point of view and it is probable that so long as the leaders of any Burma government see no other alternative which offers better results and better safeguards for their country's security, they will continue to pursue a neutralist policy firmly based on their *entente cordiale* with Communist China. Whether such a policy, which seems to make the Burma government more dependent upon decisions taken in Peking and less free to take the "right" action when it chooses, can still be called "positive neutrality" is open to question. What does seem clear is the fact that Burma's relationship to Communist China is not simply one of "friendly" relations between two sovereign states, but has become one which, from the Burman point of view, might be characterized by the slogan from George Orwell's *1984* — "Big Brother is Watching You!"

— VI —

BURMA'S PARTICIPATION IN THE UNITED NATIONS

T HE record of any nation's participation in the United Nations is a good test of that nation's application of its foreign policy. The variety of issues and problems coming before the General Assembly require a continuous process of decision-making by each member nation, in which inconsistencies or deviations from announced principles are apparent. There is a sharp focus of public attention on positions taken on resolutions before the General Assembly or its standing committees which is not found with respect to specific actions taken by a nation outside of the United Nations. For the more powerful nations, the United Nations is at once a public forum, a locus of power politics, and an instrument for the conduct of foreign policy. For the smaller nations, like Burma, the United Nations is a public forum, a convenient mechanism for conduct of diplomacy, a source of economic and other kinds of assistance and, only on occasion, an instrument of foreign policy.

Since 1945, both large and small nations have found that there are both advantages and disadvantages to United Nations' membership. There are many times when a large nation has no desire to subject some aspect of its foreign policy to UN debate and to the glare of worldwide publicity. Many large nations have preferred to carry out their foreign policy objectives without reference to the United Nations. All of the large nations, however, have consistently used the mechanism of the Security Council and the General Assembly to advance their foreign policy objectives. They have also been able to overcome some of the disadvantages of their UN membership by adopting alternative courses of action.

A small nation, like Burma, generally has more difficulty in over-coming some of the disadvantages of UN membership and of making full use of the advantages of such membership. Yet for large or small nations, their record in the General Assembly does provide a yard-stick with which to measure the application of their publicly an-nounced foreign policy principles. Because each nation must go on record on a variety of international issues and problems, it is com-pelled to keep its policies under review. In this study of Burma's foreign policy since independence, Burma's record in the United Nations provides a means by which the basic principles of its foreign policy can be analyzed in the light of their application on issues in which the Burma government has had a vital interest and on other issues of less vital interest on which the Burma government had to take a position. In doing this, it is first necessary to examine briefly the advantages and disadvantages of UN membership for the con-duct of Burma's foreign relations. This will be followed by an exam-ination of two problems brought before the United Nations in which Burma had a vital interest — the Korean War and the pressure of KMT troops in upper Burma. A brief survey of Burma's position on a selected group of problems will provide a basis for some conclu-sions.

Advantages and Disadvantages of UN Membership

The Nu-Atlee agreement provided for British sponsorship of Bur-ma's admission to the United Nations. The new Burma Government was quick to apply for membership in the United Nations and Burma became a member early in 1948. It is doubtful whether the AFPFL leaders stopped to consider what positive advantages might accrue from joining the United Nations beyond the assumption that the security provisions of the UN Charter might serve to protect their independence. It is certainly true that the AFPFL leaders, like those of other small, new, and independent nations, did not stop to con-sider what disadvantages there might be to UN membership. It was taken for granted that membership in the United Nations was a nat-ural consequence of independence and a symbol of the achievement of national sovereignty. In the intervening years, Burma's leaders have learned much and at present view their country's participation in the United Nations with mixed feelings, as do the leaders of many other nations.

First of all, the United Nations must be considered a world forum. It is the one place where the statements of representatives of any nation on any issue can achieve the maximum publicity. Concentrated at the UN headquarters in New York are all the mechanisms and organs of mass communications, the representatives of the world press and radio networks, the facilities for getting attention around the world. For a small, somewhat isolated nation, like Burma, this is often a real advantage. If Prime Minister U Nu or any high Burman official makes a speech in Rangoon, it will receive relatively little attention in the world press, and official reports to other governments will be limited to those having missions in Burma, and on receipt in foreign offices may well be overlooked by high officials. On the other hand, when the representative of Burma speaks in the General Assembly or in its committees, he has a much larger official and public audience. An illustration of this is found at the time of the Hungarian crisis in the fall of 1956. The Burman representative in the Assembly spoke in justification of Burma's strong stand condemning Soviet intervention in Hungary and ended with the words, "There, but for the grace of God, go we." Not only was Burma's departure from a "neutral" position noticed officially by all governments, but the Burman representative's speech received a worldwide press.[1] In the same period, speeches by U Ba Swe, then Prime Minister, in Colombo, Bombay, and New Delhi, taking the same position, were not widely reported. His press conference held on his return to Rangoon, in which he affirmed Burma's official stand, was virtually unreported abroad in the press and was not even known by some diplomatic representatives in Burma.

Burma has a limited number of diplomatic missions in other countries, and news reporting from Burma is spotty and in the hands of local representatives of only a few international news services. The forum of the General Assembly is, therefore, a distinct advantage as a means of publicizing Burma's policy on a given issue. The record of Burma's conduct of foreign relations, however, gives little evidence that Burman officials have fully appreciated this advantage, certainly not to the same extent as some other small nations.

The foregoing advantage, however, is offset in many instances by a disadvantage that may even cause embarrassment in the conduct of a country's foreign relations. If the United Nations Assembly and its committees are a forum for both small and large nations, they are also a forum where every participant must "stand up and be counted." It is certain that many issues have been debated before the Assembly committees on which the Burma Government did not wish to take a stand, about which Burma leaders knew very little, and perhaps cared even less. Nevertheless, the Burma representatives must vote, almost daily, during Assembly sessions on a whole host of problems and issues. To be sure, the Burma government can instruct its delegation to abstain on questions with which it is not familiar, but abstention for these reasons does Burma no credit.

The General Assembly also has some of the aspects of a legislature in its proceedings. At every session there are a few issues that do concern Burma and on which the Government wishes to take a stand and make its position known. If the Burma delegation hopes to do more than publicize its position, that is, if it hopes to be influential in adoption of a particular resolution, then its delegation must be ready and willing to lend support to the proposals of other members regarding questions about which it may have much less concern. This kind of political "vote-trading" is no less a feature of the United Nations Assembly than of any legislature in any free country. Disadvantages which may result from this kind of politics, however, are somewhat offset for Burma in the operation of the so-called Afro-Asian bloc at the UN. As an active member of this group, the Burma delegation is able to join with other nations generally pursuing a policy of nonalignment with either bloc in the cold war. By so doing, the Burma government may be better able to obtain support for its position on a specific issue, while still retaining considerable freedom of action.[2]

When the Burman Government has taken a position the leaders believe to be right, as on the Hungarian issue, and that position is contrary to Soviet policy, it finds itself subjected to considerable pressure from the representatives of the Communst bloc. Maintaining an "independent" and "neutral" policy under these circumstances is often difficult, and Burman officials at the UN and in Rangoon have stated privately that they wish Burma did not have to expose its foreign policy to such intense public gaze on every problem, large or small, that is brought before the United Nations.

Another disadvantage for Burma, linked to the above, is the fact that the Burman officials have had little experience to guide them other than that gained in the world of the United Nations. One sophisticated Burman representative expressed it as follows:

We have had no experience with the 'old diplomacy' when a nation's foreign policy was its own business and could be kept away from public gaze. We only feel at times that in the United Nations we are involved in 'gold-fish bowl diplomacy,' constantly forced to explain our position on obscure problems about which we know little, constantly having to justify our policies to the press in New York, and we must be continually alert to political pressures from all sides. Under these conditions, diplomacy — particularly United Nations diplomacy — can become a strain on the very few seasoned officials we have available.

The second aspect of Burma's participation in the United Nations affecting the conduct of its foreign relations is the fact that the United Nations is one central, almost worldwide diplomatic mission. Headquartered in New York are the diplomatic representatives of more than a hundred nations, as well as the services of a highly qualified staff of specialists in the UN Secretariat. This is a decided advantage to a small and relatively poor nation such as Burma. The Government of Burma maintains diplomatic relations with over twenty-five countries but has established diplomatic missions in a fewer number of capitals. At United Nations headquarters, however, it is possible for the Burma representatives to undertake official or semiofficial business with representatives from all of the member nations. Foreign Office officials in Rangoon have stated that Burma cannot afford too many diplomatic missions abroad and, at present, does not need them because of the facilities afforded at the United Nations headquarters in New York.

Not only does the existence of the UN provide a means of easy and inexpensive official contact with many nations, it also enables the Burma representatives at the United Nations to become acquainted with the problems of other nations and learn much more about them than would otherwise be the case. Likewise, the facilities of the UN Secretariat, as well as those of the UN Specialized Agencies, provide the Burma Government with a vast amount of information that it would be difficult to obtain through bilateral means.

It is doubtful if the Burma Foreign Office and its representatives at the UN have fully realized this advantage or have made effective use of UN facilities, and information from UN sources. UN materials, reports, studies, and the like flow into Rangoon and are distributed throughout the government, presumably to the government office within whose responsibility the subject falls. For the most part, this large amount of documentation becomes lost or stored away, and no records are kept of the total flow. The Burma Government is still not organized to utilize these UN services.

A third aspect of Burma's participation in the United Nations is found in the complex structure of the organization. After being admitted to membership in 1948, the Burma Government had to determine the extent to which it would seek membership in the various organs of the UN and in its specialized agencies. For a small nation, lacking trained personnel in all fields at home, representation in the various organs and agencies in the UN system has been a severe strain on its small trained man-power resources and a strain on its budget. Between 1947 and 1949, Burma joined eight of the Specialized Agencies of the UN.[3] In 1952 Burma became a member of the International Bank for Reconstruction and Development and the International Monetary Fund. Burma was one of the sponsors of the International Finance Corporation, and the Burma Government was an original party to the General Agreement on Trade and Tariffs. In addition to membership in the above agencies, Burma has participated actively in the Economic Commission for Asia and the Far East (ECAFE), and in December, 1955, was elected to the Trusteeship Council of the UN.

During the first years after independence, there is no doubt that the Burmans derived a feeling of pride and prestige from participation as an equal member with larger nations in the UN itself and in these UN agencies. As the years passed, however, the Burma Government, like the governments of other small and relatively poor nations, began to realize the burden which this participation imposed on its sparse man-power resources. This burden has three aspects to it. First, there is the need for Burma representatives at the meetings of the UN Assembly, the Trusteeship Council, and the

Specialized Agencies. The number of these meetings reaches almost astronomical proportions for a small delegation. What it means for Burma in practice is the appointment of persons who can ill be spared from the government or other activities. It also presents a dilemma not easily resolved. Rotation of representatives has the advantages of giving more Burmans wider experience and knowledge, thus making them more useful at home. Constant rotation, however, does not give Burma adequate representation, since the subjects and procedures at these large numbers of meetings demand experience and skill in "multilateral diplomacy," as well as technical knowledge of the working of international meetings. The solution is an unhappy compromise in which representation is changed frequently, but there is also a tendency to appoint persons with previous experience in the UN field, and such persons are often badly needed in the government at home.

The second aspect of this burden results from the assistance given Burma by the UN agencies. Almost all of the agencies of which Burma is a member are providing some kind of assistance to Burma at present, involving the assignment of specialists to various units of the Burma Government.[4] To be effective, these UN specialists have to work closely with officials in the government, but as advisers and consultants. This does not represent, therefore, a net increase in man power available for administration and execution of projects. At present, the UN specialists are only a fraction of the total number of foreign specialists and technicians at work with various government departments and agencies. While there is little question but that Burma has derived benefits from the services of these technicians, there is no question but that lack of coordination of their services and only partial utilization of their skills have reduced the benefits that might be expected. Time after time, able Burman officials have complained privately that either they could not find time to use these specialists effectively or that time spent on helping the specialists do their job prevented them from carrying out their own assignments efficiently.

Directly linked to the above problem is another that grows out of the nature of international organizations. Although the officials of the UN and its various specialized agencies would be the first to assert that their organizations only undertake those projects that are requested by member governments, in practice this is not always followed. As one small illustration of this point, the author spent a total of forty-five hours in the first six months of his residence in Burma conferring with representatives of UN agencies who had come to Rangoon to get some UN project started and wished some advice and assistance. Although generalizations are dangerous, it is fair to say that not only do the Burma officials have to spend a lot of time working out UN projects which their government has requested, but they also have to spend an undue amount of time conferring on projects of an international character that some UN agency believes will be useful. Many are "pilot projects" or studies that have only an indirect bearing on the immediate development plans of the Burma Government.

The third aspect of the burden of Burma's participation in the United Nations is the "paper work." There must be preparation for every UN meeting, not only for the agency itself, but for the numerous committees, study groups, and auxiliary conferences held under its auspices. In most cases this involves considerable work by too-busy officials, so that their representatives will be able to participate in these meetings effectively. There is a prestige element in this also. It does not do to have a Burma representative to a UN meeting ignorant of the subject under consideration, or lacking in instructions from the Burma Government on important questions that come up for a vote. Just as American Foreign Service officers complain of the immense amount of paper work, reporting, and information gathering that Washington imposes on them, Burma officials, too, are beginning to complain that UN organs and agencies are requiring an increasing amount of information, studies, and statistics from their government departments. Again, a prestige element is involved in failure to fulfill these requests.

What this all adds up to is the fact that many officials of the Burma Government, very conscious of Burma's own deficiencies in trained man power and efficient administrators, are beginning to feel that the burdens of United Nations participation may well outweigh the benefits derived. This does not apply to such substantial benefits as World Bank loans or sizeable monetary contributions, or to projects of the UN Technical Assistance Administration, but taken together with all of the many bilateral aid programs and agreements, the Burman official sometimes feels so inundated with help from abroad that he has little time to do the work for which he is paid by his government.

A most important result of the foregoing considerations is to render the conduct of Burma's foreign policy much less effective than it should be. There is too little time for thoughtful preparation of foreign policy positions on issues and problems confronting Burma. There is too little time for the officials concerned to absorb and digest the information needed in order to make wise decisions. There are too few qualified persons available. As one Foreign Office official expressed it, "If I could have just half the persons who are busy representing Burma at United Nations sessions, and the meetings of specialized agencies and international conferences, on full time duty in the Foreign Office, we would have much more efficient conduct of our foreign relations."

Finally, for a small nation, the United Nations may be utilized as an instrument of its foreign policy. Using the UN for this purpose is something that has not been carefully considered by Burman officials. In discussions, they point, quite rightly, to the one case which Burma has brought before the UN — the KMT problem. So far as it is known, there has been little consideration given by Burman officials as to how Burma can use its UN membership to advance its foreign policy objectives in general. This has been due to scarcity of able staff and lack of time for long-range policy planning. An additional factor was a general reluctance on the part of U Nu and his colleagues to plot a more vigorous course ahead in the conduct of their foreign relations.

Some of the foreign policy problems of a small nation like Burma in the UN are illustrated by the two examples of Burma's participation in the UN given in the sections which follow. Burma's record in the UN on the Korean War issue illustrates the problem of a neutral nation in the arena of power politics. Burma's presentation of the KMT case before the UN illustrates the difficulties of cold war politics for a small nation which takes the Charter at its face value.

The Korean War

Between the 1948 session of the General Assembly, Burma's first as a UN member, and the outbreak of the Korean War in June, 1950, the problem of Korea was only one of many international issues in which the Burma Government had some interest. This was the period when the AFPFL leaders were attempting to formulate their foreign policy concepts and events within Burma were of overriding importance to them. As noted previously, U Nu and his colleagues were fearful that the insurrections in Burma would lead to foreign intervention and threaten the independence of their country. They were uncertain where they could get help or how they might protect their country from outside interference. At the United Nations the Burma delegation proceeded cautiously, reflecting Burma's desire not to become embroiled in world politics.

On December 8, 1948, in Committee I (The Political and Security Committee) Burma voted in favor of a U.S.-Australian-Chinese (Nationalist)-sponsored resolution "to regard the Seoul (Southern) Government as the only legal government of the Republic of Korea." Burma opposed a Soviet effort to challenge the legality of the Seoul Government.[5] In taking this position the Burma chief delegate, U Pe Kin, explained that his government was "extremely perturbed at the tendency among certain powers to take the easiest course in solving a difficult situation . . . by proposing the partition of a country into different zones" and he feared this kind of division might become permanent. The Burma delegate asserted his government would not recognize either government in Korea since it did not want to contribute to the division of a country. Since Burma's primary concern was unification of Korea, U Pe Kin stated that his delegation would not oppose a Czechoslovakian proposal to invite representatives of the Northern Zone of Korea to participate in the Assembly's discussions of the problem, but would abstain.[6] He explained that Burma would not support an invitation to North Korean representatives because of their refusal to admit United Nations representatives to their territory. Burma voted for the establishment of a United Nations Commission for Korea to work toward unification.

In the 1949 session of the General Assembly, the Burma delegation was treated to a first hand view of vitriolic cold war politics. The report of the UN Commission for Korea was not optimistic and was critical of the Republic of Korea as well as the North Korean regime. Debates in Committee I were a clear reflection of the contest between the two power blocs and of the conditions which had caused the division of Korea into two zones. Committee I voted to continue and strengthen the UN Commission over stiff Soviet opposition. Burma supported this move.[7] Likewise Burma joined a large majority of Committee I to defeat a Soviet proposal to abolish the UN Commission and brand its work illegal interference in Korean affairs. While it is not known how much pressure was brought on Burma by the Communist bloc during these two Assembly sessions, it should be noted that during 1948 and 1949, Burma had not yet established diplomatic relations with the Soviet Union and perhaps its leaders felt free to make decisions on specific issues as they understood them.

The attack by North Korean forces on the Republic of Korea began on June 25, 1950, and was followed by the well-known immediate action of the UN Security Council. On June 27 the Security Council requested UN member nations to render all assistance possible to the UN in repelling the North Korean attack, and the next day UN Secretary-General Lie transmitted this request to all member nations. The Burma Government replied by a cable (dated July 8th), as follows:[8] "In acknowledging receipt of your cablegrams . . . I have the honour to say that the Government of the Union of Burma supports the stand taken by the Security Council in regard to Korea at its meeting of 25 and 27 June, 1950. My Government very much regrets, however, that it is not in a position to render any effective assistance."

When the General Assembly met in its fifth session in the fall of 1950, the immediate issues in Korea confronting it concerned the continuation of the United Nations Commission and permission for United Nations forces to advance into North Korean territory. On October 4, 1950, Committee I adopted "by a thumping vote of 47 to 5" a joint Western proposal which contained an "indirect but clear authorization for General MacArthur to move across the 28th parallel" in order to repel North Korean forces.[9] This same resolution established a new United Nations Commission for the Unification and Rehabilitation of Korea (UNCURK). Carlos Romulo, Philippine Chief Delegate, stated that the Asian members of Committee I had played an important role in drafting the joint eight-nation proposal. Burma voted for the resolution in Committee I and in the Assembly.

In the deliberations of Committee I on the eight-nation resolution, the Soviet Union countered with three resolutions, the first calling for a cease-fire, withdrawal of UN forces, and elections organized separately in North and South Korea; the second condemning the United States bombing in Korea; and the third denouncing the UN Commission and calling for its abolition. Burma joined the majority of Committee I to reject the first Soviet resolution, abstained on the vote which defeated the second, and joined the majority again to defeat the third Soviet resolution.[10]

In explaining the position of the Burma Government, the head of the delegation took the position that Burma did not think "the United Nations harbored any spirit of revenge against the population of North Korea" and it would be a mistake for the victorious enemy in a civil war to treat his enemy harshly. Burma contended that the aspirations of North Korea should not be overlooked and further that, while occupation of North Korea by UN forces was a military necessity, it should be the absolute minimum to ensure law and order. The Burma delegation suggested that some means must be found to find people who really represented the population of North Korea so that unification of the country could take place rapidly and nationwide elections could be held.[11]

A careful study of the debates on the eight-nation and Soviet resolutions in Committee I and of the speeches by the Burma representatives, shows clearly the influence of Soviet pressure and propaganda. The Burma delegates chose to ignore the nature of the North Korean attack and particularly its Soviet sponsorship. They chose to ignore the evidence of Soviet control over the government and people of North Korea. The Burma government and its UN delegates apparently adopted the view that the Korean War was no different in character than any other civil war between two contending sides in a country and therefore supported any Soviet proposals for a cease-fire and for representation of the North Korean regime. In taking this position, the Burma Government was pursuing its policy concepts of "independence" and "non-alignment" and at the same time reflecting a certain suspicion of the Western nations, a natural attitude for any excolonial country.

Because of the veto in the Security Council, the United States proposed a "Uniting for Peace" resolution that was designed to make possible Assembly initiative in collective measures against aggression when deadlock prevented the Security Council from acting.[12] The proposal was placed before the Assembly while the Korean experience was fresh in the minds of the delegates. Speaking on this subject in Committee I, the Burma delegate first recalled his Prime Minister's statement in Parliament supporting the official stand on Korea:

. . . What was foremost in our thoughts was the expectation of United Nations assistance when our country is subjected to aggression by a stronger power. We have pinned our faith to the United Nations Organization on that score . . .

. . . So far as I can see it will never do for us to try to be too clever and sit on the fence. If we are foolish enough to try that sort of trick, we ourselves will find ourselves face to face with aggression some day . . .

. . . A small weak nation like ours . . . can never successfully defend ourselves, alone. Fortunately there is a world organization to prevent aggression, the United Nations, of which we became a member. To be quite frank, I was not free from doubts at first . . . Korea has dispelled these doubts. But it is a fact that as soon as aggression started in South Korea the United Nations went to its assistance. This has set up a noble precedence (precedent) . . . This is the great hope, the only hope for small member nations like us.

He then asserted that, therefore, Burma felt obliged to make some contribution when the United Nations opposed any aggression.[13] Burma would "support any measures designed to prevent threats to the peace or act of aggression, which . . . the draft resolution appeared to do." [14] In an apparent answer to the Soviet contention that the resolution violated the United Nations Charter, Burma's chief delegate, U Tin, said his government viewed the plan "not so much from the legal point of view but rather as an instrument to make the United Nations effective in its primary function of preventing threats to the peace in any part of the world." [15] Although for internal reasons Burma would be unable for some time to implement part C of the resolution, which requested member nations to make elements of their national armed forces available for service as United Nations units, she hoped that this fact "would not vitiate" her "acceptance of the principles embodied in the draft resolution." [16] Burma was subsequently included in the membership (proposed by Great Britain)[17] of the Collective Measures Committee, which the "Uniting for

Peace" resolution set up to report to the Security Council and the Assembly "on methods, including those of part C of this resolution, which might be used to maintain international peace and security in accordance with the charter . . ."[18]

On November 3, 1950, the Security Council received a report from the United Nations Unified Command to the effect that with the crossing of the 38th parallel, operations were in progress to destroy all North Korean forces; three days later the Unified Command noted the approach of United Nations forces to the Yalu River and the appearance of Chinese Communist troops in battle.[19] On November 8, the Chinese People's Republic was invited to participate in Security Council deliberations on the new situation in Korea; and on November 10, six Western nations (including the United States, Great Britain, and France) presented to the Security Council a joint resolution to prevent a spread of the Korean conflict to other areas, affirming the United Nations' intention of respecting the Chinese border and calling attention to the grave danger entailed in further Chinese intervention.[20] The Chinese People's Republic refused (on November 11) the Security Council's invitation, on the grounds that their representative would be prevented from discussing foreign (UN) armed intervention in Korea and United States aggression against China. However, Peking representatives later left for New York to participate in discussions of Formosa, arriving on November 27.[21] On November 27, the Security Council added to its agenda the complaints of armed invasion of Formosa and of aggression against the Republic of Korea; representatives of the Chinese People's Republic and of the Republic of Korea were invited to the Council table.[22] Three days later the Security Council rejected (1-9) a Soviet proposal on withdrawal of United States troops from Taiwan and a Soviet-sponsored Chinese People's Republic resolution on withdrawal of armed forces from Taiwan and Korea. On November 30 the six-power resolution was vetoed by the U.S.S.R.[23]

On December 4, the sponsors of the vetoed six-power resolution asked the Assembly to take up the matter of Chinese intervention in Korea; the General (Steering) Committee of the Assembly recommended inclusion of the item on the Assembly's agenda the next day.[24] It was at this point that the so-called Arab-Asian bloc, including Burma, made the first of a long series of moves to ease tension and to work toward a peaceful settlement of the Korean War through compromise. On December 5, the delegation of thirteen countries (including Burma), headed by Sir Benegal Rau of India, appealed to Communist China and North Korea "immediately to declare that it is not their intention that any forces under their control should cross to the south of the 38th parallel." [25] It was reported that representatives of those countries (such as Burma) in the group which had recognized Communist China were planning talks with the Peking representative in New York. [26]

Committee I began consideration of the six-power resolution on December 6, 1950, and the thirteen-member Arab-Asian bloc became very active in attempting to prevent hasty action so as to give time for private talks with the Chinese Communists through the Indian Embassy in Peking. In general, the Arab-Asian bloc (including Burma) favored a peace conference with Communist China represented and opposed any attempt to condemn the Chinese Communist regime as an aggressor. For those nations like Burma which had recognized the Peking regime, there was now the double pressure from both big nations of the Communist bloc. It was obvious that a certain amount of antiwestern bias, combined with fear of antagonizing the Soviet and Chinese Communist partners, induced these nations to take a neutral position.

The Cease-Fire Commission resolution was adopted by Committee I on December 13, and by the Assembly on December 14, over Soviet bloc opposition in both cases. The Cease-Fire Group, of which Assembly President Entezam was chairman, began immediately to establish contact with the Chinese Communists and the United Nations Command. [27] On December 23, President Entezam received a statement from Foreign Minister Chou En-lai declaring the Cease-Fire Group illegal and refusing to make any contact with it. The Chinese Communists requested as a basis for negotiation withdrawal of all foreign troops from Korea and Taiwan, settlement of Korea's internal affairs by the Korean people, and membership for Communist China in the United Nations. [28]

The Arab-Asian bloc met this rejection with renewed efforts toward joint action. They discussed the possibility of pressing their Far Eastern conference proposal through the Assembly, and simultaneously their representatives consulted with the United States and the Soviet Union delegations to sound out alternative possibilities for ending the war.[29] It was rumored that the Indian Ambassador in Peking was still negotiating toward a cease-fire, while in Washington the State Department was carefully contacting members of the Arab-Asian bloc to keep them informed of current American policy.[30]

On January 6, 1951, it was reported that United States diplomats in almost all the non-Communist United Nations member countries were endeavoring to build up support for branding the Chinese Communists as aggressors in Korea.[31] Nevertheless, on January 11 the United States declared its willingness to accept a peace plan suggested by the Cease-Fire Group which would arrange an immediate cease-fire, provide for the withdrawal of all non-Korean armed forces by stages, and for a conference between the United States, Great Britain, Soviet Russia, and the Chinese People's Republic to work out a settlement of Far Eastern problems, including those of Formosa and Chinese membership in the United Nations.[32] Evidently the United States was ready to continue its support of the Arab-Asian approach until it was satisfied that Communist rejection was final. The Soviet Union was described at this time as being "careful not to discourage comparatively neutral governments' striving for compromise"; however, the outlook for its acquiescence in the cease-fire plan was not considered bright.[33]

On January 17, Foreign Minister Chou En-lai issued his country's second rejection of the United Nations' terms for a cease-fire. Communist China would not consent to a cease-fire first and negotiations later. It proposed instead that a seven-nation conference on Far Eastern problems, to be held in China, negotiate an early cessation of Korean hostilities.[34] The next day the United States told the United Nations that it considered the cease-fire efforts a failure and that the time had come for collective measures against Communist China. On January 19, the United States announced that it would introduce a resolution which would find the Peking regime guilty of aggression in Korea, would recommend that the Collective Measures Committee consider appropriate sanctions, and provide for a good offices committee to be available for possible peace negotiations in the future.[35] Arab-Asian opposition to this move had crystallized even before the resolution was introduced (January 20) in Committee I. The Arab-Asian nations based their position on a conviction that

Communist China had not ruled out the possibility of a negotiated peace; that its proposals should not be discarded without careful consideration; and that alternative proposals — specifically the calling of a Far Eastern Conference to discuss a cease-fire as soon as there was a substantial lull in hostilities — were not necessarily predestined to failure.[36]

On January 22, India informed Committee I that the Chinese Communists had agreed to the possibility of a limited Korean cease-fire as a preliminary step in a seven-power conference on the settlement of general political problems.[37] The Chinese offer was remarkably similar to the earlier Cease-Fire Group recommendations and may well have indicated a real desire to start negotiations. Over American opposition, Committee I adopted an Indian motion for a forty-eight-hour adjournment in view of the new development,[38] and the Arab-Asian bloc went into action immediately. In a series of conferences they drew up a revised draft resolution for a seven-power conference "to secure elucidations and amplifications" of the new Peking stand "and to make any incidental or consequential arrangements toward a peaceful settlement of the Korean and other Far Eastern problems.[39] The draft resolution, submitted to Committee I on January 24, was criticized as being much too weak; in fact, the complaint was reportedly raised that the plan did not even go as far as Peking had on the question of a cease-fire.[40] The resolution's sponsors, however, believed that they had the private support of many members of the North Atlantic alliance and made known their willingness to accept any clarifying amendments.[41] By January 26, with the help of Canada, the Arab-Asian bloc was ready to write into their resolution a specific provision for cease-fire consultations prior to the seven-power conference, but there were already strong indications that the United States would be able to summon the necessary two-thirds majority for its resolution and that the most that the bloc could hope for would be a defeat of the motion condemning the Chinese Communists.[42] The Soviet Union, while indicating that it considered the Arab-Asian plan inadequate, announced that in the interests of a peace settlement it would not "take exception" to it.[43]

On January 29, the Indian delegate told Committee I that his country had been advised "on the highest authority" that adoption of the United States resolution would put an end to all hopes for a peaceful settlement in Korea; it was also "reported authoritatively that . . . Peking . . . had accepted the Arab-Asian resolution in its latest form." [44] The United States-sponsored resolution had been revised to allow the proposed Collective Measures Committee to defer its recommendations for sanctions against the Chinese Communists if the Good Offices Committee should report "satisfactory progress in its efforts" to secure a cessation of hostilities. [45] (There was open evidence of a profound difference of opinion among United Nations members on the question at issue.) [46]

Although no vote was taken on either draft resolution, an announcement by Canada that she would abstain in the vote on the Arab-Asian plan made it doubtful that the bloc would receive the necessary majority support. [47] The main decisive factor seems to have been one of principle: given the common objective of peace in Korea, was it more important to reassert United Nations prestige at this point by passing moral censure on the Chinese Communists, or was it more important to secure a cessation of hostilities, even though this could only be achieved through negotiations between equals?

The Burma delegate stated his government's position as follows: "The problem at hand," said Mr. Barrington, "extended far beyond a mere finding of whether or not Communist China had committed an act of aggression," for this reason Burma and other Asian nations had not given up "attempts to seek a peaceful and honourable settlement of all existing issues in the Far East" through "direct and free discussion between the governments most directly concerned." [48] Until January 17, 1951, "at least 50 delegations" (including the Western powers) had been willing to negotiate on such broad questions as Formosa and Chinese representation in the United Nations without having first to condemn Peking as an aggressor in Korea. Why, then, when Peking had twice indicated its preparedness to enter discussions, was it "deemed essential in certain quarters that such a condemnation should now take place? [49] It was hardly realistic," he said, to believe that "the United States draft resolution would leave the door open to negotiations"; the supporters of that resolution seemed quite "determined to close the door upon negotiations" just when conditions were more favorable than before; no government which had just been labeled an aggressor could "be expected . . . to cooperate with those who had condemned it." [50] Moreover, it was quite clear to Burma — "both from the draft (United States) resolution . . . and from the debate in the Committee" — that no one envisaged truly effective sanctions against this aggression; and Burma saw "little comfort" for "the small nations which had put their faith in the system of collective security" in the passing of a "mere moral judgment." [51] Burma would oppose the United States resolution and would therefore reserve her position on representation in the proposed sanctions committee to which she would automatically be appointed by virtue of her membership in the Collective Measures Committee.[52]

On January 30, Committee I rejected the Arab-Asian draft resolution by sections, although the Soviet bloc joined the sponsors of the plan to support all but the cease-fire proviso after failing to win support for an amendment which would have specified that the proposed conference cover the withdrawal of foreign troops, settlement of Korean affairs by the Koreans, and withdrawal of American forces from Formosa.[53] At the same time the Committee approved 'the United States resolution. Of the sponsors of the Arab-Asian resolution, only two — India and Burma — joined the Soviet bloc in opposition; the others abstained.[54] When, on February 16, the Additional Measures Committee held its first meeting to consider sanctions against the Chinese People's Republic, Burma's seat was empty.[55]

Votes taken early in February, 1951, on two Soviet charges that the United States had committed aggression against Communist China are of certain use in determining the degree to which Burma had disassociated herself from United Nations policy in Korea after the condemnation resolution was passed. On the first Soviet motion, which would have declared the United States guilty of invading and blockading Formosa, Burma joined Indonesia and Yugoslavia in abstaining.[56] On the second Soviet motion, however, which would have condemned the United States for air attacks against Manchuria, Burma joined the majority of delegations in opposition.[57]

It was not until April, 1951, that the Arab-Asian bloc renewed its efforts to secure a Korean settlement. A report of April 4 stated that a series of caucuses would begin the next day, as the delegates believed the "psychological time" had arrived for a new approach to the Korean situation.[58] The same report commented on the political importance of the Asian and Arab nations to both the Western powers and the Communist nations; and it was later reported that the Arab-Asian bloc would coordinate their efforts with the existing United Nations Good Offices Group.[59] Nothing of importance resulted from the caucuses. Later in April, however, a North Korean peace feeler in the form of a demand for a conference caused further Arab-Asian bloc activity. Working mainly through Indian diplomatic representatives in Peking, the bloc was able to ascertain that no significant policy changes were contemplated by the Chinese Communists.[60]

On May 17, Committee I adopted a United States resolution, the product of the work of the Additional Measures Committee, which called for an arms embargo against the Chinese Communists and the North Koreans.[61] Although the resolution was a direct outgrowth of the January 30 condemnation of Communist China, Burma and India changed their position from opposition to abstention.[62] Burma was reported at this time to have pledged not to permit exports of articles covered in the embargo.[63] The next day in the General Assembly, Mr. Barrington explained that the resolution would "have no practical effect so far as . . . (his) country . . . (was) concerned," since "Burma's trade with China . . . (was) not appreciable and none of the materials listed in the . . . resolution . . . (entered) into such trade as . . . existed." [64] Burma's position on the original condemnation resolution, however, had not changed. She would consequently be "unable to support the present proposal which . . . would serve only to make more difficult a situation . . . already extremely difficult." [65]

On June 23, 1951, the Soviet Union suggested that hostilities in Korea be ended and discussions be opened for mutual withdrawal from the 38th parallel. Six days later the Commander-in-Chief of the United Nations Command notified his counterpart on the Communist side that upon receipt of an indication that an armistice meeting was desired, he would be willing to suggest a date for meeting. On July 10, armistice negotiations at Kaesong opened between the United Nations and the North Korean-Chinese Communist Commands. By November 27, after a two-month suspension of negotiations (by the Communists), from August 23 to October 25, tentative agreement had been reached at Panmunjom on a two and one-half-mile demilitarization zone.

On December 3, eleven nations introduced a resolution in Committee I providing that nations then outside the UN would be invited to join in any action that the United Nations might take against future acts of aggression. The resolution was sponsored by the United States, Britain, France, and eight other members of the Collective Measures Committee. Burma, Egypt, and Mexico — all members of the Committee — refused to join in sponsoring the resolution.

Evidence of Burma's policy of "non-alignment with power blocs," which often led its UN representatives into voting on both sides, is found in the resolution presented in Committee I on January 7, 1952. On January 6, the Soviet Union introduced a resolution calling for a "high-level meeting" of Security Council members in a special session with the objective of bringing an end to the Korean hostilities and promoting a settlement. This Soviet resolution was countered the next day by another resolution sponsored by the same eleven members of the Collective Measures Committee as that of December 3. On January 8, in Committee I, the Burma representative stated that "one reason why his delegation, which had taken part in the work of the Collective Measures Committee, had not been a sponsor of the eleven-nation resolution was that it wished to hear the views of the delegations which had not been represented on that Committee." The Burma delegate asserted that his government believed that collective measures were necessary and would support the eleven-nation draft resolution. He qualified this support, however, by stating that Burma would find it necessary to abstain on some parts, such as paragraph 1 and 2 of the operative part, but it particularly welcomed paragraph 10. In giving support to this eleven-nation draft resolution, however, the Burma delegate stated that he wished to make it clear that Burma was not aligning itself with any "bloc" but was only interested in the promotion of collective security. U Myint Thein (first Ambassador to Peking) then went on to say that while Burma could not support paragraph 1 of the operative part of the Soviet resolution, Burma would support paragraph 2, particularly in view of the statement of the Soviet representative that the Security Council should not take over the negotiations for an armistice but merely assist in a settlement.

When the final vote came in Committee I on the eleven-nation resolution calling for members of the United Nations to take preliminary steps necessary to provide armed forces on recommendation of the Assembly if a veto should prevent the Security Council from taking action, Burma voted with the Western powers, while only Argentina, India, and Indonesia abstained. This resolution also called for extending the Collective Measures Committee for another year. In the voting on each part of the resolution, Burma abstained on the "second operative" part of the resolution calling on UN members to have armed forces units available for service as UN units. The very large vote in favor of the resolution as a whole (only the Soviet group of five nations cast negative votes) and the fact that only two members of the Arab-Asian bloc abstained were regarded at the time as a sign of lack of real solidarity among the so-called "neutral" nations. This seemed obvious since those members of the Arab-Asian bloc that voted for the resolution did so in the face of rather thinly veiled threats by the Soviet Union.

On January 9, Committee I approved a Soviet proposal for a special Security Council session, but with definite restrictions introduced by the Western nations. Burma voted for the resolution as finally amended but abstained from voting on the Western amendment when it was offered. On January 12, the resolution calling on members of the UN to keep armed forces in readiness for possible use under a UN Assembly recommendation was passed by the General Assembly. Burma voted for the resolution; the Soviet bloc voted against it; and India, Indonesia, and the Argentine abstained.

In discussions of the Korean armistice problem in Committee I during the latter part of January, Burma took the position that as a small nation it did not want to get involved in the recriminations being exchanged between the two big power blocs. The Burman delegate always had something good to say about some part of each resolution introduced by members of either bloc. On February 2, a joint session of Committees I, II, and III met on Korean problems, and Burma, along with almost all of the Arab-Asian nations, voted in favor of Western-sponsored resolutions postponing Security Council discussion while armistice negotiations were in progress and against Soviet-sponsored resolutions on the same subject.[66] The voting on this resolution in the General Assembly on February 3 did not change. In this same meeting of the Assembly, the Burma delegate joined the American delegate in urging the Soviet Union not to make a political propaganda forum out of the ECAFE meeting then in session; and when the Soviet delegate accused the United States of economic aggression in Asia, the Burma delegate, acting as chairman, ruled him out of order.

In May and June, 1952, the charges by the Chinese Communists that the United States had been using "germ warfare" in Korea received a full airing in UN Security Council sessions and in the world press. On this question the Burma Government took a firm position in rejecting the charges as unproved. The question again came up at the fall session of the General Assembly, and Burma maintained its earlier position.

On October 23, the General Assembly voted (54 to 5) to ask the Republic of Korea to participate in discussions on the Korean question. Burma voted for this resolution. On a Soviet resolution to ask representation from the North Korean government, Burma joined with India, Indonesia, Iran, Pakistan, and Yemen in voting for it, although the resolution was defeated (38 to 11).

The key question — condemning Communist Chinese intervention in the Korean War as aggression — caused a shift in Burman attitudes. The Burma representatives took pains to explain their position carefully, by inference dissociating themselves from India and Indonesia. In the Burman view, the United Nations should have defined aggression, and in Committee I discussions on this subject, the Burma representative took a very active role, although the United States position was against any definition of aggression at this time. When the February 1 vote on condemning Communist China occurred finally in the Assembly, Burma voted "no" on the grounds that this action would only make a peaceful settlement more difficult and that nothing was to be gained by calling a country an agressor when it was extremely doubtful that effective sanctions could be applied to halt the aggression.

From this time on, the voting record shows that although Burma still did not follow India on all questions, the Burma Government apparently was becoming more and more aware of its position as the small neighbor of a large Communist China. In the subsequent period, also, the spread of hostilities in Indo-China caused the Burmans to fear that their country might yet be caught up in "another Korea" situation. The speeches made, as well as evidence collected in this study, indicate that Burma tended to abstain on votes where Communist pressure was exerted and on resolutions sponsored by the U.S.S.R. or Communist bloc states. Burma generally abstained rather than vote *with* the U.S.S.R. on most resolutions of this kind. This shift in voting was justified by the Burma representatives as a matter of principle. In explaining their votes, the Burma delegates adhered to the proposition that Burma stood for a peaceful settlement of the Korean affair, which could only be achieved by bringing all parties together around a peace table. Since Burma had entered into diplomatic relations with Communist China, it had already taken a stand favoring admission of the Communist Chinese regime to the United Nations and could hardly vote contrary to that position on Korean questions. On the other hand, the Burman votes do not show as decided a leaning to the Communist bloc as do the recorded votes of India and Indonesia. The brief summary given below reflects this position.

On 28 resolutions in Committee I between February 1, 1951 and December 8, 1954:

> Burma voted with the United States — 12 times
> India voted with the United States —   4 times
> Burma abstained — 10 times
> India abstained —   18 times
> Burma voted with the U.S.S.R. — 6 times
> India voted with the U.S.S.R. —   5 times

An analysis of the resolutions shows that on six occasions on which Burma voted with the U.S.S.R. the proposals all called for participation of the North Korean regime and of Communist China in truce discussions and in the Korean peace conference to be held after the armistice. Burma was elected to the Collective Measures Committee but did not participate in this Committee after the cease-fire in Korea in late December, 1951, on the grounds that it "had its hands full with guerrilla activities on its borders." Nevertheless, Burma voted with the United States consistently to extend the life and activities of this committee.

Although it was apparent from speeches by the Burma representatives that the Burma Government was less than satisfied with the success of the UN in bringing about a cessation of the Korean War, Burma voted for the General Assembly resolution on January 12,

1951, which called on all members to keep military units in readiness to act as part of UN forces in case of new aggression. On this resolution only India and the Argentine abstained while the Soviet bloc voted "no."

On subsequent resolutions regarding Korea, the Burma voting pattern was maintained with constant justification statements by Burman delegates that their votes demonstrated "non-alignment" and "independence of action." The Burmans saw no inconsistencies in their voting behavior and since their positions taken in the UN seemed not to have affected, one way or another, their "friendly relations" with both the nations of the Communist bloc and those of the Western bloc, they became even more certain of both the validity and the workability of their basic foreign policy concepts.

The Issue of Kuomintang Troops in Burma[67]

On March 25, 1953, Burmese Foreign Minister Sao Kun Hkio cabled the Secretary-General of the United Nations filing Burma's complaint regarding aggression against it by the Chinese Nationalist regime on Formosa. The cable charged the Nationalist Government with directing and supporting guerrilla activity in Burma and requested that the United Nations brand Nationalist China as an aggressor.[68]

A few days later U Nu gave Burma's views on the possible UN course of action then viewed as most desirable. According to *The New York Times,* "Prime Minister U Nu said today he hoped the United Nations would instruct the Formosa Government to order Nationalist Chinese forces in North Burma to surrender their arms and submit to internment.[69] U Nu expressed the view that repatriation of the Nationalist troops "would raise too many international complications . . . 'We don't know what the attitude of Red China would be if we asked Taipeh to repatriate these forces,'" the Burmese leader explained.[70] On March 25, U Nu had stated, "that at that moment relations between Red China and Burma were good, and the Chinese were kept informed about and appreciated the strenuous efforts being made by the government to overcome the KMT nuisance."[71]

U Nu's remarks nevertheless indicated that the Burmans were as yet uncertain as to Communist China's attitude toward whatever action the UN might take, and this attitude clearly loomed as a crucial factor in all Burman attempts to solve the KMT problem. In this regard, U Kyaw Nyein had gone so far as to state, the previous August, that the Burmans were concerned about Chinese Nationalist troops in their country "only because this situation could give the Peking Government a claim for intervention." [72]

On March 31, noting that "Formosan troops were attacking the armed forces along the entire 800 miles of the eastern border of Burma and within Burmese territory," the Burman delegation requested that their complaint be included on the General Assembly agenda.[73] The request was approved.

Shortly thereafter, American Ambassador William J. Sebald met with U Nu in Rangoon to discuss the situation. According to *The New York Times,* Ambassador Sebald offered to mediate with the Nationalist Government regarding the presence of their troops in Burma and asked for a cease-fire during their repatriation. U Nu was reported to have set a definite time limit within which the KMT troops would be obliged to lay down their arms and leave Burma.[74]

In any case, Justice U Myint Thein, chairman of the Burma UN delegation, presented Burma's complaint against the Chinese Nationalist Government before the UN Political Committee on April 17. U Myint Thein gave a detailed account of aggressive activities in Burma by the Nationalist intruders and presented a considerable amount of evidence to back up Burma's claim that the KMT troops in northeastern Burma under general Li Mi were being supported and controlled by the Chinese Nationalist regime in Formosa. Included in evidence were a number of captured directives from the Nationalist Government to Li Mi's forces, reports of Li Mi's Taipeh visit, the fact that Li Mi's original group of roughly 1,500 poorly equipped stragglers had grown to a force of 12,000 well-armed men, and even supporting statements by Chinese Nationalist officials.[75] The Burmans introduced a resolution calling for the condemnation of Nationalist China as an aggressor nation and for the UN to take appropriate action to bring about the disarming and interment or withdrawal of Chinese Nationalist troops in Burma.[76]

Replying to Burma's charge, the Chinese Nationalist representative, Dr. Tsiang Ting-fu, stated that "My government has no control over the Yunnan Anti-Communist and National Salvation Army," and that in entering Burma, "that Army has acted contrary to the wishes and orders of my government." Admitting paradoxically that "We do have some influence over General Li Mi," Dr. Tsiang promised in conclusion that his government would exercise its "moral influence" to help bring about a solution to the problem, but opposed the Burma draft resolution and rejected Burma's "monstrous charge" of Nationalist aggression.[77]

Various compromise resolutions were subsequently discussed, and on April 22 an amended Mexican proposal was adopted by a vote of 58–0, with Burma and Nationalist China abstaining. The resolution was adopted by the General Assembly on the following day by a vote of 59–0, with only Nationalist China abstaining. It provided that the United Nations should: (1) deplore and condemn the presence of foreign forces in Burma; (2) declare that these forces must be disarmed and either agree to internment or leave forthwith; (3) request all states to respect Burma's territorial integrity and political independence; (4) urge all states, on the request of Burma, to assist in the peaceful evacuation of these forces; (5) urge all states to refrain from assisting these forces; (6) invite Burma to report on the situation to the Eighth Session; and (7) urge the continuance of negotiations now in progress between member states.[78]

Although the resolution failed to name the Chinese Nationalist Government as aggressor as Burma had requested, the Burman delegation voted for the Mexican resolution when it came up before the General Assembly after having abstained in the Political Committee vote on the previous day. Chief Burma delegate U Myint Thein explained that "In view of the unanimity displayed in the Political Committee and because of Burma's dedication to democratic ideals and to peace and peaceful ways, the Government of Burma felt that they would have to identify themselves with a resolution which after all fully recognized the intolerable state of affairs in Eastern Burma and sought settlement of the issue in a peaceful way." [79]

On May 8, the United States proposed a four-power (Burma, Nationalist China, Thailand, the United States) conference to discuss means of solving the guerrilla problem. The Burma Government at first rejected the proposal, stating that Burma did not wish to attend a conference including the Chinese Nationalists. The Burma

Government took the position that such a conference should, without Burma's participation, draw up a plan and submit it to Burma for consideration.[80] But the Burmans later modified their stand, agreeing to the formation, under UN auspices, of a Four-Nation Joint Military Commission to discuss the means and procedure for evacuating Nationalist troops from Burma. It will be noted that whereas Burma had previously opposed evacuation in favor of interment because of uncertainty regarding Communist China's attitude toward the former measure, they now accepted, possibly after some expression of Peking's approval, evacuation as a preferable solution.

The Four-Nation UN Commission met in Bangkok on May 22, 1953. The Burma delegates at first refused to sit with their Chinese Nationalist counterparts. By the middle of June, however, the Burmans were reported to have been impressed by the sincerity of American efforts to bring about the evacuation of Li Mi's forces.[81] Representatives of all four powers began meeting as a Committee of the whole, and on June 22, the American Ambassador to Thailand, Edwin F. Stanton, announced full accord on evacuation procedure. The plan drawn up by the Four-Nation UN Commission called for Nationalist troops to cross over into Thailand, from where they would be flown or shipped to Formosa. The evacuation was to be completed within three or four weeks provided that Li Mi's soldiers obeyed orders.[82]

When the Commission attempted to implement the plan through direct negotiations with leaders of the guerrilla forces in Burma, however, the latter were far from cooperative. According to *The New Statesman and Nation,*

The KMT commanders in Monghsat . . . refused to guarantee the security of the Burmese represenatives. When talks were transferred to Bangkok, these five KMT saboteurs launched such wild propaganda that the American and Formosan representatives rebuked their irresponsibility. Their next line was the announcement that they would not withdraw from Burmese territory until ordered by General Li Mi. When the Committee ordered the General to Bangkok, he pleaded illness and sent his deputy and two staff officers on July 7. . . . General Li Mi told Chiang Kai-shek that he would on no conditions issue orders to his National Salvation Anti-Communist Army to withdraw from Burma where their sole mission was to act as a barrier between the Chinese Communists and their opposite numbers in Burma.[83]

The Commission fared no better with General Li Tse-feng who claimed to have succeeded Li Mi as commander. The former likewise refused to accept evacuation to Formosa, claiming that most of his troops were indigenous to the border area and that evacuation would violate the principle of "voluntary repatriation" established in Korea.[84]

Burma's representatives continued to press the American delegation to "take a stronger line with the recalcitrant jungle generals," [85] while Defense Minister U Ba Swe provided further evidence of Burma's growing annoyance by stating on July 30 that Burma would ask the UN to unseat Nationalist China and brand it an aggressor unless the guerrillas were evacuated.[86]

Evacuation negotiations continued throughout the summer as did sporadic fighting between Burman and KMT troops. On September 16, 1953, Burma's Ambassador to Thailand, U Pe Khin, finally submitted a demand to the Chinese representatives on the Joint Military Commission that Nationalist China agree to the evacuation of 5,000 of the 12,000 Nationalist troops in Burma within three weeks and the remainder within three months.[87] The demand was designed to counter the possibility of a token withdrawal stretched out during the coming General Assembly session. The Chinese Nationalist representatives refused to accept both the Burman demand and a compromise proposal put up by the United States. The American chairman "severely censured" this attitude, while the Burma delegation walked out of the conference.[88] Notwithstanding this breakdown in the negotiations, the American chairman of the Commission requested that the evacuation proceed as planned. With the agreement of Thailand and Nationalist China, staging points were set up.

On September 25, the Burma Government again brought the problem before the United Nations. Chief Burman delegate U Myint Thein stated that the complaceny of some UN members had "alarmed us," and compared this complacency with concern over "certain developments in the Kingdom of Laos . . . where no lack of volunteers were willing to resort to extreme measures . . . to put out the fires inspired by people with a different political ideology." [89] Citing the failure of the UN-established commission and of the Chinese Nationalist government's refusal to accept responsibility for Chinese Nationalist troops in Burma, he requested a few days later that the issue be placed at the head of the UN Political Committee's agenda. On October 4, the Political Committee voted to do so notwithstanding a request by American delegate Lodge for delay, pending the promised start of the evacuation.[90]

On October 29, the Evacuation Committee announced from Bangkok that Burma had agreed to a cease-fire until November 15 to permit the evacuation of about 2,000 troops to Thailand en route to Formosa. The Nationalists pledged to disavow and cut off supplies to the guerrillas remaining in Burma after those willing to return to Formosa had been evacuated.[91]

Defense Minister U Ba Swe had complained earlier in the month that it was becoming "more and more apparent that the Nationalists sought only a token evacuation."[92] On October 31, U Myint Thein outlined his government's attitude toward the proceedings thus far in somewhat greater detail. Speaking before the UN Political Committee, the Burma delegate acknowledged with "deep gratitude" American efforts toward a solution, but added, "Without meaning to be ungrateful, I venture to state that in dealing with the authorities on Formosa, moral pressure is not enough. If something more than that, such as a threat of an ouster from their seat in the United Nations, were conveyed to the authorities on Formosa, or if the United States would go a step further and threaten to suspend aid, I assure you the Kuomintang army will disappear overnight."[93] On November 5, he stated before the same committee that the evacuation of only 2,000 men and disavowal by Formosa of the remainder was "no consolation" and "not the semblance of a solution."[94]

Meanwhile, on October 28, American Embassy officials in Bangkok had contracted with a private airline to carry Nationalist troops to Formosa at the rate of 200 per day. The governments of Thailand, Nationalist China and the the United States agreed to defray the cost. On November 5, the UN Political Committee shelved the issue, and the evacuation began two days later.

The evacuation proceeded in a manner hardly satisfactory to the Burma Government. At first, Thai police refused to permit Burman observers at the staging points.[95] Burman representatives were allowed to join other members of the Joint Military Commission at these points only after the Government of Burma made an official complaint to the Thai Government. Shortly after arriving at the evacuation sites, the Burman observers complained that many of the evacuees were women and children and that combatants should be evacuated first. Some of the soldiers being evacuated had been recruited only ten days before, while others were unarmed or carried obsolete weapons.[96] Nor had the KMT troops in Burma ceased their activities. On November 22, Nationalist guerrillas joined a strong force of Karen rebels in an attack on a passenger train and an armed escort train between Rangoon and Moulmein.[97]

At Burma's request, the UN Political Committee renewed consideration of the KMT problem on November 17, 1953. At this time, U Myint Thein complained that most of the evacuees were "dead-wood" and that the few weapons which had been surrendered were of ancient vintage. He again stated that the United States could bring about a solution by cutting off military aid to the Chinese Nationalist Government.[98] A. J. Carey, the American representative on the joint Military Commission, reported that 1,103 troops had already reached Formosa, but acknowledged that few weapons had been surrendered.[99]

The debate before the Political Committee centered around an eight-nation draft resolution which had been presented on the same day.[100] The resolution expressed concern over the failure of the evacuees to surrender their arms and requested the United States to work for the evacuation of the estimated 10,000 Nationalist troops still in Burma.[101] The resolution was adopted by a vote of 51–0 with 6 abstentions. Burma agreed to an extended cease-fire and the issue was dropped from the UN agenda.

The evacuation dragged on throughout the winter of 1953–54. On May 30, 1954, General Li Mi, now in Formosa, announced the formal dissolution of the Yunnan Anti-Communist National Salvation Army.[102] But on July 1, Chinese Nationalist troops were again reported to be fighting Burmese units in Kengtung.[103] On July 30, the Four-Nation Joint Military Commission announced, however, that the program had been completed with the evacuation of 7,000 men and their dependents, the remaining troops deciding to stay.[104]

On August 20, Burma submitted a new request to the UN Secretary-General that "Burma's complaint regarding aggression against it by the Government of Nationalist China" be placed on the agenda of the General Assembly.[105] In their complaint, the Burma Government described results obtained thus far as a "token evacuation." This request was approved, and on September 29, Burma submitted a report to the UN charging that "about 6,000 Chinese Nationalist troops were still hugging the Thai-Burma border, ostensibly to resort to an anti-Communist drive, but primarily to enrich themselves by controlling the opium trade and manufacturing counterfeit currency."[106] James Barrington, who had replaced U Myint Thein as Chief Burma delegate, added that "Their continued existence represents a threat, not only to our country, but to the peace and tranquility of the whole of Southeast Asia."[107]

A third UN resolution was adopted deploring the fact that numerous foreign forces remained in Burma and that they were better armed and equipped than when the evacuation began. But the Burma representative acknowledged that the evacuation which had already been carried out "represented the limit of what could be accomplished by international action" and that the disposition of the remaining Nationalist troops was their own responsibility.[108] The Burma Government requested no further action and on October 15, 1954, the issue was discussed for the last time in the United Nations.

The Burma government could hardly regard that United Nations action on the one case it had taken to that body as satisfactory. From the Burman point of view, the case was clear cut. Here was a body of foreign troops on Burman soil acting as insurgents against the government and clearly being supplied from a nation (Taiwan) with which Burma had no formal diplomatic or other relations. Since the Chinese Nationalist government was clearly dependent upon the United States for its viability, the Burma government saw no reason why the United States could not bring effective pressure on the Chinese Nationalist government to force the evacuation or surrender of the refugee Kuomintang troops in Burma. It acknowledged the assistance of the United States in arranging for the partial evacuation of these troops, but was disappointed because of its failure to obtain stronger United Nations support.

The result of this experience in the United Nations was to make most Burman leaders feel that their original hopes that membership in the United Nations offered a small nation like theirs protection and succor against outside interference were misplaced. The remnants of the Kuomintang troops remaining in Burma have continued to give trouble and in March, 1961, a foreign supply plane was shot down by Burma air force fighters, thus proving to the Burmans that the Chinese Nationalist government was still guilty of complicity in supporting the KMT troops against the Burma government. In this instance there was no desire to reopen the case in the United Nations.

Thus, Burma's experience with the Korean War issue and with its attempt to get help in solving the KMT problem caused considerable disillusionment about the United Nations in Rangoon. The Burman leaders have often asserted that reliance on the United Nations for protection of their sovereignty and security is a dubious foundation and that Burma "does not want to become another Korea or a Congo." It is quite possible, therefore, that disillusionment with the United Nations as a protector of the security of small states has made it easier for the Burma government to work more closely with Communist China and to place greater reliance on its neutralist policy which dictates friendly relations with all countries.

Burma's Neutralist Policy in UN Politics

Before 1954, although the Burma government generally followed the position taken by other neutralist members, its justifications for voting were more often based on independent reasoning quite different from that of India. After 1954, when closer relations had been established with both the U.S.S.R. and Communist China, there was a tendency for the Burma delegation to join with India more often or at least not take a position contrary to that of the majority of the Afro-Asian bloc, a group constantly growing in number. This voting pattern is shown with respect to a number of the key issues on the General Assembly's agenda prior to 1960.[109]

As would be expected, the Burman government has consistently espoused the cause of anticolonialism. It supported the Indonesian Government's case against the Netherlands on West Irian. This general position on colonial questions often resulted in the Burma delegation voting affirmatively for Soviet bloc resolutions, but even here the Burma delegation often qualified its support for such resolutions by insistence that recommendations should involve an orderly process and be designed to relieve tensions rather than provoke further trouble.

This attitude led the Burma delegation to vote with the United States on many occasions when a reasonable compromise could be worked out, and it led Burma to abstain on many Soviet-sponsored resolutions which Burma believed were provocative or were presented for the primary purpose of embarrassing the United States and its allies. As was true on Korean questions, the Burma government did not blindly follow the lead of India, for on colonial issues both India and Indonesia have rather consistently opposed United States-sponsored resolutions by negative votes or abstentions and supported Soviet-sponsored resolutions by affirmative votes more often than Burma.

On issues involving international peace and security, the general line adopted by the Burma government has been consistent with its basic foreign policy concepts. The Burma delegation supported resolutions which it believed would serve to reduce tensions between the east and the west and conciliate the disputants. In many cases, the Burman explanation of their position differed from those of India and other members of the Afro-Asian bloc. While little is known of the inner discussions of representatives of this group at the United Nations, the Burma representatives have continued to try to arrive at a position based on their independent judgment of what was the "right" action on each issue as it arose.

On general issues of disarmament and control of nuclear weapons, the Burman position has been consistently that of a small nation having no responsibility in this field of international relations and therefore able to express freely whatever viewpoints appeal to it. This is not to say that the Burma government has acted irresponsibly, but to point up the fact that Burma is in reality a spectator in the nuclear weapons contest, with all of the spectator's freedom to criticize all contestants and the umpires as well.

Both in and out of the United Nations, the Burma government urged agreement on disarmament, has urged agreement on control of nuclear weapons, and asserted that all testing of nuclear weapons should be stopped pending such agreements. In general, this has placed Burma more often on the side of the Communist bloc, except when members of the Afro-Asian bloc have attempted to develop a compromise formula. On these occasions, the leadership in such attempts has usually come from India, and the proposed formulas have satisfied the Soviet Union more often than the United States.

Burma's interest in the control of nuclear weapons is real, and the Burman press since 1953 has paid considerable attention to this problem. Generally speaking, however, the attitudes of the Burman leaders and of the press have been more moderate and more tolerant than those found in India and other "neutralist" countries. When the Soviets launched their "Sputniks," the non-Communist Burmans and the non-Communist Burman press reported the events, but there was very little gloating or sly innuendoes such as were found elsewhere. In conversations with Burmans during this period in the fall of 1957, almost no Burmans remarked on this development unless an American raised the subject first. The general attitude of the Burmans seemed to be that the Soviet achievement had not in any way shaken their confidence in the scientific, technical, and industrial capabilities of the United States, which they admire very much. On other questions of peace and security, the Burma Government usually adopted a somewhat cautious position. Although political groups in Burma have publicly supported the withdrawal of all foreign troops from every country and Burman officials have taken this position publicly on occasion, it has not reflected a firm foreign policy position of the government to date. Burma has tended to take a moderate position, to support any attempts at peaceful solution of issues which seem reasonable. In many instances before 1960, this led Burma to vote with the United States or to abstain on Soviet-sponsored resolutions. The Burman leaders have not been under severe pressure to justify their position when it places them on the side of the Communist bloc, but whenever they have taken the opposite position on the side of the United States or in opposition to the Soviet bloc, the Burma representatives in the United Nations have almost uniformly taken pains to justify their stand as an "independent" determination and as no sign that they are "leaning" toward the "Anglo-American bloc." There is little question that, since 1951 in the United Nations, and particularly since 1960, the Burma representatives have been very conscious of Communist power and anxious not to take any position that might antagonize the Soviet Union or Communist China.

It is well known that the Burma Government has consistently supported membership in the United Nations for Communist China.[110] This position the Burma leaders believe to be the only one consistent with their relations with Peking. On the issues of membership for Communist bloc nations, however, the Burma Government has taken a more "neutral" stand or followed the lead of the "neutralist" majority. They have refused to endorse membership for either the North Vietnam or South Vietnam or North Korean regimes. Their justification is that they believe peace and security are best served by uniting these divided countries and that they believe membership in the United Nations for divided regimes would make eventual unification more difficult, if not impossible. Again, it is possible this earlier stand would be modified under present circumstances.

As set forth in the foregoing sections, the Burmans view the United Nations with mixed feelings. They regard membership as indispensable but are becoming increasingly aware of the particular burdens of membership for a small nation. Apart from those who have represented Burma at meetings of the United Nations and the Specialized Agencies, there is very little knowledge about the history or operations of the United Nations among the literate public in Burma. There has been no official United Nations information office in Burma until quite recently. Material produced about the United Nations is not easily available and what little is available does not get distribution. The Burma Government has been conscientious in providing for some sort of celebration on United Nations' day in October. This "once-a-year" attention to the United Nations does little to inform the literate public about the organization. The English-language press reports United Nation meetings with fairly good coverage, but always in terms of issues being debated and with no information as to what the function of the organs of the United Nations are or how they operate.

United Nations specialists in Burma, including a resident representative of the United Nations Technical Assistance Board, do almost nothing to publicize the United Nations or even to explain what they are doing in Burma, except to those Burman officials with whom they are officially in contact. The United Nations specialists keep to themselves to a considerable degree and have made little effort even to inform other foreign specialists of their work or their competence, so that there has been little or no coordination of UN activities in Burma. As with many of the small nations, to a large majority of Burmans with any interest in the world, the United Nations has not yet become a living organism, but is still something of a faraway abstraction. It has never directly affected their daily lives nor do they feel it has influenced the actions or policies of their government.

The General Assembly sessions of 1960 and 1961 may well go down in history as the turning point for the United Nations as did the sessions of 1931 and 1932 for the League of Nations. At the 1960 session, there were more heads of state and prime ministers present than ever before. Khrushchev proposed universal disarmament and banged his shoe on his desk in the Assembly hall. Prime Minister U Nu was absent. For the future of the UN and for Burma's participation in it, the most important developments occurred in the 1961 session. It was quite clear that the members from outside Europe and the western hemisphere held a substantial majority and the large increase in membership from Africa would certainly subject the character of the UN to change in the future. Even more important was the vigorous attempt of the U.S.S.R. to gain control of the organization with its "troika" proposals. Although the unaligned nations refused to accede to the Russian proposals, the Soviet veto on the Goa resolution in the Security Council and their general silence and inaction on India's invasion of Goa showed clearly some portents for the future of the UN as an organ designed to maintain international peace and security. There is little question that many leaders of both large and small nations view the future of the United Nations with grave doubts and can only hope that the small, new nations will see its real usefulness to them as a safeguard of their independence.

For Burma, the 1960 and 1961 sessions of the UN Assembly coincided with its new *rapprochement* with Communist China. In these two Assemblies, the Burma Government sought safety in numbers on most resolutions of importance and more often than in the past followed the Indian Government's lead. The voting record of these two Assembly sessions does not reveal a real solidarity among the African and Asian members except on the question of support for the position of the Secretary-General where the Soviet Union suffered a real defeat. On other issues, there was a tendency for the newer African nations to propose extreme resolutions and for the "older" excolonial states of Asia to seek a milder compromise. On seven test votes on crucial issues in the fall session of 1961, Burma followed India's lead on six and abstained on the seventh. With the election of U Thant of Burma as Acting Secretary-General, it is possible the Burma government will tend to be even more cautious than it has in the past and will avoid any position which might seem to antagonize the Communist bloc.[111]

It would be unfair to conclude that the leaders of Burma are thoroughly disillusioned about their country's membership in the United Nations. It is certain, however, that from their own experience, they have found no compelling reasons to place greater reliance on the United Nations for maintenance of their own peaceful relations with other nations and their own security. Their memories of World War II devastation in Burma and the problems this caused for their independent government are still very clear in their minds. They have seen the UN in Korea and in the Congo. They want no more fighting in Burma under any auspices or from any source. To date, they believe they have found the formula for a successful foreign policy largely through bilateral relationships and in maintaining "friendly relations with all countries." They do not view the United Nations with great enthusiasm, but will probably continue to participate in the United Nations and its various specialized agencies as long as a majority of the growing number of new and "neutral" nations pursue the same course.

—— VII ——

AFTER FOURTEEN YEARS—AN EVALUATION

IF the consistent application of a few basic principles in foreign relations is a measure of success, then Burma's policy of neutralism must be counted successful. If widespread acceptance of a foreign policy within a nation is evidence of its validity, then neutralism has been the "right" policy for Burma. After fourteen years and now under the second administration of the armed forces, the people of Burma still find their nation's independence and territorial integrity intact. They see no disputes, no serious troubles on the horizon to mar their "friendly relations" with other nations, including the members of both power blocs. Their country's representatives sit in the world's councils and they take pride in the election of one of their political leaders, U Thant, to the high post of Secretary-General of the United Nations. They are not happy about their government, they find much to criticize about the present state of economic and social progress in their country, but no important Burman voices have been raised against their country's policy of neutralism in world affairs.

There is little question therefore, that "positive neutrality" as a cornerstone of Burma's foreign relations is considered a success in the eyes of all but a very few Burmans. The declaration by General Ne Win's Revolutionary Council that his government would continue the policy of "positive neutrality" and "cordial relations with all nations" was virtually taken for granted by Burmans who have any real interest in or voice in their country's foreign relations. It is not sufficient, however, to count Burma's neutralist policy a success only because the Burmans believe it to be or because Burma is still independent to date. If this study has any value, it should provide a basis for some answers to a number of questions implicit in any evaluation of Burma's neutralism.

First, has Burma's continued independence as a nation been primarily caused by its policy of neutralism or have circumstances and actions in international affairs, over which the Burma government has had little influence, developed in such a way as to permit Burma to follow a neutralist course as an independent nation? To state this question in another way, have successive Burman governments stuck to their concepts of neutralism regardless of varying circumstances or have peculiar events, circumstances, and the actions or inaction of other nations shaped Burma's neutralism?

Second, has Burma's consistent neutralism either helped or hindered development of friendly relations with those nations whose good will and assistance were essential to Burma's development since 1948? Again, have these "friendly relations" been more the result of a neutralist policy or of circumstances or events not directly related to Burma's foreign policy? Third, if the assumptions implicit in the foregoing questions are correct, then Burma's policy of positive neutrality can be regarded as successful, not because it has been inherently "good" or "right" but because the Burma government has been fortunate in being permitted to choose this course. This implies that most foreign policy decisions have been "re-actions" to the events or issues of the moment. It is fair to ask, therefore, whether at any time since independence, the Burman leaders could have chosen alternative policies or courses of action other than neutralism and whether such options were seriously considered. Finally, has Burma's neutralism really been tested? If Burma's independence and security were seriously threatened, would positive neutrality serve to protect the nation's interests or would it have to be abandoned for some other alternative? The test here is Burma's internal strength. After fourteen years what progress has been made toward a stable political system, a viable economy, and an integrated society?

Factors Affecting Neutralism

By September, 1947, the AFPFL leaders were given responsibility for charting the course for their new nation through a peaceful agreement with Britain for transfer of power in January. There were no strings attached to this freedom. They could choose their own form of government. They could choose to remain within the British Commonwealth or go their own way. They could choose to join the United Nations or not. To many of the Burman leaders, this wide freedom of choice was sweet to their taste. In domestic policy the choice was not too difficult, for all were agreed that Burma was to be a socialist state, although many differed on its structure and on the means by which it could be created. In foreign affairs there was not, in fact, as much choice. Internal politics dictated independence from the British Commonwealth. The bipolar world of the cold war was a fact which the Burman leaders recognized. They did not wish to take sides with either power bloc. It must also be recalled that neither side urged Burma to do so. In addition, there were certain underlying factors which heavily influenced the Burman leaders toward a posture of nonalignment.

First of all, the influence of Buddhism, its "otherworldliness" has always affected Burman attitudes toward people and events. To the Buddhist, merit is gained by serving the *phongyis*, by building pagodas, performing the proper ceremonies at the proper times, and often seeking, through meditation in a monastery, to divorce mind and body from the world outside. The precepts of the Buddha are held up as a guide to living, but the realities of daily life often lead the Burman to act in whatever way will best serve his selfish interest of the moment or help him adjust to new circumstances. In politics, the Burman is quick to take advantage of weakness and is not overscrupulous in the methods he employs to advance his interests. Acceptance of Buddhism by the majority of Burmans has always been tempered by a heavy dose of realism, a pragmatic approach to life.

In another sense, Buddhism for the Burmese is more than a religion or a way of life. It represents tradition, a cultural past, and encompasses habits of thought and conduct which are legacies of centuries. The "Buddhist way" embraces those elements in their culture which Burmese regard as their own and hence provide them with a sense of security against the unknowns — the many insecurities — which have flooded in upon them during the past two decades of war and insurrection. There seems little question but that U Nu's sweeping election victory in 1960 was testimony to the desire of a large number of Burmans to cling to the traditional ways — to rid themselves of the disruptions caused by modernization and rapid change.

In the light of all this, the AFPFL leaders were probably acting as traditional Burmans in adopting an independent foreign policy — a policy of neutralism, in which their country was beholden to none and free to go its way as best it could. The split in the AFPFL in 1958, while it was certainly a power struggle among the leading politicians, was also, in part, a contest between those who wanted to make the country over, to create a socialist state, industrialized and modern, as rapidly as possible, and those who resisted this trend, who were content to go more slowly, reaping all the personal benefits of political power along the way. The lack of any large-scale support for the Communist and pro-Communist parties and their own internecine quarrels is further evidence of this.

A second underlying factor in the formulation of Burma's neutralist policy can be found in the ideological orientation of the AFPFL leaders. They were nurtured in Marxism, but it was Marxism passed on to them through the medium of the British and Indian Communist parties. As has been stated, it is doubtful whether many of the young leaders in the Burma independence movement ever became serious students of Communist doctrine. With few exceptions, they were willing to regard Marxism as the means by which they might achieve independence for their country, not as an end in itself. When later confronted with hard decisions, they were willing to modify or to postpone the application of Marxist doctrine in order to solve immediate problems or achieve immediate, short-term ends.

Nevertheless, the desire of the young Burma leaders of the independence movement for an early resolution of Burma's status, was buttressed by the Marxist-Leninist-Stalinist position on colonialism. Even apart from their Marxist leanings, General Aung San, U Nu, and their colleagues can be characterized as anticolonialist. At this point, a distinction must be made between an attitude of anticolonialism and antiwesternism. Too often, the leaders of an independence movement who express attitudes of "anticolonialism" are said to be "antiwestern." This is not always true as the history of the independence movements in Asia reveals. The Indonesians, for example, were anticolonialists because they were intent on securing their total freedom from Dutch rule. Once free from colonial status, the Indonesian government has not been consistently "antiwestern," in the sense of refusing economic aid and other assistance from "western" (and therefore, "colonial") nations. The history of postwar Burman policy has demonstrated that the AFPFL leaders, and almost all Burma politicians have retained, on the whole, friendly feelings toward the British and toward the United States. Even in postwar relations with Japan, the Burmans have welcomed Japanese assistance in economic development provided under the reparations agreements and have tended to separate their feelings about the Japanese military occupation during the war from their atitudes toward Japanese civilians after the war.

In Burma, it was very natural that the Burman independence leaders should be against colonialism in all forms, since they were struggling for freedom from the colonial rule of the British. This alone would have induced them to adopt a foreign policy after independence of no entangling alliances with their former masters or other colonial powers. Their espousal of Marxism as a guide to their post-independence domestic and foreign policies fitted in very well with their attitudes of anticolonialism. In this general line of thinking, the AFPFL leaders did not differ too much from those in other Asian colonies.

The key to adoption by the AFPFL leaders of an "independent" foreign policy for their country, however, does not lie in their espousal of Marxism or their feelings of anticolonialism. The record presented in this study demonstrates that the real key is found in the postwar policies of the Soviet Union toward the Asian cuntries about to attain their independence. In Burma, particularly, for reasons already set forth, the AFPFL leaders were probably more receptive to close ties with the Soviet Union than were those of any other Asian nation. Had the Soviet Union in 1948 or 1949 used the tactics which have been employed with considerable success since 1955, it is quite probable that Burma would now be a communist satellite for all practical purposes. In 1948–49, the Burma government needed arms quickly to suppress the Karen and communist insurgents. The Burma government needed loans and other economic aid to offset the expenses of suppressing the severe and almost successful insurrection. Had the Soviet Union offered arms freely and without any "strings" and had the Soviet Union offered credits for

economic development purposes, it is probable that the AFPFL leaders would have accepted such assistance gladly. That they did not
ask for Soviet help was due to their success in obtaining arms and
loans from India and the British Commonwealth on their own initiative and because of the quick response of Prime Minister Nehru and
his government.

It is not known whether the AFPFL leaders ever considered seriously asking the Soviet Union for the assistance they badly needed
in 1948–49. The public policy and actions of the Soviet Union, however, indicate that it is possible such a move was rejected, if considered, because of the virtual cold shoulder given the new Burma by
the Soviet Union. Radio Moscow's castigation of U Nu and other
Asian leaders as "running dogs of the imperialists" and the Kremlin's
policy of insisting that only an armed seizure of the government by
force would fulfill Moscow's definition of a "truly liberated country"
were hardly calculated to endear the AFPFL leaders to the Soviet
Union from which they had openly stated they hoped to "draw their
inspiration."

The plain, blunt fact is, that the Burman Marxist leaders in 1948–
49 were rebuffed by the Soviet Union which, so far as is known, offered no help to the new "Leftist State" but on the contrary was
supporting the very factions working to undermine the new government. As has been stated, this was a shock to the Marxists among the
AFPFL leadership. It is no wonder that they failed to understand
the policy of the Soviet Union. And it is no wonder that the circumstances of Soviet policy in 1948–49 was a most important factor influencing the adoption of an independent, and later neutralist foreign
policy. Nor did the Chinese Communist regime after its quick recognition by the Burma government in December, 1949, perform any
better. While it is true that the Chinese Communist regime did not
overtly or significantly interfere in Burma's internal affairs in support
of the Burman communists, nor use the presence of refugee KMT
troops in Kengtung as an excuse for interference, all of this was negative action. As an Asian revolutionary government, hailed by many
political elements in Burma for its success, the Peking regime remained aloof in its relations with Burma until 1953–54. The reasons
for this may be logical, but the important point here is that a socialist government in Burma had no indication from Peking that its basic

Marxist orientation was even understood, much less appreciated and supported. On the contrary, just enough support was given the Burman communists from across the northern border to make the AFPFL leaders and particularly the Burma Army staff officers suspicious of Chinese Communist intentions.

So it was, that in the first two and one-half years after independence, when the AFPFL leaders were trying to formulate a foreign policy, the policies and actions first, of the Soviet Union and then of Communist China, were coldly correct, unsympathetic, and even suspect. The AFPFL had nowhere to turn for material assistance in their nation's development than to the Western nations. When they found that loans and economic aid of different kinds could be obtained from the West without any "strings attached" they were more and more confident that a policy of "independent neutrality" — essentially noncommitment to either side in the cold war — was a workable foreign policy. By the time the Communist bloc got around to changing its policy toward the southern Asian nations and was ready to offer economic aid, barter agreements, and other forms of assistance, the AFPFL leaders were too convinced of the "rightness" of their neutralism and had learned enough so that they were not taken in by Communist bloc promises. The record of the rice barter deals between Burma and the Communist bloc states shows that the AFPFL leaders were acting with political realism and some sagacity. They used these arrangements when they desperately needed them in 1953–55, but were just as quick to reduce their commitments on rice agreements and on the Soviet "gift" projects, once they did not need them any longer.

The unfolding of events, therefore, and in particular the policies pursued by the Communist bloc toward Burma compared to the friendly attitude of the Western nations and their receptivity to Burman requests for economic assistance "without strings" have continually conditioned the AFPFL leaders to believe that their policy of "non-alignment" coupled with the precept of accepting aid from any source so long as no "strings are attached" has been the "best" and the most workable foreign policy they could devise. In one sense, it has enabled Burma to have the "best of all possible worlds" — to be able to keep on friendliest terms with the big nations in both the Communist and the Anglo-American blocs and to avoid antagonizing anybody. It is only natural that the Burman political leaders attribute this seeming success of their foreign policy to their own efforts rather than to outside circumstances or to the policies of other nations.

This brings us to a third factor influencing the development of Burma's neutralism. At the outset, U Nu and his colleagues recognized the inescapable fact that Burma was a small, weak nation. They had few illusions of potential strength. They did not believe that they should strive to develop any kind of a power position in Asia, by any means. Intent first of all, on the internal economic, social, and political development of their new nation, the AFPFL leaders wanted to avoid entanglements or involvements in power politics. They wanted to be "friendly with all nations." They acted to get rid of any form of foreign economic domination left over from colonial times by a policy of nationalization, later modified to permit investment of foreign capital in controlled "joint venture" schemes. Most of the Burman political leaders, because of their Marxism, their anticolonialism or both, honestly feared that Burma might again become the object of great power exploitation. They assumed that the Western nations still harbored predatory instincts. They believed that the Soviet Union was not such a power, but after 1950 they were uncertain about the intentions of Communist China. This uncertainty was based in part on the record of earlier Chinese empires, on the war experience of having large bodies of Chinese troops within their territory, but most of all on the simple fact that they recognized, perhaps instinctively, that a land of empty spaces will always be a potent lure to a big country teeming with underfed people particularly if it is a neighbor.

Furthermore, the AFPFL leaders in 1948–49, responsible for plotting Burma's course in the world of nations, were forced to make their own assessment of the kind of an international world into which they had taken their new nation. Their assessment was simple and clear-cut. They declared publicly that the world of 1948–49 was dominated by the power struggle between the Soviet bloc and the Anglo-American bloc. In this contest, they decided that another world war was an ever present possibility. Their experience at the United Nations confirmed their assessment of the bitterness of the cold war struggle. The Korean war, followed by the war in Indo-China, confirmed their fears of another holocaust in which they were certain that Burma would suffer as it had in the Second World War. This assessment strengthened their belief that an "independent" policy, one of "non-alignment" and "friendly relations with all countries" was the only effective course to pursue. Their fears of another world war led them to interpret their basic foreign policy principles so as to leave them as much freedom of action as possible, but more importantly to provide a basis for taking whatever action they could as leaders of a small nation to ease tensions and help bring about peaceful settlement of disputes. These attitudes led to quick acceptance of these principles as a panacea for the ills of the world or even of Asia. As U Nu and others made clear and as the Rangoon press attempted to point out, these principles, like the precepts of the Buddha, were valid only if acted upon. As political realists, the Burmans were willing to let actions by Communist China be the best evidence of their validity. The Burma border trouble caused some doubts as to Communist China's willingness to abide by these principles, but peaceful settlement of the problem of border demarcation again convinced the Burman leaders that their basic foreign policy principles were right and that they worked.

The varying attitudes and circumstances noted above are examples of the manner in which the evolution of Burma's neutralism has been influenced in practical terms. In the fourteen years since independence, it seems as if any one set of circumstances or events which might have influenced the AFPFL leaders seriously to modify their government's neutrality policy, has always been balanced by another set of circumstances or by certain attitudes which have tended to convince these leaders of the validity of neutralism. Theoretically, the Burma government could have chosen a different course. Theoretically, the Burma government could have remained within the Commonwealth, and even if not a member of SEATO, could at least have allied itself defensively with other members of the Commonwealth as has Malaya. Or, again, theoretically, the Burma government could have aligned itself with the Soviet Union and the Communist bloc states, a more compatible position ideologically, but the time when this could have been done passed without any real interest or response forthcoming from Moscow or Peking. No Burman politician has ever felt that he should advocate that Burma go begging to nations of either bloc. Such an attitude is incompatible with

Burman feelings, cultural inheritance, and Burma's embryonic nationalism. A policy of neutralism, therefore, both fits the Burman background, Burman attitudes and has been dictated, in the minds of the Burman leaders by unfolding events and circumstances.

The Scope of Burma's Foreign Relations

A big power in the international world is almost obligated to carry on relations with all other nations, large or small, for its recognition is always sought by new states and there are always many reasons for establishing relations quite apart from immediate and tangible self-interest. A small nation has a certain freedom to choose those states with which it will have diplomatic and other relations. Here, specific factors affect the scope of the foreign relations of a small nation. These may be budgetary, trade possibilities, the need for economic and technical assistance or geographic location, cultural and historical ties. Again a new small state, when recognized by a big power or a lesser state, traditionally is under an obligation to reciprocate and establish at least a minimum diplomatic relationship.

There is some freedom for a small nation in determining the general scope of its international relations. Ambassadors from a small state can be accredited to more than one country. Establishment of formal diplomatic relations can be postponed indefinitely even if there has been mutual recognition. Finally, the United Nations headquarters offers one alternative to establishment of formal relations because a small nation, represented at the United Nations can conduct negotiations, obtain information, and arrange agreements for trade by direct contact with representatives of other nations with which it has not formal relations or official representation.

In determining the scope and character of its foreign relations, the leaders of a small state must always be conscious of its weakness. A big power may very well attempt to avoid serious disputes with other states, particularly other powers, but in the nature of international politics, clashes of interests between a big power and other nations, large or small, seem unavoidable. A large nation has available a variety of instruments of national power, including armed forces, which it can use to carry out its policies, to settle or to alleviate disputes with other nations. A small state is usually denied, or at least partly denies itself, many of these instruments of power. It is therefore incumbent on the leaders of a small state to so define the scope and character of its foreign relations and so conduct its foreign policy as to avoid any disputes with other states which might affect its independence or its ability to maintain itself.

Another test of the effectiveness of the foreign policy of a small nation, therefore, is whether its policy has been so constructed and executed as to permit the maximum of profitable relations with other nations, large or small, and whether its foreign policy and actions have resulted in a minimum of serious disputes with other nations which might affect its independence or its ability to maintain itself. This test can be applied to Burma's neutralist foreign policy by first determining whether the Burman leadership recognized the problem of the small state in international politics as outlined above and whether in carrying out a neutralist foreign policy Burma has obtained maximum benefits and had a minimum of serious disputes with other countries.

Initially, the government of Burma established relations with the United Kingdom, the United States, India, Nationalist China, and Pakistan, certainly a natural and obvious requirement. Although an exchange of notes in London provided for Burma-Soviet diplomatic relations, official establishment of embassies did not take place until the late summer of 1950. Burma's hasty recognition of the People's Republic of China in December, 1949, automatically severed its previous relations with the Republic of China, but official relations were not opened in Rangoon and Peking until the summer of 1950.

Once official relations had been established with the nations most important to Burma's interests, the Burma government was freer to decide the scope and character of its relations with other nations. In expanding its foreign relations the AFPFL leaders seem to have been guided by three considerations. First, any economic development in the country depended upon sale abroad of Burma's surplus rice crop. Therefore, it was vital that Burma open relations with any nations which were actual or potential customers for Burma rice. Second, the Burma government could only fulfill its ambitious schemes for a socialist state by obtaining outside foreign assistance in the shape of loans, grants, trade agreements, credits, and technical assistance. Therefore, it was vital that Burma have relations with those countries which might supply some elements of economic aid. Third, the

AFPFL leaders had determined that Burma's foreign policy should be based on the principle of "friendship with all countries." Therefore, it was necessary for Burma to open relations with countries which might not be customers for Burma rice or might not be able to supply some form of economic assistance, but with which Burma needed to have official relations for geographic, historical, or other reasons.

In 1948–49, therefore, Burma opened relations with Indonesia, a primary rice customer, with Israel, a potential supplier of technical assistance, and with Japan, through trade missions, a prime supplier of economic aid in the form of reparation and a rice customer as well. Official relations with Thailand were natural, since the two countries were neighbors even though competitors in the world rice market. Relations with Ceylon were natural because of the common heritage of Buddhism and also because Ceylon is a rice customer. Expansion of Burma's foreign relations followed in subsequent years an orderly pattern influenced by the three factors mentioned above.

Official relations between Burma and Egypt, Yugoslavia, France, and Italy were established between 1950 and 1954. The very close relations between Burma and Israel and with Yugoslavia have already been noted. It is an interesting testimony to the effectiveness of the "friendly relations with all countries" concept that close relations with Israel have not prevented Burma from maintaining friendly relations with Egypt (and later with the United Arab Republic) and other Muslim states like Indonesia, Pakistan, and Afghanistan. Nor have close and friendly relations between Burma and Yugoslavia, characterized by a personal friendship between U Nu and President Tito, apparently affected adversely Burma's relations with the Soviet Union, Communist China, and other Communist bloc states such as Poland, Czechoslovakia, or Rumania with which Burma has had official relations since 1955.

Burma was one of the UN members which failed to carry out the intent of the United Nations General Assembly resolution of 1949 by recognizing the Republic of Korea as the government of Korea. In this instance, the Burma government took the position that, to recognize the government of one part of Korea and not of the other, or even to recognize both Korean regimes, would be to perpetuate a divided country, a condition the Burma leaders regarded as not conducive to international peace. The Burma government took the same position with regard to divided Vietnam although "good-will" missions from each of the Vietnam governments and Burma have been exchanged several times. In the case of divided Germany, the Burma government did not apply its principle of nonrecognition of a divided country. The Federal Republic of Germany was a recognized source of economic assistance and formal diplomatic relations were established in 1956.

In the case of these divided territories, the Burman leaders found themselves in a dilemma of conflicting interests. The government accepted a trade mission from East Germany and by 1958 this mission had a small permanent representation in Rangoon. It also became clear after 1960 that neither the Soviet Union nor Communist China regarded nonrecognition of the Korean and Vietnamese regimes as a satisfactory policy. On the other hand, if the Burma government had entered into formal relations with both the Communist and non-Communist governments of Korea and Vietnam, such action could not have been regarded with enthusiasm in either Peking or Moscow and, what is more, there would have been no logical reason for Burma not to have reestablished relations with the Chinese Nationalist government on Taiwan.

Prime Minister U Nu and his colleagues solved this dilemma of foreign relations in a typical and practical fashion, which at the same time demonstrated that aspect of the "psychology" of neutralism which leads neutralist countries to take positions favorable to that of the Communist bloc in the absence of any fear of retaliation by the Western nations. In 1961 the Burma government announced that it had entered into trade relations with the Communist People's Republic of Korea, and with the Communist Ho Chih-minh regime of North Vietnam involving exchange of consular relations. It was carefully stated that these new relationships did not imply that Burma was "recognizing" either of these two governments. Thus the Burma government apparently gained the advantages it sought while technically adhering to the principles of nonrecognition of divided territories. It is interesting to note that in the same year Burma completed its establishment of diplomatic relations with all state members of the "Communist camp" including Outer Mongolia.

As new African states have come into existence in the past few years, the Burma government has extended official recognition to most, but not all, and it would appear that economic considerations are taken into account as well as the natural desire of Burma, an ex-colonial territory, to recognize the independence of other excolonies. Burma early agreed to official relations with the Philippine Republic but did not provide for an exchange of diplomatic missions and establishment of legations in Rangoon and Manila until 1959. A number of Burman officials have visited Mexico and have been intrigued with the way in which the Mexican government has gone about dealing with economic, social, and political problems in an environment and under circumstances similar to those faced in Burma. This is about the only Latin American nation in which Burmans have shown any interest or with which they seem to feel that official relations might prove profitable.

While it is not hard to see the reasons for development of Burma's relations with certain nations and not with others, the basic question for a small nation like Burma is whether a policy of developing relations with a large number of countries of diverse interests and members of both power blocs in the present world has, in any way, adversely affected Burma's interests. To be practical, has establishment of official and "friendly" relations with any nation or group of nations hindered Burma's ability to dispose of its rice surpluses or to obtain needed economic assistance of any sort? The record of Burma's foreign relations reveals a negative answer. For example, Burma's continuing "friendly" relations with Communist China and other Communist bloc states, including the Soviet Union, has not prevented or apparently affected expansion of U. S.-Burma economic aid programs or of economic aid and technical assistance from Britain, West Germany, or other Western nations. Nor has Burma's acceptance of considerable economic assistance from the Anglo-American bloc adversely affected Communist bloc assistance to Burma or its general relations with the Communist nations. Again, close ties with Israel and Yugoslavia have not adversely affected Burman relations with the U.A.R., with General Nasser personally, with other Muslim states like Afghanistan or Indonesia, or with either the Soviet Union or Communist China.

It would seem, therefore, that Burma's development of friendly relations with a sizeable number of nations having conflicting interests in world politics has been profitable and has not hindered the Burma government in the pursuit of its policy goals or in obtaining the practical economic and other assistance it has desired. This conclusion would tend to support the old thesis that a small nation existing in a world of predatory states does well to play off one against the other and to spread its "interest" eggs in as many baskets as possible. This element has not been absent from the minds of the Burman policy-makers, but the record would indicate it has not been a paramount or primary factor in determining the scope and character of Burma's foreign relations. "Friendly relations with all countries" and "economic aid from any country so long as it does not infringe Burma's independence" are principles of very wide application, ones which can encompass a considerable variety of actions in foreign relations. To the Burman leaders, these principles of their foreign policy have worked well because they have shown good results, and to date, no really adverse consequences.

Again, the question may be raised as to whether the advantages Burma has derived from carrying on profitable relations with a variety of countries of diverse interests have been the consequence of the policies themselves and their effective execution, or have these good results for Burma been a matter of luck or because of circumstances in this rapidly changing world over which Burma has had little or no control. Part of the answer is to give credit to the Burman leaders for initiating relations with those nations able to supply Burma's practical needs for disposal of surplus rice, for economic aid and technical assistance. Consistent adherence to the principle of non-alignment with either power bloc has been of advantage to the Burma government in negotiations for economic aid since the AFPFL leaders have repeated again and again that they do not regard any economic agreement which they say "has no strings attached" as compromising their "independent" and "neutral" foreign policy. It must be recognized, however, that at any time, any one of the major nations could have denied help to Burma unless the Burma government was willing to make at least a negative commitment that it would not accept aid from a member of the rival bloc. Fortunately for Burma, the general pattern of postwar international politics has been otherwise. Small nations in need of help have generally not been penalized because they sought and obtained help from a member of a rival power bloc or another nation which followed a neutral policy. In fact, the postwar record of foreign aid by members of both power blocs is such that a good case can be made for a foreign policy or neutrality by any underdeveloped country. If a small country accepts aid from a member of the Communist bloc, it is likely to get discreet offers of aid from one or more of the western nations and vice versa. This has happened to Burma, and has tended to reinforce the Burma leaders' belief in the success of their neutrality policy.

Another test of effectiveness of a small nation's foreign policy is whether its basic principles or the government's execution of foreign policy in specific situations has resulted in serious disputes with other nations or not. Indonesian policy and actions, for example, brought about a very serious dispute with the Netherlands over West Irian (Dutch New Guinea) and with Communist China over the status of Chinese in Indonesia. In the case of Burma, there have been a number of situations which could have resulted in serious international disputes. To date, the Burma government has been able to act in such a way as to prevent this from happening.

Implicit in the adoption of "friendly relations with all countries" as a basic concept of Burman foreign policy was the corollary principle of peaceful settlement of disputes. This was stated by U Nu to be necessary if Burma was to maintain friendly relations with all countries. Burma was more fortunate than Indonesia in some ways since it inherited only one potentially serious territorial dispute, that of the undemarcated border with China. When Britain transferred power to the new Burma government, it acknowledged Burma's sovereignty over all territory it had controlled in the colonial period. Burma had no "West Irian" problem. Again in Burma, the Chinese resident minority was small and had never attained the virtual retail trade monopoly of the much larger Chinese population in Indonesia. In the prewar period, however, there were nearly a million Indians in Burma and this population did have a place in the economy similar to the Chinese in Indonesia. Japanese conquest drove most of the Indians out and the Burma government's land policies prevented those who returned from reestablishing their prewar position. Likewise, Burma's policy of nationalization prevented any significant reestablishment of British or other foreign enterprises in the country after 1948. Compensation for nationalized concerns was arranged for through negotiations and never became a matter for dispute between the governments concerned.

In the years 1951–54, the Burma government faced a potentially dangerous dispute arising from the presence of refugee Kuomintang troops in upper Burma. The Burma government sought a peaceful solution to this problem, first by obtaining assurances from Communist China of noninterference and next by submitting this problem to the United Nations. Although the Burma government was less than satisfied at the final solution, the problem was alleviated as a result of its efforts at a peaceful solution. Again the problem of border demarcation which threatened to develop into a crisis in Sino-Burman relations was finally settled by negotiations and agreement. It was in connection with the preliminary agreement in principle on the border problem that U Nu voiced the principle that in international relations it is "sometimes necessary for a nation to forego its legitimate claims in the interest of maintaining peaceful relations with other nations." Recognizing the disparity in power of Communist China and Burma in this case, the Burma government did not stick at technicalities or insist on rigid legal arguments. The border settlement was one of accommodation.

The record of Burma's action in the two disputes mentioned and its record in its relations with other states show that the Burman leadership took the initiative in translating its precept of "friendly relations with all countries" into action. By exchanges of visits and conferences, the Burma leaders have been able to settle minor differences between their country and Thailand over border problems. They were able to create an atmosphere of friendly relations despite historic Thai resentment for Burmese sacking of the old Thai capital of Ayuthia. Although Thailand is a member of SEATO, which Burma has refused to join, and is also a competitor in the world rice market, the initiative taken by the Burman leaders has created a general aura of good will in Thai-Burman relations.

Burma also shares a border with East Pakistan and this has involved the two governments in a number of disputes of a local nature. Arakanese Muslims migrated to East Pakistan in the early years after 1948 because of the insurrections in Burma and the violence perpetrated by the *Mujahids* on the Burma side. Later the flow was reversed when conditions in Burma became more stable and those in East Pakistan became worse. During the whole period, there has been a continuing problem of smuggling, sometimes on a considerable scale. For the most part, local officials on each side of the border have attempted to handle the problem, but in the fall of 1959 the problem became much more serious and armed clashes occurred. The military caretaker government of General Ne Win acted quickly to deal with this problem. As a result of agreement with the Government of Pakistan, a Joint Commission was established by the two countries in January, 1960, to handle this and all other border problems. The Indian population in Burma, most of them heartily disliked by the Burmans, has caused difficulties from time to time, but so close have been the relations between U Nu and Premier Nehru that the two governments have been able to prevent any of these difficulties from assuming the character of a serious dispute.

The record of the Burma government in applying its principle of "friendly relations with all countries" has been good. When U Nu took office again in 1960, he could truthfully say that Burma was on friendly terms with all countries and was not involved in any serious international disputes. He could attribute this situation in large part to the initiative taken by his government in peaceful settlement of such disputes as arose over the preceding years. And he could state that this record demonstrated the validity of Burma's policy of nonalignment, friendly relations with all countries, and adoption of positive efforts to ease international tensions. Such was the Burman belief in the success of their "positive neutrality" that when General Ne Win asserted the new military government in 1962 would continue this policy, it was accepted as a matter of course by the public.

Alternative Choices in Foreign Policy

Throughout this study it has been emphasized that circumstances and events seemed always to have combined in such a way as to reinforce what may have been the natural predeliction of U Nu and his associates for a policy of "independence" and nonalignment. In the formative years when neutralist principles were being developed by U Nu and his close associates, two extreme choices were certainly open to them. First, between 1947 and 1951, the AFPFL leaders *might* have decided to associate their nation closely with the Soviet bloc, or they might have limited their foreign relations to the West and to the uncommitted states, so as to have followed what many would have regarded as a "pro-Western" foreign policy. Those who advocated the first course were mostly the underground Communists engaged in trying to overthrow U Nu's government. Those who advocated the second course were mostly older politicians or Burmans who had strong western sympathies because of education or association with the British or Americans. In one of his earliest statements on foreign policy, U Nu asserted that although Burma drew much inspiration from the U.S.S.R., "Burma was no Czechoslovakia, but was three thousand miles away" and "within the Anglo-American sphere of influence." Hence, he said, Burma must have friendly relations with all countries and "no alignment with power blocs antagonistic to each other." (This was before 1949 and the capture of mainland China by the Chinese Communists.)

Burman acceptance of the concepts of "anticolonialism" made them fearful of too close ties with the West, hence their insistence on economic aid "without strings." Realistic appraisal of what might be expected in economic aid from the Communist bloc was tested in later years and left the AFPFL leaders chary of any policy which would lead to greater economic dependence on the Communist bloc states. Communist control of the mainland revived many old fears of Chinese expansion across the Yunnan frontier, but after 1950 these fears were less of armed invasion than simply the "spilling over" of the rapidly increasing Chinese mass into underpopulated Burma. Thus, at no time during the past fourteen years has there been a particular combination of circumstances or events which clearly dictated that the AFPFL leaders or the military choose sides in the cold war.

If the above is valid, Burma's neutralist policy would seem to have been shaped by history, particular combinations of international events, geographic location, and the good luck of not having become a bone of contention in the cold war contest like Laos or Vietnam. Nevertheless, it is still pertinent to ask whether there have been less extreme, but no less clear alternatives before the Burma leaders, which, had they been chosen, would have resulted in significant modifications in their neutralism.

In the first place, there have been two periods when the Burma government might have "aligned" itself much closer with the United

States and its allies. In 1952–53, just as the AFPFL leaders were beginning to breathe easier because they believed that the Karen and Communist insurgency no longer posed a threat to the government's existence, their government was beset with two major problems. The Korean war cease-fire and armistice caused a fall in the world rice market to a far greater extent than had been anticipated. Not only did the world price levels drop to a new low, but some customers for Burma's rice were reluctant to buy as much as in previous years. The rice export bubble burst and with it Burma's hopes of high foreign exchange earnings to pay for foreign imports needed in an overambitious economic development program. Equally grave was the infiltration of several thousand refugee Kuomintang troops into northeastern Burma.

At this point, the Burma government had an alternative choice to continued neutralism. It could attempt to obtain help from western nations for its rice problem and through loans tide itself over the foreign exchange crisis. It could have approached the United States directly for help in evacuating the KMT troops from upper Burma. These options were given consideration, but the United States was unwilling to act vigorously to aid Burma in disposal of its surplus rice, since the U. S. had agricultural surpluses of its own to deal with and it was equally unwilling to put pressure on the Chiang Kai-shek government in Taiwan and work with this government on rapid evacuation of the KMT troops. Had the American government in the summer of 1953 developed a new declaratory policy for southeast Asia, emphasizing support for "national independence" as it did after 1960 and implemented this policy by action to assist Burma, it is not unthinkable that the Burman leaders would have reacted favorably. The result could have conditioned the AFPFL leaders to a more favorable attitude toward a SEATO alignment and a consequent weakening of ties with the Communist states.

Without this American initiative, however, the AFPFL leaders were unwilling to take any lead on their own. They cancelled the U. S. economic assistance program, became increasingly annoyed with delay in evacuation of the KMT troops and what they felt was a weak U. S. stand on this subject in the UN, and turned to the Communist bloc for help. Burman disappointment in U. S. policy, lack of

U. S. action and Burman disillusionment over the UN's role as protector of small nations has already been explained. Disappointment with the Western nations was not permanent, however, and there was a second period when the Burma government might well have chosen to develop much closer ties with the United States and its Western allies.

The second chance came in the period 1956–59. This was the period of the border clashes with Communist China, the Suez case, and the Hungarian revolt. It was also the period when Burma's political system was saved from collapse by sudden agreement on a military caretaker government which was generally anticommunist and favorable to ties with the west. At this time the United States did come to Burma's assistance with a renewed and larger economic aid program. Beyond this, however, the American government seemed paralyzed by the growing trouble in Laos and Vietnam, by the Berlin crisis and the great spurt of the Soviets in "space spectaculars" — the "sputnicks." Attitudes in Burma were not unfavorable toward the West, but there was little response except a willingness to provide more economic aid. Whether a more positive response by the United States would have made the Burman leaders feel they could resist the growing blandishments and pressures by the Communists, of course, is speculation, but it presented a real possibility. In both examples given above, it must be noted that a Burman choice of closer ties with the U. S. and its allies was not alone Burma's to make. It would have been taken by U Nu, in the first instance, or General Ne Win in the second instance only because of positive action by the United States — assurances by the U. S. of a positive response to such a choice by the Burma government.

In the second place, it is fair to ask the question, was there any time during which it would have been possible for the Burman government to have so far departed from middle-of-the-road neutralism as to have virtually aligned itself with the Communist bloc. In retrospect, it would seem that there were two such periods. As has already been stated (in Chapter I) the Burma government was most favorably disposed toward the Soviet Union in 1948–49, at the beginning of the country's independence. At this time, if the Soviet Union had made firm efforts to woo this new Marxist-Socialist government in

Asia, it is quite likely that the Burman leaders would have responded readily and closer ties at that time might well have led to real alignment at a later date.

In 1953–55, another opportunity presented itself to the Burma government to develop much closer relations with the Soviet Union and Communist China. The Communist nations had come to Burma's aid with their rice barter agreements. Burma was suddenly "discovered" by the "big-wigs" of Communism, the Five Principles were signed, and U Nu and Chou En-lai fraternized at Bandung and in Rangoon. Khrushchev and Bulganin received a warm welcome in Burma and "gave" the Burma government five "projects." But there were sour notes in this "new" relationship. The port of Rangoon was tied up for weeks while cement from behind the "Iron Curtain" was unloaded under the rice barter deals only to solidify with the coming of the rains. The Soviet "gift" projects turned out to be less than "gifts" and only three were ever carried to completion, engendering little enthusiasm in Burma for Soviet aid.

Barter trade with the Communist bloc was not satisfactory and by 1956 the Burman government had obtained new customers for its rice and new grants and loans which made reliance on the Communist bloc no longer necessary or desirable. Had effective and concerted action been taken by the Communist bloc nations between 1953 and the end of 1955, in developing closer economic and political ties with Burma, virtual alignment with the bloc rather than neutralism, might have been effected. Nevertheless the good relationships developed at this time between Burma and Communist China provided a foundation for the *rapprochement* effected in 1961 which has brought Burma closer to a modification of its neutralist foreign policy than at any time in the past fourteen years. This may mean that there will be less opportunity for the Burma government to choose a course that is in any way adverse to the interests of the Communist bloc in the future.

The foregoing presentation emphasizes clearly a point about Burma's neutralist foreign policy which few Burmans would admit publicly and many have not carefully considered at all. If it is a reasonable inference that the Burma government could have chosen an essentially different course than neutralism, that is, one of alignment with the west or with the Communist bloc at the periods noted above when circumstances were favorable for such action, it is obvious that lack of response or action by either the Western nations or those of the Communist bloc was mainly responsible for it not doing so. To state this conclusion more bluntly, at no time since 1948 does it seem that the major nations of either power bloc deemed Burma important enough in the furtherance of their interests to make a concerted effort to win the Burma government to their side. Burma has been left to pursue its policy of neutralism as much by the inaction of the major nations as anything else.

In view of both internal and external events, and of the foreign policies of the major contestants in the cold war, it has been possible for the Burma government to pursue a course of nonalignment. Other courses could have been chosen at different times, but the fact that Burma as a country has not yet become a bone of contention between the forces in the cold war, such as Korea, Laos, or Vietnam and the fact that political factionalism in Burma itself induces compromise would have made it difficult after 1950 for the Burma government to have abandoned its neutralist policy. The foregoing outline of possibilities has been presented to a number of knowledgeable Burmans, who agree that changes were possible at the periods indicated, but who insist they were not very probable. These Burmans and others point out that it is a fact that the nations of neither power bloc have thought it worth while to date to make a sustained effort to capture Burma for their side in the cold war and that, consequently, while Burma has been fortunate in this respect, it has largely been due to their government's adherence to a neutralist foreign policy. It is thus fair to conclude that for Burma, and in Burman eyes, neutralism has been a viable foreign policy carrying with it far less risk to date of direct involvement in the cold war and less danger to the country's independence than any other policy.

Dangers from Within

If the Burmans who count are unsure of the future or are uneasy about the present, it is not because they oppose their government's foreign policy of "positive neutrality" or advocate a different course. Their uncertainty or unease stems from their doubts about the capability of their government, whether under civilian or military control, to so manage Burma's affairs as to turn a small, "weak" country into a small, "strong" nation capable of surviving the vicissitudes of the unsettled world of the 1960's. During the past fourteen years, the Burma government has survived severe internal insurrections, but at a time when the insurrectionists received no significant support from outside Burma's borders as such groups have in Laos and Vietnam today. Since independence, Burma has survived two periods of near political chaos (in 1958 and in 1962), in each case resulting in a take-over of the government by the military. Fortunately, none of these internal difficulties have attracted sufficient attention from the principal contestants in the cold war to make Burma a bone of contention such as Laos and Vietnam.

The fact, however, that Burma has so far escaped serious threats to its independence and integrity, should not delude anyone into thinking that Burma is safe for the future, or that a nonaligned Burma, friendly with all nations is exactly what the rulers in Moscow and Peking desire. In the eyes of the Chinese Communists, the United States has been and remains the "principal enemy." As Mao Tse-tung has written,[1] "The main blow of the revolution should be directed at the chief enemy . . . As for secondary enemies, we should adapt a dual revolutionary policy towards them. Work hard to keep them neutral, or even make allies of them when possible, while isolating their reactionary elements so as to concentrate our forces to fight against the principal enemy of the moment."

A basic question, then, is whether the Burmans have been able to so strengthen their government, their economy, and their society during the past fourteen years as to be able to sustain their "positive neutrality," their "friendship with all nations," and their acceptance of economic aid "without strings," against new and possibly more serious threats to the integrity of their nation than have confronted them in the past. An answer to this question requires a summary look at Burma's progress to date. Four major internal problems have worried many intelligent Burmans from the beginning and still concern them because they are far from being solved. First, there is the problem of how best to plan the economic development of Burma and, more importantly, how to develop an effective and efficient management of a largely state-owned and state-controlled economic system. Second, there is the problem of how to utilize most effectively the human resources of the country and how best to provide for the trained man power needed by any new, excolonial country. Third, there is the problem of how to attain a politically stable system in a country of diversity and among a population not yet used to the sophisticated concepts of parliamentary democracy. Finally, there is the complex and puzzling problem of creating a *nation,* a sense of national unity, an identity transcending those of geographic location, or ethnic-linguistic groups. It is, again, the problem of most new, excolonial nations which have inherited a plural society. To what degree can local, parochial separatisms be recognized without vitiating all efforts to build a national identity among all the peoples of Burma? It is the progress toward solutions of these internal problems, which, more than any other factors, may determine the future viability of Burma's foreign policy of neutralism.

The story of Burma's economic development since 1948 is illustrative of the many problems confronting most of the new nations. Although the Burman economy has probably not fared much worse than that of other new nations in Asia, its development has certainly fallen short of Burman and foreign expectations.[2] Acceptance of economic assistance from any nation, so long as it did not infringe on Burma's sovereignty, is a principle many Burmans in the government have been proud of and have adhered to consistently. The record shows, however, that economic aid from too many sources can be embarrassing and can present difficult problems of coordination in economic planning for the government.

Chou En-lai's announcement in Rangoon in January, 1961, that the Peking regime was granting Burma a credit in the equivalent of 30 million pounds sterling with interest payments only after ten years caused the U Nu government to urge publicly that Chambers of Commerce, all government departments, and any private groups send in suggestions as to how best this credit might be used. For in early 1961, the Burma government did not need this credit but it could hardly refuse to accept this evidence of "friendly cooperation" and "peaceful intentions" being demonstrated by its big northern neighbor, Communist China. Effective economic planning involves more than taking a public opinion poll, so to speak, as to how best to "spend" a sudden, unexpected, accrual of foreign credits.

Economic planning in Burma had its ups and downs before 1958, due in considerable part to events or circumstances outside of

Burma's control. Unfortunately, the political crisis of 1958, as has been explained, caused an almost complete halt in the execution of the existing economic plan. The first Ne Win government ousted two American advisory groups, but showed little capability in managing Burma's economy effectively. The third U Nu government during 1960 and 1961 struggled valiantly to produce a new four-year plan which was finally approved in mid-1961. This plan presumably will be carried out by Ne Win's successor "Revolutionary Council" government.

The present military regime, however, must overcome almost four years of slowed-down economic development. Projects under way have somehow moved ahead, a few have been completed, but internal political squabbles, pressures, and probably too much government by committee have hampered the whole decision-making process in the government, whether under civilian or military control. Even more serious has been the inability of the Burma government to coordinate the large variety of government-operated or controlled projects with the economic aid and technical assistance received from the widest variety of sources — international agencies, uncommitted nations, and nations who are members of both the big power blocs. A continuance of the spoils system, and political patronage, together with an insufficient number of expert managers and administrators has meant slow and very uneven progress. The first Ne Win government attempted with considerable success to "purge" the government of patronage appointees and "economic insurgents." The present Ne Win government has pledged to undertake this same process once again.

Interrelated to these difficulties, have been the many disagreements over the relative emphasis to be given to the public and to the private sectors of Burma's economy as well as the emphasis to be given to industrialization and to agricultural development. The recent "Manifesto" of the Revolutionary Council under General Ne Win, can hardly be said to chart a clear course for the country's future economic growth.[3] All of these disagreements and very general, unprecise statements of objectives have been characteristic of Burman politics and political leaders since independence. They have been complicated by excessive bureaucratic meddling by politicians (and possibly by the military during its periods of rule), by a lack of managerial skills, and very inadequate delegations of authority and responsibility. Many Burmans attribute weaknesses in economic planning and failures in coordination and efficient management of projects to a general unwillingness of most Burmans in public life to adopt the concept that public service for the welfare of one's country is a worthy end in itself rather than a means of enhancing personal and family position, power, and prestige.

Implicit in the foregoing is the seeming unwillingness of Burmans in the government to look very far ahead to the consequences of economic policy decisions. There seems to be a tendency, remarked upon by Burmans and by foreign observers, to make *ad hoc* decisions and "let the future take care of itself." Burmans have asserted that such an attitude is not a sign of weakness, since the Burman economy and the Burman government have "demonstrated their powers of survival to date." It does not follow, however, that a far from stable Burman economy can survive forever on a day-to-day basis or on faith. There is the danger that the most recent *rapprochement* between Burma and Communist China (referred to in Chapter V), with consequent increase of pressure for expansion of Sino-Burman commercial and cultural relations could well result in such an increase of Chinese Communist influence over Burma as to make the country far more dependent upon its northern neighbor than a strict interpretation of neutralism would envisage. The question which Burman leaders have not yet answered is whether a country with very uneven, not too well-planned or coordinated economy can sustain a foreign policy of neutrality or nonalignment, against undoubted pressures from one side in the cold war.

A second internal problem, still unsolved by either the civilian or military governments in Burma is that of effective utilization of the country's human resources. In all aspects of economic, political, and social development in a new nation, the need for rapid expansion of its trained man power has been so often reiterated as a primary requirement as to be largely taken for granted. Most educated Burmans are fully cognizant of this need, but over the past fourteen years only "barely perceptible progress" has been made in the utilization and training of Burmans to help solve the nation's problems.[4] Full use of any country's human resources is primarily an educational task, but it is much broader in scope than the development of a formal educational system. Means must be found by which persons possessing some education or training can be given opportunity and incentives to further perfect their skills, or learn new skills and generally increase their knowledge. Some effort must be made to use trained people regardless of their racial or linguistic affiliations. Unless such discrimination is sharply reduced there will be a continued waste of trained man power as almost any educated Shan or Kachin or Chin or Karen will point out.

In this area, real progress is not easy to assess because some yardstick must be chosen as a measurement. Compared to the educational system which existed in 1941 under British rule, the Burma government can show substantial progress in the numbers of children in school, the increase in the numbers of schools in the country, and the considerably expanded enrollments in technical schools and in the universities. Likewise, many, many more Burmans are being given the opportunity for vocational and technical training than ever before. There is no doubt about the capacity of the people of Burma to learn anything or to acquire any skill given an opportunity and adequate incentives. The essence of the problem is not in the numbers being trained or in their capacity for training, it is in the quality of the training itself. It is the low quality of the educational product of Burma's schools and colleges and institutes which has caused grave misgivings among many Burmans and more among foreign residents of Burma who are there to assist in Burma's development.

When the new government was established in 1948, one of its major goals was a rapid expansion of educational opportunities for its citizens. For a variety of reasons, thorough revision of the school curricula, production of necessary textbooks, visual aids and above all, expansion of effective teacher training were given inadequate attention and educational progress lagged badly. Although some effort was made to provide all the requisites of a good educational system mentioned above, surveys and reports of educational commissions over the past fourteen years still point to the fact that educational facilities are only barely adequate to meet part of the demand of Burmans for some kind of an education. What is worse, many of the educational methods in use today are little changed from those introduced by the British at the beginning of the century.

Burman leaders have not been unmindful of these difficulties but it is a question as to whether very many of them are fully conscious of the close correlation between economic and political development and the educational process or how well they understand the importance of *quality* in educational training as opposed to the numbers trained. In part this has been a matter of priorities. Expenditures on economic development projects, in particular the urgency of those projects which would decrease Burma's dependence on imports or provide foreign exchange earnings have meant that there has been a much lower expenditure of money and effort on educational development. There has been a failure on the part of many Burmans to realize that while a hydroelectric power installation or a brick factory or textile mill can be planned and with good management be brought to completion according to schedule, the training of a sufficient number of Burmans to administer government operations and enterprises, to carry on the day-to-day business of a modern state takes much longer and, in one sense, requires more skill in planning and execution, by more people than do noneducational enterprises.

It is not unfair to say that there has been very little progress in developing the standards of education necessary to produce the kind of trained people Burma needs. There are far too few teachers and too few well trained teachers, at all levels in the educational system. In no other segment of Burman life have British colonial practices and ideas been clung to so tenaciously than in the schools and the universities. The British system made a certificate or a university degree dependent upon passing examinations and a premium was placed on rote-memory learning. The tragedy of this continuance of the British colonial inheritance is that for fourteen years the number of qualified and trained young people needed for government service, for management of economic enterprises, and a variety of other tasks is not only pitifully small but those who are trained have generally not learned to think. Nor have they been given much opportunity to learn how to analyze problems.

Lack of effective educational progress is understandable. What is regrettable is the fact that in two years of U Nu's third government no visible efforts were initiated to improve the quality of training in the educational system. Students still resist successfully any attempts to raise academic standards and the profession of teacher gets very little of the recognition it needs to raise the quality and level of teaching in all the schools, colleges, and universities. A major and very obvious consequence of the failure to improve the quality of education in Burma is an ineffectiveness in government administration and in government-operated enterprises which must be seen to be believed. There are, of course, some exceptions, but unfortunately they do not seem to inspire much imitation. Pilot projects have a way of remaining interesting but not becoming instructive. Young people who have passed their examinations by a rote-memory process are not well equipped to apply and integrate their knowledge by a reasoning process. They are happier following the rule book and the regulations.

Again there is danger for the future in the failure of the Burma government to make effective use of its greatest resource, the people of Burma. In the old colonial society, education was the open door to a particular kind of employment which gave superior social status to the employee. The educated person had relatively limited responsibilities and there was very little knowledge gained of the complexities of the world outside the colony. So long as this inherited colonial type of education is perpetuated, as it has been to a considerable degree in Burma, graduates of high schools and universities are unlikely to seek work in the rural areas, even on government projects. They gravitate to or remain in the cities and larger towns, often taking less than satisfactory jobs or even ones for which they are not trained, because to earn a livelihood otherwise would lower their social status as an educated person. Too many of them become the educated "half-employed" or unemployed. In Burma, as in other excolonial countries, the students and the unhappy graduates are the prime targets of Communist propaganda and subversion.

The country-wide All-Burma Student's Unions have been heavily infiltrated by the Communists for many years. Likewise, the Rangoon University Student's Union, which manages affairs for the 12,000 students at the major university in Burma, has been under Communist control since 1952 at least, with the possible exception of one or two years in the intervening period. If Peking and/or Moscow ever intend to develop a truly hard-core Communist organization in Burma, well organized enough to become a potent political force, the students in Burma's schools and the recent graduates provide some prime material.[5] These products of Burma's educational system have learned very little about the world in which they live. They know almost nothing about the politics of the cold war or the economic systems of the Western nations or of the Communist bloc. Very, very few have ever learned to think for themselves although they are all very free in expressing opinions on almost any subject. Yet like all young people, they are eager for change, for progress, for advancement for themselves.

The present leaders of Burma, both civilian and military grew up in virtually the same educational environment, yet they have had the hard experience of political or military responsibility, of managing the affairs of a nation, and many of them have learned a great deal. Eventually, these men will be replaced by Burmans who never experienced British rule or Japanese occupation or the excitement of participating in a successful independence movement. Many of those who will rise to positions of leadership in the coming years will have had just as much impulsion toward Marxism as did U Nu and his associates. They will bring with them, not the feeling that they made their independent nation and must somehow make it succeed, but quite different feelings evidenced by the growing egocentrism now manifested in Burma. If Peking and/or Moscow decide it is to their interest to make the effort, and should hold out to a Burma government in the future a promise of continuing independence within a Communist "Co-Existence Prosperity Sphere" then "liberation"—Communist style — will have as much appeal to a new generation of Burmans in control of the government as did the promises of the Japanese in 1942.

A third major problem, about which many Burmans are truly concerned and which seems little nearer solution now than in 1949, is that of attaining a stable political system for the country. As has been stated, Burman politics is the politics of factionalism, of the interplay of contests for personal power and position. The most often voiced criticism by Burman citizens is against self-seeking politicians who appear unwilling to subordinate their ambition for personal gain and prestige to the welfare of the country as a whole. The civil servants, many of whom are hard working and dedicated public officials, found great relief during the first six months of the military caretaker government because "the politicians were off our necks." These feelings were modified during the remainder of Ne Win's term because of the propensity of the military to make snap decisions and take arbitrary action. What most Burmans hoped, was that the gains made during the military government period — more law and order in the country, reduction of graft and corruption, and a generally greater feeling of security — would be maintained and even built upon by the third U Nu government.

At first, with U Nu's Union Party holding an overwhelming majority in the parliament, it appeared that the optimists had some ground for their hopes. As the months wore on it seemed that the technique of government followed by the Union Party was to appoint more and more committees and commissions to consider and "coordinate" the "16,000 problems" U Nu asserted were confronting his government. U Nu himself, appeared to vacillate in his role of both Prime Minister and party leader. At one time he expressed the wish to resign, then decided to divest himself of responsibility for the party organization. This position he soon changed by assuming a new title in Burman politics of "Party Boss." In 1961, when problems were no less pressing than earlier, U Nu left the capital for a forty-five day meditation period on the top of Mount Popa where he refused to permit government business to reach him. While the committees and commissions considered, debated, and reported, little progress seems to have been made in resolving fundamental problems of political disunity. To make matters worse, by the end of 1961, Burmans were openly discussing the fact that U Nu's Union Party, like the old AFPFL had begun to fragmatize, to split into contending cliques and factions. This factionalism was taken advantage of once more by the Communists, both above and underground, to press their demands.

By the end of January, 1962, the same political *malaise* of 1958 had set in and with the same result. Political disintegration was forestalled by the military *coup d'état* of March 2. As in 1958, the military, through their Revolutionary Council, acted swiftly and arbitrarily. Civil servants have the politicians "off their necks" but the army officers are once more at their sides to give the orders. Whether this will be a change for the better, it is too early to say. One thing is certain, achievement of political stability of any permanent character in a new nation is not to be obtained by fiat or to be gained by arbitrary acts in an atmosphere of chauvinism. But it was not a consideration of the long-range future that prompted General Ne Win, Brigadier Aung Gyi and their military colleagues to act. It was the obvious and immediate need for a strong government, an executive strong enough to stop the "deteriorating situation," to bring the country under a single control that brought about Ne Win's second government. Only the months or years ahead will prove whether the military can do what U Nu and his political associates failed to achieve.

A fourth problem for any Burma government and one on which only little, if any progress has been made, is to be found in the present condition of Burman society. As Furnivall pointed out, Burma has had a plural or fragmented society. British rule was established within what could be considered at the time Burma's natural frontiers. Within these boundaries, however, live over four million non-Burmese speaking peoples, some in still primitive tribal conditions. In 1948, these minority peoples had nowhere to go but to the Union of Burma and some, like the Karens, were so diffused among the Burmese in the south and southeast that no linguistic boundary even for administrative purposes could have been drawn to provide them with a separate area within the Union. The Burma Constitution made unusual provisions for these minority groups by giving the Chins, Kachins, Shans, and Karens separate states within the Union and giving these minorities a majority of representatives in the upper house of parliament, the Chamber of Nationalities and cabinet posts for their representatives.

Nevertheless, the separatisms or fragmentation of Burman society which existed in pre-British times and which the British did little to alleviate continued to persist and even seems to have become more virulent. Shans, Kachins, Chins, and Karens still regard themselves as separate nationalities within the Union of Burma. For political reasons, U Nu apparently felt it necessary to accentuate these differences during his third administration by promising both the geographically separate Arakanese and the Mons, who are Burmese-speaking Buddhists for the most part, autonomy as new states within the Union. Further divisive tendencies showed themselves in September, 1961 when a conference of minority groups was held in the Shan State capital of Taunggyi from which *Burmese* politicians were barred. Demands for secession and for an independent Shan state were made by some of the younger extremist delegates at this conference. Thus it would seem that the various ethnic-linguistic groups within the Union, after fourteen years, are no nearer the point of assimilation into a larger Burman nationality and citizenship than in 1948. They feel discriminated against by the Burmese dominated government in all sorts of ways and the Burmese majority, proud of their Burmese history and their Burmese kingdoms continue to feel superior to their fellow citizens of a different race and language. This growing disunity and the failure of U Nu's government to bring any real semblance of national unity into Burma as a whole was another major cause for the military take-over in March, 1962.

It is not just a question of educating these minority peoples to a point where they feel a real identity with the Burmese and others as citizens of a single nation, Burma. If this was all, the problem would be serious enough. What is the essence of the problem of Burman society is no less than the problem of nationhood. Burma is an independent state but is not yet a nation. This problem faces almost every excolony when it becomes independent since all these excolonial countries inherited arbitrarily drawn colonial boundaries usually enclosing a congerie of ethnic-linguistic groups. The failure to date, of the Burma government to inject into the minds of the people of Burma, minority groups and all, a sense of true nationalism, a feeling of loyalty to their nation which would transcend loyalty to locale, racial or linguistic group or family or faction, has handicapped the government at every turn. Divisive tendencies due to race or language or locale are compounded by other divisive tendencies due to political factionalism, family loyalty, ideological differences, and sheer parochialism. The net result, as in so many of the new nations, is an almost total lack of anything like national unity about which their leaders talk so much.

In the world of cold war politics, the existence in Burma, as in many of the new nations of which Laos and the Congo are only current examples, of these divisive tendencies, these feelings of separatism, this truly fragmented society, is no less than an open invitation to infiltration and subversion from the outside. The Burman leaders have always been afraid of this happening and U Nu said many times, that outside interference, support for or subversion of some of these separate groups in Burma was the greatest danger to the country's freedom. There is a weakness in Burman reasoning on this problem, however, to which few Burmans will admit if they recognize it at all. Because Burma was a British colony and the present Burman leaders were nurtured in the Marxist-Leninist view of colonialism, they always seem to regard the possibility of interference or subversion by Western nations or Western interests equally as dangerous as Communist subversion. Many Burmans seem to believe that the United States and the European "imperialist" powers still cherish some secret ambition to subvert Burma's independence, not by armed invasion but by support of a separatist group within the country, or by a combination of economic, political, and cultural means. Of course, this is what the Burmans are constantly being told by the Communists. Hence U Nu's insistence on economic aid "without strings" which, as far as western economic assistance is concerned, he has stated has had no strings attached at any time.

This Burman attitude, also found in many of the new nations, is based on their little knowledge of nineteenth-century colonialism as continually interpreted by the Communists and does not seem to permit acceptance of the concept that nations' actions and policies can and do change. Such an attitude naturally reinforces the concepts of neutralism, but as such, tends to becloud the nature of the cold war in the decade of the sixties. If the Burman leaders harbored as deep suspicions of Communist intentions and designs as they do of Western intentions, then their neutralism might have more of the character of impartiality about it. Whereas the actions of the Western nations since 1945 hardly support the deep Burman suspicions of the danger of western subversion in their country, the Burmans, like other neutralists, refuse to accept the openly declared intentions of both the Soviets and the Chinese Communists as posing any danger to their independence. Their attitude seems to be one of accepting Communist declarations like the "Five Principles" at face value and of refusing to change unless events prove them wrong. To the outside observer, this attitude seems much like that of a homeowner who doubts an inspector's warning that faulty wiring in his house may cause a fire and who asserts he will wait until the fire breaks out before he will take action.

This ambivalent attitude of the Burmans, like that of many leaders in other neutralist countries, is understandable, if regrettable. It is understandable, for if Burmans were to admit the illogic of their refusal to take seriously Communist intentions to "liberate" Asian countries, this would necessitate a fundamental reorientation of their foreign policy to a posture other than "positive neutrality." It is regrettable, because it induces in Burman leadership acceptance of a double standard of judgment on cold war issues — the application of one set of values to the actions and policies of Western nations and a different set of values to those of the Communist nations. The failure of Burman leadership to achieve a substantial degree of national unity and to significantly diminish those divisive tendencies, parochialisms, linguistic and ethnic differences which have plagued the territory since precolonial days gives to the Chinese Communists particularly, the opportunity for further dividing and weakening Burma to the point where its government can be bent to the will of Peking.

The failure of the Burma government, whether civilian or military, to make significant progress toward solution of the four major problems summarized in this section leads to one conclusion in which may be summed up an evaluation of Burma's policy of neutralism to date. If the leaders of Burma, or any small, relatively weak nation, espouse a neutralist policy based on principles of "non-alignment," "friendly relations with all nations," "economic aid from any source if no strings are attached," and at the same time permit changing circumstances and events to dictate their day-to-day decisions, then the success of such a nonalignment or neutralist policy will be in direct proportion to their ability to make effective and consistent progress toward economic viability, political stability, and national unity within their country. In the case of Burma, continued failure to solve any one of the four major internal problems previously summarized — all of which are interrelated — could result, not necessarily in a national collapse, or a sudden armed invasion, but in the gradual erosion of the capabilities of the Burman leadership to draw a line beyond which a foreign policy action would lead to alignment or growing dependence upon Communist China and the Soviet bloc.

If any Burma government is not strong enough to sustain a policy of neutralism and protect its independence in the face of growing Communist influence, then the Western nations would either have to initiate counteraction or see their own influence in Burma steadily diminish. Burma's neutralism then, particularly the basic principles which U Nu enunciated and the military have pledged to continue would have to be radically reinterpreted or discarded altogether. Many Burmans would not accept this line of reasoning, for like the people of all new, excolonial countries, many have confidence that they can deal with Communism when it comes but until then, they will not worry about it. Unfortunately there are very few Burmans who have studied history thoroughly, who know the details of the Communist take-over of Czechoslovakia in 1948, or the Soviet take-over in North Korea between 1945 and 1950 or who take a continuing interest in events in Laos and Vietnam. Furthermore, to accept the line of reasoning presented above, for many Burmans, would mean a reorientation of their thinking; it would serve to further unsettle them in their unsettled society in a very unstable world. It is understandable that they avoid facing up to such a change, but the conclusions reached in the chapter on Burma's relations with Communist China are merely reinforced by the foregoing discussion and should be considered by those who are interested in Burma's future welfare as an independent nation.

— VIII —

NEUTRALISM: VIABLE POLICY OR FATAL TRAP?

In preceding chapters it was suggested that while the Burmans regard their foreign policy of neutralism as successful to date, it may have led them into such a close *rapprochement* with Communist China as to have virtually nullified, in fact, the practical application of those principles upon which their neutralist foreign policy has been based. It is the purpose of this concluding chapter to examine neutralism briefly in a broader context, based upon this case study of Burma's foreign policy.

It is recognized that Burma's geographic contiguity with Communist China has always involved special considerations for the Burman policy makers different from those which might apply to many new, excolonial nations like Ghana, for example. Nevertheless, what can be learned from the Burman experience as a neutralist nation has a number of broad applications. In Asia, the present situation of Laos, of Cambodia, and of Nepal, the first hopefully to become a "neutral and independent nation" through Soviet-American agreement, and the latter two following a neutralist policy by declaration, makes this broader examination pertinent.

Neutralism as a Cult

As more and more of the new, excolonial nations have declared their adherence to a policy of neutralism or nonalignment, the relationships of these neutrals in conferences, in the United Nations, and through expressions of their leaders have almost assumed the form of a cult, endowed with certain elements of mysticism and taking on an air of exclusivity. Anxious to avoid entanglements with the cold war contestants, yet painfully aware of their dependence upon them and of the fact that isolationism in the modern world was impossible, the leaders of Burma and other new nations have endowed the concept of neutralism with properties suggestive of certain religious groups — a "holier than thou" attitude in their dealings with the committed nations. Expressions of these feelings can be found in the many assertions by U Nu, General Ne Win and his staff officers, and Burman representatives at UN sessions which have been echoed by many of the representatives of the newer nations. Time and again the neutralists have contended that their very posture of nonalignment makes them more "objective" in judging the rights and wrongs of crucial international issues than those nations which are committed to one side or other in the cold war. Yet there have been few instances in which the Burma government or any group of the neutral nations have offered carefully conceived and constructive proposals for solutions of the very problems they assert they can judge better than others.

When issues or problems arise that affect their individual, vital interests, however, these same neutral leaders act as all good nationalists have always done in justifying their contentions, often adopting the very line of reasoning they have been most critical of the western nations for following. This occurred when the Burma government was pressing its case in the UN on the presence of Kuomintang refugee troops in upper Burma. The Kashmir dispute, the Goa case, and the dispute over West Irian provide similar examples of these neutralist attitudes by the leaders of India, Indonesia, and others which support their cause.

This apparent development of a "cult" of neutralism stems basically from feelings of both egocentrism and ethnocentrism characteristic of all new nations. For in one sense, the excolonies which have become independent since World War II are the "status-seekers" in the world community, since few of them have either the resources or the capabilities of becoming "power-seekers." There is little doubt but that, in the minds of the AFPFL leaders during the first six years of Burma's independence, their new nation needed to establish a "status" position for itself in the world. These leaders desired greater recognition for their nation but were handicapped by uncertainty as to whether they could even maintain the independence of their country. Fear of interference from outside in support of the Communist or Karen insurrectionists or the KMT troops was a constant concern of the Burman leadership. In the first six years of independence, the Burmans who counted politically had very mixed feelings about their country, their past, and their identification in the strange new world of power politics. They had little time to get these feelings sorted out in their minds under the pressures of events, as one severe crisis succeeded another.

By 1953–54, the situation had begun to change in Burma's favor. The very fact that the AFPFL government had survived crises which could easily have caused its collapse gave the Burman leaders a greater feeling of confidence. The fear of outside interference had diminished after the "correct" attitude taken by the Chinese Communists on the KMT problem. The end of hostilities in Korea and Indo-China removed the fear of imminent world war in the Far East. The willingness of the Western nations and of India to provide economic aid to Burma was balanced by the willingness of the Communist bloc countries to relieve Burma of its unexpected rice surpluses in 1953–55.

In the six years after 1954, Burman attitudes both changed and hardened from those of the previous six years. Many Burman politicians retained a warm feeling for the Soviet Union and an admiration for its achievements. This was hardly reciprocated. As more Russian technicians and advisers appeared in Burma, it was obvious that they came because they were sent and that they were generally incapable of developing warm and friendly relations with the Burman people. Burmans who went to the Soviet Union found themselves in a totally strange world and perhaps sensed that they were not being welcomed as friends but as persons who could be used for Soviet purposes. Initial admiration for Communist China was at first enhanced by the fact that the Chinese seemed much more compatible to the Burmans as Asians than did the Russians. The problems confronting Communist China seemed more familiar to the Burmans. They admired the "discipline" of the "hard-working" Chinese masses. Yet most Burmans who went to Communist China did not return convinced that Communism was the solution to Burma's problems. Whatever admiration Burmans felt for the "progress" made by their northern neighbor was more than balanced by their realization of the potent mass of the Chinese population. To a Burman unused to living in a crowded and overpopulated country, the sheer weight of the Chinese mass population was something frightening to contemplate. Hearing reports of the continuous flow of persons across the border, the politically literate Burman could not but worry about the future of his small, underpopulated and open country, so close to the pressing Chinese hordes.

Earlier suspicions of the intentions of Western "colonial" nations were considerably ameliorated after 1954. The United States, Great Britain, members of the British Commonwealth, and other Western nations had willingly accepted Burman conditions for economic aid "without strings." Japanese reparations had provided a most important "lift" to Burman plans for economic development. If the Western nations harbored any "designs" on Burma, as the communist parties and leaders contended, then the record of Western economic aid provided no evidence of this. Although American experts might have preferred to see American aid channelled into certain types of projects rather than others, Burma government requests were honored without much objection. Earlier questions about the American aid program were all but forgotten after 1956 when a whole series of agreements were made for increased American assistance.

Perhaps most important of all was the fact that beginning in 1952, Burma began to achieve a more widely recognized status in the world of nations. In this year Burma began its participation in the Colombo Plan. By 1952 it had become a member of all the United Nations specialized agencies and had begun receiving various kinds of assistance from them, including the United Nations Technical Assistance Administration. Likewise, Burma had become one of the so-called "Colombo Powers." In the meetings of this group, the Burman Prime Minister, U Nu, participated as an equal with the Prime Ministers of India, Indonesia, Pakistan, and Ceylon in dealing with international problems of concern to their respective nations.[1] This participation allowed Prime Minister U Nu to have an important part in planning the Bandung Conference of Asian-African nations held in Indonesia in 1955.[2] For the smaller nations of Asia and particularly Burma, this has been a high point in their international relations. The "glow" of the Bandung Conference has faded now and annual celebrations of this event have begun to lose their lustre since no efforts were made, or perhaps were possible, to make the meeting at Bandung a start of continuing association.

Although Bandung was a high point of achievement and recognition by Burma as a nation, any disappointment felt regarding its outcome or in the lack of similar action since has not diminished Burma's status in the world, at least in the eyes of the Burmans. Development of close and friendly relations with uncommitted states has given Burma a position in which the Burman leaders feel they are not alone in the world but have the moral, and even material support of other nations who have achieved a status position. To their ties with India, which date from the beginning of their independence, Burma can add the close and friendly ties developed with Israel and Yugoslavia and the fact that as a neutral nation, Burma is also on good terms with General Nasser and the U.A.R. as well.

Another contribution to the Burman feeling that their country has achieved a real status in the world community after 1954, has been the attention paid to Burma by other nations and the most important members of the two power blocs. Increasingly after 1954, the Burma government has been host to heads of states, prime ministers and foreign ministers from the Communist bloc, the free nations and the uncommitted nations. As state guests these individuals were given the usual fanfare of official greetings, the drive in from the airport amid (some) cheering crowds, visits within Burma, and the usual state functions. Burman officials from U Nu down, as well as General Ne Win and his staff officers, who have gone abroad since 1954 have been accorded VIP treatment. When abroad on official missions, whether in the Communist bloc or in the free nations, Burman officials are well taken care of, their reasonable wants met, and they are wined and dined lavishly. This is heady stuff for the representatives of a small nation which has been isolated from contacts with other nations within the memory of most of the Burman officials who receive such treatment.

It is no wonder that most of the Burmans in politics are firm supporters of their government's neutrality policy. It has permitted them to travel to Israel, to the United Arab Republic, to the United States and to Communist China, to the Soviet Union and to Japan and Western Europe. Since 1954, Burma has naturally been requested to send representatives to all UN conferences, a large number of intergovernmental meetings on atomic energy and the international law of the sea, and to hosts of privately sponsored conferences. In these meetings, the Burman representatives are treated with respect, they have an equal voice with those of the big powers, and their views are listened to. All of this means that the politically literate Burmans, those who really have a determining voice in the politics of their country, have begun to exhibit characteristics of egocentrism. They have been convinced by experience that their government's policy of neutrality has been workable, and has paid dividends both to their government and to themselves as Burmans.

As a result, more and more Burmans have come to believe that neutralism permits their country to be friends with all nations and beholden to none. This has permitted growth of the sentiment that Burmans should run their own affairs as they please with as little advice from outside as possible. The latest expression of both this egocentrism and of *Burmese ethnocentrism* is to be found in the recent Manifesto of General Ne Win's Revolutionary Council. (See Appendix IV.) In his analysis of this aspect of Burman attitudes, Lucien Pye concludes:[3]

The Burmese politician is equally ill at ease and unsure of himself in dealing with Westerners, who in a sense represent the other extreme of acculturation continuum and who like the peasant have not had to change their identities. In these relations the Burmese politician is decidedly more effective when the circumstances cast the foreigner in the unambiguous role of opponent whose every intention and design must be vigorously resisted. Such situations offer the politician proof that he is true to his Burmese identity and that he can resist the attraction of the foreign. Most particularly, the Burmese politician seems to derive satisfaction from those confrontations in which he is able to criticize the West on the basis of Western values, for these provide him with the opportunity to prove that he is acculturated to the modern world while at the same time he is true to his separate identity as a Burman. He can feel that in changing his standards of judgment, he has not lost his sense of loyalty.

Similar illustrations could be found among the political leadership of almost all of the newer, excolonial nations. These attitudes, these uncertainties, which express themselves in egocentrism, even chauvinism in foreign affairs, are interconnected with the "cult" of neutralism, for nonalignment, in the minds of neutralist leaders, means self-reliance and justifies whatever kinds of relationships they assert they have with the aligned states or the big powers of either bloc. The "mystique" of this cult of neutralism enables many of these leaders to take refuge in their desires to be free of any entanglements or obligations to the aligned nations in the face of actions or policies which, in fact, prejudice their principles of neutralism.

Neutralism as a Semantic Trap

It is significant that in India and Burma, the "oldest" of the neutralists among the new nations, use of the label *neutralist* or *neutralism* to characterize their respective foreign policies was not the choice of Prime Minister Nehru or of Prime Minister U Nu in the first years after independence. Both leaders seem to have realized from the beginning that the kind of foreign policy they wished their governments to pursue — "non-alignment with power blocs antagonistic to each other," "friendly relations with all nations," and "acceptance of economic aid from any nation so long as it did not infringe their sovereignty," — could not be described as "neutrality" in the historic context of that term in international relations. Hence both Nehru and U Nu, seeking for succinct descriptions of their basic foreign policy concepts, most often used the word "independent."

Beginning with the Korean war, however, and increasingly thereafter, Western journalists and officials began to describe the nonalignment policies of Burma, India, and other nations as *neutralist* and to label their leaders *neutralist*. Explanations by Nehru and by U Nu of the essential elements of their nonalignment policies were to no avail. Protests from writers and scholars that this new usage of *neutralist, neutralism, neutral,* and *neutrality* was improper and debased rather precise terminology by making the older definitions of these words meaningless, were to no avail. U Nu expressed his unhappiness over this semantic development most precisely in his speech at the National Press Club in Washington in 1955.

The terms *neutral* and *neutrality* as describing the status or policy of a state in international relations had become endowed before 1939 with precise meanings. All students of international law are familiar with the so-called "Laws of Neutrality" and both in national and international courts as well as in national legislation and international agreements, the status of a neutral state and the policy of neutrality were accepted in international practice along with a set of criteria by which the policies and actions of a neutral nation might be judged. Neutrality was generally held to require a state to refrain from taking part either directly or indirectly in a war between two nations. Neutrality was considered to be more than nonbelligerancy, but nevertheless was more of a negative than a positive posture. The neutral state in time of war was restrained, if it followed international custom, from a wide range of activities which might be construed as participation on one side and thus give rise to a declaration of war or other acts by the opposing side which would end such a neutral status.

Throughout a century before World War II, the status of a neutral state and a policy of neutrality implied as strict impartiality as possible. This did not mean complete stoppage of relations with the belligerents in a war, or a wholly negative policy. On the contrary, it was regarded as proper for a neutral to engage in nonmilitary relations with belligerents so long as such activities were conducted without favoritism — with impartiality. With the passing of adherence to the old customs and rules of international law when even after World War I undeclared wars became more frequent, it was obvious that in proportion to the extent and scope of a war between great powers, each side would make the most strenuous efforts to prevent nations from following a neutral policy and attempt to enlist them on their side against their opponents.

Among Western nations, the breakdown of American neutrality policy in two world wars, tended to stimulate the idea that neutrality was untenable and somehow "wrong." Since the Western nations in both world wars regarded their cause not as something which could be impartially judged, but as a cause which was morally "right" it followed that a policy of neutrality, once the big battles had been joined, was morally wrong. It is not surprising, then, that when realization that the postwar world was not to be the world of a managed peace under the aegis of the United Nations, but had turned out to be a world of "cold war," Western statesman and Western publicists, who believed in the "rightness" of the struggle against Communism, regarded a policy of nonalignment as similar to neutrality or neutralism and inveighed against it. It was natural, then, that use of *neutralist* and *neutralism* to describe the status and policies of such states as India, Burma, Indonesia, and others was widely accepted after the outbreak of the Korean war. From the Western point of view, the war in Korea was not war in the old sense of the last two world wars, but a punitive action by the world community through the United Nations, against an aggressor attempting to destroy the integrity of an independent state. In such a concept, there could be no real neutrality by members of the United Nations unless they failed to honor their obligations under the UN Charter. In this context, Secretary of State Dulles' contention that "neutralism" was immoral is understandable. (Some would contend it was unfortunate as well.)

So it was that Burma and other nations following a nonalignment policy had the labels *neutralist* or *neutralism* thrust upon them, with the implication in Western capitals, particularly in the United States, that such a posture was not only "immoral" but also required that they follow a strict course of impartiality. Since 1950, newspapers have been full of statements asserting that Burma or some other neutral nation was "leaning toward the Communist side" or toward the Western side perhaps capped by some semantic absurdity that a particular nation was more "neutral" toward the Communists than toward the West.

U Nu and other leaders of nonaligned countries soon realized that if they accepted the label neutralist as best describing their foreign policy, the result might be to limit severely their freedom of action and to make them so subject to pressures from each bloc in the cold war as virtually to paralyze action in the interests of strict impartiality. In short, the post Korean war usage of the terms *neutral, neutrality, neutralist,* and *neutralism,* had so denatured the older and more precise meanings of this terminology as to make it useless for their purposes. Yet U Nu and the leaders of the nonaligned nations have been so trapped by widespread usage of the terms neutralism and neutralist and their own usage of this terminology, that it is difficult to see how they can escape from this semantic trap. They have been forced to adopt the posture of Humpty Dumpty in his conversation with Alice: "I don't know what you mean by 'glory,'" Alice said. "I meant, 'There's a nice knock-down argument for you.'" "But 'glory' doesn't mean a 'nice knock-down argument,'" Alice objected. "When *I* use a word," Humpty Dumpty said, in a rather scornful tone, "it means just what I choose it to mean, — neither more nor less."

U Nu, Nehru, and other leaders have constantly sought to escape from the semantic trap of neutralism by use of other terms to describe their foreign policy — such as "non-alignment" "un-committed" and the like, and by use of qualifying adjectives such as "positive," and "dynamic." They have sought to escape from the implications of impartiality as a standard for their actions by asserting that their neutralism includes the principle that each government will take the "right" action on any issue as it may judge it at a given time. For U Nu and other neutral leaders have realized that in the present world, almost every action they take in relations with important nations can be interpreted as partisan. Furthermore, as this study of Burma's foreign policy shows, the Burma government can neither afford to be strictly partial in its foreign relations or in its position on all international issues, nor has it wished to be in the past.

So firmly has the neutralist label been fastened upon any nation pursuing a policy of nonalignment in the cold war that such nations cannot ignore it, or divest themselves of it. At the large Conference of these nations in Belgrade in September, 1961, almost all of the representatives tried successfully not to let the terminology of neutralism creep into their vocabulary, calling the meeting officially the "Conference of Unaligned States" and using the phrase nonalignment whenever possible. Worldwide reporting of this meeting, however, was under no such restrictions and in both the Communist and non-Communist press, *neutral, neutrality, neutralism,* and *neutralist* were used freely and interchangeably.

This semantic trap, from which the nonaligned nations have been unable to escape so far, is more than a matter of words. The implication that any action which openly espouses a policy of nonalignment, and is therefore, immediately dubbed *neutralist,* must strive to follow a course of impartiality is very clear. In the cold war contest, neither bloc is enthusiastic about neutralism as a status or a posture in foreign affairs. If unwilling to force a change in policy in a given case, such as that of Burma, both the Communist bloc states and the Western allies will put pressure on the Burma government not to show favoritism to the other side. When Burma or another neutral does seem to act partially, it is criticized only by the opponents of the side it has seemed to favor. Such a situation has induced in the leaders of Burma and similar neutral nations a constant attitude of wariness in their foreign relations. They hesitate to take a needed action or to adopt a logical position they believe to be "right" on some international issue for fear of criticism from one side or the other of the cold war. Their only comfort is derived from each other, but such are the differences between the neutral nations, that to date there have been few instances of the development of close and really profitable ties among many of them.

U Nu was probably right, after 1948, to insist as long as he could that Burma was following an "independent" foreign policy. In his mind and apparently in Nehru's as well, this meant no entangling military or political alignments or alliances with the cold war contestants. It did not rule out economic, cultural, or other ties such as Burma and India have developed, nor did it rule out political or military arrangements with other nonaligned states in the earlier years. An independent foreign policy, certainly in the minds of Burman leaders, was one designed to give them maximum freedom of action in future and unforeseen contingencies. It is equally certain that many arrangements between Burma and Communist bloc states were not made enthusiastically by the Burman leaders. But, labelled as neutralists, they were forced to make such arrangements since these might serve to demonstrate their impartiality or "neutrality" in view of continuing agreements with non-Communist nations for economic aid and other assistance.

Since U Nu, General Ne Win, and other Burman leaders have tried hard to de-emphasize the label "neutralist" for their foreign policy and have attempted to present it as an "independent" policy, their lack of success may well have diminished their ability to make hard or courageous decisions on the basis of "right" action. It may be contended, therefore, that "neutrality" as a policy is more likely to prejudice independence of action than otherwise and that a nation cannot have it both ways. It is therefore questionable whether President Kennedy's policy of supporting a "neutral and independent" Laos is not opening the same semantic trap for a new Laos government as Burma was almost "pushed" into. Burmans and other leaders of neutral nations are far from happy about the terminology of neutralism and have sought to escape from semantic difficulties with little success thus far. Too great preoccupation with terminology, however, is bound to obscure the more basic problem. Can the security and independence of a small country be protected by a policy of neutralism? Words are not enough.

Neutralism as Policy

Basic to the decisions made by U Nu and his colleagues in 1947–48 on the kind of foreign policy their new, small, Socialist state was to follow, was an estimate of the kind of international world Burma had entered. The Burman leaders made this judgment and almost without exception, they believe their estimates were correct. They saw the world divided by the contest of the big powers in a cold war. As they looked at their immediate problem of building a new nation, they wanted as little to do with this international contest as possible. They knew enough to feel that withdrawal from the world was not the answer. They determined to keep on friendly terms with all nations and to avoid involvement with the big power blocs if they could.

At the start, the Burma leaders did not believe they would have to become too dependent on other nations for assistance in developing the economy of their Socialist state. A variety of circumstances, not the least a series of violent insurrections, led the AFPFL government to seek and to accept economic aid from a growing number of nations, including members of both big power blocs. In accepting this help, U Nu and his associates, perhaps half-consciously, realized that by this process the Burma government was creating ties which might at some point vitiate their basic policy of nonalignment or neutralism. They began with the principle that only such foreign aid as was offered "without strings attached" would be acceptable. The effectiveness of this part of their neutralist policy, however, depended upon exercise of careful judgments, not just on each aid agreement, but on the longer-term consequences of economic ties with those nations furnishing the bulk of the assistance.

The Burman leaders believe that they have made good judgments on the whole. By taking economic help from a variety of sources, foreign governments and international bodies, they feel they have not prejudiced their neutralism or their independence of action. They may not have been able to obtain all the economic help from outside they wanted, but they have not gone begging. During U Nu's third government and in the brief period of General Ne Win's Revolutionary Council government, there have been no intimations from Burman leaders that their country's economic condition was so serious as to need large-scale assistance from the outside. These facts buttress Burman belief in the success of their neutralist policy.

There are two elements in this presumed success, however, which must be emphasized. The first is the fact that as a small nation, Burma is not only underpopulated, but normally has a large rice surplus which is the mainstay of its foreign exchange earnings which can be used for internal development. This has been fortunate for Burma since the government has not been under the pressure of population growth as has India. A second element, less well recognized by many Burman leaders, is the fact that Burma's limited resources have not been any great inducement to foreign predators throughout its history. In the nineteenth century, other European powers had neither the will nor the strength to contest gradual conquest of Burma by the British. In the present century, Japan's attention to Southeast Asia was much more directed at Indonesia for its resources than at Burma and other territories. Neither the Soviet Union nor Communist China, to date, has apparently regarded Burma as a high-priority target for either economic or strategic reasons. Thus the Burma government has been able to trade and obtain aid from a large number of nations, members of both power blocs as well as neutrals, without seeming to prejudice its nonalignment policy or prevent its maintenance of friendly relations with all.

In the political realm of foreign relations, until 1960, the Burma government had been able to steer a tenable neutralist course. At the United Nations, Burman representatives had consistently explained their government's positions on crucial issues from somewhat different points of view than those of other leading neutrals. Burma's voting record on such issues before 1960 shows less partiality than that of India or Indonesia. Apart from U Nu's one attempt to involve himself and the Burma government in the role of mediator between the United States and Communist China, the Burma government has been conservative in its actions and statements on crucial international disputes. It has not taken the lead in the so-called Afro-Asian bloc at the United Nations or in the various meetings and conferences of neutral nations since Bandung. Burman leaders have had too many problems at home to act the role other than that of the "quiet" neutral in international politics.

Since 1960, however, the Burma government's implementation of its neutralist principles has undergone gradual changes which call into question the viability of neutralism as a safe policy for a small, internally weak nation. Many factors have been responsible for these changes, internal and external, and it has obviously been the interaction of both internal circumstances and changing international situations which have produced them.

First, Burman leaders and their representatives abroad have increasingly adopted the view of the East-West struggle held by India, Indonesia, and many of the new neutral nations. This view holds that a posture of neutralism or nonalignment means not taking sides in the cold war contest, but it results in a strange paradox. Out of the tendency of the neutral nations to assert, for example, that nuclear testing is wrong no matter which bloc undertakes it, comes an unwillingness to make logical judgments on resumption of nuclear tests by one side in violation of a clear undertaking given by both the U.S.S.R. and the United States. As currently expressed, the neutral nations seemed to have developed a double standard of judging the policies and actions of the cold war opponents. In the clear case of the Soviet Union's violation of the nuclear test-ban on the eve of the conference of unaligned states in Belgrade, the neutrals, Burma included, were unable to bring themselves to criticize the Soviet Union unilaterally as they have not hesitated to do concerning many American policies and actions. In Western nations, there has developed a deep suspicion that a policy of neutralism induces a willingness to apply different standards of judgment to the Communist bloc than to the free World allies.

Refusal to apply logical standards of judgment to both sides in the cold war simply means that politically, the neutrals are aligning themselves with one side on many crucial questions and problems. Burma's leaders and those of other neutral states generally deny that this is a departure or a break in their policy of neutralism, but it has been so regarded in Western nations and it is implied in the favorable expressions coming from Peking and Moscow when such a double standard of judgment is expressed. On the other hand, when a neutral nation deals with a problem vital to its national interests, it acts as nations have done in the past, ignoring the fact that such action may be similar to that for which it has roundly criticized the United States or one of its Western allies.

The paradox arises again from the semantics of neutralism which implies impartial judgments and actions. It would be difficult indeed for Burma or other small, neutral nations to refrain from positions or policies which are not in effect alignment with one side or the other in the cold war. That Burma's leaders deny their favoritism to the Communist position is being "un-neutral" there is no question. It does not look that way to others, however, and Western nations cannot be blamed for doubting Burma's pretensions at nonalignment.

A second change, noticeable since 1960, which can affect the viability of Burma's neutralist policy, has resulted from application of the principle of "friendly relations with all nations." In the earlier years U Nu, and even in 1958, General Ne Win, expressed considerable, and understandable pride in the fact that their government had been able to develop friendly ties with all other nations and had no serious disputes with any. Successful application of this principle, however, is not just a matter of Burma's initiative. Friendly relations in the world community is a two-way street. When other nations make overtures for "expanding" friendly relations with Burma, the Burma government can hardly reject them out of hand and still follow its principles. Thus, the Burman leaders had little choice but to accept the Soviet "gift" projects, even though they were less than enthusiastic about the end results. Although the Burma government reduced its commitments for rice deliveries to Communist bloc states after the series of barter deals between 1953 and 1955, it could hardly have turned down the later offers of Communist China in 1959–60 for increased rice purchases under arrangements less satisfactory than with some of Burma's non-Communist customers. Finally, Communist China's sudden offer of a large credit in 1961 under the atmosphere of "expansion of friendly relations" between the two countries could hardly have been refused or even modified.

The foregoing would seem to indicate that if neutralism means following a policy of friendly relations with all countries, it has in fact become a limitation on the freedom of action of the neutralist state. It tends to prevent a neutral government from being selective in those arrangements which are proposed to it by members of the Communist bloc. Since the policy of the United States and the un-committed nations has not been one of "dumping" unasked for aid and credits on developing nations, Burma and other neutralist na-tions, by attempting to be impartial friends with all, have found themselves drawn into closer ties of all kinds with the Communist bloc. To the degree that this situation continues and these ties ex-pand further, the whole policy of neutralism is prejudiced and the neutrals find it more and more difficult to maintain even a semblance of impartiality in the cold war contest.

A third change in the workings of Burma's neutralism since 1960, directly related to the one described above, is the view taken by Burman leaders of how best to protect their nation's security. "Friendly relations with all nations" means, in effect that the Burma government must weight each major move in economic or other re-lations with a particular state in terms of its possible effect on "friendly" relations with other states. Burman leaders are somewhat proud of the fact that their government has been able to keep on good terms with nations at odds with each other, like India and Pak-istan, Egypt and Israel, Yugoslavia and the Soviet Union, the United States and Communist China. But there remains the question, in case of a clear threat to the nation's integrity and independence, not to be resisted by Burman efforts alone, where would Burma turn for help? Is it possible that maintaining friendly relations with all nations means Burma has no real friends in time of need?

In the first few years of independence, U Nu stated on several oc-casions that a small, new nation should consider whether it should seek powerful allies who would help protect its freedom from out-side threats. Many politicians objected to this idea and those who had been against Burma becoming a member of the Commonwealth argued equally against any alliances with any power for any purpose. Faced with internal insurrections, the Burman leaders increasingly adopted the view that the most serious threats to Burma's security and integrity were internal. Many of them asserted that Burma had nothing to fear from any armed aggression by Communist China or any other nation. They believed there was danger that support might be given to the insurrectionists from the outside by the Communist bloc or by the West. They were convinced they could best avoid such assistance by a policy of nonalignment and friendly relations with both sides. They believe they were proved correct.

U Nu and his colleagues, however, did not ignore the danger of Burma's embroilment in a situation in which Burma's independence might be threatened by overt attack from outside its borders. When the invasion of south Korea was followed by swift United Nations action, U Nu and many of the non-Communist Burman leaders applauded this move and took the position that the United Nations had proved it could protect a small nation, and that consequently there was no need for Burma to seek allies. As the Korean war dragged on and the amount of loss of life and property became known, the Burmans quickly changed their minds. Their disillusionment with the UN was not complete but found expression in the widely heard phrase, "We don't want to become another Korea." United Nations action in the Congo has strengthened, rather than weakened this attitude. Likewise, as the Burman leaders have seen events unfolding in Vietnam and in Laos, they are fearful of reliance on any outside help because they have been a battleground in one war and do not want to see what they have accomplished destroyed.

At present, they see American Marines in Thailand and the danger that this neighboring country might become embroiled in the warfare going on in Laos and Vietnam. The original basis for their neutralist policy plus unfolding circumstances in Asia, first in Korea and now close at home, have conditioned the Burman leaders to believe that somehow they must maintain friendly relations with the nearest and most powerful neighbor, Communist China, if they are to avoid having their integrity threatened either by overt attack or by internal subversion. The net result of these evolving attitudes has been to lead the Burma government to enter into a new period of *rapprochement* with one major contestant in the cold war struggle. In making this change of course, the Burmans publicly assert that they are steadfastly following the principles of their neutralist policy. Privately many of the more knowledgeable Burmans are not so sure.

It is this change of course in relations with Communist China, finally, which is the most important indicator that for Burma, at least, neutralism may not turn out to be a viable foreign policy. The circumstances leading up to this new Sino-Burman relationship have already been described. Certain consequences of this change since 1960 can be summarized here. First, Peking's willingness to settle the problem of border demarcation with Burma on terms not unfavorable to the Burmans was not due wholly to Communist China's adherence to the Five Principles of Peaceful Co-Existence or friendship with Burma. Peking desired to use this settlement as an instrument in its negotiations with Delhi, and did. More than this, as payment for the border treaty, the Chinese Communists extracted from the Burma government a treaty of nonaggression and friendship which, in effect, sealed its ties closer with Burma. Under this treaty, as previously set forth, the Burma government may not enter into any military alliance with another country which can be interpreted as "directed at" Communist China. Although the words "military alliance" are used, the Communists have been used to giving their own special meanings to well-understood terms for a long time. By this treaty, Burma's freedom of action has been limited.

In the second place, the agreements signed by General Ne Win in Peking in January, 1960, pledged both countries to expand their economic and cultural relations. An immediate consequence of this was the offer of the large Chinese Communist credit followed by an increasing number of exchanges of technical and military "good-will" missions and steps taken to increase Chinese Communist technical assistance in Burma as well as to develop further the trade routes into Yunnan and expand trade itself. As a corollary to this changed Sino-Burman relationship, in the few months of General Ne Win's second regime in 1962, his Revolutionary Council has taken more drastic steps than any predecessor Burma government to reduce Western influence in Burma. Elimination of the activities of the private American Ford and Asian Foundations' activities in the country, as well as cancellation of English-language teaching programs under American and British auspices have already been undertaken at a time when there seems to be an increase of Communist missions, technicians, and cultural troupes coming to Burma.

Because the rulers in Peking believe firmly that neither Burma nor any other excolonial nation will be "liberated" until Western influence has been eliminated and these nations are well on the road to

"Socialism" as defined by the Communists, there have been no overt criticisms of Ne Win's military regime as "un-democratic" or "fascist" as there were during his interregnum between 1958 and 1960. Today, Burma constitutes for Communist China a valuable outlet to the world, an actual and potential resource of food and a window, if not a door, on the Bay of Bengal. It is no wonder that the Peking press and radio speak highly of General Ne Win's Revolutionary Council and have no criticism for the Council's manifesto on "The Burmese Way to Socialism."

It is hard to escape the conclusion, that under changing circumstances, Burma's pursuit of a neutralist foreign policy has led the Burma government perilously close to alignment with Communist China. It makes little difference whether General Ne Win and his Revolutionary Council continue to stand by Burma's "positive neutrality" as descriptive of their foreign policy, if actions and events seem clearly to demonstrate that their government and country have come within the sphere of influence of Communist China to the extent that relations with Western nations are confined to formal "government-to-government" arrangements and the Chinese Communists can exercise a virtual veto on Burma policy and actions. If these conditions continue, Burma's "positive neutrality" can become nothing more than a verbal declaration, but it will be of "positive" assistance to the Communists of Peking and Moscow whose long range goal is not the "neutrality and independence" of the small, new nations in Southeast Asia or elsewhere, but a status of dependency to themselves.

The Risks of Neutralism

The conclusion stated above indicates that, at least in the author's opinion, neutralism has not been a viable policy for Burma under the conditions of 1962, but instead has led Burma close to being trapped into a status of dependency on Communist China. It may well be that fortune and circumstances will favor Burma in the future, as in the past, and that by one means or another the Burma government may be able to escape such close alignment with its big northern neighbor as to maintain its integrity. The case of Burma, however, may be unique for obvious reasons and it cannot be inferred that because neutralism may have turned out to be unviable for one country it is equally so for other small nations elsewhere whose situation may be quite different. It is pertinent, therefore, to summarize the risks of a neutralist policy for a small nation as they have been revealed by this specific study of Burma's policy.

First, there is the risk thaat continued adherence to neutralism, which must include attempts to stay on friendly terms with all nations — with the members of both power blocs — induces a psychology of compromise. Fear of offending a "friendly" nation often leads a government to place undue value on settlement of any differences to the point where peaceful settlement of differences becomes an end in itself. In the case of Burma's leaders and those of many other neutral nations, their public assertions in their own capitals, on visits abroad, and in the United Nations, give the general impression that if only the major contestants in the cold war would sit down and negotiate any and all disputes between them, "international tensions would be immeasureably relieved." At many conferences and in many UN Committee sessions, representatives of neutral nations have expressed great impatience at the willingness of the United States or its allies to stick firmly to some proposal and not to "compromise" with the Communist states represented. It is here, most often, that the neutral nations' representatives have increasingly displayed their adherence to a double standard of judgment in East-West issues.

Not only does the policy of neutralism seem to induce an undue willingness to compromise on international issues, it also makes more difficult bilateral relations between the neutral nations and members of the Communist bloc. Resistance to Communist pressure seems much more difficult for the neutralists because of their feelings about the Western nations, their recent rulers, because of the compatibility of their desires and goals with Communist ideology and most important, because the leaders of Burma and of other neutral nations are not sure what they might suffer if they stand up to the Communists. It is an ironic commentary on the present world that nations which have much to gain from close association with the free nations of the northern half of the globe incline toward closer relations with the totalitarian Communist world for fear of losing what they are sure to lose if they become dependencies of Moscow or Peking.

Second, there appears to be the risk that a neutralist nation may become so intent on balancing its commitments to either side of the cold war so as to maintain a "neutral" posture, that its leaders will be unable or unwilling to determine clearly just what the limits or bounds of their neutralist policies and actions should be. In very practical terms, if Burma or Indonesia or any other similarly situated neutralist nation decides to take a Soviet-constructed steel mill or sugar mill, is this kind of commitment likely to create further ties which may limit the neutral nation's freedom to accept similar economic assistance from western nations? Should acceptance of credits from the Communist bloc be limited in amount, duration or not, without an attempt to balance this relationship by roughly equal credits from non-communist sources? Similar questions could be asked concerning military assistance, equipment, weapons, and a range of other items. The source from which these items will be requested and accepted is something which the government of a country will have to determine.

There is little evidence that the Burman leaders or those of very many small, neutralist countries have taken the time or have been willing to establish their own criteria by which they can set the bounds of their neutralist policy. Most such decisions are taken under pressures of domestic problems and internal politics and are made without much in the way of a guideline which could enable them to realize that specific kinds of relations with one nation or group of nations may have a way of accumulating to the point where such close ties are created as to go beyond the bounds of nonalignment to dependency.

A third risk in the pursuit of a neutralist policy is found in the tendency pointed out in this study of the people of a small neutralist state to express their national independence in truculence, chauvinism, and egocentrism. Again, in the very practical and very vital day-to-day struggles of the cold war, the major nations involved have had their patience tried many times. American patience with the neutralist policy of Nehru and Krishna Menon began to wear very thin after the Indian armed seizure of Goa and was expressed in the American Congress by efforts to reduce the current appropriation of aid to India as a result. Events in other neutral nations and attitudes of extreme nationalism or even antagonism to the West also have a way of accumulating feelings and emotions that can result in action not at all to the liking of the neutral nations. Likewise, if the Soviet Union has refrained from taking more vigorous steps in Asia and elsewhere to advance Communist interests, it has most certainly not been the existence of neutralist policies by the possible objects of such action that has deterred the Kremlin. It is not certain that the Chinese Communists view the present world and the dangers of nuclear war in the same way as do their Soviet Allies. No very satisfactory formulas have yet been found that may act as deterrence to Chinese Communist action outside their borders. It is certain that Burma's neutralism and its consequent *rapprochement* with Peking would not deter Mao Tse-tung and his colleagues in the slightest from extensive attempts to turn Burma into another Laos or another People's Republic on the model of that of Ho Chih-minh's.

Under what conditions, then, might a policy of neutralism based on principles of nonalignment, friends with all nations, and no aid "with strings" succeed for a small, excolonial nation? First, it is still a valid principle in international politics that "only the strong can be free." Effective neutralism under which a nation is able to act independently and can so determine the nature and scope of its relations with other states as to remain free of economic, cultural, political, or military entanglements, requires strength of will on the part of its leaders. It requires careful thought and planning as to what course will preserve its independence in the face of new situations and changing international conditions. But strong-willed leaders are not enough. A small nation's ability to assert and to maintain its integrity and to withstand pressures from the outside can be measured in direct proportion to the degree to which its government has been able to develop a viable economy, a stable political system and inculcate in its people a sense of national unity and national purpose.

If a policy of neutralism is only viable under the above conditions, then very few of the new, excolonial nations could qualify as being strong enough to make a policy of neutralism workable. There is another side to the coin. Since 1945, an increasing number of nations have adopted a neutralist policy and have still been able to maintain their integrity and independence, *not* because of any inherent "rightness" in this policy but because, for a variety of reasons and in a variety of changing circumstances, the major contestants in the cold war have been unwilling to use their power to force a change.

Neutralism as a status for small nations is not wholly satisfactory to either the Communist bloc states or to the United States and its allies. Both Moscow and Peking regard neutrality as incompatible with their view of the world as they hope it will become. At the most, neutralism is tolerable in some cases because it has not been worth while for either Communist partner to force a given neutral nation into relations of dependence. The risks do not justify the effort in some cases and in other cases, such as Burma, the advantages gained to date from a close relationship with a friendly, neutralist country are sufficient in terms of current Communist goals. Certainly, the United States and its allies would prefer that many neutralist nations, if not all, so managed their foreign affairs as to avoid any possibility of Communist capture or infiltration and subversion. This is the meaning of President Kennedy's phrase, "a neutral and an independent Laos."

To admit that neutralism as a policy has been successful in preserving their independence to date mainly because the major powers in the two opposing blocs of the cold war have permitted them to do so would be very unpalatable for Burma's leaders or for those of most other small, neutral nations. Yet the fact remains that the cold war contest is not only a conflict between different ideologies, different economic and political systems, but is also a contest for influence over the uncommitted nations. For the Communist bloc partners, no less than the United States and its allies, view any substantial increase of influence by their opponents as a direct threat to their national security. The leaders of the small, neutralist nations, for the most part, do not like to view the cold war in this light. Their own ideological preconceptions, their underlying antagonisms to Western nations because of their colonial past, influence them toward seeing any extension of the cold war as a threat to their future development. Noninvolvement, nonalignment, therefore, seems to present the only possible course by which they can preserve their freedom.

This study of Burma's foreign policy should demonstrate that strict noninvolvement and nonalignment would only be a viable policy if Burma, or any similar neutral nation, were able to maintain itself with only the minimum of any kind of relations with the members of the two power blocs and were able to so control their internal affairs as to prevent any significant infiltration from any outside source prejudicial to their security. Such a policy would also dictate a political system not subject to "pro-West" or "pro-East" influences. It would mean that the cold war contest could not be fought out over domestic issues between factions with ties outside the country. In the present complex interdependent world, such isolation is not possible and for the new nations it is undesirable.

In the final analysis, and in the light of this study of Burma's foreign relations it would appear that neutralism as presently defined in policy and action is less than a viable policy. More and more it appears to lead a small, weak, excolonial nation toward the fatal entrapment of dependency upon the Communist bloc. And whether such growing dependence is manipulated by Peking or by Moscow, the end result is the same. If the reasoning in this study is substantially valid, then neutralism as a foregn policy for a small, excolonial nation is inconsistent with true independence in foreign affairs, since in the present state of world politics, neutralism has lost almost all the connotations of "impartiality" which the word "neutrality" implied before 1939.

It would seem, therefore, that Nehru and U Nu as principal architects of nonalignment policies for new nations were right in the beginning in asserting that they desired their governments to pursue an "independent foreign policy" taking action they believed right in each case. For a nation that pursues an "independent" foreign policy can decide to make whatever alignments seem desirable in its national interests and it is not required to justify them by proving that it is not "leaning to one side." A nation pursuing an "independent" foreign policy can take sides on international issues or can refuse to take sides without having to show that its action in either case is "bringing it nearer to the Communist bloc," or makes it "lean closer to the Anglo-American bloc." For any small nation to act with such independence, its leaders would have to adopt a more carefully thought-out criteria of judgment than that demonstrated in the past by Burmans or those of many other small nations. They would have to have the courage to stand by their convictions and stand up to pressures from the major powers. In so doing, however, they would earn far more respect than many new nations have gained to date. Such a posture would annoy the Communists, but it would give to the small nations a common interest in preserving the sovereign independence of each other and would gain the support of the larger and more powerful nations of the free world. In the long run, dropping all the terminology of neutralism and standing on the principle of the sovereign right of independence might contribute as much to development of a world of law and order as anything else. For only in a world of law and order can the weak become strong and in this effort remain free to manage their development in their own way and in their own time.

APPENDIXES

NOTES

INDEX

—— APPENDIX I ——

BURMA RESEARCH PROJECT PAPERS

1. Historical Factors in Burma's Foreign Policy. By Oliver E. Clubb, Jr.
2. Burma at Independence: A Balance Sheet. By William C. Johnstone.
3. Burma's Foreign Policy, 1947–1957: A Content Analysis. By Kenneth L. Neff and William C. Johnstone.
4. Burma's Relations With Communist China: A Case Study. By Isabelle Crocker and William C. Johnstone.
5. Burma's Foreign Economic Relations, 1947–1957: A Case Study. By John H. Badgley. Distributed as a publication of the Rangoon-Hopkins Center for Southeast Asian Studies, Rangoon University.
6. The Effects of the Karen Insurrection on Burma's Foreign Policy: A Case Study. By William M. Rideout, Jr.
7. Burma's Foreign Policy and the Korean War: A Case Study. By Isabelle Crocker, Kenneth L. Neff, and William C. Johnstone.
8. The Effect of Chinese Nationalist Military Activities in Burma on Burman Foreign Policy. By Oliver E. Clubb, Jr. Distributed by the RAND Corporation, Santa Monica, California as P-1595-RC, January 20, 1959.
9. Burma's Participation in Asian and Afro-Asian Conferences: A Case Study. By Isabelle Crocker and William C. Johnstone.
10. Burma's Participation in the United Nations: A Case Study. By Kenneth L. Guenther and William C. Johnstone.
11. Burma's Position in South and Southeast Asia. By Richard H. Butler and William C. Johnstone.
12. Notes on Decision-Making in Burma's Foreign Policy. By William C. Johnstone.
13. A Study of Factors Affecting Burma's Foreign Policy, 1947–1957. By William C. Johnstone and Associates.
14. Burma After a Decade of Independence. By William C. Johnstone.
15. A Decade of Burma's Foreign Policy: Findings and Conclusions. By William C. Johnstone and Associates.
16. Burma's Foreign Policy in the Next Decade: Indicators of Change. By William C. Johnstone.
17. Observations on Contemporary Burma: 1959. By William C. Johnstone. Distributed by The RAND Corporation, Santa Monica, California, as Research Memorandum, RM-2535-RC, May, 1960.
18. A Chronology of Burma's International Relations, 1947–1958. By William

C. Johnstone and Associates. Distributed as a publication of the Rangoon-Hopkins Center for Southeast Asian Studies, Rangoon University.

Note: In addition to the persons listed above as contributors to the research project papers, Jean McEwen Haiken, Nana Bigelow Vreeland, and David Pfanner gave invaluable assistance in the collection of materials and preparation of preliminary draft studies during 1956 in Washington. Special acknowledgement is due Mrs. Helen Neff and Mrs. Rose Calder, Staff Associates at the Rangoon-Hopkins Center for Southeast Asian Studies who developed chronological materials, maintained the files and provided secretarial and typing assistance to the Director and members of the research project staff.

—— APPENDIX II ——

SINO-BURMAN TREATIES

Agreement Between the Government of the Union of Burma and the Government of the People's Republic of China on the Question of the Boundary Between the Two Countries.

The Government of the Union of Burma and the Government of the People's Republic of China,

With a view to promoting an over-all settlement of the Burmese-Chinese boundary question and to consolidating and further developing friendly relations between Burma and China,

Have agreed to conclude the present Agreement under the guidance of the Five Principles of Peaceful Co-Existence and have agreed as follows:

Article I

The Contracting Parties agree to set up immediately a joint committee composed of an equal number of delegates from each side and charge it, in accordance with the provisions of the present agreement, to discuss and work out solutions on the concrete questions regarding the Burmese-Chinese boundary enumerated in Article Two of the present Agreement, conduct surveys of the boundary and set up boundary markers and draft a Burmese-Chinese boundary Treaty. The joint committee shall hold regular meetings in the capitals of the two countries or at any other places in the two countries.

Article II

The Contracting Parties agree that the existing issues concerning the Burmese-Chinese boundary shall be settled in accordance with the following provisions:

(1) With the exception of the area of Hpimaw, Gawlun and Kangfang, the entire undelimited boundary from the High Conical Peak to the Western extremity of the Burmese-Chinese boundary shall be delimited along the traditional customary line, that is to say, from the High Conical Peak northward along the watershed between the Taiping, the Shweli, the Nu (Salween) and the Tulung (Talon) Rivers on the one hand and the Nmai Nka River on the other, up to the place where it crosses the Tulung (Talon) River between Chingdam and Nhkumkang, and then along the watershed between the Tulung (Talon) and the Tsayul (Zayul) Rivers on the one hand and all the upper tributaries of the Irrawaddy River, except for the Tulung (Talon) River, on the other, up to the western extremity of the Burmese-Chinese boundary. The joint committee shall send out joint survey teams composed of an equal number

of persons from each side to conduct surveys along the above mentioned watersheds so as to determine the specific alignment of this section of the boundary line and to set up boundary markers.

(2) The Burmese Government has agreed to return to China the area of Hpimaw, Gawlum and Kangfang which belongs to China. As to the extent of this area to be returned to China, it is to be discussed and determined by the joint committee in accordance with the proposals put forward and marked on maps by the Governments of Burma and China on February 4, 1957 and July 26, 1957, respectively. After determining the extent of this area to be returned to China, the joint committee shall send out joint survey teams composed of an equal number of persons from each side to conduct on-the-spot survey of the specific alignment of this section of the boundary line and to set up boundary markers.

(3) In order to abrogate the "perpetual lease" by Burma of the Meng-Mao triangular area (Namwan Assigned Tract) at the junction of the Namwan and the Shweli Rivers, which belongs to China, the Chinese Government has agreed to turn over this area to Burma to become part of the territory of the Union of Burma. In exchange the Burmese Government has agreed to turn over to China to become part of Chinese territory the areas under the jurisdiction of the Panhung and Panlao tribes, which are west of the boundary line from the junction of the Nam Ting and the Nampa Rivers to the No. 1 marker on the southern delimited section of the boundary as defined in the note exchanged between the Chinese and the British Governments on June 18, 1941. As to the extent of these areas to be turned over to China, the Chinese and the Burmese Governments put forward proposals marked on maps of July 26, 1957 and June 4, 1959, respectively. The area where the proposals of the two governments coincide will definitely be turned over to China. Where the proposals of the two Governments differ as to the area under the jurisdiction of the Panhung tribe, the joint committee will send out a team composed of an equal number of persons from each side to ascertain on the spot as to whether it is under the jurisdiction of the Panhung tribe, so as to determine whether it is to be turned over to China. After the extent of the areas under the jurisdiction of the Panlung and Panlao tribes to be turned over to China has been thus determined, the joint committee will send out joint survey teams composed of an equal number of persons from each side to conduct on-the-spot survey of the specific alignment of this section of the boundary line and to set up boundary markers.

(4) Except for the adjustment provided for in paragraph (3) of this Article, the section of the boundary from the junction of the Nam Ting and Nampa Rivers to the No. 1 marker on the southern delimited section of the boundary shall be delimited as defined in the notes exchanged between the Chinese and British Governments on June 18, 1941. The joint committee shall send out joint survey teams composed of an equal number of persons from each side to carry out delimitation and demarcation along this section of the boundary line and set up boundary markers.

Article III

The Contracting Parties agree that the joint committee, after working out solutions for the existing issues concerning the Burmese-Chinese boundary as enumerated in Article II of the present Agreement, shall be responsible for drafting a Burmese-Chinese boundary treaty, which shall cover not only all the sections of the boundary mentioned in Article II of the present Agreement, but also the sections of the boundary which were already delimited in the past and need no adjustment. After being signed by the Governments of the two countries and coming into effect, the new boundary treaty shall replace all old treaties and notes exchanged concerning the boundary between the two countries. The Chinese Government, in line with its policy of being consistently opposed to foreign prerogatives and respecting the sovereignty of other countries, renounce China's right of participation in mining enterprises at Lufang of Burma as provided in the notes exchanged between the Chinese and British Governments on June 18, 1941.

Article IV

(1) The present agreement is subject to ratification and the instruments of ratification will be exchanged in Rangoon as soon as possible.

(2) The present agreement will come into force immediately on the exchange of the instruments of ratification and shall automatically cease to be in force when the Burmese-Chinese boundary treaty to be signed by the two Governments comes into force.

Done in duplicate in Peking on the twenty-eighth day of January 1960, in the Chinese and the English language, both texts being equally authentic.

For the Government of
the Union of Burma

(signed) Ne Win

For the Government of the People's
Republic of China

(signed) Chou En-lai

Treaty of Friendship and Non-Aggression
Between the Union of Burma and the People's Republic of China

The Government of the Union of Burma and the Government of the People's Republic of China,

Desiring to maintain everlasting peace and cordial friendship between the Union of Burma and the People's Republic of China,

Convinced that the strengthening of good neighborly relations and friendly cooperation between the Union of Burma and the People's Republic of China is in accordance with the vital interests of both countries,

Have decided for this purpose to conclude the present Treaty in accordance with the Five Principles of Peaceful Coexistence jointly initiated by the two countries, and have agreed as follows:

Article I

The Contracting Parties recognize and respect the independence, sovereign rights and territorial integrity of each other.

Article II

There shall be everlasting peace and cordial friendship between the Contracting Parties who undertake to settle all disputes between them by means of peaceful negotiation without resorting to force.

Article III

Each Contracting Party undertakes not to carry out acts of aggression against the other and not to take part in any military alliance directed against the other Contracting Party.

Article IV

The Contracting Parties declare that they will develop and strengthen the economic and cultural ties between the two States in a spirit of friendship and cooperation in accordance with the principles of equality and mutual benefit and of mutual non-interference in each other's internal affairs.

Article V

Any difference or dispute arising out of the interpretation or application of the present Treaty or one or more of its articles shall be settled by negotiations through the ordinary diplomatic channels.

Article VI

(1) The present Treaty is subject to ratification and the instruments of ratification will be exchanged in Rangoon as soon as possible.

(2) The present Treaty will come into force immediately on the exchange of the instruments of ratification and will remain in force for a period of ten years.

(3) Unless either of the Contracting Parties gives to the other notice in writing to terminate it at least one year before the expiration of this period, it will remain in force without any specified time limit, subject to the right of either of the Contracting Parties to terminate it by giving to the other in writing a year's notice of the intention to do so.

In witness whereof the Prime Minister of the Union of Burma and the Premier of the State Council of the People's Republic of China have signed the present Treaty.

Done in duplicate in Peking on the twenty-eighth day of January, 1960, in the Chinese and English languages, both texts being equally authentic.

For the Government of the Union of Burma	For the Government of the People's Republic of China
(signed) Ne Win	(signed) Chou En-lai

— APPENDIX III —

A HARD LOOK AT MR. TENDER

by U Law Yone
(*The Nation,* Rangoon, March 2, 1957)

"The most publicized man in Burma today is U Nu. His name literally means, 'Soft, tender or green,' all of which belie his character. He once told Thakin Soe, 'You be the Lenin of Burma, and I'll be your Maxim Gorki.' But U Nu has since shown himself to be more adept at politics than he ever was at play writing. The gentle dreamer who abhorred guns and could not kill a snake has developed into a fighter who revels in the rough game of politics. He will never be a Stalin, but there is a good deal of granite in his make-up. There is no particular triumph in his return to the Premiership today. He never really quit.

"U Nu is 50 years old, and looks about ten years younger. But I have seen him gaunt and unhappy. Then he looks his age. The rest of the time he tries to keep his weight down (about 155 lbs.) and to present a brave exterior. His features are regular, his hands well shaped and his fingers well kept, and a smile sits naturally on his moon face. But he worries. When he worries he gets sick, and the sickness gets him in the stomach.

"The secret of U Nu's success is his keen sense of observation; that, and an almost uncanny intuition. The most grievous mistake that anyone can make is to think that he is a simple character. There is more complexity in his little finger than in the entire physiology of most people. In him naiveté and shrewdness are so unevenly blended that one never knows which will be uppermost at any given moment. I am constantly amazed by his instant grasp of complicated matters and his inability to take in commonplace situations.

"U Nu is an easy person to talk to. He leads one along, keeps the conversation going smoothly, and contributes in an anecdotal way. When one comes away from a visit with U Nu, one has the distinct feeling of having talked too much. On his part, U Nu says much about the past, little about the present and nothing at all about his future plans. And he does all this without appearing cagey. In point of fact, most people get the impression that he is an unusually frank and uninhibited person. This is because they fail to recognize what a subtle individual he is.

". . . .U Nu is accessible from the side of flattery and, to do him justice, from that of kindliness. The flattery works better if it is open, even blatant.

"But this in a leader is a dangerous weakness and leaves him open to the sycophants who always surround powerful men.

"None the less, the man is extremely human. It is possible to get a rise out of him, and when it is all over, to laugh together over it. On one of several occasions when something I published got under his skin, he wrote a rude letter and got his parliamentary secretary to sign it. We detected his hand and gave him tit for tat. In the end, he got so angry that he ordered my arrest. It needed the joint efforts of U Kyaw Nyein, U Tun Win and Bo Khin Maung Gale and several others to dissuade him. At the next press conference he still looked displeased at me. 'Your friends saved you,' he grumbled, but there was no more venom in him.

"Another time he spoke sharply to me for criticizing everything. 'You can afford to tickle us with your pen,' he said, 'you don't have to *do* anything.' 'Mr Prime Minister, that's one of the privileges of my profession.' Through the years, I think he has come to appreciate this fact. He must also learn that it is not sufficient for him to be convinced that what he is doing is right. It must appear so to others. In the very first chapter of "How to Win Friends and Influence People," which he has translated, there occurs the story of the man who killed at a bank robbery, then killed an innocent policeman, and several others, before he was taken. Just before he died, he scribbled, 'I am a kind man.'

"U Nu is often dubbed the leader of the mob, rather than of a party. That is not true. No party is going to retain a leader it can dispense with without loss to itself. The day he ceases to be useful to the party, it will have no compunction about jettisoning him. His ability to draw the crowd, his homespun tales, his salt-of-the-earth phraseology, are, of course, distinct assets, but over and above these is a warm personality and an intuitive short-cut to decision. When he went to China, I felt more or less certain he would come back a cropper. He came back with the 'Package Deal' a measure which could not be called a great feat of diplomacy, but which certainly confounded his critics. Another man would have been better prepared to wrangle with the Chinese, but could hardly have got off as lightly.

"U Nu has always prided himself on his ability to write books and plays. I am sure he could earn a comfortable living by writing, but I am afraid he would never be happy if he divorced himself from politics. It has got into his blood, until now he would be warped and frustrated if he tried to drain it out. Even his religion is mixed with politics. When he rises early to be at his devotions, the man is entirely sincere. His religion gives him great solace. But there have to be outward shows and manifestations to incite the people to take *their* religion seriously. So also, with honesty. He feels that it is not enough that he should be above bribery. It has to be proved, hence he makes a fetish of turning over the smallest gift to the nation. I think it is childish, but then I am not as fanatical as he in trying to make every minister into a Caesar's wife, beyond reproach.

"I have talked with several of U Nu's 'inner circle' and the concensus of opinion is strikingly like what Alanbrooke said of Churchill, ... 'He has an unfortunate trick of picking up some isolated operation, and without ever really having it looked into, setting his heart upon it.' When he once gets into these moods he feels everybody is trying to thwart him and to produce difficulties . . . Perhaps the most remarkable failing of his is that he can never see a whole strategical problem at once. His gaze always settles on some definite part of the canvas and the rest of the picture is lost. Because of this failing, U Nu has often pulled a boner, which is not surprising, but he has the knack of recovering his stance, which astonishes his enemies as well as his friends.

"The complaint is sometimes heard that U Nu is tending to become more and more dictatorial. His past actions refute this charge. A dictator is made of sterner stuff. He does not compromise once his mind is made up. I can think of many occasions on which his colleagues have talked him round. As I said to a certain Minister once, 'If U Nu ever becomes a dictator, you'll be to blame.' U Nu can be extremely touchy and he can say scathing words, but in any argument it is better to stand your ground with him, even if he flares to the sky, rather than take umbrage yourself and mutter behind his back. He admires guts even in a political opponent. 'Burma under the Japanese' is nothing if not a tribute to Dr. Ba Maw's courage.

"U Nu is first and last a popular leader. He is disqualified for the details of administration. That is where the weakness of his government is most apparent. From morning till night, he wears out his secretaries with notes and memoranda, but such is the system in Burma that few of his ideas get translated into action. And it is quite useless to prod him to fire a subordinate. A Burman judge shrinks at whipping a prisoner. U Nu, the Burman Prime Minister, is congenitally incapable of sacking a man for incompetence. Perhaps there is a reason for this, but short of doing a psychograph I cannot discover it. It may be that knowing himself to be a dreamer and a visionary, he feels he cannot be too hard on a subordinate for being unpractical. Before he eloped with his wife, U Nu planned the whole operation, then stood her up because he could not find the motor boat!

"But while he cannot hurt individuals, U Nu can fire whole outfits. He very nearly sacked the whole of the SAMB; he got rid of ECA at one fell swoop, and, at one time, after he had agreed to accept six million pounds from the Commonwealth, he bundled the Ambassadors out of his house. These things would have been avoided if the people concerned knew his real character. He hides his mounting irritation until the moment arrives when he erupts. That is why one has to be extremely careful in dealing with him. One may put up one's feet in his presence, slap him on the back and address him as 'old boy' and he will stand it as long as he thinks one is not deliberately offensive, but the moment one tries to patronise him or offer a calculated insult, he reacts violently.

"Somebody who knows U Nu well once told me, 'Don't get friendly with U Nu. You'll get nothing out of it except being dragged to the Indian movies.' That is not altogether unsound advice. When U Nu goes to see a film he goes to be entertained. Weird phantasies suit him best because in that way the man of imagination tries to break away from the life of practical politics. He is a greater Walter Mitty than any man I know. Burma is his stage. The play that is being put on is his play, and he is acting the main part. It is complicated enough to shatter the nerves of most living persons. He can hardly be expected to relax with more social problems at the cinema.

"Perhaps it is because his mind is so busy that his bodily needs are so few. With such big gaps in education and knowledge, he nevertheless has an accumulation of facts and quotations so neatly pigeon-holed in the recesses of his memory, that he is able to bedeck his speeches with aphorisms wherever he goes. And all the time he is observing and adding to his storehouse, his alert mind separating the weighty from the trivial. He seems to gain a little from each person he associates with, whoever he may be. But while sophisticated in his thinking, he is not so in his personal habits. He eats at 9 and again at 5. Not for him is the utterly un-Burman institution called lunch. Most times he eats whatever is placed before him, but let him be upset and he complains like a child. Cleanliness is, to him, next to godliness. 'I don't mind if my daughter marries a beggar,' he said recently, 'but he should be a clean beggar.' He is, of course, a great health faddist and swallows vitamin tablets with every meal. He can stand the cold but shuns the draught like the very devil.

"Who are U Nu's friends? We can parade in our mind's eye a succession of ministers, religious leaders, politicians, businessmen and clowns. Now and again we hear of someone who is extra thick with him, but never lasts. The fact of the matter is that U Nu is a self-reliant person with a great sense of destiny. In his career, there are no Grey Eminences, no permanent court jesters. Perhaps the only exception is U Thant, and U Thant never talks about him, not because he does not know or because it would take too long. To all questioners, U Thant answers with one word, 'mercurial,' and that is a very apt description. I am not sure that this singular lack of attachment on U Nu's part is not a virtue. When I recently told U Nu that U Thant was down with overwork, the reply I got was typical, 'It's a miracle he didn't go down last year or the year before that.' It was not a callous remark, but coming from U Nu the best tribute he could pay to a loyal friend. U Thant, too, knows how to speak his language.

'What keeps you so busy these days, Ko Thant?' U Nu once asked.

'You,' was the unhesitating retort.

"When it comes to strangers, however, U Nu can turn on the charm. He is such a believer in the 'personal contact' approach to problems and so alive to the possibilities of human relationships, that people who have watched him operate have been known to reply, 'Did he translate Dale Carnegie, or did Dale Carnegie translate him?'

"I can best illustrate his uncanny habit of doing the right thing at the right time by an incident during his American tour. At that time the Majority Leader in the Senate was William Knowland, a man whom U Nu had deliberately snubbed in Burma because at the time Knowland came to Rangoon, the KMT incident was rankling in U Nu's breast. But, when invited to address the American Congress, U Nu was received and introduced by Knowland as though he were a long lost friend. This disturbed U Nu afterwards, and he wrote a letter of apology for the cavalier treatment accorded him in Burma. When, later, U Nu dropped a brick over the 'admission of China into the UN' issue, we thought, 'Now for the Knowland blast.' It never came and now we know the reason why.

"This innate sense of fairness, and even humility, is what sets U Nu apart. The apology to Mr. Sloss, the great goodwill shown to Sir Archibald Cochrane ('the Governor I used to abuse whenever I had nothing better to do'), the admission to Bo Tun Sein, ('I am sorry I have not taken my parliamentary duties more seriously,') and the ability to say to anybody, 'I have been a fool, I apologise,' are the best insurance against U Nu ever turning out to be a dictator."

—— APPENDIX IV ——

THE BURMESE WAY TO SOCIALISM

(Manifesto of Burma Revolutionary Council: Rangoon, April 30, 1962)

Our Belief

The Revolutionary Council of the Union of Burma does not believe that man will be set free from social evils as long as pernicious economic systems exist in which man exploits man and lives on the fat of such appropriation. The Council believes it to be possible only when exploitation of man by man is brought to an end and a socialist economy based on justice is established, only then can all people, irrespective of race or religion be emancipated from all social evils and set free from anxieties over food, clothing and shelter and from inability to resist evil, for an empty stomach is not conducive to wholesome morality, as the Burmese saying goes, only then can an affluent stage of social development be reached and all people be happy and healthy in mind and body.

Thus affirmed in this belief the revolutionary Council is resolved to march unswervingly and arm-in-arm with the people of the Union of Burma towards the goal of socialism.

Fundamentals of Our Policy

In setting forth their programmes as well as in their execution the Revolutionary Council will study and appraise the concrete realities and also the natural conditions peculiar to Burma objectively. On the basis of the actual findings derived from such study and appraisal it will develop its own ways and means to progress.

In its activities the Revolutionary Council will strive for self-improvement by way of self-criticism. Having learnt from contemporary history the evils of deviation towards right or left the Council will with vigilence avoid any such deviation.

In whatever situations and difficulties the Revolutionary Council may find itself it will strive for advancement in accordance with the times, conditions, environment and the ever changing circumstances, keeping at heart the basic interests of the nation.

The Revolutionary Council will diligently scan all ways and means whereby it can formulate and carry out such programmes as are of real and practical value for the well-being of the nation. In doing so it will critically observe, study and avail itself of the opportunities provided by progressive ideas, theories and experiences at home or abroad without discrimination between one country of origin and another.

Socialist Economy

The fundamental concept of socialist economy is the participation of all for the general well-being in works of common ownership, and planning towards sufficiency and contentment of all, sharing the benefits derived therefrom. Socialist economy aims at the establishment of a new society for all, economically secure and morally better, to live in peace and prosperity.

Socialist economy therefore opposes any pernicious economic system in which man exploits man, and self-interest and self-seeking are the motivating forces.

Socialist economy does not serve the narrow self-interest of a group, an organization, a class, or a party, but plans its economy with the sole aim of giving maximum satisfaction to material, spiritual and cultural needs of the whole nation.

Socialist economy is the planned, proportional development of all the national productive forces.

Productive forces is the collective term for natural resources, raw materials, instruments of production, accumulated capital, peasants, workers, intelligentsia, technicians, know-hows and experiences, skills, etc.

Socialist economy proportionally plans, on the basis of the population and productive forces, for sufficiency and abundance of consumer goods. While improving the standard of living and increasing the purchasing power of the nation it also expands production. Socialist economy thus solves the problem of unemployment and ensures security of a means of livelihood for every individual.

In order to carry out socialist plans such vital means of production as agricultural and industrial production, distribution, transportation, communications, external trade, etc., will have to be owned by the State or cooperative societies or collective unions. Among such ownerships state ownership forms the main basis of socialist economy. State ownership means ownership by the whole nation itself, whereas ownership by co-operatives or collectives means group ownership by respective concerns. But as all forms of ownership will have to operate within the framework of socialist national planning, they are interdependent.

In building up an economy according to socialist plans every able individual will have to work according to his ability. The material and cultural values that accrue will be distributed in accordance with the quantity and quality of labour expended by each individual in social production.

In our Burmese socialist society equalitarianism is impossible. Men are not equal physically and intellectually in the respective quantity and quality of service they render to society, and differences are therefore bound to exist. But at the same time social justice demands that the gaps between incomes be reasonable, and correct measures will be taken to narrow these gaps as much as possible.

A Socialist Democratic State will be constituted to build up a successful socialist economy. A Socialist Democratic State is based on, and safeguards its own socialist economy. The vanguard and custodian of a Socialist Democratic State are primarily peasants and workers, but the middle strata and those who will work with integrity and loyalty for the general weal will also participate.

Parliamentary democracy called the People's Rule came into existence in history with the British, American and French revolutions against feudalism. It happens to be the best in comparison with all its preceding systems.

But in some countries the Parliamentary Democracy has been so abused as to have become only the means by which the opportunists and propertied people deceive the simple masses.

In the Union of Burma also, Parliamentary Democracy has been tried and tested in furtherance of the aims of socialist development. But Burma's Parliamentary Democracy has not only failed to serve our socialist development but also, due to its very defects, weaknesses, and loopholes, its abuses and the absence of a mature public opinion, lost sight of, and deviated from the socialist aims, until at last indications of its heading imperceptibly towards just the reverse have become apparent.

The nation's socialist aims cannot be achieved with any assurance by means of the form of Parliamentary Democracy that we have so far experienced.

The Revolutionary Council therefore firmly believes that it must develop, in conformity with existing conditions and environment and ever changing circumstances, only such a form of democracy as will promote and safeguard the socialist development.

These then are the fundamentals of socialist economy.

Programme for Transition to Socialism

Reorientation of Views. In marching towards socialist economy it is imperative that we first reorientate all erroneous views of our people.

Fraudulent practices, profit motives, easy living, parasitism, shirking and selfishness must be eradicated.

We must so educate the people that to earn one's living by one's own labour and to see dignity in one's own work comes into vogue. We must educate, lead by example and guide the people away from the base notion that it is beneath one's dignity to work by the sweat of one's brow.

Attempts must be made by various correct methods to do away with bogus acts of charity and social work for vainglorious shows, bogus piety and hypocritical religiosity, etc., as well as to foster and applaud *bona fide* belief and practice of personal morals as taught by ethics and tradition of every religion and culture. We will resort to education, literature, fine arts, theatre and cinema, etc. to bring into vogue the concept that to serve others' interests is to serve one's own.

Administrative Machinery

In our road to socialism the existing bureaucratic administration is a big stumbling block. To achieve our socialist aims with effect, this machinery is impossible. Steps will have to be taken to remove this bureaucratic machinery and lay firm foundations for a socialist democratic one.

Defense Services

The existing defense services will also be developed to become national armed forces which will defend our socialist economy.

Economy

The Union of Burma is an economically backward agricultural country. The national productive forces need to be continually developed to build up socialist economy. That is why various productions that would be compatible with existing conditions and time will have to be planned and developed. While modernizing the agricultural production which forms the main basis of the national economy such industries as would be commensurate with the natural resources and capabilities of the country will also be developed. In doing so national private enterprises which contribute to national productive forces will be allowed with fair and reasonable restrictions.

On the full realization of socialist economy the Socialist Government, far from neglecting the owner of national private enterprises which have been steadfastly contributing to the general well-being of the people, will even enable them to occupy a worthy place in the new society in the course of further national development.

The Question of Nationalities

As the Union of Burma is a country where many indigenous racial groups reside, it is only when the solidarity of all the indigenous racial groups has been established that socialist economy which can guarantee the welfare of every racial group can be achieved. In striving towards fraternity and unity of all the races of the Union we will be guided by what General Aung San, our national leader, said at the AFPFL Conference held at the middle terrace of the Shwedagon Pagoda on January 20, 1946.

A Nation is a collective term applied to a people, irrespective of their ethnic origin, living in close contact with one another and having common interests and sharing joys and sorrows together for such historic periods as to have acquired a sense of oneness. Though race, religion and language are important factors it is only their traditional desire and will to live in unity through weal and woe that binds a people together and makes them a nation and their spirit a patriotism.

We, the peoples of the Union of Burma, shall nurture and hug a new patriotism as inspired by the words of General Aung San.

Social Service

Education. The Revolutionary Council believes that the existing system unequated with livelihood will have to be transformed. An educational system equated with livelihood and based on socialist moral values will be brought about. Science will be given precedence in education.

Our educational target is to bring basic education within the reach of all. As regards higher education only those who have promise and enough potentialities and industriousness to benefit from it will be specially encouraged. The Revolutionary Council believes that other social services such as health, culture, etc., shall flourish in direct proportion to the tides of socialist success like the lotus and the water's height, and will accordingly work towards this end.

Religion

The Revolutionary Council recognizes the right of everyone freely to profess and practise his religion.

Organizational March

In marching towards the goal of socialism the Revolutionary Council will base its organization primarily on the strength of peasants and other working masses who form the great majority of the nation. It will also march hand-in-hand with those who will work with integrity and loyalty for national interest and well-being of the people.

The Revolutionary Council will therefore carry out such mass and class organizations as are suitable for the transitional period, and also build up a suitable form of political organization.

When political organizational work is carried out Socialist democratic education and democratic training will be given to the people so as to ensure their conscious participation. The Revolutionary Council believes and hopes that there will come about democratic competitions which will promote Socialist development within the framework of socialism.

The aforesaid are in outline the belief and policy of the Revolutionary Council of the Union of Burma.

Responsibility of the People

The Revolutionary Council has faith in the people and in their creative force.

The Revolutionary Council believes that the people will, with an active awareness of their duties and responsibilities, play their part in full in this national Revolutionary progressive movement and programme under the leadership of the Revolutionary Council.

The Revolutionary Council reaffirms and declares again that it will go forward hand-in-hand with the people to reach the goal of socialism.

Let us march towards socialism in our own Burmese way.

The REVOLUTIONARY COUNCIL
OF THE UNION OF BURMA

Rangoon, April 30, 1962

NOTES

Chapter I

Introduction

1. There is still no general agreement as to whether *Burman* or *Burmese* is the proper appellation for the people of Burma as a whole. In this study, *Burman* is used to refer to the nationals of the country, Burma. *Burmese* is used to designate the ethnic-linguistic majority of the total population of Burma. *Burman*, literally "of Burma" carries with it no historical connotations of race or language, while *Burmese* has been commonly applied to the majority ethnic-linguistic group in Burma by the people of Burma. No Shan, Kachin, Karen or Chin wants to be called a *Burmese* in Burma since this ethnic-linguistic pride characterizes the attitudes of large numbers of the minority population of the country. High officials, who are *Burmese* by race and language, tend to use this word as applying to all the people of Burma. Those who are aware of the problem of unifying the people of the country to the point where they accept identification with Burma, the nation in their hierarchy of loyalties, tend to use the term *Burman*.

2. J. E. Spencer, *Asia East By South — A Cultural Geography* (New York, 1954), p. 208.

3. *Ibid.*

4. This was well illustrated during the course of the Round Table discussions in London in 1931 between delegates from Burma and British officials concerning Burma's future political status. See *Burma Round Table Conference,* November 27, 1931–January 12, 1932 (London: H. M. Stationary Office, Cmd 4004, 1932), proceedings, statements of the Shan States representative, the Sawbwa of Hsipaw, p. 61; the spokesman for the Burmese majority, U Tharrawaddy Maung Maung, p. 65; and the Karen representative, Mr. Sidney Loo-Nee, p. 86.

5. J. S. Furnivall, *South Asia in the World Today*. In book of the same title, ed. Phillips Talbot (Chicago, 1950), p. 4.

6. See particularly John F. Cady, *A History of Modern Burma* (Ithaca, 1958).

7. This summarization is drawn from the unpublished dissertation by Oliver E. Clubb, Jr., "The Dynamics of the Burmese Independence Movement" (The Johns Hopkins University School of Advanced International Studies, Washington, D. C., 1961). Mr. Clubb obtained a considerable amount of original material in Burma between 1956 and 1958, supplemented by interviews with leading members of the independence movement. See also John F. Cady.

8. In 1930–31, the young leaders of the independence movement began using the honorific *Thakin*, a form of address hitherto reserved exclusively for European men such as the similar honorific *Sahib* in India. They asserted that by this move Burmans would be restored from a position of subservience to

Europeans to one of equality. This form of address was used until after independence and became a kind of badge of honor. It was also used to designate the young leaders of the independence movement, as "the Thakins" or "the Thakin movement," and as late as 1962 was used to designate the left wing faction of U Nu's Union Party.

9. See Thein Pe Myint, *What Happened in Burma* (New York: Institute of Pacific Relations, 1944), p. 3 ff., for an account of the origins of the BRP, also called the NRP (National Revolutionary Party). Thein Pe added *Myint* to his name after the war.

10. The *Dobama Asiayone* (literally, "We Burmans Association") was organized late in 1930 under the leadership of Ba Thaung. Thakins Nu (U Nu), Aung San, Hla Pe, Lay Maung and Thein Pe Myint were all members. This organization was one of many such groups established during the prewar period. Neither this nor any of the many other political groups in Burma attained the cohesiveness of the Indian Congress Party.

11. Khin Myo Chit, *Three Years Under the Japanese* (Rangoon, 1945), p. 4.

12. Thakin Nu, *Burma Under the Japanese* (London, 1954), pp. 1–2.

13. See *The Nation*, Rangoon, for January 16, 1949, for an account of this episode.

14. This agreement is described by Thein Pe Myint in *What Happened in Burma*, p. 3. General Ne Win was also a member of this group.

15. See Boh Yan Naing, *Yebaw Thoun Geik Hmantan Gyi* (The Journal of the Thirty Comrades). Trans. in *Amoutha* (The Nationalist), Rangoon, August 16, 1956. Thakin Ba Sein led a rightist minority faction that was expelled from the *Dobama Asiayone* in 1938. His group was thereafter known as the "Ba Sein Dobama Asiayone."

16. U Ba Swe, *Guide to Socialism in Burma* (Rangoon: Government Printing and Stationary Office, 1956), p. 1. See also Dr. Maung Maung, "Profile: U Kyaw Nyein," Rangoon, *The Guardian Monthly* (March 1955).

17. Bo Yan Naing, one of the BIA leaders, claimed he entered Burma with 24 men, a force that grew in numbers to several hundred by the time he engaged the British forces at Shwedaung. For an account of this battle, see Sir William Slim, *Defeat Into Victory* (London, 1956), pp. 45–47.

18. Thakin Nu, *Burma Under the Japanese*, p. 20.

19. Willard H. Elsbree, *Japan's Role in Southeast Asian Nationalist Movements* (Cambridge, Mass., 1953), p. 17.

20. *Ibid.*, p. 21.

21. F. C. Jones, *Japan's New Order in East Asia* (London, 1954), p. 132.

22. International Military Tribunal, Tokyo, preliminary interrogations, interrogation of Ba Maw, Sugamo Prison, May 22, 1946.

23. See Burma Intelligence Bureau, *Burma During the Japanese Occupation* (India, 1943).

24. For additional details of these developments see U Tun Pe, *Sun Over Burma* (Rangoon, 1949); Khin Myo Chit, *Three Years Under the Japanese*; and Thakin Nu, *Burma Under the Japanese*.

25. See Chapter VI for more recent evidence of this.

26. U Kyaw Min, *The Burma We Love* (Rangoon, 1945), p. 78 ff.

27. See Slim, *Defeat Into Victory*, p. 510.

28. See Thakin Nu, *Burma Under the Japanese*; Thein Pe Myint, *Sit Atwin*

Kha Yi Thar (Wartime Traveler), trans. (Rangoon, 1953); also J. H. Brimmel, *Communism in Southeast Asia* (New York, 1959), pp. 185–194.

29. See Dr. Maung Maung, "Profiles of Thakin Than Tun and U Kyaw Nyein," Rangoon, *The Guardian Monthly* (October 1956 and March 1955).

30. *Ibid.*

31. Various sources indicate that the new BCP looked to the Indian Communist Party for guidance until well into 1948.

32. When the armed communist insurrection against the new AFPFL government broke out in 1948, the top ranks of the insurgents were filled with wartime resistance leaders and some regular units of the Burma deserted to them.

33. Slim, *Defeat*, p. 519.

34. The AFO was renamed the AFPFL (Anti-Fascist People's Freedom League) in August, 1945.

35. Burma Office, "Statement of Policy. . . ." (London: H. M. Stationary Office, May 1945).

36. Vice Admiral The Earl Mountbatten of Burma, *Report to the Combined Chiefs of Staff by the Supreme Commander, Southeast Asia* (London: H. M. Stationary Office, 1951), p. 201.

37. Mountbatten, pp. 144, 201–202.

38. *Ibid.*, pp. 202–203 and Slim, pp. 519–520.

39. Aung San, *Presidential Address*, delivered by Major-General Aung San at the second session, Supreme Council, AFPFL (Rangoon, May 16, 1946), p. 32.

40. See *The Statesman*, Calcutta, July 20–21, 1946; also Mountbatten, pp. 199–201; and F. S. V. Donnison, *Public Administration in Burma* (London, 1953), p. 109.

41. *The Statesman*, Calcutta, July 16–17, 1946.

42. Aung San, *Presidential Address*, p. 25. See also J. S. Furnivall, "Twilight in Burma: Reconquest and After," *Pacific Affairs* (March 1949).

43. Aung San, pp. 33–35.

44. Dr. Maung Maung, *Burma in the Family of Nations* (Amsterdam, 1950), p. 106.

45. Government of the Union of Burma, Department of Information, *Burma's Fight for Freedom* (Rangoon, 1948), pp. 41 and ff; also Hugh Tinker, *The Union of Burma* (London, 1957), p. 21.

46. Other members of the Burma delegation included the Socialist leaders Thakin Mya and Kyaw Nyein; the right-wing opponents of Aung San: U Saw and U Tin Tut. U Tin Tut was a senior member of the prewar civil service and returned to Burma with Dorman-Smith in 1945. He quickly allied himself with Aung San's goals, joined the AFPFL and was said to have been the only one of the prewar civil servants whom Aung San fully trusted. He was assassinated in September, 1948.

47. The new Burma government, however, was able to retain its "membership" in the "sterling bloc" and thus gain certain financial and trade advantages.

48. U Saw was later tried and executed for the crime.

49. *Burma's Fight For Freedom*, p. 36. Dr. Ba Maw reportedly refused to join the AFPFL because he felt it had been too opportunistic in turning against

the Japanese and working with the British. Thakin Ba Sein also refused to join because he felt the AFPFL was too much dominated by the leftists.

50. *Burma's Fight For Freedom*, p. 42.

51. Aung San, pp. 12 and 33–35.

52. *The Statesman*, Calcutta, July 18–21, 1946.

53. Dr. Maung Maung, *The Nation*, Rangoon, January 8, 1949.

54. Dr. Maung Maung, "Profile: Thakin Than Tun," Rangoon, *The Guardian Monthly* (October 1956).

55. This union again went on strike against the government in February, 1949, as a means of support for the Communist insurgents.

56. Dr. Maung Maung, "Profile: U Ba Swe," Rangoon, *The Guardian Monthly* (March 1956).

57. See Brimmell, *Communism*, pp. 189–190 ff.

58. Thakin Than Tun was also Aung San's brother-in-law as they had married sisters.

59. Thakin Nu (speech), November 27, 1947, Government of the Union of Burma, Ministry of Information, *Towards Peace and Democracy* (Rangoon, 1947), p. 20.

60. Dr. Maung Maung, *Burma*, pp. 190 ff.

61. Thein Pe Myint, "Political Memoires," unpublished ms., p. 474.

62. Thakin Nu (speech), November 27, 1947.

63. See *Towards Peace and Democracy*, pp. 16 and 23–38.

64. See Brimmell, *Communism*, pp. 193–194. Also M. R. Masani, *The Communist Party of India* (New York, 1954), p. 90, and Ruth T. McVey, *The Calcutta Conference and the Southeast Asian Uprisings*. Interim Report Series, Southeast Asia Program (Ithaca, 1958).

65. Thein Pe Myint, "Memoires," p. 474.

66. *Ibid.*

67. Government of the Union of Burma, *Burma and the Insurrections* (Rangoon, 1949), p. 4 and ff.

68. Thein Pe Myint, "Memoires," pp. 499–500.

69. *Ibid.*, p. 488.

70. Dr. Maung Maung, *Burma*, p. 114. He states that a committee of 111 were "fully occupied" at the height of the Constituent Assembly's work. U Chan Htoon, for some time on the Supreme Court of Burma, was an adviser, as was U E Maung, holder of many cabinet posts. In the final stages, the services of Sir Benegal Rau, chief adviser to the Indian Constituent Assembly, were made available to the Committee.

71. U Nu, "Sowing the Seeds of Freedom," speech before the Constituent Assembly, September 24, 1947, text in *Towards Peace and Democracy*, pp. 2 and 5–6.

72. Material in this section is primarily based on John H. Badgley, *Burma's Foreign Economic Relations, 1948–1957 — A Survey* (Rangoon: The Rangoon-Hopkins Center for Southeast Asian Studies, 1959).

73. The cattle population of Burma did not reach its prewar level until well into 1958.

74. One serious problem for the new Burma government was virtually solved by the Japanese occupation. Moneylenders and money lending organi-

zations had foreclosed on large numbers of Burman village debtors in the pre-war depression years. One group, Indian Chettyars from Madras, were reported to have taken possession of nearly 40% of the delta rice lands by 1941. Most of these alien titleholders had fled Burma in 1942 and before they could reassert their claims after the war, a Burma Agricultural Relief Act was passed, can-celling all debts incurred before October 1, 1946.

Chapter II
The Formative Period — 1948–1953

1. U Nu, Convocation Address, Rangoon University, December 2, 1953. Note: Nu dropped the honorific "Thakin" in 1952 and thereafter resorted to the traditional Burmese "U."

2. See Cady, *A History of Modern Burma*, pp. 582 ff.

3. *The Nation*, Rangoon, May 26, 1948, text in *Towards Peace and Democracy.*

4. Text in *Towards Peace and Democracy*, p. 117.

5. Cady, p. 585.

6. *The Nation*, Rangoon, June 17, 1948.

7. William M. Rideout, Jr., "The Karen Insurrection — A Case Study," unpublished ms. (Rangoon, 1957).

8. Rideout, and Cady, p. 589 ff.

9. *Ibid.*

10. "Dacoit" means robber or bandit.

11. The conference representatives were: Prime Minister Nehru, India; Dr. Evatt, Australian Minister for External Affairs; Mr. De Silva, High Commissioner for Ceylon in India; Mr. Bottomly, British Secretary for Overseas Trade; and Mr. Malcolm MacDonald, Commissioner-General for Southeast Asia.

12. *The Nation*, Rangoon, May 8, 1949.

13. The total number of Kuomintang refugee troops who fled into northeast Burma and into the mountainous areas of Laos has never been accurately determined. Reports place the number between fifteen and fifty thousand.

14. *The Nation* gave page one prominence to the full statement on June 8.

15. U Nu, "Bullets Versus Ballots," speech before Parliament, September 28, 1949, Government Printing and Stationary Office, text in *From Peace to Stability* (Rangoon, 1951), p. 22.

16. See *The Nation*, Rangoon, August 25 and 29, 1949, and *The New York Times*, November 25, 1949, reporting a speech by Liu Sho-chi urging formation of national liberation armies in Asian countries to achieve "national independence" and "people's democracy."

17. The Chinese Communists reverted to the older name for the capital, "Peking" (northern capital) in place of the designation given during the Chiang Kai-shek regime, "Peiping" (northern peace).

18. See *The Nation*, Rangoon, October 9, 10, and 11, 1949.

19. Reuters' dispatch to *The Nation*, Rangoon, December 3, 1949.

20. The public announcement was made in Rangoon on the same day and on December 17, the Chinese Nationalist Government, now on Taiwan, broke off diplomatic relations with Burma, recalling its Ambassador and his staff.

21. See *The Nation*, Rangoon, December 12, 1949. K. M. Pannikar, Indian Ambassador to the Chinese Nationalist Government at the time, who was in New Delhi on consultation, states the Burma government specifically requested the Indian government to delay its own recognition of the new Chinese People's Republic so that Burma could be the first Asian nation to do so. K. M. Pannikar, *In Two Chinas* (London, 1955), p. 68.

22. Tibor Mende has written that, "When Burma's first Ambassador prepared to present his credentials to Mao Tse-tung and was advised that only a deputy would receive them, he refused on the ground that he brought credentials from one sovereign state to another and could not present them to one of lesser dignity than the head of the nation. The Russian Ambassador in Peking intervened to advise his colleague to follow the example of other countries and meet Mao Tse-tung's deputy. U Myint Thein cabled Rangoon for instructions and was told that unless he could present his letter to the head of the Chinese State, he should return home. Shortly afterwards he was received by Mao Tse-tung." Tibor Mende, *Southeast Asia Between Two Worlds* (London, 1955), p. 154. The above was confirmed by the author in personal conversations in Rangoon. It is interesting to note that the Chinese Communist Government accorded the same treatment to Colonel (now Brigadier) Aung Gyi, appointed Ambassador to Peking by General Ne Win in the early part of 1959, and with the same results.

23. U Nu, "Insurrection: An Analysis and a Remedy," speech in Rangoon, December 11, 1949, in *From Peace to Stability*, pp. 51–53.

24. U Nu, "The Political Scene," speech at a mass meeting in Rangoon, February 27, 1949, in *Towards Peace and Democracy*, p. 181 and ff.

25. In *From Peace to Stability*, p. 86 and ff.

26. See Badgley, *Burma's Foreign Economic Relations*.

27. The agreement provided for US$8–10 million of grant aid.

28. *Pyidawtha*, translated freely as "welfare state" more literally means something like "people and government cooperate for happiness."

29. The termination permitted completion of existing projects and the Burma government continued the services of the two American advisory groups under direct contracts which were not finally terminated until February, 1959, by the Ne Win government.

30. U Hla Maung, a prominent member of the inner clique of the AFPFL, had held many responsible party positions and had been Mayor of Rangoon before he headed the Burma side of the U. S.-Burma aid program. He is a Burmese Muslim, however, and apparently did not have the confidence of many leaders in the Burmese Buddhist community.

31. *The Nation*, Rangoon, April 9, 1952.

32. The Burma government also reached a friendly agreement with Britain on settlement of the preindependence debt and with the Indian government on the old debt arrangements terminated when Burma was detached from India in 1935.

33. U Nu, "Internal and External Problems," speech before Parliament, Rangoon, March 8, 1951, in *From Peace to Stability*, pp. 195–196.

34. Italics are the author's.

35. *The New York Times*, June 26, 1951.

36. *Ibid.*, July 2, 1951.

37. *Ibid.*, July 20, 1951.

38. U Nu, "Towards a Welfare State," speech at the first Union Welfare Conference, official English trans. printed by the Government of the Union of Burma, Ministry of Information (Rangoon, 1952), pp 28–31.

39. U Nu, "Advice to University Students," Convocation Address, Rangoon University, Government of the Union of Burma, Ministry of Information, text in *Forward With The People* (Rangoon, 1955), pp. 88–89.

Chapter III
"Positive Neutralism" — 1954–1958

1. *Economic Survey of Burma, 1954,* Government Printing and Stationary Office (Rangoon, 1954), p. 5. GNP was K. 4,079 million for the 1952 fiscal year. Foreign exchange reserves passed the K. 1,000 million mark in late 1952 and the postwar high was reached in June, 1953 at K. 1,269 million. *Note:* Because of high world rice prices up to the fall of 1953, the State Agricultural Marketing Board (SAMB) was able to make huge profits for the government by maintaining low paddy prices and exporting rice at approximately twice the domestic price. These export earnings were the major portion of funds the government depended upon to finance capital formation from the public sector.

2. Quarterly Bulletin of Statistics, Government Printing and Stationary Office (Rangoon, 1st Quarter, 1955).

3. See *The New York Times,* July 3, 1955 and *The New Times of Burma,* July 2, 1955.

4. Official Records, Tenth Session of ECAFE, February, 1954, p. 71.

5. *The New Times of Burma,* July 2, 1953.

6. *The New York Times,* October 14, 1954.

7. *The New Times of Burma,* October 16, 1954.

8. China was to supply coal, silk and cotton textiles, paper, agricultural implements, light industrial products, handicrafts, enamelware, porcelain, canned products, pharmaceutical and medical substances, and cigarettes in amounts to be determined jointly.

9. U Nu, "Towards a Welfare State," speech on August 4, 1952, Government Printing and Stationary Office, text in *Burma Looks Ahead* (Rangoon, 1953), p. 116.

10. Since 1948, the concept that "aid without strings from any source is acceptable so long as it does not infringe Burma's independence," has had constant lip service, but no reference can be found to the application of this idea in conjunction with barter trade prior to the negotiations with Communist China in 1954.

11. U Nu, *The Nation,* Rangoon, November 23, 1954.

12. *The New Times of Burma,* June 12, 1953.

13. *The New Light of Burma,* July 4, 1953.

14. *The Burman,* March 10, 1954.

15. *The New Times of Burma,* November 8, 1954.

16. *The People's Daily,* Rangoon, October 20, 1954.

17. *Taing-Lone-Kyaw,* trans., Rangoon, November 5, 1954.

18. *The New York Times,* May 9, 1956.

19. *The Nation,* Rangoon, May 29, 1956.

20. Just four years after the termination of the original United States aid program, the wheel had turned full circle and a new U. S. aid program was in full operation.

21. In summary, the "Five Principles" are: (1) reciprocal respect for the integrity and territorial sovereignty of both states; (2) nonaggression; (3) non-interference in the affairs of the other state; (4) equality and mutual benefit in all relations; and (5) adherence to the principle of peaceful coexistence. These principles had first been expressed in the Sino-Indian joint agreement and declaration on Tibet the previous April and formed part of the Nehru-Chou En-lai communiqué released on June 28, the day Chou arrived in Rangoon from India.

22. U Nu, Martyr's Day Speech, July 19, 1954, official English trans., Government of the Union of Burma, Ministry of Information (Rangoon, 1954), pp. 1, 3, ff.

23. U Nu, speech before Parliament, September 27, 1957, official English trans., Government of the Union of Burma, Ministry of Information (Rangoon, 1957). It might be noted that in this speech, as well as in his earlier one of July 19, U Nu does not seem to take into account the position of the Soviet Union and its possession of nuclear weapons.

24. Jawaharlal Nehru, speech before Parliament, March 17, 1950, Government of India, Ministry of Information and Broadcasting, New Delhi, 1954, p. 144.

25. Jawaharlal Nehru, speech before Parliament, June 12, 1952, Government of India, Ministry of Information, pp. 216–217.

26. Jawaharlal Nehru, "Defining Foreign Policy," speech before Parliament, Ministry of Information, February 17, 1953, p. 219. Almost all of this speech was taken up with the Kashmir dispute.

27. English texts and reports on these speeches in *The New Times of Burma* and *The Nation*, Rangoon, for September 15 and 16, 1954.

28. *The Nation*, Rangoon, September 30, 1954.

29. *Ibid.*, October 23 and November 20, 1954.

30. *Ibid.*, January 18, 1955.

31. U Nu, *An Asian Speaks*, speeches in the United States (Washington, D. C., 1955).

32. *The New York Times*, October 5, 1956.

33. *Ibid.*, September 6, 1956.

34. See Chapter V for further evaluation of the significance of these border incursions.

35. See *The Nation*, Rangoon, *The New Times of Burma* and *The Guardian Daily*, Rangoon, for November 10, 11, and 12, 1956.

36. In a speech before the All-Burma Peasant's Organization (ABPO) reported in *The Nation*, Rangoon, September 24, 1956.

37. Text in *The Nation*, Rangoon, October 3, 1956.

38. Statement dated November 2, 1956, official text from *The New Times of Burma*, November 9, 1956.

39. *The New Times of Burma*, November 9, 1956.

40. For further details of the Burma government's action in the United Nations, see Chapter VI.

41. *The New Times of Burma*, November 10, 1956 and *The Nation*, Rangoon, November 11, 1956.

42. Reported in *The Nation,* Rangoon and *The New Times of Burma,* November 20, 1956.

43. See *The New York Times,* November 21 and December 12, 1956, also *The Nation,* Rangoon and *The New Times of Burma,* for November 22, 1956.

Chapter IV

Political *Malaise* — And Its Aftermath 1958–1962

1. See "A Hard Look at Mr. Tender," profile of U Nu by U Law Yone, editor of *The Nation,* Rangoon. Text in Appendix III.

2. Factual information for this period has been drawn from a chronology of events and statements prepared by the staff of the Rangoon-Hopkins Center for Southeast Asian Studies based upon thorough coverage of the Rangoon press and other Burma publications as well as personal interviews by the author and staff members.

3. See *The Nation* and *The Guardian Daily,* for May 9, 10, 11, and 13, 1958.

4. Tinker, *Union of Burma,* p. 60, fn. 2, states that according to Burmese chronicles, *Pyusawhti* was a warrior who reigned around 167 A.D., and that it was hoped that the use of this legendary hero's name would give prestige to the scheme.

5. On June 23, the Burma War Office released official figures on insurgent surrenders. The release stated that from the start of the insurrection up to June 9, 1958, 36,733 rebels had surrendered. For the period from October, 1957 to June 9, 1958, 7,420 insurgents had surrendered. This total included 2,001 White Flag Communists (from Thakin Than Tun's CPB); 212 Red Flag Communists (Thakin Soe's BCP); 2,192 PVO's; 463 KNDO's; and over 2,500 "others."

6. *The Nation,* Rangoon, June 11, 1958.

7. See Sein Win, "The Split Story," *The Guardian Daily,* Rangoon, 1959.

8. See *The Nation,* September 25 and 26, 1958; *The Burman,* September 25, 1958; and *The Guardian Daily,* September 24, 25, 26, and 27, 1958.

9. Two days before the takeover — just before dawn on September 24 — the author counted from the upstairs porch of his house on Prome Road, Rangoon, fifty-one truck loads of fully armed troops in battle dress with mounted guns moving into the city from the Mingaladon army encampment.

10. *The Nation,* Rangoon, September 25 and 26, 1958.

11. *Ibid.*

12. *The Nation,* September 28, 1958.

13. See *The Nation* and *The Guardian Daily* for September 29 and 30, 1958.

14. A. Kaufman, "The Events in Burma," *International Affairs* (Moscow, October 1959), pp. 96–100.

15. In his exposé of Soviet intelligence activities in Burma, Aleksandr Y. Kaznacheev (Soviet Embassy information officer who defected to the American Embassy in Rangoon) states that the article in question was received by the Soviet Embassy in Rangoon and "planted" in *The Bharat Times,* then reprinted by "friendly" newspapers in Rangoon. *The New Leader,* New York, January 18, 1960.

16. The original Ne Win cabinet: Justice U Chan Htun Aung, Judicial and Foreign Affairs; U Khin Maung Pyu, Home Affairs, Immigration and Information; Justice U Thein Maung, Deputy Premier, Social Welfare, Religious Affairs, Health, Relief, and Rural Resettlement; U San Nyunt, Transport and Communications, Marine and Civil Aviation; U Ka, Education and Union Culture, Agriculture and Forests, Land Nationalization; U Chit Thoung, Industry, Mines, Labor and Housing; U Kyaw Nyein (not the U Kyaw Nyein of the Stable AFPFL) Finance and National Planning; U Ba Kyar, Trade Development, Cooperatives and Supplies. Brigadier Tin Pe was shortly appointed Minister for Housing and Public Works. Other Cabinet posts were filled by representatives of the states in the Burma Union.

17. One of the most visible accomplishments was a garbage removal campaign in Rangoon, along with considerable street repair and elimination of hundreds of the scavenger "pi" dogs. Unfortunately these "clean-up" campaigns were conducted almost entirely by the troops and did not catch on with the general public. Refugee villages and huts in the city were torn down and the refugees "re-settled" in two large "satellite" towns on the outskirts.

18. This action seems to have been caused by military impatience with foreign advisers attached to the previous government and not by identifiable "anti-Western" feelings.

19. Burma Army officers who visited Israel were much impressed by the community defense system in that country and arranged for over fifty Burma army families to be given training in these communities.

20. There was a sudden influx of Russian visitors in addition to a large number of Russian technicians working on the "gift" projects. The author had several encounters with them at Rangoon University and it was all too obvious that their chief interest was to learn as much about Burma politics and about American activity in Burma as possible.

21. See Chapter V for additional discussion of these episodes.

22. *The Nation,* December 27 and 30, 1959.

23. See further discussion of the border problem in Chapter V.

24. *The Guardian Monthly* (editorial), Rangoon, March 1960.

25. See also Chapter V.

26. *The Guardian Monthly* (editorial), October 1960.

27. See *The Nation,* March 2, 3, and 4, 1962. The author was in Rangoon for the last eight days of January, 1962, and was able to talk with a variety of competent observers, both Burman and foreign. It was apparent at that time that a military takeover was imminent. Few doubted it would happen, but there was disagreement over "when."

Chapter V

Burma's Relations with Communist China

1. See A. M. Halpern, "The Chinese Line on Neutralism," *China Quarterly* (January–March, 1961), pp. 90–115. Also, same author, "Why are the Chinese Nervous?" The RAND Corporation, No. P-1987, May 1, 1960.

2. See *The Nation,* Rangoon, September 9, 1950.

3. Reported in *The Nation,* November 8, 1950.

4. *The Nation,* May 3, 1951.

5. See *The New York Times,* March 9, 1951, for summaries of press conference and report.

6. UN General Assembly, 6th Plenary Session, November 6, 1951, proceedings, p. 100.

7. Quoted in Chap. II.

8. See Chaps. II and VI for more detailed discussion of this point.

9. The "Five Principles" in summary, were: (1) mutual respect for territory and sovereignty; (2) nonaggression; (3) noninterference in internal affairs; (4) equality and mutual benefit; and (5) peaceful coexistence.

10. *The Bamakhit,* Rangoon, June 26, 1954. (trans.)

11. *The Burmese Review* and *Monday New Times,* Rangoon, June 28, 1954.

12. *Oway,* Rangoon, June 29, 1954. (trans.)

13. Collected Speeches, in *For World Peace and Progress,* Rangoon, Ministry of Information, 1954.

14. *The Nation,* September 23, 1954 and *The Burman,* October 15, 1954. It is to be noted that a nonaggression treaty was signed in January, 1960.

15. *The New York Times,* November 14, 1954.

16. *The Burman,* November 14, 1954.

17. *The New York Times,* December 1, 1954.

18. *Ibid.*

19. *The Nation,* December 21, 1954.

20. *Ibid.,* December 24, 1954.

21. *The New York Times,* July 26, 1955. Note: It is interesting that the "Five Principles" as such, were not included in any of the formal resolutions at Bandung.

22. *U. S. News and World Report,* "Peaceful Coexistence as it looks to Asia," interview with U Nu, Washington, August 5, 1955, pp. 80–83.

23. U Nu, Speech to the Overseas Press Club, text in "An Asian Speaks," Washington, July 6, 1955.

24. *The New York Times,* July 2 and 7, 1955.

25. Text of this speech in full in *The New Times of Burma,* Rangoon (English) November 4, 1956. It is interesting that Peking Radio also broadcast the full text in English.

26. *The Nation,* June 24, 1956.

27. *The Nation* and *The New Times of Burma,* August 18, 1956.

28. Possibly identical to the "Central Committee of the People's Liberation Armies of Southeast Asia"; see *The Nation,* January 10 and 28, 1952.

29. *The Nation,* January 26, 1952.

30. *Ibid.,* January 14, 1952.

31. *The Tribune,* Rangoon, January 24, 1953.

32. See *The New Burma Weekly,* Rangoon, January 17, 31, and February 7, 1959. Than Maung, according to his biography, had been active in student politics, Chief Editor of the *Mandalay Sun* in 1942, and AFPFL organizer in 1946. After travelling in the Communist bloc states of eastern Europe in 1947, he became a Communist Party member and joined Thakin Than Tun's underground in 1949. In 1959, he "entered the light" and helped to re-establish the *Mandalay Sun.*

33. *The Nation,* April 19, 1959. The term "yebaw" (comrade of boldness) is an honorific title appropriated by former members of the Burma Independent Army. "Bo" literally "Captain" (in the Army) has been used as an honorific by insurgents.

34. *The Nation,* May 28, 1949.

35. *The New York Times,* February 1, 1951. This report drew a spirited denial from the Burman Ambassador to the United States, U Aung Nyet Kyaw, published in a letter to *The New York Times,* February 26, 1951.

36. *The New York Times,* March 9, 1951.

37. See *The Nation,* May 19, 1951 and *The New York Times,* July 8, 1951.

38. *The Nation,* June 2 and 25, 1951.

39. *The New York Times,* August 13, 1953.

40. *The New Burma Weekly* (Than Maung articles).

41. See editorials in *The Nation,* June 25, 1954; *The Hanthawaddy,* July 29 and August 18, 1954; and *The Tribune,* August 5 and 24, 1954.

42. See, for example, *The Nation,* September 17, 1954 and October 22, 1955; also *The Hanthawaddy,* February 7, 1955. Similar stories appeared in *The New York Times* beginning in May 1955.

43. See *The Nation,* June 8, 9, and 11, 1959 and *The New York Times* for the same dates.

44. See particularly, Daphne E. Whittam, "The Sino-Burmese Boundary Treaty," *Pacific Affairs,* Summer, 1961. Miss Whittam provides footnote references to a number of articles on the border dispute. Also, Dorothy Woodman, *The Making of Burma* (London, 1962), chaps. xvii and xix.

45. See Whittam and also *The Nation,* November 17, 1950, September 17, 1958; and *The New York Times,* November 18, 1950 and July 13–16, 1953.

46. It is interesting to note that in a book by Theodore Shabad, *China's Changing Map* (London, 1956), the author reproduces two maps. The first (p. 176) shows almost all of the Kachin State as disputed territory, as well as a large part of the Wa State. Another map (p. 264) shows almost all of Assam down to the Bhramaputra river as disputed territory between India and China, as well as the whole northern area of the Kachin State in dispute between China and Burma. The author acknowledges that a Vaughn S. Gray prepared the maps for this book and that material was obtained from "Chinese Russian and Western sources."

47. They were: Miss Daphne E. Whittam, an associate editor, and staff member On Myint.

48. The Mission was headed by the Burman Ambassador to Peking, U Win Maung. Other members were: James Barrington, Permanent Secretary of the Foreign Office; U Zanhta Sin, head of the Kachin State; Sima Duwa Sinwa Nawng, and Duwa Zau Lun of the Kachin State Council; Major Shan Lone, Secretary of the Kachin State Ministry; and U Khin Nyunt of the Foreign Office. The Mission was joined in Peking by U Ohn, Burman Ambassador to the U.S.S.R. who later became confidential adviser to U Nu. Since the Burma Foreign Office had no real research staff at the time, it had called in Professor Gordon T. Luce to assist in getting material together from the archives, but persons interviewed have stated that this material was incomplete, since many of the prewar records were in London and Burma government archives were scattered and unorganized. It has been asserted that this Burman Mission to Peking was

forced to rely considerably on material produced by the Chinese. See *The Nation* and *The New Times of Burma,* October 20, 23, 25, 29, and 30, 1956.

49. The new U. S. aid agreements were signed in March, 1957 and provided for a total of US$42.3 million of which 17.3 million was to be in Burmese kyats from the proceeds of sale of U. S. agricultural produce under the P. L. 480 agreements.

50. See texts of these treaties in Appendix II.

51. In 1961 the Peking regime signed a border settlement treaty with Nepal but with "special points" to be adjusted later, particularly concerning territorial sovereignty over Mount Everest.

52. Author's italics.

53. Text of the Sino-Burman loan/credit agreements in *The Asian Recorder,* Bombay, February 5–11, 1961, pp. 3772–73.

Chapter VI

Burma's Participation in the United Nations

1. This was revealed by a spot check in Washington and among foreign diplomatic representatives in Rangoon in response to the question, "Do you know what Burma's position was on the Hungarian issue in 1956?" Without exception the affirmative replies referred to this speech at the UN.

2. See Thomas Hovet, Jr., *Bloc Politics in the United Nations* (Cambridge, Mass., 1960), chaps. iii and iv.

3. These are: The Food and Agriculture Organization (1947); The International Labor Organization (1948); UNESCO (1949); The World Meteorological Organization (1947); The World Health Organization (1948); The International Civil Aviation Organization (1948); and the Universal Postal Union (1949). See Frank N. Trager, Patricia Wolgemuth and Lu-yu Kiang, *Burma's Role in the United Nations, 1948–1955* (New York, 1956).

4. According to a survey by the Burma government in 1957, there were over 60 specialists from 7 UN agencies assigned to various departments of the Burma government. The total number of foreign specialists assigned to the Burma government at this time was over 300.

5. *The New York Times,* December 9, 1948.

6. United Nations, General Assembly, Third Session, Part I, Committee I, Summary of Meetings, 232nd meeting, December 7, 1948, pp. 976 ff.

7. *The New York Times,* October 4, 1949.

8. Security Council Official Records, Supplement for June, July, and August, 1950, Document s/1950, p. 74. Note: The Burma Government later contributed 400 tons of rice to UN forces in Korea valued at US$49,943.

9. *The New York Times,* October 5, 1950.

10. General Assembly, Fifth Session, Committee I, 353rd meeting, October 4, 1950, vol. I, pp. 60–61.

11. General Assembly, Committee I, 351st meeting, October 3, 1950, pp. 60–61.

12. Presented to Committee I in the form of a joint draft resolution on October 9, 1950.

13. General Assembly, Committee I, 367th meeting, October 18, 1950, pp. 147 ff.

14. *Ibid.*

15. *Ibid.*

16. *Ibid.*

17. *The New York Times*, October 29, 1950.

18. General Assembly, Fifth Session, Annexes, vol. III, Agenda item 68, Document A/C.1/576/, Rev. 1, p. 7.

19. "A Korean Chronology: December 27, 1945 to July 27, 1953," United Nations *Bulletin*, 15.3:78 (New York, August 1, 1953).

20. *Ibid.*, pp. 78–79.

21. *Ibid.*, p. 79.

22. *Ibid.*

23. *Ibid.*

24. *Ibid.*

25. *The New York Times*, December 6, 1950. Quotation is from the appeal.

26. *Ibid.*, p. 15.

27. "A Korean Chronology," pp. 79 and 108.

28. *Ibid.*, p. 108.

29. *The New York Times*, December 27, 28, and 30, 1950; January 1 and 3, 1951.

30. *Ibid.*, December 27 and 30, 1950.

31. *Ibid.*, January 7, 1951.

32. "A Korean Chronology," p. 108.

33. *The New York Times*, January 12, 1951.

34. "A Korean Chronology," pp. 108–109.

35. *The New York Times*, January 19 and 20, 1951.

36. *Ibid.*, January 19, 20, 21, and 22, 1951.

37. *Ibid.*, January 23, 1951. For text of Chinese statement see General Assembly, Fifth Session, Committee I, proceedings, 429th meeting, January 22, 1951, vol. II, p. 525.

38. *The New York Times*, January 23, 1951.

39. *Ibid.*, January 23 and 24, 1951.

40. *Ibid.*, January 25, 1951.

41. *Ibid.*, January 24 and 25, 1951.

42. *Ibid.*, January 27, 1951.

43. *Ibid.*, January 26, 1951. The Soviets did introduce two brief amendments.

44. *Ibid.*, January 30, 1951.

45. General Assembly, Fifth Session, Supplement No. 20 A (A/1775/Add. 1.), Resolution 498 (V) — (also called A/1771), p. 91.

46. *The New York Times*, January 30, 1951.

47. *Ibid.* For text of the debates, see General Assembly, Fifth Session, Committee I, 434th and 435th meetings, January 29, 1951, vol. III, pp. 571–573.

48. *Ibid.*

49. *Ibid.*

50. *Ibid.*

51. *Ibid.*

52. *Ibid.*, pp. 578–579.

53. *The New York Times,* January 31, 1951.
54. *Ibid.*
55. *Ibid.,* February 17, 1951.
56. *Ibid.,* February 8, 1951.
57. *Ibid.*
58. *The New York Times,* April 5, 1951.
59. *Ibid.,* April 6, 1951.
60. *Ibid.,* April 16 and 19, 1951.
61. *The New York Times,* May 18, 1951.
62. *Ibid.*
63. *Ibid.,* May 19, 1951.
64. General Assembly, Fifth Session, Plenary meetings, 330th meeting, May 18, 1951, vol. II, p. 736.
65. *Ibid.*
66. India was absent on one vote because it was Chairman of the Neutral Nation's Repatriation Commission. Indonesia voted with India without exception.
67. Material in this section is based upon a study by Oliver E. Clubb, Jr., "The Effect of the Chinese Nationalist Activities in Burma on Burma's Foreign Policy." (Listed in Appendix I)
68. United Nations Document A/2375. "Kuomintang Aggression Against Burma," March 23, 1953. (Also published by Ministry of Information, Rangoon, 1953)
69. *The New York Times,* March 30, 1953.
70. *Ibid.*
71. *The Nation,* Rangoon, March 26, 1953.
72. *Ibid.,* August 11, 1952.
73. General Assembly, Seventh Session, April 1953, proceedings, p. 31.
74. *The New York Times,* April 21, 1953.
75. Just as the Burma government was on the point of bringing the issue before the UN, for example, the Chinese Nationalist Government Chargé d'affaires in Bangkok was reported by *The London Times* to have stated that the "12,500 troops under General Li Mi were under the direct command of the military headquarters in Formosa; that, so far as his government was concerned, they were deployed in undemarcated territory where the authority of the Burma government was at least questionable; and that their operations were really an extension of the struggle against Communism in Korea, Indo-China, and Malaya." *The London Times,* March 30, 1953.
76. "Kuomintang Aggression Against Burma," pp. 31–43.
77. *Ibid.,* quoted on pp. 56–57.
78. General Assembly, Document A/C.1/L.44, Rev. 2, 1953.
79. "Kuomintang Aggression Against Burma," p. 99.
80. Royal Institute of International Affairs, "Chronology of International Events and Documents" (supplement) (London, 1945–1955) vol. ix, No. 10, p. 295.
81. *The New York Times,* June 12, 1953.
82. *Ibid.,* June 23, 1953.
83. *The New Statesman and Nation,* London, August 8, 1953.
84. *The New York Times,* July 24, 1953.

85. *Ibid.,* July 31, 1953.
86. *Ibid.*
87. *Ibid.,* September 7, 1953.
88. *The New Light of Burma,* Rangoon, September 19, 1953.
89. General Assembly, Eighth Plenary Session, 446th meeting, September 25, 1953, proceedings, pp. 172–173.
90. *The New York Times,* October 5, 1953.
91. *Ibid.,* October 30, 1953.
92. *Ibid.,* October 6, 1953.
93. *Ibid.,* November 1, 1953.
94. *Ibid.,* November 6, 1953.
95. *The Nation,* Rangoon, November 8, 1953.
96. *The New York Times,* November 28, 1953.
97. *Ibid.,* November 25, 1953.
98. *Ibid.,* November 28, 1953.
99. *Ibid.*
100. The eight nations were: Australia, Canada, India, Indonesia, New Zealand, Norway, Sweden and the United Kingdom.
101. *The New York Times,* November 28, 1953.
102. *Ibid.,* May 31, 1954.
103. *Ibid.,* July 1, 1954. Chinese irregular troops were similarly reported to have been assisting Karen insurgents in battles with the Burma army as late as March 27, 1954. See *The New York Times,* March 28, 1954.
104. *The Burman,* Rangoon, August 22, 1954.
105. *Ibid.*
106. *The New York Times,* September 30, 1954.
107. General Assembly, Ninth Plenary Session, 845th meeting, September 29, 1954, proceedings, p. 145.
108. General Assembly, Ninth Session, 1954–55, Ad Hoc Political Committee, Sixth Meeting, proceedings, p. 17.
109. See Hovet, *Bloc Politics,* chaps. iii and iv, also Trager, *Burma's Role.*
110. Hovet.
111. It is to be noted that there has been an increasing solidarity on some issues among the increasing number of African members of the UN and very often the Asian members of the Afro-Asian bloc have taken more conservative positions.

Chapter VII
After Fourteen Years — An Evaluation

1. Mao Tse-tung, *On Contradictions,* English ed. (Peking, 1960). Quoted by Li We-han, *Peking Review,* March 9, 1962, pp. 8–9.
2. For a thorough and detailed analysis of Burma's economic difficulties, see Louis J. Walinsky, *Economic Development in Burma 1951–1960* (New York, 1962).
3. Text of this manifesto in Appendix IV.
4. These conclusions are based on the author's personal observations and experiences during 1957–59 while serving as Visiting Professor of International Relations at the University of Rangoon. See also Walinsky.

5. On July 3, 1962, about two weeks after the start of the University terms, Rangoon University students staged protest demonstrations against the High-School examination system and new regulations regarding student hostels. During the next three days the demonstrations got out of hand, professors' cars were overturned and the Rector and some faculty besieged in their houses. On July 7, Burma Army units were called out to break up the mobs. Soldiers opened fire on the students reportedly killing some fifteen persons and wounding nearly thirty others. Charging that communist agitators were responsible and that the Military would not permit such unruliness, the Army on July 8 blew up the Student Union building at the University and General Ne Win ordered all universities and colleges closed until further notice. None had been reopened by the end of August. This arbitrary action by the military only served to disrupt the process of higher education in Burma rather than spur students to more serious efforts.

Chapter VIII
Neutralism: Viable Policy or Fatal Trap?

1. U Nu participated in the following conferences of the "Colombo Powers": Conference on Indonesia, New Delhi, January, 1949; Second Indonesian Conference, New Delhi, March, 1949; First Colombo Conference, Colombo, Ceylon, April, 1954; Bandung Preparatory Conference, Bogor, Indonesia, December, 1954; Bandung Conference, April, 1955; and Second Colombo Conference, New Delhi, November, 1956.

2. For a fuller account of the Bandung Conference, see George McT. Kahin, *The Asian-African Conference* (Ithaca, 1956), and Carlos P. Romula, *The Meaning of Bandung* (Chapel Hill, 1956).

3. Lucien W. Pye, *Politics, Personality and Nation-Building. Burma's Search for Identity* (New Haven, 1962), p. 263.

INDEX

A SELECTED LIST OF OTHER RAND BOOKS

THE FREE PRESS

Dinerstein, H. S., and Leon Gouré. *Two Studies in Soviet Controls: Communism and the Russian Peasant; Moscow in Crisis*. 1955.

Garthoff, Raymond L. *Soviet Military Doctrine*. 1953.

Goldhamer, Herbert, and Andrew W. Marshall. *Psychosis and Civilization*. 1953.

Leites, Nathan. *A Study of Bolshevism*. 1953.

———— and Elsa Bernaut. *Ritual of Liquidation: The Case of the Moscow Trials*. 1954.

HARVARD UNIVERSITY PRESS

Bergson, Abram. *The Real National Income of Soviet Russia since 1928*. 1961.

Fainsod, Merle. *Smolensk under Soviet Rule*. 1958.

Hitch, Charles J., and Roland McKean. *The Economics of Defense in the Nuclear Age*. 1960.

Moosteen, Richard. *Prices and Production of Machinery in the Soviet Union, 1928–1958*. 1962.

MC GRAW-HILL BOOK COMPANY, INC.

Leites, Nathan. *The Operational Code of the Politburo*. 1951.

Mead, Margaret. *Soviet Attitudes toward Authority: An Interdisciplinary Approach to Problems of Soviet Character*. 1951.

Selznick, Philip. *The Organizational Weapon: A Study of Bolshevik Strategy and Tactics*. 1952.

FREDERICK A. PRAEGER, INC.

Dinerstein, H. S. *War and the Soviet Union: Nuclear Weapons and the Revolution in Soviet Military and Political Thinking*. 1959.

Speier, Hans. *Divided Berlin: The Anatomy of Soviet Political Blackmail*. 1961.

Tanham, G. K. *Communist Revolutionary Warfare: The Viet Minh in Indochina*. 1961.

PRINCETON UNIVERSITY PRESS

Baum, Warren C. *The French Economy and the State*. 1958.

Brodie, Bernard. *Strategy in the Missile Age*. 1959.

Davison, W. Phillips. *The Berlin Blockade: A Study in Cold War Politics*. 1958.

Johnson, John J. (ed.). *The Role of the Military in Underdeveloped Countries*. 1962.

Smith, Bruce Lannes, and Chitra M. Smith. *International Communication and Political Opinion: A Guide to the Literature*. 1956.

Wolf, Charles, Jr. *Foreign Aid: Theory and Practice in Southern Asia*. 1960.

ROW, PETERSON AND COMPANY

George, Alexander L. *Propaganda Analysis: A Study of Inferences Made from Nazi Propaganda in World War II*. 1959.

Melnik, Constantin, and Nathan Leites. *The House without Windows: France Selects a President*. 1958.

Speier, Hans. *German Rearmament and the Atomic War: The Views of German Military and Political Leaders*. 1957.

———— and W. Phillips Davison (eds.). *West German Leadership and Foreign Policy*. 1957.

STANFORD UNIVERSITY PRESS

Gouré, Leon. *The Siege of Leningrad, 1941–1943*. 1962.

Kecskemeti, Paul. *Strategic Surrender: The Politics of Victory and Defeat*. 1958.

———— *The Unexpected Revolution: Social Forces in the Hugarian Uprising*. 1961.

Leites, Nathan. *On the Game of Politics in France*. 1959.

Trager, Frank N. (ed.). *Marxism in Southeast Asia: A Study of Four Countries*. 1959.

OTHER PUBLISHERS

Buchheim, Robert W., and the Staff of The RAND Corporation. *Space Handbook: Astronautics and Its Applications*. Random House. 1959.

Hsieh, Alice L. *Communist China's Strategy in the Nuclear Era*. Prentice-Hall. 1962.

Rush, Myron. *The Rise of Khrushchev*. Public Affairs Press. 1958.

Whiting, Allen S. *China Crosses the Yalu: The Decision to Enter the Korean War*. Macmillan. 1960.